KEYWORDS

KEYWORDS

Essays on Philippine
Media
Cultures
and Neocolonialisms

Rolando B. Tolentino

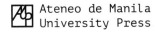

Ateneo de Manila
University Press

ATENEO DE MANILA UNIVERSITY PRESS
Bellarmine Hall, Katipunan Avenue
Loyola Heights, Quezon City
P.O. Box 154, 1099 Manila, Philippines
Tel.: (632) 426-59-84 / Fax (632) 426-59-09
E-mail: unipress@admu.edu.ph
Website: www.ateneopress.org

Book and cover design by Karl Fredrick M. Castro

Screen images from the personal collection of the author.
Photo stills from Karl Fredrick M. Castro.

The National Library of the Philippines CIP Data

Recommended entry:

    Tolentino, Rolando B.
        Keywords : essays on Philippine media
    cultures and neocolonialisms. – Quezon City :
    Ateneo de Manila University Press, [2016],
    c2016.
        vi, 376 pp ; 22.86 cm

    ISBN 978-971-550-761-5

    1. Mass media and culture – Philippines
    Historiography. 2. Philippines – Colonial influence.
    3. Popular culture. I. Title.

302.23   P94.65.P5   2016   P620160249

CONTENTS

Introduction: Keywords, Philippine Media Cultures and Neocolonialisms

T his book takes off from the classic Marxist work *Keywords: A Vocabulary of Culture and Society* by Raymond Williams, a seminal listing of contemporary socio-economic and political concepts that influence and are influenced by culture.[1] Instead of the usual etymological origins of words, Williams expounds not just on the origin but also on the evolution—including the socio-economic and political contradictions—of cultural concepts whether or not the contemporary trajectory of such concepts was generated from the origin and rise of the concepts, or has moved elsewhere. Relationally, I intend this book to imbibe the keywords integral to the understanding of Philippine media cultures and neocolonialisms.

The essays discuss the daily moment and monumental epoch of keywords in Philippine cultural politics that shape and are shaped by their media cultures and neocolonialisms. The plural forms in the title emphasize the multiplicity of cultural experience and, therefore, cultural expressions and politics in media cultures. Terms and concepts, such as those discussed here—empire, development, abjection, geography, primordiality, hysteria, sovereignty, fatherland, masses, judiciary, piracy, vagination, and domesticity—form some of the significant keywords that world the experience of Philippine neocolonialisms. I use media texts and cultures to articulate the contestation over the cultural politics that brought about the origin, rise and development, and even demise or resurrection—the formation and transformation—of the various aspects and thick descriptions of Philippine neocolonialisms. Keywords, therefore, are integral in the worlding—the substantiation or the "keyworlding," if you will—of the experience in Philippine neocolonialisms, and its media representations that signify specific class, gender and sexuality, race and ethnicity antagonisms and complicities.

I opt for the aptness of the concept of neocolonialism to analyze the depth, spread, and contours of the Philippine state. On the one hand, such neocolonialism is imbibed in the semifeudal, semicolonial character of the Philippine state. By semifeudal, I refer to the continuing land ownership patronage that defines the electoral politics and public governance of the Philippine state; by semicolonial, the continuing and intensifying peripheral emplacement of the Philippine state under the rubric of the United States empire, and newer imperial and imperialist nations and formations, such as Japan, China, or South Korea, and Asia Pacific Economic Council, World Trade Organization, General Agreement on Trade and Tariff, among others. Interestingly, both semifeudal and semicolonial also denote the imperatives of culture of the Philippine state. While statistics, for example, indicate the increasing number of workers in urban centers, the main form of employment hiring practice, subcontractualization, has eroded the traditional definition of the worker capable of radical transformation within a liberal setup that, in turn, has negated the subcontractual hire as a non-legal entity within neoliberalism. Such major class transformation of the "worker" still falls under the rubric of the semifeudal and semicolonial Philippine state: the new worker remains intermittently under the patronage of local and global businesses; in the case of the worker in the "sunshine industry" of business process outsourcing, the historic opportunity to be a multinational worker within the national sphere, which has been predicted to outpace the usual reliable source of gross domestic product of the Philippine state: overseas contract workers; and the middle-class effect of such historic political and economic turns, giving rise to a unique entrenchment in the global communicative capitalism: given the nation's low middle-end global status, the propensity of its citizens to possess cellphones and use the internet;

to participate in social networks; to reconstitute the diasporic family; and to find low-level individual economic growth through participation in international sites offering subcontracted term paper and thesis research, English tutorials, and even internet sex acts. In other words, as Facebook's relationship status would say then, "it's complicated." And it is through selected keywords using media cultures that substantiate the experience of Philippine neocolonialisms that we can understand how the Philippine state operates and reconstitutes itself under global neoliberalism.

On the other hand, similar to neoliberalism taking off from the liberalism of the Enlightenment, neocolonialism accounts for the not-so-radical break from the colonial to the postcolonial Philippine state. It is only in the granting of independence by the United States to the Philippines on 4 July 1946 that the country was formally outside the control of a foreign colonial power for the first time. Many historians have already attested to the bogus independence, especially from the United States, because by 1946, the country was already economically, politically, and culturally entwined in the United States' affairs. The post-World War II period also marked the quest for national independence of former colonies, all of which evoked a relational quasi-independence modality of the postcolonial Philippine nation. Instead of thinking of neocolonialism as a radical break—as what has been critiqued of postcolonialism—from colonialism, there is material evidence, especially in culture, that the old ties still bind, and that the Philippine state has, at best, only imagined modernities still within the U.S. empire, and other expanded imperial and imperialist formations. I use neocolonialisms to represent the variety of applications to Philippine state formation and transformation, i.e., it draws from all its past colonialisms (Spain, United States, and Japan) and newer purveyors of imperialisms (Japan, South Korea, Hong Kong, Singapore, Saudi Arabia, European Union, China, WTO, GATT, World Bank, International Monetary Fund, and Asian Development Bank, among others).

As I use media texts and cultures to expound on Philippine neocolonialisms, for this Introduction, let me turn to another important apparatus of the Philippine state to initially illuminate how ideological apparatuses are mobilized for and on its behalf. As a kind of flashforward to the contemporary Philippine state, as I begin with chapters on empire and development, the next section on education and the production of surplus labor are integral to understanding the conditions of the possible under the Philippine state— both source of sadness and emasculation on the one hand, and from which resistance and the people's movement draw inspiration for its social formation and transformation, on the other hand. It is able to draw historical and social contexts to jumpstart the understanding of ideological apparatuses servicing neocolonialisms that substantiate the continuities and discontinuities of the Philippine state.

Education and Surplus Labor in Philippine Neoliberalism

Kristel Tejada's death note read:

> *Mahal na mahal ko ang pamilya ko. At lahat din ng iba pang nagmamahal sa akin. Di ko lang talaga rin kinaya. Sana mapatawad at ipagdasal niyo ko. Salamat sa lahat magkikita pa ulit tayo. Sorry pero kailangan ko lang talagang gawin 'to* (I love my family very much, and all those who love me. I just could not take it anymore. I hope that you will forgive me and pray for me. Thank you for everything and we will see each other again. Sorry but I really need to do this).
> ... *Tandaan* (Remember): Without true love, we're nothing.[2]

K
E
Y
W
O
R
D
S

Tejada, a sixteen-year-old, first-year college student of the Behavioral Sciences program, took her own life on 15 March 2013 after being forced to file a leave of absence from the University of the Philippines-Manila (UPM), the nation's premier state university. She filed her form two days prior to her death. Since February, however, she had been attending classes unofficially after failing to settle her tuition debt and only after requesting special permission from her professors.

UP matriculation is based on a scheme called "Socialized Tuition and Financial Assistance Program (STFAP)," a gradated rate of per unit payment based on the family's annual income. Tejada's bracket was D, the second to the lowest, and at the time of her dismissal from the university, she had incurred a debt of PhP 10,000 (USD 250). With a monthly household income of PhP 10,000, the family with a brood of five could hardly afford her schooling. Tejada's appeals for late payment were all denied and she was required to surrender her school ID to her college.

Tejada embodied the corporeal disenfranchisement of youths who, together with their families, dreamed of a college education, but whose dreams exceeded their own underclass capacities. In this essay, I use Marxist concepts to analyze and problematize the ideological formation in and through education in Philippine neoliberalism. The first part discusses the function of labor in state formation or, more specifically, how labor—and its naturalizing component, education—is integral to the role of the state. The second part discusses the intensification of neoliberalism in education that bifurcates laboring corporeality from overseas contract workers to the more recent experience of contractual youth labor in business process outsourcing (BPO), located in various national cities. This involves the reengineering of Philippine education that supposedly caters to the global benchmark of twelve-year basic education (K-12) and short-circuited, shortsighted tertiary education. The last part synthesizes the function of education in the experience of Philippine neoliberalism, allowing for the naturalization of middle-class desires and elite-only access to these desires.

Many colleagues, students, and alumni in and outside UP were shocked by Tejada's death. A university official, however, called it a "very isolated unfortunate case" on the one hand, but also reasoned on the other hand, "as in any organization or institution, there are specific guidelines in relation to punctuality. This is not to repress any student but this is a means of putting order, uniformity, and equality among all UP students."[3] What Tejada's death signifies in the more recent trajectory of Philippine neoliberalism is the preeminent role of education as the marker of both middle-class accessibility of desire and inaccessibility to historical claims. The bodies of the desiring young are diminished in the instance of contact with and rearing by Philippine education. Tejada's death reifies the diminishment of youthful bodies earmarked for labor by flooding them—through necrophilic education—into the "reserve army of [postindustrial] labor" that seals their common fate and consigns their collective future. Unwittingly mobilized in Philippine education, Tejada and all her contemporary and succeeding generation of youths are transformed into the exigencies of capital, which as Marx, in one of his definitions, uncannily states as "capital is dead labour, that, vampire-like, only lives by sucking living labour, and lives the more, the more labour it sucks."[4]

Philippine Education, Labor, and the State

Commodore George Dewey's triumph against the aging Spanish armada in Manila Bay on 1 May 1898 signaled the start of U.S.

intervention in the Philippines, later to trigger its military takeover on 14 August 1898, which marked the formal ceding of the Philippines by Spain through the signing of the Treaty of Paris on 10 December 1898. The colonial swap left the on-the-verge-of-independence Philippines at a standstill. Spanish colonial education, albeit limited to local elite, provided the critical impetus for articulating and transforming the colony to the wishful desire for a sovereign status. Jose Rizal and his *ilustrado* cohorts, educated in the colonial schools and in Europe, espoused for reforms within the Spanish empire, calling for due recognition of its Philippine colony. Andres Bonifacio, the supposedly self-taught leader of the Katipunan, led the call for revolutionary change. Even before U.S. colonialism, the Philippine revolution was already led by local elites, specifically Emilio Aguinaldo, who took over from Bonifacio after ordering his death.

U.S. colonialism espoused "benevolent assimilation" (William McKinley), and rested on the idea of the locals ("Our Little Brown Brothers") as infants and wards who needed rearing under civilized ways. The brutal pacification drives provided one polar end of colonial design by the U.S. empire, and public school education provided the opposite end. As with the pacification drives, colonial education entailed the logic of subjugation. As a matter of fact, the first teachers were American soldiers who knew the logic of colonial education, "officers commanding the garrisons of towns in all parts of the archipelago manifested their belief in a policy of native concilia-tion by the warmest support and advocacy of education."[5] For David Barrows, Director of Education in the Philippines, "native education" provided a guise for the U.S. army to provide a conciliatory gesture "even while engaged in the work of subjugation."[6]

The task was later taken on by a group of about five hundred volunteer teachers called Thomasites, having landed from the ship USAT Thomas in August 1901, that provided the intellectual labor power to harness the ideological formation of the Philippine colonial state. The idea of transplanting political and economic institutions was also carried out in education, "[T]he American system of public schools was transplanted without changing its content, method or character."[7] In a kind of colonial power mimicry, the U.S. empire was reproduced in the Philippine colony through a rhetoric of "in our image" that used the logic of transplantation or an inter-harnessing of the efficiencies of the agricultural sector for circulation in the empire. Native education ensured the filling up of vacancies in the bureaucracy of the new Philippine colony, such as civil service work in the local municipalities, tax offices, post offices, police and the military branches, and of course, public education. From this lowly variant of American education, Barrows hailed in 1910, "Now a great middle class is forming."[8]

Such euphoria, of course, was intermittently correct. However, in the mid-1920s, the colonial bureaucracy was already filled up, and education no longer provided the edge for social mobility.[9] Furthermore, in a survey of the Monroe Commission in 1925, "fourth year high school students had a reading ability equal to American children in grade five."[10] The teaching of English was supposed to train the colonial subjects in the ways of enlightened democracy and patriotism, but with little impact. The right to vote was, among other things, only exercised by those who had skills in the English language. As a result of the emphasis in Philippine colonial design, colonial education resulted in its own fiscalization and bureaucratization, from the colonial to the local levels. Prior to the Japanese invasion, estimates placed the number of schools at twelve thousand, teachers at forty thousand, and pupils at 1.95 million.[11] The bureaucracy kept on growing. By 1958–1959, there were 110,000 public school teachers, seventy thousand of whom were women.[12] By 2013, the number of public school teachers was around six hundred thousand.[13]

The emphasis on colonial education was primordially necessitated by the economic requirements of the U.S. empire. The economic logic of laissez-faire was used to underwrite the actual costs of the colonial education. Laissez-faire was an "economic freedom" that went beyond U.S. political charter or constitution, and could only be exerted by Filipinos themselves. Externally located in colonial relations, however, Filipinos' pedagogical contact with laissez-faire had to be under the guise of "temporary or permanent American supervision."[14] Co-terminus with the introduction of public education of the natives was the engineering of land ownership in the Philippines. The crux of the debate was that given the already six million acres of cultivated lands, with an additional forty million acres earmarked for future cultivation, and on U.S. ownership of 90 percent of all lands, including most of the area for timber and mineral deposits, what would be the sufficient size of homestead land for the establishment of a modern estate?[15]

What colonial education has resulted in is the formation of an elite subclass that has attained limited access to middle-class comfort, but on the wholesale, the mobilization of excess bodies in the service of semi-feudal, semi-colonial relations. As James LeRoy states in 1904, "In the present state of education and initiative of the Filipino masses, they must, in most regions, be laborers in crowds on large estates."[16]

The tropical requirements for capital accumulation precluded Filipinos from engaging in direct capitalist praxis. In addition, for LeRoy, hundreds of years of peonage under Spain makes it highly improbable for Filipinos to be able to exercise this economic freedom.

The transformation of land from the hands of the public to the private sector allows for surplus accumulation by capitalists at the expense of the workers. Marx had discussed this along two axes: first, the workers who are leased lands for a sufficient price but still not commensurate to the wages paid to them; and second, the role of the immigrant workers who are brought in through profits generated by the government, and that keep steady the supply of labor at a cheap cost. This is known as "the great secret of 'systematic colonization'" that proclaims "that the capitalist mode of production and accumulation, and therefore capitalist private property, have for their fundamental condition the annihilation of self-earned private property; in other words, the expropriation of the labourer."[17] The colonial empire bestowed the economic logic of laissez-faire only to American colonizing capitalists and their local cohorts. The workers were doomed to sustain the privatization of public lands to ensure their indebtedness to the U.S. empire and to sustain the proliferation of surplus bodies for ready hiring.

Education proved to be the smokescreen to ensure the bitter choice of accepting laissez-faire practice in the Philippine colony. It ensured the steady supply and cheapening of labor—even literate laborers—that generated the necessary capital accumulation for the colonial powers. It materialized the U.S. empire's benevolent assimilation: allowing for functional literacy to develop yet at the same time forbidding this literacy from transforming into a mass critical state, to become anti-U.S. imperialist, for example. Through the further introduction and proliferation of popular media (e.g., printed literature and the movie), such functional literacy was necessary to savor the newer colonial subjectivity and to make accessible some markers of middle-class colonial citizenry offered by the U.S. empire.

Philippine Education, Neoliberalism, and the Containment of Labor Mobility

U.S. colonial education ensured the integration of the Philippines into its capitalist division of labor. What has become of the Philippine state is its lingering and continued conversation with the U.S. capitalist network, especially in neoliberalism. After declaring martial law in 1972, Ferdinand Marcos adhered to structural adjustment loans that greatly funded education but with consequences, such as support for courses that propelled national development drives, textbook development, national collegiate entrance examination, and vocational training, among others. Relative to its Southeast Asian neighbors, Philippine education and other services were greatly underfunded. By 2010, according to a *Manila Times* editorial: "For every 100 pupils who enter Grade 1, only 86 will continue till Grade 2. Over the last 30 years, this has been the highest dropout rate (14 percent) in the basic school cycle. By Grade 4, only 76 will still be in school. By Grade 6, only 67 of the original 100 would still be enrolled—and only 65 will finish elementary school. Of the 65 children who graduate from Grade 6, only 58 will move on to high school. And of the 58 who enter high school, only 42 will graduate."[18]

Out of 100 pupils who enter the first grade, only ten will complete college.[19] To be a college student in the Philippines is already an elite act, to graduate from college is even more elitist. Similar to the American colonial education, recent developments offer little to emancipate Filipino labor. The opportunity for social mobility via education has become extremely limited and elitist. The quality of education also does not translate into jobs that one has been trained for. Philippine tertiary education has been instrumental in under-employment, or does not create a fit between graduated programs and market demands. Market demands have historically emplaced Philippine labor in 3D (dirty, dangerous, and demanding) jobs both nationally and internationally. With some half a million college graduates every year, 18 percent will be unemployed.[20]

The quality of Philippine education has also been declining, as can be gleaned from this report:

> UNESCO says in its National Education Support Strategy (UNESS) that the quality of elementary education in the Philippines has deteriorated over the years as indicated by the low achievement rates for students. In the 2007–2008 school year (2008–2009 figures have not been released) the pass rate was 64.81 percent in mathematics, 63.89 percent in science, 57.90 per cent in English, 61.62 percent in social sciences and 73.18 per cent in Filipino. All scores were low compared to the desired 75 percent cut-off score, UNESCO said.
>
> For the same year the Philippines ranked 41st in science and 42nd in mathematics from among 45 countries in the Trends in International Math and Science Survey, according

to UNESCO. As for secondary education, the UNESCO says that the quality "is not far from that of the elementary level as indicated by the poor performance of fourth-year students in the National Achievement Test."[21]

The lack of government investment systematically disenfranchised education as a public service for a public good. Deprived of the quantity and quality of teachers, classrooms, facilities, and textbooks, the student's value—precisely as effect of a systemic excess lack—is always already undervalued, making it a conducive resource for capital exploitation and accumulation.

The privatization of Philippine education is structured not only by government neglect but also by high private sector stakes. Basic education is 80 percent in the hands of the government, 20 percent in the private sector. However, on the tertiary level, education is inversely skewed in favor of the private sector: 80 percent private, 20 percent government.[22] Individuals become highly reliant on their own resources, including labor, in the procurement of tertiary education. In order to further conform to global standards of K-12 (Kindergarten and twelve years of basic education), the program was introduced in 2011 for full implementation by 2018, and envisioned to replace the ten-year basic education.[23] After finishing junior high school, the student is given a TVET (Technical Vocational Education and Training) certificate that already allows for basic employment. Senior high school becomes a filtering program to allow feeds to three tracks: academic, technical-vocational-livelihood, and sports and the arts. What the K-12 program will realize is the immediate employability of basic education graduates, and the non-necessity of tertiary education for all. The latter all the more renders tertiary education—to what will now be a year less than the present load—as an even greater elite marker.

While the United Nations benchmarks 6 percent of gross domestic product to be spent for education, the Philippines only spends 2.6 percent (USD 318 per person) for education, one of the lowest when compared to its Asian neighbors, such as Thailand, which spends USD 1,048 per person.[24] Next to Cambodia, the Philippines also has the largest student-to-teacher ratio for the elementary level in Southeast Asia, at 60–80:1.[25] The Filipino youth is disenfranchised through education. Underfunded, ill-equipped, lacking quality jobs, the youth—for the most part—are condemned to become exploited excess labor bodies in the service of neoliberal capitalism. With newer pedagogical jargons introduced in the

KEYWORDS

Asia Pacific Economic Cooperation (APEC), the thrust for "life-long education" is deemed translatable to retooling and re-skilling in the light of massive layoffs, and furthers labor contractualization and flexibilization.[26] "Universal mobility" means a standardization of programs and curricula across member countries in order to assure the quality of free movement of professionals and laborers.

With dwindling budgets in education, state universities and colleges (SUCs) are not even just encouraged but required to corporatize to generate additional sources of income. Additional income comes largely from school fees. In a study of select state universities and colleges in their experience with corporatization, it was found that school fees account for 94 percent of additional income, while 6 percent comes from business income.[27] Students, through fees generated from them, subsidize public tertiary education, and have allowed "improvements and significant effect on SUCs' growth in terms of number of program offerings, number of faculty and extension projects."[28] UP, a national university in the Philippines, has developed through time as an elite outpost: "UP draws from the wealthiest and most educated families in the population, in which 58% of fathers have finished college and 77% are professionals or administrators."[29] It is only within the private sector that the high-tuition Catholic schools are "skewed to the wealthy as UP."[30]

UP's alignment with the elite was already observed in 1991. However, more recent developmental goals have concretized UP's placement with elite education. UP's privileged academic position has allowed it to be the only state university to excel even among the best private institutions. It nurtured the hope of the best and the brightest, especially for the underclass, to have access to quality tertiary education. However, the introduction and continuous tweaking of the STFAP have allowed for a social reengineering of its student population. In 1989, the initial implementation of STFAP doubled the per-unit matriculation fee, from PhP 150 to PhP 300.[31] This was further increased in 2007 to PhP 1,500 per unit. In school year 1991–1992, 20 percent of UP's students were full scholars (full tuition fee waiver and monthly allowance), but in 2010–2011 it was down to only 2 percent. The dwindling support of the national government to UP and UP's own mechanism for income generation or systematic disenfranchisement of the underclass have favored the upper class. STFAP's history proved that it was developed to generate income from students, and not to socialize the cost of education in UP.

Contrary to STFAP's failure to support the underclass's education, the program is one of the most sought-after UP legacies for the rest of the SUCs. The Commission on Higher Education (CHED), the agency tasked with quality assurance in tertiary education, has mapped out STFAP as a key program to be implemented by all SUCs. In its "Roadmap for Public Higher Education Program," CHED endeavors to re-rationalize tertiary education through its greater bureaucratization aimed at "maximizing the system's contribution toward developing competent and high-level human resources and generating knowledge and technologies needed for advancing the country's national development and competitiveness."[32] In what seems like a re-versioning upgrade—similar to software and hardware development—the value-added rhetoric of greater applicability of tertiary education in national development and global competitiveness, albeit paradigmatically problematic, resurfaces. Education is reinstrumentalized as an "instrument of poverty alleviation" and a "vehicle for technologically-driven national development and global competitiveness."[33]

The basic premise of Philippine education remains unresolved, if not altogether reaffirmed: that education produces the affordable labor for national development and global competitiveness, which means it remains functionally skilled and appropriate-able (exploitable) in global capitalism. SUCs are poised to be self-reliant ("maximize resource generation") on the one hand, and inclusive ("expand access . . . among lower income and disadvantaged groups)—primarily through STFAP and other scholarship and loan programs—on the other hand.[34] The SUCs have been left for remedial and reiterative work, with CHED relying mostly on initiatives and progress generated by private institutions: catering to the poor and disadvantaged, focusing on priority programs in instruction, research, and extension, "which the private sector cannot adequately provide," including geographic areas not serviced by the private sector.[35]

The response has been two-fold and begins in various points in contemporary Philippines. Education has prevented the rise of a strong middle class, allowing for a sizeable graduate population since the 1970s to become overseas contract workers (OCWs). In a study by anthropologist Raul Pertierra, both parents and children who aspire to higher education do so as a form of "political involution": the most important reason for parents to work overseas is to finance their children's education, but the desire by parents to persevere is that the children themselves can also become OCWs.[36] As a result of the prioritization of fiscal mobility, political citizenry is deprioritized: "Lacking political clout or economic muscle, the middle class is forced to adopt the strategies of exclusion typifying the elite. In the process, they may ensure individual success but at the cost of public structures which, in the end, are the only guarantors of values of competence and achievement characterizing the middle class."[37]

The 2000s offered another multinational node to Philippine education, working in the nation-space under the sunshine industry of BPO. The optimism in BPO work is unmatched in economic history:

> According to the Business Processing Association of the
> Philippines, the BPO industry revenue is targeted to reach
> US$13.4 billion for 2012 (the year-end financial report for 2012
> has not yet been released as of this time). This is an increase of
> 22 percent over 2011's revenues of $11 billion. The projection
> for 2013 is an even larger $16 billion with over 926,000 Filipinos
> being employed in various BPO jobs, up from 770,000 for 2012.
> By 2016, the IT-BPO industry is expected to rake in $25 billion—
> almost 9 percent of the Philippines' GDP, and employ 1.3 million
> Filipinos.[38]

Even as the industry is able to generate some eighty to one hundred thousand new jobs, the tight labor market remains a complaint of employers.[39] Forty-nine percent is the ideal rate, but only five to ten percent gets hired.[40] Untrained and unskilled for BPO jobs, prospective laborers are being trained through a coordinated effort among employers and the government.

Health issues remain a high concern for call center workers. Night shift is preferred by employers to service clients abroad, particularly the U.S., and is also preferred by workers because of untaxed differential premium pay. Health issues about the eyes, cough, voice disorders, and insomnia are prevalent in call center workplaces, as are restless leg syndrome, obstructive sleep apnea, and stress. As a result of health and work issues, BPO offices allow for leisure comforts to cushion the work load and attrition of workers. According to Executive Director Joselito Uligan of the Contact Center Association of the Philippines, "This is the only industry where companies provide facilities like gym, spa, cafeteria, gaming rooms and even day-care centers. They even allow Facebook access. There're a lot of things we provide to our people that other companies in other industries don't, won't, can't, or couldn't."[41] The gentrified lifestyle is also manifested in the redevelopment of urban landscapes, allowing for the construction boom in office spaces in Manila and other major cities. This urban redevelopment creates an atmosphere of economic takeoff. In laborers' bodies, the gentrification is individually witnessed in the acquisition of gadgets and 24/7 services that cater to this new army of laborers in the boom industry. The underside of this middle-class lifestyle, however, involves sexual promiscuity as the increasing HIV incidence rate among workers would indicate.

What OCWs and BPO workers share in common is the low-end quality of available jobs: dead-end, contractual, high-risk, and alienating work. The mismatched quality and quantity of students and graduates produced in the educational system allow capitalists to appropriate Filipino laboring bodies for capital accumulation. Rendered docile subjects in education, laborers are further reified as docile in low-end quality of available employment. Having found two specific niches in the global and sexual division of labor, the mobility of Filipino laboring bodies is contained, allowing for limited collective growth and criticality. By being categorized as contractuals, laborers are not deemed as a thorough political entity with rights, especially the right to organize into unions and to strike. The euphemism of "human rights" is made to stand for the most basic of individual entitlements, not for a collective political expression.

Education in the Service
of Neoliberalism

According to Terry Eagleton, "To study an ideological formation, then, is among other things to examine the complex set of linkages or mediation between its most articulate and least articulate levels."[42] The ideological formation in and through education perpetuates state formation and transformation in neoliberalism. It involves meaning, or the signification process, and "non-meaning" or the invisibility of the very operation of signification, even as such invisibility exerts an impact on the becoming of ideology and its ideological practices. My contention is that ideological formation in Philippine education has moved from a cultural imposition that routinizes and sedentizes meaning to a praxis similar to popular culture and other mediated youth experiences: a service sector formation that can demand entertainment and leisure comforts (similar to those amenities in the BPO workplace). More attuned to a middle-class fantasy, commercialized and privatized education now demands value-for-money, greater efficiency and openness, service with a smile, harnessing of the client's agency, and industry partnership, among others.

Like popular culture, education is generated for income and profit, acclimatizes middle-class culture as its benchmark, is entwined in a sado-masochistic commodity fetishism, is urban-based, and is experienced in the pleasure mode. Like media, education is mass-generated for a private good—the good of the individual client. It has moved toward greater privatization of the good, negating the principle of education as a public good that empowers the individual to empower the public. Also like media, education hides the true motive for the generation of information and service—profit. Anecdotal accounts, days and months prior to Tejada's death, portray this imbrication to a newer education drive or a newer ideological formation in and through education. According to her parents, Tejada wanted to become a student of UP and when she did become a first-year college student, "She loved studying. She loved UP. She believed that financial limitations shouldn't be a hindrance to education. She didn't expect that the system implemented last year would defeat her."[43]

Tejada's feeling of betrayal by the system was accumulated through her short stint at UP. She skipped classes after missing deadlines for payments, and her ID had to be forcibly returned to UP. Yet, every morning, she would still wake up thinking she was going to the university. Similar to the capitalist imperative of "no work, no pay" to laborers, Tejada's violent predicament was rendered by the university's "no pay, no service" imperative, treated no differently to the services for utilities. Like laborers fired or laid off, Tejada had very little recourse. Her death, however, became a powerful drive to question the very forces, meaning, and non-meaning in the ideological formation of education. It ransomed ideology, temporally heralding an end-of-ideology as the educational system has reached a cultural turn. For the first time, the calls for the scrapping of STFAP and the fight for full state subsidy have efficaciously been significant.

Education's ideology is rationalized by agencies such as UP and other SUCs, and by the state. Efficiency in the delivery of services meant efficiency in collecting tuition fees, generating other sources of income, managing income, cutting costs and services, or shifting resources to high-demand courses. It involves acts of self-deception: that such things have to be done to make education more relevant and competitive. Or on the level of Tejada until her death: that UP was worth living for. Rationalization also involves legitimation or "the process by which the ruling power comes to secure from its subjects an at least tacit consent to its authority."[44] Immediately after hearing of Tejada's death, UP announced that it was just in the process of announcing actions intended to liberalize STFAP. In this claim, UP was legitimizing its 24/7 drive toward bettering the lives of its clients and the nation. And thus, UP's legitimation claims for the better individual good, or even for the glory of the state, universalize its existence as the premier state university, still affording access to those who do not have newer historical access and claims to it.

Tejada's story is heart-wrenching, and so are the stories of the hundreds of thousands who have not had access to tertiary education, who were fortunate to have entered but have dropped out, who graduated and have landed in unemployment and underemployment. A book such as this on Philippine media cultures and neocolonial-isms employs a relational affective resonance. But it is the mapping out of media cultures and its integral function in neocolonialisms that allows for sites of resistance and collective possibilities to also be foregrounded. This is where I draw a kind of purposive strength on why I write the way I do.

K
E
Y
W
O
R
D
S

Such individual choice, as a Philippine scholar and citizen, also generates support from the political and cultural solidarities I have formed and that have formed me. I am grateful to colleagues from the Congress of Teachers and Educators for Nationalism and Democracy (CONTEND) for inculcating the continuing need for consciousness-raising, mobilizing, and organizing; to the Manunuring Pelikulang Pilipino (Filipino Film Critics Group) for making annual film viewing an integral work in the filtering, at least for myself, of alternative and oppositional aesthetic possibilities; and to the University of the Philippines, where friendships and comradeships abound, and for harnessing its 1970s radical history in asserting its political present and future.

Foremost in the support to gather these essays and to rework them toward the found theme on keywords and neocolonialism is the Center for Southeast Asian Studies of Kyoto University where I had stayed from October 2007 to April 2008 as visiting research fellow. I wish to also thank Rica Bolipata-Santos and Maricor Baytion, Ateneo University Press directors, for guiding the project to its fruition in this book form. To the work and friendships of the Ateneo Press staff, and copyeditors Randy Bustamante, Linda Bulong, and Mel S. Bulong for making the publication process lighter than how it usually is.

I am also thankful for the feedback of the blind referees that shaped this Introduction and final version of the manuscript.

"Film in the Age of Empire: Cinema, Gender and Sexuality in the U.S. Colonization of the Philippines," *Bulawan: Journal of Philippine Arts and Culture* (2001): 68–79.

"Animating the Nation: Animation and Development in the Philippines," in *Animation in Asia and the Pacific,* edited by John Lent (UK: John Libbey Publishing, 2001), 167–80.

"Dogeating/Dogeaters: Abjection in Philippine Colonial and Neocolonial Discourse," *Philippine Studies: Have We Gone Beyond St. Louis?,* edited by Priscelina Patajo-Legasto (Quezon City: University of the Philippines Press, 2008), 665–82.

"Popular Discourse of Vietnam in the Philippines," *Philippine Studies* 50, no. 2 (2002): 230–50.

"Primordial Milk: Japanese Cinema's Representation of the Philippines," *Transglobal Economies and Cultures: Contemporary Japan and Southeast Asia* (Quezon City: University of the Philippines Press; National University of Singapore, 2004), 275–311.

"Local/Global Nation and Hysteria: Japanese Children's Television in the Philippines," in *Image and Reality: Philippine-Japan Relations Towards the 21st Century,* edited by Rolando S. Dela Cruz (Quezon City: Institute of International Legal Relations, U.P., 1997), 239–62.

"Sovereign Nations, Sovereign Bodies: Japanese Legal Culture, Animation Studies, Security and Sovereignty," *Danyag* (UP-Visayas Journal of Humanities and Social Sciences) 3, no. 2 (Dec 1998): 121–40.

"Popular as Political: The Fatherland, Nationalist Films and Modernity in South Korea, Taiwan and the Philippines," *Kritika Kultura* (2003).

"The Fatherland, Nationalist Films and Modernity in South Korea, Taiwan and the Philippines," *Public Policy* 3, no. 1 (Jan–Mar 1999): 82–101.

"Masses, Power, and Gangsterism in the Films of Joseph 'Erap' Estrada," *Kasarinlan* 25, nos. 1–2 (2010). "Political Economy of Ideas," http://journals.upd.edu.ph/index.php/kasarinlan/article/view/1998.

"Lack and Excess in the Filmic Representations of Justice," *Mindanao Forum* (Official Journal of the MSU-Iligan Institute of Technology) 21, no. 2 (Dec 2008): 75–96.

"The Poverty of Justice: Postcolonial Condition and Representations of Justice in Contemporary Philippine Cinema," *Cinema, Law, and the State in Asia* (New York: Palgrave Macmillan, 2007), 85–100.

"Piracy Regulation and the Filipino's Historical Response to Globalization," *Social Science Diliman* 5, nos. 1–2 (Jan 2008–Dec 2009): 1–25.

"Vaginal Economy: Cinema and Globalization in the Post-Marcos Post-Brocka Era," *Humanities Diliman* 7, no. 2 (2010), http://journals.upd.edu.ph/index.php/humanitiesdiliman/article/viewArticle/1988.

"Globalizing National Domesticity: Female Work and Representation in Contemporary Women's Films," *Philippine Studies*, Social Fantasies, 57, no. 3 (2009): 419–42.

ENDNOTES

1   Raymond Williams, *Keywords: A Vocabulary of Culture and Society* (Croom Helm, 1976), later revised into *Culture and Society*. Another expanded version was published by Fontana in 1983, and Blackwell published *New Keywords: A Revised Vocabulary of Culture and Society* in 2005, expanding on Williams's original work.

2   Quoted in Reiner Padua and Evelyn Macairan, "New Enrolment Ruling: If Only Kristel had Known," *Philippine Star*, 17 Mar 2013, accessed 12 May 2013, http://www.philstar.com/headlines/2013/03/17/920669/new-enrolment-ruling-if-only-kristel-had-known.

3   UP Manila Chancellor Manuel Agulto, quoted in "UP: Student's Death an 'Isolated Unfortunate' Case," *Sun Star*, 18 Mar 2013, accessed 12 May 2013, http://www.sunstar.com.ph/breaking-news/2013/03/18/students-death-isolated-unfortunate-case-273547.

4   Karl Marx, "The Limits of the Working Day," *Capital* Volume 1, accessed 12 May 2013, http://www.marxists.org/archive/marx/works/1867-c1/ch10.htm#S1.

5   David P. Barrows, "What May Be Expected from Philippine Education?" *The Journal of Race Development* 1, 2 (Oct 1910): 160.

6   Ibid., 159–60.

7   W. C. Grimes, "Organization and Administration of Education in the Philippine Islands," *The Phi Delta Kappan* 10, no. 6 (Apr 1928): 175.

8   Barrows, "What May Be Expected," 162.

9   See Daniel F. Doeppers, *Manila 1900–1941: Social Change in a Late Colonial Metropolis* (Quezon City: Ateneo de Manila University Press, 1984).

10   Chester L. Hunt and Thomas R. McHale, "Education and Philippine Economic Development," *Comparative Education Review* 9, no. 1 (Feb 1965): 69–70.

11   Pauline Crumb Smith, "A Basic Problem in Philippine Education," *The Far Eastern Quarterly* 4, no. 2 (Feb 1946): 143.

12   Hunt and McHale, "Education," 69.

13   Dona Z. Pazzibugan, "Teachers May Receive P5K to P35K in Bonuses," *Philippine Daily Inquirer*, 5 Mar 2013, accessed 12 May 2013, http://newsinfo. inquirer.net/368597/teachers-may-receive-p5k-to-p35k-in-bonuses.

14   James A. LeRoy, "'Laissez-Faire' in the Philippine Islands," *Journal of Political Economy* 12, no. 2 (Mar 1904): 191.

15   Ibid., 195.

16   Ibid., 198.

17   Karl Marx, "The Modern Theory of Colonization," *Capital* Volume 1, accessed 12 May 2013, http://www.marxists.org/archive/marx/works/1867-c1/ch33.htm.

18   *Manila Times* editorial, quoted in Karl Wilson, "School Drop-Out Rates Highlight Lost Decade of Education in the Philippines," *The National,* 28 Jun 2010, accessed 12 May 2013, http://www.thenational.ae/news/world/asia-pacific/school-drop-out-rates-highlight-lost-decade-of-education-in-philippines#full.

19   Juan Edgardo Angara, cited in Paolo Romero, "Angara: Quality Education for All," *Philippine Star*, 30 Apr 2013, accessed 12 May 2013, http://www.philstar.com/headlines/2013/04/30/936537/angara-quality-education-all.

20   National Statistics Office, cited in Darwin G. Amojelar, "Lots of Jobs for College Grads but Do They Want the Work?" *InterAksyon*, 14 Jan 2013, accessed 12 May 2013, http://www.interaksyon.com/business/52619/lots-of-jobs-for-college-grads-but-do-they-want-the-work.

21   UNESCO, cited in Wilson, "School Drop-Out Rates."

22   Robert P. Cooney, "Education in the Philippines Part II," accessed 12 May 2013, http://www.wes.org/ewenr/wenrarchive/RP_EdInThePhilippPart2Spr89.pdf. Also in Estelle James, "Private Higher Education: The Philippines as Prototype," *Higher Education* 21, no. 1 (Mar 1991): 189.

23   See Official Gazette, accessed 12 May 2013, http://www.gov.ph/k-12/#Implementation.

24   UNESCO, cited in Wilson, "School Drop-Out Rates," and also cited in "Primer on 'Scrap STFAP,'" 22 Apr 2013.

25   Alliance of Concerned Teachers, cited in Wilson, "School Drop-Out Rates."

26   See Ramon Guillermo, "Rationalizing Failures: The Philippine Government in the Education Sector," Courage Online from Education for Development Magazine, Ibon Databank, Dec 1997, accessed 12 May 2013, http://www.skyinet.net/~courage/position/act-edanalysis.htm. "Life-long education" and "universal mobility" are examples drawn from Guillermo.

27 Renato F. Malate, "Corporatization of State Universities and Colleges: Impact on Higher Education," *The Threshold* 4 (Jan–Dec 2009), 84.

28 Ibid., 82.

29 LeRoy, "Laissez–Faire," 203.

30 Ibid.

31 For the development of STFAP, see "Primer on 'Scrap STFAP.'"

32 CHED, "Roadmap for Public Higher Education Reform" (2011), 1.

33 Philippine Development Plan 2011–2016, quoted in CHED, "Roadmap."

34 Ibid., 2.

35 Ibid., 3.

36 Raul Pertierra, "The Mythology and Politics of Philippine Education," *Kasarinlan: Philippine Journal of Third World Studies* 10, no. 3 (1995): 113–14, accessed 12 May 2013, http://journals.upd.edu.ph/index.php/kasarinlan/article/viewArticle/1686.

37 Ibid., 119.

38 Business Processing Association of the Philippines, cited in Romel Panabi, "Demand for BPO Work Remains High in 2013," accessed 12 May 2013, http://www.likejobs.com/articles/demand-for-bpo -employees- remains-high-for-2013.

39 Joselito Uligan, Contact Center Association of the Philippines, cited in Benito D. Estopace, "BPO Workers Opt For Jobs Overseas," *Business Mirror*, 3 Apr 2013, accessed 12 May 2013, http://www.abs-cbnnews.com/business/04/02/12/bpo-workers-opt-jobs-overseas.

40 Business Processing Association of the Philippines, cited in Panabi, "Demand for BPO Work."

41 Uligan, quoted in Estopace, "Jobs Overseas."

42 Terry Eagleton, *Ideology: An Introduction* (London: Verso, 1991), 50.

43 Blesilda Tejada, mother, quoted in Erika Sauler, "For Kristel Tejada, Studying Was a Coping Mechanism," *Philippine Daily Inquirer*, 18 Mar 2013, accessed 12 May 2013, http://newsinfo.inquirer.net/375303/for-kristel-tejada-studying-was-a-coping-mechanism.

44 Eagleton, *Ideology*, 54.

KEYWORDS

Empire

Gender and Sexuality in U.S. Colonialism

Film critic Ella Shohat, in invoking the need to synthesize feminist and postcolonial cultural critiques, mentions a basic absence of a connection in the writings of historiography of cinema: that "the beginnings of cinema coincided with the height of imperialism between the late nineteenth century and World War I."[1] So, too, in this space of absence is the negation of the language of "engenderment" and sexualization that have punctuated the rise of imperialism and that have been articulated in cinema. This essay maps out the relational fields in the language of engenderment and sexualization specific to the U.S. colonization of the Philippines. It outlines the modes by which the Philippines is engendered and sexualized, and how its feminine engenderment and sexualization become integral to the U.S. imperialist project of enlightenment and modernization. In particular, the essay provides a close textual reading of pioneering films, implicating notions of territorialization and bodies. I relate how these films open to a symptomatic reading and which, in turn, implicate how its own use of the language of engenderment and sexualization becomes necessary to articulate the imperialist project.

Colonialism, after all, gets codified through a rhetorical practice of engenderment and sexualization. By rhetorical I mean not just the verbal representation but also the material forces that substantiate language and other forms of representation. Poised in the language of machismo and patriarchy (virgin land, conquest, and benevolent assimilation, for example), colonialism is materialized not only through the political and economic institutions but also through the covert practice of a superior race—culturally represented as the virile colonialist male—saving and conquering an inferior race. Films rhetorically pose a covert colonialism. Our present fascination with Hollywood films, for example, provides evidence for the continuing American homogenization of our own culture. Such national fascination and cultural imperialism have their historical roots with the introduction of films—especially those that seek to represent Filipino-American relations—in the country. Films become museums of the everyday, socializing citizenship toward the American cultural paradigm. As museum displays, films act as cultural artifacts, providing historical and social testimonies of moments that define past and present nationhood and collectivity. This notion also finds affinity with what used to be popular museums in the U.S. at the turn-of-the-twentieth century, when exhibitions, like films, used spectacles to represent the triumphs of civilization, including the conquest of inferior races.

KEYWORDS

As an issue of hegemonic historiography, the U.S. history of violent suppression of Filipino anti-colonial struggles is erased as the "little known war," consequentially rewriting U.S. involvement as one of "immaculate conception" which "mystifies the origins and motivations of American foreign policy" as especially anecdotal and ambivalent.[2] By mapping the language of engenderment and sexualization involved in the U.S. colonization of the Philippines, I foreground some basis of critique of this dominant historiography, positioning such "immaculate conception myth" within the very terrain of the political economy of such engenderment and sexualization.

I begin this essay by rereading some basic historical texts of colonialization, mapping out how these texts are fueled by a libidinal economy that is articulated in the language of engenderment and sexualization. By constantly returning to the ideals of the imperialist project—enlightenment and modernization in general—I further draw some linkages to the consequent turn to transnationalism and late capitalism as these are presently experienced. The second half of the essay is devoted to a reading of the three short films, implicating issues raised in the first section. I focus the discussion in my reading of these films on the issues of territorialization (frontier myth, war, colonization) and territorialization as experienced through bodies (marking, differentiating, engendering, sexualizing, and racializing). I turn to the larger concept of the exhibition—a popular experienciation of display and representation, development and progress, travel and space—as a relational field in which some issues raised in film cohere with the imperialist project. My intention is to make the connections between film and the age of American empire-building more historically and culturally specific.

The turn of the twentieth century signaled U.S. rise as a global power. With a need to expand its markets and assert its growing dominance, the U.S. turned to a declining colonial power. Spain provided little resistance to U.S. conquest of its territories (Cuba, Puerto Rico, and the Philippines). Admiral George Dewey's overwhelming victory against the Spanish armada in Manila Bay was greeted with astonishment and national pride. William McKinley set the tone for enlightened colonization in 1898. In a remark to a Methodist Delegation, he pounded on the dilemma of colonizing the Philippines:

> I thought first that we would take only Manila; then Luzon;
> then other islands, perhaps, also. I walked on the floor of the
> White House night after night until midnight; and I am not
> ashamed to tell you gentlemen, that I went down on my knees
> and prayed Almighty God for light and guidance more than
> one night.... And one night it came to me this way... there
> was nothing left for us to do but to take them all, educate
> the Filipinos, and uplift and civilize and Christianize them,
> and by God's grace do the very best we could by them, as our
> fellowmen for whom Christ also died. And then I went to bed,
> and went to sleep and slept soundly, and the next morning
> I sent for the chief engineer of the War Department (our
> mapmaker), and I told him to put the Philippines on the map of
> the U.S.[3]

This was precisely in contrast to Spain's mode of colonization, described oxymoronically as *"backward* colonialism." After introducing the *pueblo* (town) and *hacienda* (plantation) systems, there was little concern left for the welfare of the people. The Spanish language and education were privileged spheres for the colonizers and the local elites. Spain's colonization positions the Philippines in the feudal feminine where sexual power is realized on ignorance or repression of knowledge.

Interestingly, however, McKinley's confession directs to the notion of religious epiphany as the moment of enlightenment. Epiphany becomes the moment of realization of the connective sense and power of the imperialist project, i.e., the connection of individual condition (McKinley's anguish and torment) with the object of the condition (Philippines) to the larger "benevolent" project (the manifest destiny of the U.S./imperialism). Grounded on the ethos of Protestantism, epiphany becomes the individual's realization of himself in the larger structure that holds the individual and society together. McKinley's moment becomes emblematic of the Anglo-Saxon tradition of enlightenment, allowing individual torment to foreground the justification for the violent suppression of dissent in the name of a larger cause. His simple command to the chief engineer to position the Philippines in the U.S. map would have serious reverberations and ramifications in various socio-political and economic spheres, all subsumed into the knowledge that the individual is doing the right thing. Note McKinley's shifting positionings of "I" and "we," where the "I" refers to his individual torment, and "we" to implicate the collective bodies of people supposedly backing the rubric of the imperialist project. In invoking to "do the very best *we* could by them," "we" comes at the crucial point that calls the nation into a decisive national action, one marked by benevolence and necessity, one of manifest destiny.

Consequently, McKinley is calling for the construction of the Philippines as approximating the imperialist ideals, a clay to be molded into the ideal subjects of enlightenment. His invocation of the Philippine image is a desire for mimetic power: "the ability to mime, and mime well, in other words is the capacity to Other."[4] In thus prescribing "to educate the Filipinos, and uplift and civilize and Christianize them, and . . . do the very best we could by them," McKinley is juxtaposing the concept of the old and the new in which modernity becomes the imperative to conquer the inferior feudal formation. Embodying the logic of the "white man's burden," McKinley was repositioning the colonized to some figurative shadow of the white man. Inversely taken, therefore, the colonized is already engendered: uneducated, abjected, uncivilized, pathetic. These are the very qualities of the Spanish colonization and feminization of the Philippines. The same inversion produces the Philippines as ripe for conquest and submission to a more powerful benefactor/exploiter.

McKinley's feminized figure of the Philippines is to bear some semblance of the qualities of the civilized. However, the colonized figure has to be constructed as sexually provocative and provoking to necessitate conquest. Seduction must come into play prior to the enlightenment objective. In January 1900, Alfred J. Beveridge's first Senate speech emphasized the unlimited resources of the Philippines:

> No land in America surpasses in fertility the plains and valleys
> of Luzon. Rice and coffee, sugar and coconuts, hemp and
> tobacco, and many products of the temperate as well as the
> tropic zone grow in various sections of the archipelago. . . .
> The wood of the Philippines can supply the furniture of the
> world for a century to come. At Cebu the best informed man of
> the island told me that 40 miles of Cebu's mountain chain are
> practically mountains of coal. . . .
>   I have a nugget of pure gold picked up in its present form
> on the banks of a Philippine creek. I have gold dust washed
> out by crude processes of careless natives from the sands of a
> Philippine stream. Both indicate great deposits at the source
> from which they come. . . .[5]

The fertile agriculture and abundant natural spaces become the site of figuration of the woman-nation. Depicted as "virginal," "under-developed" yet "overly endowed," the Philippines becomes ripe for conquest and submission by all means necessary. The exaggeration of the nation's assets puts the figure in a double-bind in relation to its own national development, why it remains underdeveloped. The fault is underscored in the relationships with Spain as the inadequate provider and with its own people as the incapable provider. Beveridge continues:

> Spain's export and import trade with the islands [is]
> undeveloped, $11,534,731 annually. Ultimately our trade, when
> the islands shall be developed, will be $125,000,000 annually,
> for who believes that we cannot do ten times as well as Spain? . . .
>   It will be hard for Americans who have not studied them
> to understand the people. They are a barbarous race, modified
> by three centuries of contact with a decadent race. The Filipino
> is a South Sea Malay, put through a process of three hundred
> years of superstition in religion, dishonesty in dealing, disorder
> in habits of industry, and cruelty, caprice, and corruption in
> government. It is barely possible that 1,000 men in all the

archipelago are capable of self-government in the Anglo-Saxon
sense.

> ... But, Senators, it would be better to abandon this
> combined garden and Gibraltar of the Pacific, and count our
> blood and treasured already spent a profitable loss, than to
> apply any academic arrangement of self-government to these
> children. They are not capable of self-government. How
> could they be? They are not of a self-governing race. They are
> Orientals, Malays, instructed by Spaniards in the latter's worst
> estate.[6]

Like its construction of a feminized position for the Philippines,
the U.S. also constructs such a position for the Orient through the
feminization of all other sources of threat—other colonizers and
other local populations. What remains, therefore, is a notion of the
U.S. as the only viable masculine project that could necessarily
dominate the Orient of its resistance and possibilities. The U.S. thus
spells the potent agent of twentieth century modernization.

The assertion of Anglo-Saxon masculinity is doubly inscribed
in this logic. Firstly, it positions the Philippines to the feminine
and woman to nature, and therefore, in need of a more enlightened
penetration for the possibility of economic and cultural ideals to
be productively disseminated. Secondly, it positions the masculine
in Spain as inept and in the Philippines as inherently immature. As
such, there is a rescue fantasy at work here: the U.S. wants to save
the Philippines from its Spanish colonizers, and to a more marginal
position, from its own kind. Thus the U.S. rhetoric inserts itself as the
only logical solution to the ineptness and political immaturity of all
other masculinities.

There is a second imperative to the U.S. evangelization of colonization of the Philippines—the possibility of further asserting its
growing dominance, its masculinity in the feminized space of the
Orient:

> [T]he archipelago is a base for the commerce of the East. It is a
> base for military and naval operations against the only powers
> with whom conflict is possible; a fortress thrown up in the
> Pacific, defending our Western coast, commanding the waters
> of the Orient, and giving us a point from which we can instantly
> strike and seize the possession of any possible foe.[7]

In summary, through the dual objective of modernization and enlightenment, the U.S. is able to maintain the Philippines as a feminized figure ripe for conquest and submission on the one hand, and education and cultural upliftment on the other. The language of the imperialist project maintains the objectifiable feminine position of the colony, precisely in order to draw the necessity of continuing domination. U.S. colonialism seeks to emplace a language of binary opposition (man/woman) in its rule of the colony. However, such emplacement is not at all an immutable position. Even with the stranglehold of colonialism, the populace resisted and dialogued in various ways, making the experience of colonialism a contentious one. Colonialism and the very language of its engendered and sexualized articulation are engaged in a contest for hegemonic and linguistic coherence with the forces they seek—but never wholly dominate. In the succeeding section, the language is mapped out in film.

Cinema's entry into the Philippines in 1897, with the introduction of the Lumière cinematograph and films, signaled the circuiting of the Philippines into several transitory periods: from Spain to U.S. colonization, and from colonialist to imperialist capitalism. Cinema comes at an opportune time when technology was transforming modernity from individual to mechanical reproduction of reality. Necessitating new markets for mass-produced commodities, the U.S. competed for a global share of cinema at a time when its factories were also bursting at the seams, producing surplus products also needing new markets. Film's coming into the Philippines marks a shift in the experience of reality. Conduit with its developmental model of colonialism, the U.S. also introduced new consumption and cultural patterns. It also involves newer requirements to colonial citizenship, such as public school education and cultural literacy for mass consumption. As such, the Philippines was a direct market for U.S. colonialism and its mass-produced commodities, film being one of them. Film itself upheld U.S. colonialism, introducing technologized ways of visualizing, representations and imaginaries of citizenship, and colonialism in general.

After military censorship rules were lifted in the Philippines, the news of the war of conquest's atrocities became materials for the short features. This further fueled the debates in the U.S. on whether or not to colonize the Philippines. Edison Company would cash in on these burning issues of the times, and produce from his New Jersey location films depicting war in the Philippines, "a bugle-call purpose [of] fanning the imperialistic emotions of the hour."[8] In 1899, he did several films, two of which are listed below, and for which Kemp Niver provides a synopsis:

Advance of Kansas Volunteers at Caloocan
June 5, 1899 (24 ft.)
    The first scene was photographed through thick foliage. Approximately two dozen men have rifles pointed at the camera position. As the films progresses, the men advance towards the camera, firing. From the left and right of the camera are men wearing American Army uniforms, who walk away, firing at the first group of men. A man carrying an American flag follows; he is shot, and another soldier picks up the flag. As the picture ends, the soldier waves the flag triumphantly.

U.S. Troops and Red Cross in the Trenches Before Caloocan
June 5, 1899 (31 ft.)
    As the camera begins, a ditch or trench can be seen in a heavily wooded area. A man attired in a U.S. Army infantry officer's uniform jumps into the ditch and brandishes a sword indicating that others should follow. Soon the trench is filled with approximately twenty men wearing American infantry uniforms. They fire their rifles over the rim of the trench, gesture as if cheering, and proceed to leave the trench. The film ends as two of the men fall wounded, and two women dressed in Red Cross nurses' uniforms are seen bending over him.[9]

These films sustained fantasies of indefatigable and heroic imperialist conquest. In the first film, the maintenance of the flag calls nationalism into fold. The war in the Philippines becomes a nationalist issue where winning is the only honorable way out. The flag's partial disappearance creates anxiety; its consequential resurfacing via a proud erect soldier waving the flag in bold movements instills pride in a nation at war. The flag becomes the phallic symbol of the nation—its sagging posture is reclaimed for erectional pride—representing the totality of the nation united in times of heroic crisis. The Black soldiers portraying Filipino insurgents disappear from screen. The menacing bodies are forced into the background and then erased. By themselves, the figures of American soldiers in uniform become a homogenized temporal image of the nation—invoking its stability even in the presence of a threat and its readiness for death in the pursuit of national ideals. The unconscious at work in this visualization is the eliding of Blacks and Native Americans' issues in

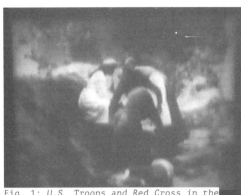

Fig. 1: *U.S. Troops and Red Cross in the Trenches Before Caloocan* June 5, 1899

Fig. 2: *Advance of Kansas Volunteers at Caloocan*

their own dealings with Anglo-Saxon society. The Blacks' enforced migration into the U.S. to work as slaves and the Native Americans' own land disenfranchisement are foreclosed in the visuals of the war simulations in the Philippines. The Blacks' own constant figuration in racial tensions (the Rodney King beating and the L.A. Uprising, for example) is also elided in this presentation.

In the second film, the U.S. war operation is presented as within war protocol, efficient, and humane. All these are posited as counter to the enemy's undertaking, not seen in the frame. The speculation of the identity and body of the enemy is alluded to only within the context of the film title. "Caloocan" becomes an unidentifiable signifier in the spatialization of the war. But atrocities in Caloocan locate the place in an unenviable position. A certain Captain Elliot of the Kansas Regiment writes:

> Caloocan was supposed to contain seventeen thousand inhabitants. The Twentieth Kansas swept through it, and now Caloocan contains not one living native. Of the buildings, the battered walls of the great church and dismal prison alone remain. The village of Maypajo, where our first fight occurred on the night of the fourth, had five thousand people in it that day, —now not one stone remains upon top of another. You can only faintly imagine this terrible scene of desolation. War is worse than hell.[10]

Similar to the first film's scenario, only the American soldiers remain standing triumphantly. However, it is the second film's erasure of the enemy's identity that coincides with Captain Elliot's statements: "they never rebel anymore, there isn't anybody left to rebel."[11]

Thus the entry of women Red Cross nurses foregrounds two issues of the feminine: the positioning of the feminine to the protocols of war and to the humanization of war. The notion of the "home" is transposed to the war zone; the nursing function, however, remains inscribed in the feminine. While seemingly invoking a proto-feminism in women's spatial movement, the presence of the nurses, however, is made conspicuous to the actual events happening in the Philippines. The magnitude of 600,000 Filipino casualties in Luzon island alone, or the involvement of 126,000 American soldiers, is obscured by the sanitized war version in film. The sanitization of the war is inscribed in women's bodies, readily risking their own lives by being placed in the trenches to perform their duties.

KEYWORDS

The spatialization in film of triumphant Anglo-Saxon soldiers
amplify the "myth of the frontier." As Renato Rosaldo explains of
Richard Slotkin's concept:

> [I]n part revolves around the hunter hero who lives out
> his dreams in spiritual sympathy with the creatures of the
> wilderness who teach him their secret lore. "But his intention,"
> Slotkin says, "is always to use the acquired skill against the
> teachers, to kill or assert his dominance over them. The
> consummation of his hunting quest in the killing of the quarry
> confirms him his new and higher character and gives him full
> possession of the powers of the wilderness." In this analysis, the
> disciple turns on his spiritual masters and achieves redemption
> by killing them. This frontier myth, which Slotkin calls
> regeneration through violence, shaped American experience
> from the westward expansion through the imperialist venture
> in the Philippines to the early rhetoric of the Vietnam War.[12]

As such, the penchant to conquer involves an identification
with the other: that which reminds the self of its modernist excess,
of its distance from the pure other. Once negotiated, the imperialist self then begins a move to erase the other, not totally, as Slotkin
and Rosaldo have suggested, but with a distance that allows for both
attraction and repulsion to instantaneously take place.

The "myth of the frontier" created a mythic binary hero who is
both pastoral and violent, or has the best qualities of the civilized
and the savage. These characterizations were to be witnessed in the
U.S. masculinist design for colonial conquest of the Philippines. On
one hand, enlightened colonization introduced democratic institutions and public school education to achieve McKinley's benevolent
ideals. On the other hand, military operations in what will be called
the "original Vietnamization" pacified any resistance to colonial rule.
This was intended to achieve McKinley's "practical" ideals. The dual
strategies for conquest gave rise to stereotypes of the Filipino population. The pastoral strategy sought to train the "infantile" natives for
future independence while the militarist strategy sought to put the
native "savages" under control.

The film, *The American Soldier in Love and War* (9 July 1903), a
three-part short feature shot by a G. W. Bitzer, further focuses on the
elaboration of a dialectics of the inside/outside in categories of impe-
rialist/native, man/woman, white/black, civilized/savage, and adult/
infant. Niver provides a description of the three segments:

The American Soldier in Love and War, No. 1 (32 ft.)

A woman is sitting at a table with her head in her arms in a set of a living room. She moves when a man in military uniform comes into the room from behind a curtain. He walks towards her and begins to comfort her. The film ends as the man in military uniform is embracing the woman.

The American Soldier in Love and War, No. 2 (31 ft.)

A painted backdrop depicts a jungle. From camera right, a man in the uniform of a Spanish-American War soldier enters. He acts as if he is wounded or exhausted and falls to the ground. Two actors, a man and woman dressed as natives, enter from camera left. The male native immediately sets upon the fallen American soldier and attempts to kill him. There is a scuffle. The woman begs for the life of the soldier as the film ends.

The American Soldier in Love and War, No. 3 (27 ft.)

This was filmed from the point of view of a theater audience. The set and surroundings convey the impression of a jungle or a desert island, with heavy foliage and an ocean nearby. The only on-stage piece of equipment is a doorway to a hut. A white man in an Army uniform with a large bandage around his head is sitting in front of the hut. Standing alongside, facing the camera, is an actor made up to resemble a large black woman. She is fanning the man with a palm fan. Another native is holding a bowl from which the wounded soldier is eating. The next action shows a man with a beard and pith helmet arriving accompanied by a white woman wearing a large picture hat. The woman rushes into the arms of the soldier. After much embracing, the soldier indicates the black woman had saved his life, and the picture closes with the white woman removing her necklace and handing it to the other woman.[13]

The film attempts to humanize the war through the figure of the soldier. Soldiers in their symbolic stature and actual work police national borders, believing that what's contained in the inside (the nation's content) is sanctified and sanctimonious, to the extent that Benedict Anderson suggests, "not so much to kill, as to willingly die for such limited imaginings."[14] It also humanizes the war through the family romance. The separation dealt by war leads to a happy resolution with the natural and logical flow of imperial conquest—the natives acknowledge their place in the order, sanctifying the imperialist figure.

Bodies prefigure in this film. David Spurr suggests that "in colonial discourse, the body of the primitive becomes much the object of examination, commentary, and valorization as the landscape of the primitive."[15] The primitive's body, in turn, becomes the marker of racial difference and inferiority. The black woman's body, for example, becomes a shield to the soldier's own body, and in which the utopian vision of the imperialist project is realized. The white woman's body, on the other hand, becomes the nurturer of the domestic space of the home and the homeland. Her transposition to the colony marks the taming of the menacing space of the other: safe enough for a white woman to be in. The hysteria over a white woman and colored man is only too easily provoked as the anti-miscegenation law in the U.S. prevented interracial marriages. However, in transposing the white woman to the space of the native, her traditional home functions also get transposed in the figure of the male and female natives. The white woman's transfer of the necklace to the female native is symbolic of the gesture to transfer domestic functions, too. This has been the criticism with bourgeoisie feminism: it enabled white women, to some extent, to be liberated from the domestic sphere only to have women of color and Third World women assume their place in the domestic and sexual economies.

The black woman is represented as the figure recognizing the node by which the imperial structure is to be deciphered. She is represented as a playful adult, while the male native who misrecognizes the node is represented as infantile—incapable of intellectual redemption. All that the male native is good for is labor provided. But the figure also marks an originary betrayal, of an allegorical selling out to the imperialist. Like Eve's position relative to original sin, the betrayer position becomes a figure of constant blame and interrogation, of having to constantly explain and exonerate oneself.

The "large black woman" and her quick gestural actions mark her with an excess of sexuality, and thus needs to be rescued from her own kind. The male native is doubly marginalized—feminized and infantilized—in this short feature. Such marginal positionings of the male are largely due to the woman's recognition of "proper" space in the imperialist order. Her xenophilia becomes a transcendental mark of her sexuality, i.e., in her defense of whiteness, she is able to retain her sexuality through film; the soldier, however, has no interest. Her energetic willingness to serve the white master foregrounds the continuing tension between her sexuality and the feminization and infantilization of the male, and how much of this positioning is to be blamed on her white fetish.

Masculine imperialist dominance has perpetuated the feminized positioning of the Philippines. Other films shot during the period and available through the Paper Print Collection of the Library of Congress are: *Rout of the Filipinos*; *Capture of the Trenches in Candaba*; *Aguinaldo's Navy*; *Battle of Mr. Ariat* [sic]; *An Historic Feat*; *Pack Train, General Bell's Expedition*; *25th Infantry*; *Bridge Traffic, Manila*; *The Escalta* [sic]*, Manila*; *A Filipino Cock Fight*; *Unloading Lighters, Manila*; *Water Buffalo, Manila*; *Troops Ships for the Philippines*; and *Filipino Scouts, Musical Drill, St. Louis Exposition*. Specific to produced war-related films, "the titles of these films alone suggest the supremacy of the white colonizers over their colonialized subjects . . . The films spoke of defeat, of the capture of Filipino soldiers—in short, of America's triumph over the Filipinos."[16]

Until the late 1910s, Edison Company would continue to shoot "actuality films." However, earlier in 1901, Thomas Edison would immediately turn heroic exploits, say, of Frederick Funston's capture of the Philippine insurgency's elusive leader, Emilio Aguinaldo, into film. *The Philippines Yesterday and Today*, for example, was produced in 1915, and "shows native life in the Philippines, mostly among savages." The reviewer would continue, "the concluding pictures of the series show the progress that is being made in redeeming and educating the people. It may readily be seen that it will take many years to fit all the natives for the responsibility of self-government."[17] Furthermore, ethnographic films were to be utilized to maintain U.S. possession of the Philippines. The quintessential enlightened colonizer, Dean C. Worcester, secretary of the interior in the Philippines, used motion pictures to illustrate how intervention accelerated the native savages' ascent into civilization under American tutelage. *A New York Times* journalist reports on his first public lecture on tribal Filipinos at Carnegie Hall:

> The savage, naked, dirty, and unkept, was shown in still photographs, while the same on-time savage, clothed, intelligent in appearance, and clean, later was shown in moving pictures. Still photography showed the huts of the savages of the early days of the American occupation, while the moving pictures depicted cleanly villages, with beautiful public buildings and neat little homes, after a few years of American rule.[18]

Photographs reflected static qualities while film reflected kinetic movements of bodies into space. Such has been the imperialist usage of film, heightening differentiating intervention on all fronts—economic, educational, cultural, etc.—to generate the temporal ideal:

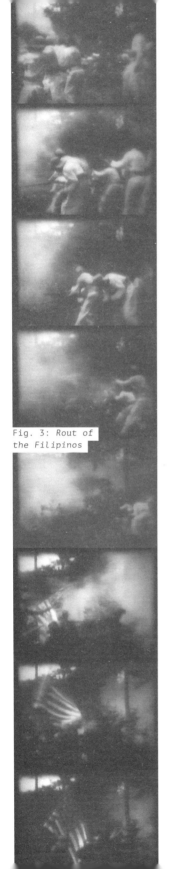

Fig. 3: Rout of
the Filipinos

Fig. 4: Filipinos Retreat
from Trenches

Fig. 5: Water Buffalo, Manila

Fig. 6: The Escalta

conquest, domination, continuing domination, or transformation into neocolonialism.

It is along this area directing to newer modes of experiencing the imperialist project that I shift to a connection of films and the world expositions. Specifically, I draw on Sharra L. Vostral's work "Imperialism on Display: The Philippine Exhibition at the 1904 World's Fair." In the Louisiana Purchase Exposition held at St. Louis, the Philippine exhibition of tribes and culture was in conjunction with the stated goals of "familiarizing the American public with incongruous tribal elements of the Philippine population . . . from lowest types of head-hunting savagery to best products of Christian civilization and culture."[19] In other words, the exhibition was to serve as a gauge to America's efforts so far to colonialize the Philippines, a sort of differentiating "before" and "after" showcase. Thus Vostral would point out:

> its more hidden agenda was to serve as a propaganda tool
> to convince the American people that the new U.S. role as a
> colonial power was a positive one. By portraying Filipinos
> as primitives and showcasing newly established reform and
> educational programs, the Philippine Commission (organizer
> of the Philippine exhibition) hoped to convince a skeptical
> public that the Philippine insurrection against American rule
> had ended and that the U.S. government had the benevolent
> intention of civilizing its "little brown brothers" (a pejorative
> term to refer to Filipinos). The commission also hoped the
> exhibit would promote interest in developing the Philippines'
> rich natural resources.[20]

As an investment, the Philippine exhibition hoped to generate a characterization of the Philippines, and the proper place of the U.S. in the Philippine national character. Thus the exhibition also was working on a spatial dialectics of the inside and the outside. The tribal component—1,100 Filipinos were quartered at the site—was the space of abjection, a primitive culture one becomes attracted to and is repulsed by. It is only the Mineralogy Pavilion, and to a larger extent, the Education Pavilion that further justified continuing U.S. presence in the islands. The imperialists proudly point to its contribution in the latter area: "The Americans, aiming to qualify the population for orderly self-government, have in three years established 2,900 primary schools in which 800 American teachers and thousands of native pedagogues are teaching 200,000 children the primary studies in English."[21] The imperialist project, when pacification was inevitably resolved by violent pacification, shifted attention to a cultural domination. The introduction of the public school system with English as the medium of instruction eventually places a tighter rein on the Philippine colonial consciousness, with many of its effects still pervasive today.

Ella Shohat and Robert Stam make the connection between cinema and ethnographic spectacle: "If cinema itself traced its parentage to popular sideshows and fairs, ethnographic cinema and Hollywood ethnography were the heirs of a tradition of exhibitions of 'real' human objects, a tradition going back to Columbus's importation of 'New World' natives to Europe for purposes of courtly entertainment. Exhibitions organized the world as a spectacle within an obsessively mimetic esthetic."[22] Furthermore, the coincidence is almost dubious—cinema's beginnings coincided with the series of world fairs marking America's unprecedented progress in human civilization.

The notion of exhibition ties in with film's intent at the turn of the century. Both were connected to the imperialist project that sought to present cases of primitiveness and, at the same time, the potentials for civilization. Only through the lingering penetration of imperialism can such potentials be maximized. The reimaging of the native—from primitiveness to civilization—works in the dual instance of attraction and repulsion. Neither one position is totally objectified. It is in the interest of the imperialist project to maintain this dual characterization of the native, for in the bottom line, the native is in itself always already the other of the colonizer.

The mapping out of the imperialist agenda is through the feminization of the native's terrain. In so doing, the imperialist assumes the patriarchal imperatives. But in conjunction with its own project and by way of differentiation from the Spanish colonial project, the drive toward modernization and enlightenment were pursued to economically and politically develop a self-sufficient entity on the one hand, and to culturally be comparable with Anglo-Saxon tradition on the other. The language of engenderment and sexualization became crucial to the U.S. colonization of the Philippines. If the development of film was to be an imperialist symptom, by the 1930s the Philippines was already producing some fifty films to reach its peak of 250 films a year. Presently, with 150 films as its annual output, it ranks third after India and the "three Chinas" as the largest producer of films in Asia. However, Hollywood continues to encroach on the local market. The struggle for visuality and representation continues to this day.

1   Ella Shohat, "Gender and Culture of Empire: Toward a Feminist Historiography of the Cinema," *Quarterly Review of Film and Video* 13, nos. 1–3 (1991): 45.

2   Epifanio San Juan Jr., "For a Critique of Contemporary Imperial Discourse," *Reading the East/Writing the West* (New York: Peter Lang, 1992), 198. In this essay, San Juan was emphasizing Peter Tarr's major critique of Stanley Karnow's *In Our Image: America's Empire in the Philippines* (London: Century, 1990): the conceptualization of U.S. involvement in the Philippines as Karnow's fantasy of "Immaculate Conception," a phrase borrowed from Stuart Creighton Miller. Tarr's essay was published in *The Nation* (5 Jun 1989).

3   William McKinley, "Remarks to a Methodist Delegation," *The Philippines Reader* (Quezon City: Ken, 1987), 25.

4   Michael Taussig, *Mimesis and Alterity: A Particular History of the Senses* (Routledge: New York, 1993), 19. Particularly specific to film, Taussig points out that "Susan Buck-Morss [suggests] that mass culture in our times both stimulates and is predicated upon mimetic modes of perception in which spontaneity, animation of objects, and a language of the body combining thought with action, sensuousness with intellection, is paramount. She seizes on Benjamin's observations of the corporeal knowledge of the optical unconscious opened up by the camera and the movies in which on account of capacities such as enlargement and slow motion, film provides, she says, "a new schooling for the mimetic powers" (20).

5   Alfred J. Beveridge, "Our Philippine Policy," in *The Philippines Reader: A History of Colonialism, Neocolonialism, Dictatorship, and Resistance,* ed. Daniel B. Schirmer and Stephen Rosskamm Shalom (Quezon City: Ken, 1987), 25.

6   Ibid.

7   Ibid., 26.

8   Erik Barnouw, *Documentary: A History of the Non-Fiction Film* (Oxford: Oxford University Press, 1983), 30.

9   Kemp R. Niver, *Early Motion Pictures: The Paper Print Collection in the Library of Congress* (Washington: Library of Congress, 1985).

10 Renato Constantino, *The Philippines: A Past Revisited* (Quezon City: Renato Constantino, 1975), 249.

11 Luzviminda Francisco, "The Philippine-American War," *The Philippines Reader* (Quezon City: Ken, 1987), 19.

12 Renato Rosaldo, *Culture and Truth: The Remaking of Social Analysis* (Boston: Beacon Press, 1989), 72.

13. Niver, *Early Motion Pictures.*

14 Benedict Anderson, *Imagined Communities* (London: Verso, 1983), 16.

15 David Spurr, *The Rhetoric of Empire: Colonial Discourse in Journalism, Travel Writing, and Imperial Administration* (Durham: Duke University Press, 1993), 22.

16 Nick Deocampo, "From Revolution to Revolution: The Documentary Movement in the Philippines," *Documentary Box* #5 (1994), 15–16.

17 Quoted in Charles Musser in collaboration with Carol Nelson, *High-Class Moving Pictures: Lyman H. Howe and the Forgotten Era of Traveling Exhibition, 1880–1920* (Princeton: Princeton University Press, 1991), 254.

18 Quoted in Rodney J. Sullivan, *Exemplar of Americanism: The Philippine Career of Dean C. Worcester* (Quezon City: New Day, 1992), 183.

19 Quoted in Sharra L. Vostral, "Imperialism on Display: The Philippine Exhibition at the 1904 World's Fair," *Gateway Heritage* (Spring 1993), 19.

20 Ibid., 19.

21 Ibid., 26–27.

22 Ella Shohat and Robert Stam, *Unthinking Eurocentrism: Multiculturalism and the Media* (London: Routledge, 1994), 107.

Development

Animation and Development

T he rise of Philippine animation—from its beginnings in the local comics, political cartoons, and commercial advertising to its present quest for a national idiom and its multinational linkages—provides an anthropological narrative in the developmental shifts that affect the nation.[1] Animation in the Philippines has animated the way development has been implemented in the nation in this century, one that vigorously attempted to poise the nation within the larger transnational grid of development. It shows the early and sustained kinetic desire of the United States-as-colonizer for the emplacement of the Philippines within its geosphere of economic, political, and cultural influence. It also represents the recent, more eclectic kineticism that so characterizes the postmodern transnational sphere. Invariably, however, even as it has continued to modernize itself, the nation is still positioned low in the present global division of economic and sexual labor and capital.

Philippine animation can be read as analogous to the modernization of both the nation-state and nation-being (and its citizenry).

This essay looks at Philippine animation—its history of production and its production of texts—as a site of contestation of imaginative geographies. The visual representation of an imagined nation produces both truth and counter-truth claims in the ways the nation has been constructed. What becomes of animation, like the cinematic medium itself, wholly conceived and technologized by the West, is a constant interrogation of the media that constructs the parameters of imagining the nation. Though the media produces the grid to imagine the nation, the articulation of the nation in animated texts provides subversive and preservative desires to the very limits set by the grid of imagination. In this essay, I investigate the history of Philippine animation's development as integral in the present circuiting of animation as both an idiom of national identity and a position in the transnational network. That the rise of animation came at a time of great authoritarian control and consolidation under Marcos, whose own construction of nation is imbricated in national and transnational ideals, presents a shift from a colonizer's drive of national development to a local take on development through transnationalism. I proceed to analyze selected animated texts that represent the contesting national desires—from the nation-state, nation-being to various claims to citizenship. This essay is intended to draw connections between animation as an essential component in producing the discourse of the nation, and the nation as the covert angst that so constitutes the production of animated texts.

K
E
Y
W
O
R
D
S

I turn to a brief discussion of the symbolic relations between postmodernism and animation as instrumental in the analysis of aesthetic and social practices in national development. Fredric Jameson's characterization of postmodernism could easily be transposed to animation, specifically in the desire to animate objects.[2] Jameson characterized postmodern culture with the emergence of a new kind of depthlessness; fundamental mutation both in the object and world itself, becoming a set of texts or simulacra; and the waning of affect.[3] There exists a reverse correlation between the dwindling conditions of art and reality in postmodernism and the continuously heightening quest for technological and narrative advantage in animation. Thus, animation provides a reversed lens to filter the postmodern condition. In this essay, the rise of animation is used to renarrativise the trajectory of Philippine development under the colonial and neocolonial conditions.

What also happens socio-politically in postmodernism is the insurmountable kinetic movement of goods, capital, and individuals brought about by multinational capitalism that produces newer

social relations among individuals and groups.[4] In the Philippines,
newer social identities that did not exist some twenty to thirty years
ago now proliferate in the landscape—overseas contract workers,
Japayuki (Filipina entertainment workers in Japan), DHs (domestic
workers in Asian countries), male guest-relations officers (nightclub
entertainers), DIs (dance instructors), youth subcontractual workers,
and so on. These newer identities, though opening up spaces of
location for marginal and disenfranchised social beings, continue to
be nominalized in official discourse. Animation's own insurmountable kineticism allows for a playing field whereby such meanings and
beings can be filtered. Using images devoid of clear-cut historical and
cultural specificity, Philippine animation figures can be analyzed to
retell various social relations in a modern and postmodern set-up
that remains inequitable and unjust. To a large extent, Philippine
animation cuts across history in its ability to condense stories and
claims of older and more recent identities.

The kineticism in postmodernism and animation lends itself well
to the analysis of Philippine development. Within this century alone,
various technological strides have been made in which the nation
was modernized. The modern nation has been caught in various
development loops, mimicking western developmental models while
seeking its own cultural vocabulary to define its own. What the
present state of development casts, however, is a grotesquely uneven
implementation. While the Philippine development project remains
unfinished, it underscores the various political and cultural forces
at work, claiming the right to speak for the nation. The interaction
between the seemingly opposing forces—the political entities on the
one hand, and cartoonists and animators on the other hand—provide
for critique of and complicity in the right to represent the nation and
its development.

The History of Animation:
Writing the Nation in the Colonial
and Transnational Imaginations

The United States' colonization of the Philippines at the turn of the
twentieth century inevitably shifted the trajectory of development
of the Philippine nation. Coming at the heels of victory against
the Spanish colonizers, Filipinos were all too ready to seize the
historic moment of defining and implementing their own vision of
nationhood. However, the United States' colonization shifted the

forces in the decisive calibration of the nation's development—from a mass-supported local leadership to a rule by feudal elites and American colonizers. Since the Philippines provided for the United States its own defining moment at empire-building, the Philippines being its first colonial venture outside its own national domain, the model of enlightened colonialism was implemented. This means that as the national resources were exploited for colonial interests, so, too, were the modern areas of cultural life—health, sanitation, education, and communication—also engineered to provide a conducive system for American capital to take root.[5] Just as the American colonial period endeavored to modernize the colony by introducing the rice thresher and artesian well (1904), electric streetcars and telephone system (1905), postal savings bank and electric iron (1906), it also introduced ice cream, movies and rat control (1899), public school system (1901), and golf clubs (1902).[6] Side by side with the economic and political circuiting of the colony, its cultural transformation was also at stake. As historian Renato Constantino stated:

> The transformation of consumption habits which was characterised by a shift to American products has been interpreted as a mark of modernisation of Philippine society; actually it was merely part of the essential continuity in the evolving economic pattern that first became discernible in the nineteenth century—the development of raw material exports based on a predominantly agricultural economy. American policy may therefore be characterised as a "ratification and rationalization of the status quo."[7]

Today's Philippine modernity has become indelibly inscribed in and by American colonialism. Philippine animation takes root from two major sources, both grounded in American-introduced capitalism: service businesses and print capitalism. The two sources, however, started with a similar beginning in cartooning. Antonio S. Velasquez, known as the "Father of the Tagalog Komiks," began in cartoonized advertising, creating characters that personify consumer products and businesses introduced in the American colonial era: Isko for Esco shoes; Tikboy for Tiki-Tiki, a children's vitamin syrup; Nars Cafi for Cafiaspirinia; Captain Cortal for Cortal; Castor for Botica Boie's Castoria; Aling Adina Comadrona for United Drug products, Charity for Philippine Charity Sweepstakes, and so on.[8] The corporate and brand mascots created by Velasquez were concentrated in the health and drug industry, a major focus of American social

Fig. 1: *Felix in Hollywood*

engineering. Even the Philippine Charity Sweepstakes was founded to primarily subsidize health programs.

Velasquez, however, was famous for creating the comic strip, Kenkoy, in 1928. Collaborating with Romualdo Ramos, a translator in the advertising department, Velasquez's Kenkoy became a success. Kenkoy reflected the contradictions of Filipinos colonized into American rule, sporting a "gleaming Valentino hairstyle [wearing] baggy pants," and speaking pidgin English.[9]

Sooner than expected, the invariably funny and lovable Kenkoy, clothed with the very human aspiration to succeed and featured with all the verities of life during the Commonwealth years, became a hit and a mass media hero. He viewed events in a light-hearted manner. He even managed to poke fun at the drama that was the westernising of the Philippines during those years. He mouthed the English *okedokey, wait a minute,* and *nothing doing,* among others, as *okedowk, weitaminit,* and *nating duwing* as English was spoken by most of the newly-colonised Filipinos.[10]

Kenkoy was translated and published in six other vernacular publications, enabling the character to reach a national audience. It also gave birth to other strips. Readers copied Velasquez's design for Kenkoy's clothing. Poet Jose Corazon de Jesus, more famous as Huseng Batute, wrote the poem "Pagpapakilala" (Introduction), subtitled as "Ay Introdius Yu Mister Kenkoy" (I Introduce You to Mister Kenkoy). Composer Nicanor Abelardo wrote the song "Ay, Naku, Kenkoy!" (Oh My Kenkoy!) and "Kenkoy Blues," a march. The character Kenkoy gave rise to spin-offs, depicting his family, parents, sweetheart, archrival, community members, sidekick, children, and others.

Kenkoy made the Philippine komiks industry. More so, it provided both humor and a cultural idiom during the anxious period of maintaining nationalism and awaiting Philippine independence. After the violent Filipino-American War (1899–1902) that claimed over six hundred thousand lives in Luzon alone, the postwar period was marked by continued resistance, specifically from the swelling labor ranks incorporated into American colonial capitalism.[11] Education, the key to social mobility for the local majority promised by the American colonizers, could no longer sustain the egalitarian dream. "By the late 1920s, the major avenues for career mobility were increasingly constricted."[12] However, from 1920 to 1930, increased production of agricultural products surged—sugar exports by 450 percent, coconut oil by 233 percent, and cordage by 500 percent. Such economic profits, benefiting the local elites, bolstered confidence in the American presence in the colony.[13] With the popular sentiment wanting independence, the Commonwealth was inaugurated in 1935, paving the way for imminent Philippine independence. By this time, however, structures of American colonial capitalism were already institutionalized and wreaking havoc in the national lives of Filipinos because of the inequitable policies enacted during the earlier period of colonial rule.

An even earlier aspect of print capitalism that provided for a more parodic introspection into the American colonial rule were the politically-oriented publications in the early 1900s—the *Telembang* and *Lipang Kalabaw* (1907). These two publications regularly featured political cartoons, commenting on the colonial figures, their policies and era. The political cartoons provided an avenue for churning social commentary at a time when the colonial set-up imposed stringent policies on the articulation and display of Philippine nationalism. As Constantino explains, the Sedition Law passed in 1901 "imposed the death penalty or a long prison term on anyone who advocated independence or separation from the United States even in peaceful means."[14] It also punished any person who would "utter seditious words or speeches, write, publish or circulate scurrilous libels" against the United States government or the Insular Government.[15] Through cartooning, with minimal use of the written word, *Lipang Kalabaw* provided an edgy commentary on the colonial condition, usually the contradictions of colonial rule that continue even in postcolonial times:

> the perennial floods of Manila, the corruption of the police, the
> frankenstein-growth of politicians sporting guns and over-sized
> egos, the Americanised manners of the emerging youth, the
> death of Spanish language and culture, the captive nature of
> the English language over traditional values, profligate lending
> scandals at the Philippine National Bank, public hospitals that
> denied citizens basic service, the gun-happy constabulary, and
> so on.[16]

Cartooning provided a dual contradictory purpose—it reified the operations of American colonial capitalism, and it also subverted the colonial set-up. While the American colonial set-up harped on liberal democracy, press freedom, and free speech, contradictory policies allowed only for their oppressive and limited articulation. Such contradiction is best embodied in the figure of the cartoonist. As Alfred McCoy observed, the Filipino cartoonists were "often the leading artists of their generation seeking survival in a colonial society with little use for their talents."[17] The Filipino cartoonists worked for both the interests of print capitalism and advertising. Like artists Velasquez and Fernando Amorsolo, other renowned Filipino cartoonists worked for the interest of both print capitalism and advertising. They served the business interest of growing areas of the service industry, creatively providing for mascots and other advertising needs. They also served the Filipino nationalist cause, drawing political commentaries through the komiks and satirical publications, even at the expense of producing racist cartoons.

American enlightened colonialism brought new levels of consciousness and opportunities for businesses. As disseminated through the public school system, English became a prominent language. English literacy was a key factor in the growth of mass circulation papers.[18] By 1939, the total circulation of all Philippine publications had reached 1.4 million, of which 722,000 were in English.[19]

It was only during the postwar and post-independence era that Philippine animation took a serious turn.[20] Philippine animation prior to 1953 was mostly focused on commercial advertising, churning out cartoons for print and television commercials. In 1953, komiks cartoonist Larry Alcala made an 8mm film, a black-and-white exercise in movement of a girl jumping rope and a boy playing with a yoyo.[21] Other pioneers in animation were Jose Zaballa Santos and Francisco Reyes, who did a cooking oil endorsement, and *Juan Tamad* (1955), a six-minute work based on a popular folklore character. Nonoy Marcelo did *Biag ni Lam-ang* (The Life of Lam-ang, 1979), a 60-minute feature on the adventures of the Ilocano epic hero, and *Annie Batungbakal* (1974), a seven-minute clip for the Nora Aunor movie. Animation in film was used for special effects, like in *Ibong Adarna* (The Adarna Bird, 1941) and *Ang Panday* (The Blacksmith, 1983). One can still observe the latent economic imperative with these animation pioneers, who worked for the advertising film businesses. There is also the political imperative, as Marcelo's feature dealt with the ethnic epic from the region of then President Ferdinand Marcos.

Such dual purpose in cartooning remains emplaced even in present-day animation. Contemporary Filipino cartoonists are also imbricated in doing multinational advertising at the same time as subcontractual animation work. The Marcos period provided a space for animation production both useful to and subversive of the national administration ideals. No other president in Philippine political history has been so conscientious in conceiving and implementing a national development program than Marcos.[22] He built massive infrastructures and enacted laws that primarily supported multinational businesses. In his dream of a *Bagong Lipunan* (New Society), unfolded after the declaration of martial rule in 1972, he envisioned to clear the national space for both nationalism to firmly take ground and foreign businesses to flourish.

With a background in animation from a New York film school, Marcelo did animation work for the administration. Though only the first episode was produced, *Tadhana* (Destiny) was envisioned to popularize Marcos's rewriting of national history. In the only episode, the war between Spain and Portugal for global colonial rights was done through zooming and intercutting images of illustrations and maps. In preparation for war, the Spanish armada moves in with the *Star Wars* theme. Marcelo also did animation for Kabataang Baranggay (Youth League), the national youth organization headed by Imee Marcos, Ferdinand Marcos's eldest child. He also did the animation sequences for an education series produced by a Marcos office intended to create local entrepreneurs. Episodes dealt with the Green Revolution themes of self-reliance in food using popular technology, such as *tilapia* (carp) raising and bee farming. However, Marcelo was also made famous by the newspaper comic strip *Tisoy*, which documented and satirized the conditions of the Marcos administration.

By the 1980s, however, the Marcos circuiting of the nation in global multinational work had already been institutionalized. The period was also marked by economic and political turmoil that led to the Marcoses' downfall in 1986. One major development in animation that grew out of Marcos's direct development policies was the operation of foreign studios in the country. Marcos used subcontractual work to entice foreign business. Harping on cheap but highly-skilled local labor, Filipino cartoonists were employed in foreign animation studios to do episodes of various Hanna-Barbera and Toei series. The Australian-based animation firm, Burbank Studios, pioneered animation subcontracting in the Philippines in 1983.[23] Given tax incentives and other investment lures, Burbank Studios initially focused on the animation needs of the local advertising market. Eventually, it also produced an educational animation series for the Middle East. Burbank Studios wanted to break into the American market. It needed the proximity of the Philippines to the United States as a base of operation, and the skills of Filipino laborers as chief resource. It trained local animators that either established their own advertising firms or transferred to other multinational studios when Burbank Studios folded in the late 1980s.

Presently, the big players in Philippine animation are FilCartoons and Philippine Animation Studio, Inc. (PASI), owned by foreigners. FilCartoons, for example, does work on *Mad Jack the Pirate* and *Toonsylvania*, cartoon shows for the American firms Saban and Dreamworks SKG. Their artists have done "much of the acclaimed work in Fox Studios' *Anastasia* and Disney's *Mulan*, among others."[24] Such developments have led critics to believe that Filipino artists have been reduced to artisans: "As 'subcontractors' for foreign animation studios, it is quite obvious that FilCartoons artists are reduced to craftsmen who follow a codified set of rules, without free rein in their art."[25] Another employment track for Filipino cartoonists involves overseas contract work, a program institutionalized during the Marcos period that relies on exporting Filipino labor for precious dollar remittances. The systematic export of Filipino labor has presently deployed four million overseas contract workers that yield some USD 6 billion annual remittances, about two-thirds of the present national budget. More and more Filipino cartoonists work for overseas Disney, Malaysian, and Singaporean studios.

Filipino cartoonists find affinity with their fellow nationals doing multinational and overseas contract work. They are hired because of their pleasing personalities, command of the English language, high skills, Western disposition, and their acceptance of lower salaries than their counterparts in the West. A recent Philippine subcontracting project was the *Chito Chat* series on MTV Asia. The character Chito provides onscreen chatter about the music video being shown.[26] Cartoonists also find themselves doing work in advertising companies like Star Animation, owned by the local entertainment conglomerate ABS-CBN. These cartoonists also did work for the children's show *Batibot*, which regularly features animation segments.[27] Recently, however, there is a slight reversal of the situation as Filipino artists and entrepreneurs came up with the *Stone* comic book series, stylishly drawn, based on Philippine lore, and sold at comic book conventions in the United States.[28]

With its immense pool of creative talents, Philippine animation has yet to commercially take off. The first and only locally animated television series, *Ang Panday*, produced in 1987, only drew a curious audience, and the first full-length commercial film, *Ibong Adarna* (1997), also proved dismal in attracting a local audience. The major figure in Philippine feature animation is Gerry Garcia. Paling in comparison to big-budgeted Hollywood and Japanese animation, local animation has yet to be commercially competitive. This is also the drawback of global competition conceived during the adminis-

tration of Marcos's successor, Corazon Aquino, and implemented
by her successors, Fidel Ramos and Joseph Estrada. Barring protec-
tionism, local businesses have yet to rise above the competition,
becoming demoted in the global division of capital and labor. The
export-processing zones started during the Marcos dictatorship
allowed for a wide-ranging incentive package to foreign businesses,
even the promise of a strike-free environment. Clark, the former
American air force base, has transformed into one such strike-free
zone. Two companies, GM Mini Computer Exchange and Cerulean
Digital Colors Animators, have located in the Clark Special Economic
Zone. There are some four hundred and fifty workers for its digital
animation work load.[29]

Animation inscribed the nation in colonial and transnational imaginaries. During its preconception, cartooning allowed for
conservative and contrary ideals of the colonial set-up to be articulated and popularized. Cartooning in advertising and print capitalism, involving the same set of artists, articulated the dual position of
colonial rule and national selfhood. Up until the mid-1980s, Marcos's
emplacement of national ideals toward the service of multinational
businesses provided a divide between business in the new world
order and the further interrogation of selfhood. FilCartoons artisans,
for example, are responsible for shows like *Chicken and Egg*, *Johnny
Bravo*, *Captain Planet*, and *Johnny Quest*. Filipino cartoonists found to
have been part of Disney's or DreamWorks' feature animations often
get high media publicity, especially in the national dailies.[30] It is only
in recent times that commerce and national ideals are again merging,
as the artists of the 1980s developed their own animation companies
that service various businesses.[31] In the 1990s, a newer breed of
animators emerged. Unlike the prior generation that made various
attempts at inscribing a national idiom in this form, the 1990s artists
are more vocal in articulating the politics of newer social movements,
such as environmentalism, feminism, social injustices, and so on.

The Production of Animated Texts: Order and Subversion of National Imaginations

The generation of independent filmmakers and media artists of the
1980s and 1990s grew up amid the political milieu of the Marcos
dictatorship and its replacement in the Aquino, Ramos, and Estrada
administrations. The post-Marcos period harped on economic growth
and strengthening of civil society. Under the Marcos dictatorship,

independent filmmakers and media artists articulated various national idioms in an attempt to unite with the larger mass movement waging a national struggle against fascism and imperialism. If during the American colonial era the Sedition Law stifled freedom of association, the press, and free expression, the Anti-Subversion Law of the Marcos dictatorship also stifled a free and full-range of artistic expression. Paradoxically, the stringent conditions of the dictatorship allowed for a wide-ranging exploration of artistic endeavors within the limited space and media format. The Marcos dictatorship provided the era of Philippine cinema's second golden age, a sustained movement of artistically and politically committed film output that started in the mid-1970s. It also provided the impetus for an independent film and video movement, which eventually reached its peak in the 1980s.

Marcos used film and animation to propagate his presidency. Directly in film, his election and reelection bids were fueled by the production of autobiographical works. He also used the censorship board to stake claims of decency and proper citizenry in the nation's most popular media. Indirectly, he used animation for a similar peda-gogical drive—to teach Filipinos to be self-reliant. During his admin-istration, the children's show *Batibot* was produced to teach children the rudiments of not only reading, writing, and arithmetic, but also national identity formation. Unlike the American show *Sesame Street* on which it was patterned, *Batibot* made great efforts in dealing with issues of cultural literacy and awareness in being Filipino. Animation was used for such identity formation purposes.

The independent production articulated the various national idioms of the nation that was experiencing great historical changes. My focus of discussion is on the independent aspect of Philippine animation that provided for animated images in the ways the nation was envisioned to be imagined, constructed, and contested. Such images, however, were imbricated in both the desire of the indepen-dent animator to envision critical images and the government that supported the mechanism for such images to materialize on screen.

The annual short film and video festival, started in 1982 by the Experimental Cinema of the Philippines, was once headed by Imee Marcos. The festival is still continued by the Cultural Center of the Philippines, providing recognition for talented animators. Most of the animation produced, like in the experimental, documentary, and feature categories, invariably commented on the Marcos dictatorship and subsequent national administrations. Like the political cartoons and komiks before them, the recent animation provided satirical commentaries on the social and political era. The brothers Mike and Juan Alcazaren produced the clay animation shorts, *Hari* (King, 1982), dealing with the power struggle among various creatures for the possession of the crown, and *Huling Trip* (Last Trip, 1983), a futuristic vision of a radioactive era where creatures eat each other in order to survive. *Spit* (1989) by Roque Lee (Roxlee) showed a character spitting saliva, then transforming into different figures and interacting with various social realist images. Claire Salaveria's *Anino* (Shadow, 1984) told the story of an artist living the life of a shadow inside a container, using charcoal drawings. Nonoy Dadivas, Fruto Corre, Pablo Biglang-Awa Jr., and Alfonso Ponce collaborated on *The Criminal* (1984) about a fugitive on the run who could not escape from himself. There is a scene in the film, of lambs jumping over a razor gate, that calls attention to the opening scene of Salvador Dali and Luis Buñuel's classic avant-garde film. There is also a self-reflexive device of the criminal seeing himself introspect through television until he is framed via media coverage in the same medium in the end. Monlee and Roxlee collaborated on *The Great Smoke* (1985), a satirical commentary on nuclear war and the eradication of the human race, and *Headset* (1983), also a satire about a man with a headset that blares rock music.

Lending themselves to allegorical readings, these animation projects covertly remarked on the construction of the Philippine nation under Marcos. Having lived through their formative period under his rule to what will be known as the generation of "Marcos babies," the filmmakers made artistic statements against the overt fascist order or its dehumanizing effect on individuals. Some of these filmmakers were even trained in Imelda Marcos's sponsored Philippine High School for the Arts (PHSA), an exclusive secondary school geared toward artistic excellence. Yet their exposure to politics, primarily in the state-run University of the Philippines, provided counter-artistic claims to their otherwise formalistic secondary training. It could even be claimed that the covert politics became the generation's own aesthetic formalism.

The animation of the 1990s provided for a more grounded elaboration of micro-social issues. Unlike the 1980s filmmakers who dwelt on covert macropolitics, the 1990s generation overtly discussed issues that tackled newer social movements. Like the impetus for the national economic takeoff and sustained growth of the late 1980s and 1990s that provided for a greater concern for middle-class economics and strengthening of civil society structures, artists were concerned less with great historical problems than with everyday issues and identities. Yet most of these films were developed from animation workshops sponsored by the Mowelfund Film Institute, a quasi-government agency also engaged in movie workers' welfare and film training.

Tita Rosel's *Anong Trabaho ng Nanay Mo?* (What is Your Mother's Job?, 1995) presented a happy child's voice narrating the mother's grueling daily schedule, only to reveal that the mother is simply in the house the whole day. Ellen Ramos's *Sa Kabila ng Bulkan* (The Other Side of the Volcano) dealt with Aetas, the indigenous people in the Pinatubo area, displaced by the volcanic eruption. Toger Tibon's *Radha Syam* (1995) presents a free visual association, using Indian religious images. The short animation calls attention to religiosity and spirituality in the present commercial age. Kris Layug's *Mr. Klean* (1995) uses various corporate slogans and logos to find the emasculated soap figure, Mr. Klean, a victim in his own universe. It engages Freud and Ford in a kind of assembly-line diagnosis of individual psychology; in the end, Mr. Klean opts to be a male underwear commercial figure, *à la* Calvin Klein.

The animation of live subjects was used in Auraeus Solito's *Suring at Ang Kuk-ok* (Suring and the Kuk-ok), where a figure embodying mother nature cries of environmental destruction and loss of traditional values. Based on tales and images of Palawan (an island in the southern Philippines which has the largest remaining virgin forest in the country), the film uses images of nature—shells, sands, fishes, leeches, leaves, and flowers—in stop-motion filming to retell the pain of, and search for, a primordial scene of bliss with nature. Joey Agbayani's *Kidlat* (Lightning) evokes the somber feel of the 1980s generation in a twisted fantasy on the election fraud. It also engages in quick-motion shots, using balloons to express the thoughts of the two male leads—the reporter searching for truth, and the politician hiding it from him. The politician's lying is signaled by the various changes in the size of the reporter's pencil. In the end, the lying politician is killed by a giant pencil, signaled by lighting and thunder. Nonoy Dadivas's *Anak Maynila* (Child of Manila) uses a draft sketch of a black-and-white character filmed against the backdrop of quick-speed shots of the city. Familiar sights, such as the Plaza Lawton, Santa Cruz Church, and Avenida areas are used as backdrop of the inner character's own moral trip to deterioration and redemption.

Animagination is a bi-annual animation festival hosted by the local animators group. It has since hosted three festivals since 1995. A bi-annual animation workshop is also spearheaded by Mowelfund Film Institute that produces some five to ten works.

Because of the systematic institutionalization of migrant work, Philippine diaspora is also represented in animation. In the United

States, the prime mover of computer animation is Filipino-born teacher Mar Elepaño, based at the University of Southern California. Having started in graphic animation, he has since moved on to more expensive high-tech computer animation which most of his local compatriots could not yet access. His *Ala Turk 1* presents graphic images fused in Herbie Hancock's music, resulting in an improvised modern impressionistic piece. *The Blue Nun* uses very tactile moving images set against the music backdrop of the vocals of Pakistani singer Nusfrat Fateh Ali Khan. Though the images are not culturally specific, the fusion of sound with slowly moving images creates a sort of East-West identity. What is being articulated in the animation is the lack of permanence, and the persistence of movement and metamorphosis in this liminal position.

There now exists a plural articulation of the nation in animation. In exploring various themes of individuality and sectoral ideals, the underlying angst that is evoked in Philippine animation is the motif of the nation, its past development and its continuing struggle to cohere itself. The animated texts of the 1980s underscored the nation as a covert presence. In the 1990s, however, the nation is fragmented, oftentimes capturing its individuals and sectors its failure to provide a just and humane society. The present stress to strengthen civil society structures and middle-class economics remains a hegemonic ideal, as the nation is enmeshed in a regional crisis, and corruption reigns over the democratic delivery of services to the people. Thus, as the nation continues to be defined, Philippine animation, given its limited annual production, continues to negotiate and to represent its place in the nation.

Philippine animation has textually represented and contextually dialogued with national development. In representing the nation, the terrain of representation involves efforts to transact with multinational business and a local audience longing for national imageries. The 1980s and 1990s have clarified such distinction, making independent animation productions represent the interest of questing for a national idiom. In contextually dialoguing with national development, cartoonists, artists, and animators have always been poised within the shadow of government, stimulating American and local capitalism. As a consequence of government efforts, animation was also used to provide further impetus to national development. It is in these parameters that animators worked, representing their historical block claims in a nation that has circuited its citizens to a transnational national development.

I am grateful to Professor John Lent for inviting me to think and write about Philippine animation. The essay was also made possible through the generous support and information shared by Ricky Orellana of the Mowelfund Film Institute.

1 I adhere to Arturo Escobar's discourse of development, "as a historically singular experience, the creation of a domain of thought and action, by analyzing the characteristics and interrelations of the three axes that define it: the forms of knowledge that refer to it and through which it comes into being and is elaborated into objects, concepts, theories, and the like; the system of power that regulates its practice; and the forms of subjectivity fostered by this discourse, those through which people come to recognize themselves as developed or underdeveloped" (*Encountering Development: The Making and Unmaking of the Third World* [Princeton: Princeton University Press, 1995], 10).

2 Fredric Jameson, "The Cultural Logic of Late Capitalism," *Postmodernism or, the Cultural Logic of Late Capitalism* (Durham: Duke University Press, 1991), 1–54.

3 Ibid., 9–10.

4 For a discussion of the specific movement of multinationalism in the Asia Pacific region, see Arif Dirlik, ed., *What is in a Rim? Critical Perspectives on the Pacific Region Idea* (Boulder: Westview Press, 1993).

5 For a discussion of the implications of American colonial policies in the various economic and cultural experiences of the Philippines, see Reynaldo C. Ileto, "Cholera and the Origins of the American Sanitary Order in the Philippines"; Warwick Anderson, "Where Every Prospect Pleases and Only Man is Vile: Laboratory Medicine as Colonial Discourse"; Michael Salman, "'Nothing Without Labor': Penology, Discipline and Independence in the Philippines under United States Rule," *Discrepant Histories: Translocal Essays on Filipino Cultures* (Philadelphia: Temple University Press, 1995), 51–82, 83–112, 113–29. Also see Daniel F. Doeppers, *Manila 1900–1941: Social Change in a Late Colonial Metropolis* (Quezon City: Ateneo de Manila University Press, 1984).

6 See Luning Bonifacio Ira and Isagani R. Medina, "What Will They Think of Next?" *Turn of the Century* (Quezon City: GCF Books, 1990), 206–25.

7 Renato Constantino, *A Past Revisited* (Quezon City: Renato Constantino, 1987), 312. Quoted from Owen, "Philippine Economic Development and American Policy: A Reappraisal," *Compadre Colonialism* (Ann Arbor: University of Michigan Center for South and Southeast Asian Studies, 1971), 104–5.

8 Cynthia Roxas and Joaquin Arevalo, Jr., "The Birth of the Komiks," *A History of Komiks of the Philippines and Other Countries* (Quezon City: Islas Filipinas Publishing Co., Inc., 1984), 19. Komiks is the indigenized term for comics.

9 Ibid., 4.

10   Ibid., 11.

11   The figure comes from the *New York Times*, quoted in Luzviminda Francisco, "The Philippine-American War," *The Philippines Reader: A History of Colonialism, Neocolonialism, Dictatorship, and Resistance* (Quezon City: Ken Inc., 1987), 19.

     The labor movement provided a sustained avenue for local resistance in the city. As Doeppers in *Manila 1900–1941* states, "The [. . .] important change may be termed the expansion and consolidation of proletarian life, as the manual employees of large modern firms formed organizations and affected some change in labor-management relations by striking."

12   Doeppers, "*Manila 1900-1941*," 3.

13   Constantino, "Past Revisited," 343.

14   Ibid., 251.

15   Quoted in Constantino, "Past Revisited," 251.

16   Alfredo Roces, "Mang Juan and Uncle Sam: The Filipino Caricaturist as Historian," *Philippine Cartoons: Political Caricature of the American Era 1900–1941* (Quezon City: Vera-Reyes, Inc., 1985), 12.

17   Alfred W. McCoy, "1900–1941: Images of a Changing Nation," *Philippine Cartoons: Political Caricature of the American Era 1900–1941* (Quezon City: Vera-Reyes, Inc., 1985), 19.

18   Ibid., 17.

19   Quoted in McCoy, "1900–1941," 17.

20   Film historian Nick Deocampo would state that Philippine animation had an earlier start, with the short animation entitled *Bloto* (1930s) inspired by the archrival of the titular character of the American cartoon, *Popeye*. This is based on a conversation with Deocampo, 1 December 1998.

21   The postwar animation history is taken from Joel David and Lena Pareja, "Animation," *CCP Encyclopedia of Philippine Art, Volume VIII-Philippine Film* (Manila: Cultural Center of the Philippines, 1994), 83–84.

22   I discuss the Marcos developmental model in "Articulations of the Nation-Space: Cinema, Cultural Politics and Transnationalism in the Philippines" (Dissertation, University of Southern California, 1996).

23   This account of Burbank Studios in the Philippines was gathered through an interview with Tom Stacey, former animation supervisor, 4 Aug 1999, Brisbane, Australia. Interview was conducted together with John Lent.

24   Poch Caballos and Vichael Angelo Roaring "Comic Quests: Unraveling the Secrets of FilCartoons and Alamat," *Philippine Collegian* 176, no. 8 (3 August 1998), 6.

25   Ibid.

26   See Howie Borja, "Chatting with the 'Chito Chat' Guys," *Philippine Daily Inquirer* (13 December 1997), E7.

27 For a feature on Star Animation, see Leah Salterio-Gatdula, "Look What's Invading the Small Screen," *Philippine Daily Inquirer,* November 1998, D6.

28 See Caballos and Roaring; Allan Hernandez, "Romancing the Stone," *Manila Times,* 22 September 1998, 19; Bert B. Sulat, Jr., "Whilce Myth," *Today's Weekender,* September 1998, 324, 1–2; and Kap Maceda Aguila, "Written and Drawn in Stone," *The Philippine Star,* September 1998, YS-8, 2–3.

29 Diego C. Cagahastian, "Film Animators Locate in Clark," *Bulletin Today,* 1 June 1998, 30. Interviewed by Cagahastian, Clark Development Corporation President Romeo D. David states, "Having these digital animation productions in the Clark Special Economic Zone will elevate the status of Filipino workers up to standards set by these hi-tech firms and would give them the chance to explore new avenues as we prepare for the electronic world of the next millennium" (30).

30 One such case is Ronnie del Carmen who did work for *The Prince of Egypt,* covered in a two-part feature article by Nestor U. Torre, "Filipino Animation Artist at DreamWorks," *Philippine Daily Inquirer,* 24 October 1998, C7 and 31 October 1998, B8.

31 The idea of commerce and art dialectically related in Philippine animation is mentioned in the interview with Ricky Orellano, Mowelfund, 1 December 1999.

Abjection

Dogeating/*Dogeaters*

A bjection has prefigured in colonialist discourse as an affect of the colonized in the instance of interlocution by the colonizer. Although historically positioned outside the West's language of discourse and discourse of language, the abject/colonized is maintained and sustained by multiple subject positions: retaining that which is tactically useful from the inside (nationalist and/or other collective perspectives, and to include the individual/personal positions), and "making do" with what is enforced upon from the outside. This essay examines the abject's position as a process obscuring and marking difference for the colonizer and colonized. As the colonizer seeks to utilize difference to perpetuate technologies of power, so too can the operations of the technology be repowered for the colonized, that is, to provide moments of crossing-over or temporal boundary collapse of the inside/outside dichotomy. For the colonized, this project marks difference of subject positions whether by maintaining the inside or recuperating the outside imago.

In "The Rani of Sirmur," Gayatri Spivak has elaborated on the West's textualization of the practices of the colonized which provides the screens and contexts to read, view, and critique these practices as object, then as abject of the Western frame.[1] For the West, it has to operationalize modes and means to understand the colonized in order to *know* the colonized, and consequently, in order to *colonize* the colonized. Elaborating on the Heideggerian notion of "worlding," to denote the Western processes of naming, containing, and locating the world of the colonized, Spivak inflects a site of strife, where contradictions of the process is exposed in the imperialist/modernist project.

Dogeating—like other pejorative categories (from the colonizer's point of view) signifying indigenous and abjected practices such as cockfighting, caning, and "women in veil," among others—acts as an activation field where contending discourses are poised in a disjunctive temporality. This essay provides some of the issues that are called upon in the activation field, hoping that such discussion provides a tactic of reempowering the position of the abject/colonized and hopefully, to extend to various practices and tactics that can move forward an agenda of older and newer social movements. I do not intend to either place dogeating in the locus of "chic-ness" arrived at by sushi or Indian or Cambodian restaurants, or the everyday-ness realized of Chinese combo platters and Italian take-out counters. Edward Said in "Representing the Colonized: Anthropology's Interlocutors" forewarns of oversimplification in dwelling with issues of representation of the colonized as a stable progression or worse, in embracing these as progressive: "To represent someone or something has now become an endeavor as complex and as problematic as an asymptote, with consequences for certainty and decidability as fraught with difficulties as one can imagine."[2]

Homi Bhabha provides a mode that might embrace some aspects of this project's discussion of the various discourses that locate, relocate, and mislocate the dogeating text.[3] Between the pedagogical mode of Western historical construction of the colonized subject and the performative mode of the colonized's enunciation of the regime of significations lies the terrain of the colonialist discourse. This terrain is riddled with ambivalence that marks for both colonizer and colonized circuits for incorporating, resisting, and subverting each other's otherness and differences. By historicizing the temporality opened in the colonialist discourse, I veer away from the "interchangeable positionalities" which I find problematic in Bhabha's text. For Bhabha, the in-between space allows for a fluidity of the temporal instance: the binary categories do not retain their borders, destabilizing and making interchangeable the relations of colonizer/colonized, object/subject, pedagogical/performative, and so on. While reversal and crossing-over are strategic for the colonized, they can also be a process of equivalence for the colonizer. By further substantiating the field with stakes in identity politics, empowerment, historicity and specificity, and difference, I hope to retain a level of personal, collective, and social politics in Bhabha's discourse.

Mapping the disjuncture of dogeating, therefore, necessitates a reconsideration of relocating, if not reinscribing, of these politics—which reconsiders the violent history of colonialism and neocolonialism in all levels of the colonized's living—as a way of moving beyond the repressive limitations of cognitively mapping the colonialist discourse. As a cartography that does not call the politics of cartography into question, colonialism and neocolonialism impress a map that seems to suggest use and abuse for both colonizer and colonized, and has functioned to provide the newness and archaicness of the language of discourse from which the colonizer incorporates and abjects the colonized. While it is important to know how the colonizer articulates its discourse, it becomes tactically important, too, to acknowledge the sense-making processes of the colonized of the discourse of their own objectification and subjectification. Dogeating, like most abjected practices, can be repowered as site of complicity when necessary and site of critique when vital.

The notion of dogeating, of eating one's pet—not just any pet but one privileged enough to be *man's* best friend—surely turns the stomach of the Western individual or the West in general. Almost cannibalistic, in abjecting the practice, however, the practitioner is also abjected. The image of the colonized is textualized, a worlding that alludes to other ideas and practices of naming and locating the "proper" place of the colonized. The West's appalled reaction, however, is no longer suspicious; if at all, the reaction is always already foreshadowed by his project of self-enlightenment: reifying and reaffirming the positions of the colonizer and colonized. After all, humanity is already emplaced in the historical locus of the dawn of the twenty-first century when "information is being doubled: every fifth year in electronics; every third year in space-research and nuclear energy."[4] It becomes contradictory, therefore, to situate a practice like dogeating in the circuits of this information technology that characterize the postmodern and transnational world. If knowledge is an incorporation of nature and culture, so much of

Western epistemology is based on the oral stage, devouring all that is outside and abjecting what the self cannot incorporate.

In this critique of Western epistemology, food discourse prefigures as symptomatic of the process and slippage of the construction of knowledge. What the West cannot contain, it abjects as excess. As the practice of dogeating continues in this information age, the practitioner remains undaunted while the West lingers in its perplexity, unable to know what it hopes not to know. Dogeating becomes a sublime strain in the Western production of knowledge.

In dogeating, the dogeater is named and located, othered as the individual is transformed to belong to a mass of people. A nation is interpollated under the rubric of savagery. The practitioner is racialized, denoted as a mass exceptionalized and naturalized as possessing an appetite for dogmeat; consequently, a nation is marginalized and disenfranchised in this Western production of knowledge. This production of knowledge is also tied to a sexualization yearned and produced, and to an emasculation of the colonized's practices. Thus, this knowledge production is also engendered, sexualized, animalized, criminalized, and feminized. To be abjected is to wallow without an inside or an outside, neither to be included nor excluded. Here lies the efficacy of the abject and abjection: to be an alternative to the operations of binary opposition that produce categories, hierarchies, and consequently knowledge. Abjection can be read in Bhabha's instance of ambivalence. This allows for a breakdown of the colonial order, a recontainment of meanings within and without the scope and borders of the binaries of pure and impure, clean and unclean, civilized and savage, colonizer and colonized, male and female.

Such shifting also pushes further the notion of abjection, as Spivak would note of Julia Kristeva's overall project, within the Christianizing and Westernizing functions of discourse. In *Powers of Horror: An Essay on Abjection*, Kristeva explores the potentials of abjection and horror in creating possibilities for the foregrounding of marginal positions. For her, abjection

> is an extremely strong feeling which is at once somatic and
> symbolic, and which is above all a revolt of the person against
> an external menace from which one wants to keep oneself at a
> distance, but of which one has the impression that it is not only
> an external menace but that it may menace us from the inside.[5]

In addition, she adds, "So it is a desire for separation, for becoming autonomous and also the feeling of an impossibility of doing so."[6] Like Bhabha's ambivalence which is recuperable for both colonizer and colonized, Kristeva's position, while critical of Western genealogy of knowledge, linking epistemology to Judaism that has produced the dual contradiction of Christianity and Nazism, refurbishes the apparatus of knowledge and can be drained of its negative effects, moving toward western purity, puritarianism, and essentialism.

In setting up this notion of Western purity, Kristeva fears contamination and thus succumbs to the problematique she herself has forewarned. This makes the problem interesting, as another layer of intervention is positioned in the use of abjection to theorize the colonized abject. Western workings of colonialism, and consequently, neocolonialism, have come to privilege and reproduce the *civilized* in their conquest and dominion over the colony and empire. To enforce *civilization* is to strive for a hegemonic moment, one which for the colonized is both based on the continuous play and antagonism of coercion and consent. On the one hand, *civilization* demands that the savage be contained through the production of the hegemonic moment. Yet the colonizer also does not want to, for it cannot, fully contain the savage and transform the colony into *full* civilization. The colonizer fears constructing a mirror system of signification for the colonized. A sharing of the colonizer's system would facilitate the production of a common language and thus, of a language of subverting the system, leading to the breakdown of the colonial logos. Of what use, then, is a colonizer, if the colony has been taken out of its aegis, out of savagery—where the savage has become civilized, where the civilized native approximates the peninsular civilized. For the colonizer, elements of the colonized's savagery remain crucial to his colonial enterprise, that which defines the logos of colonialism—to convert the native population (with emphasis on the local elites) and its resources to Western, Christianized, and civilized ways, to convert the colony as the colonizer's domain. Hence, to perpetuate colonialism, the colonizer has to absorb the savage's language and culture in the colonizer's own domain. Filipino American critic Vicente Rafael notes that the Spanish words *conquista* (conquest), *conversion* (conversion), and *traduccion* (translation) are semantically related:

> The Real Academia's *Diccionario de la lengua española* defines conquista not only as the forcible occupation of a territory but also the act of winning someone's voluntary submission and consequently attaining his or her love and affection. Conversion literally means the act of changing a thing into something else

. . . Conversion, like conquest, can thus be a process of crossing into the domain—territorial , emotional, religious, or cultural—of someone else and claiming it as one's own. Such a claim can entail not only the annexation of the other's possession but, equally significant, the restructuring of his or her desires as well . . . To be converted in this sense is to give in by giving up what one wants in favor of the wants of someone else.

Conversion . . . connotes translation. One who translates is said . . . "to express in one language what has been written or previously expressed in another." Translation as expression is linked as well to explanation (explicacion) and interpretation (interpretacion) of meaning and intention. It thus denotes events that take place within and between languages.[7]

The colonized has also worked in a similar operation. On the one hand, it perpetuates the notion of the savage as difference, to distinguish oneself from the label it has been inscribed, tactically as a way to reconfigure the gaze that is able to fascinate and reposition the colonizer. On the other hand, the colonized is forced upon by the political and economic weight of the colonizer to be conquered, converted, and translated; it, too, assimilates the gaze of the civilized because it cannot escape the "look" upon which the colonial society is made to cast its image. There are, however, other positions located in the interstices of the colonized's reworking of notions of the civilized and savage, and abjection to posit new sites of complicity, resistance, and subversion. Michel de Certeau, in repositioning the reader in the production of meaning as a counter to the divestment made by Roland Barthes's own privileging of the author, alludes to abjection as site of alternative sense-making practices: "(The reader's) place is not *here* or *there*, one or the other, but neither the one nor the other, simultaneously inside and outside, dissolving both by mixing them together, associating texts like funerary statuses that (the reader) reawakens and hosts, but never owns."[8]

This is the area that I propose as site of new or alternative contestation for meanings and practices. In viewing dogeaters/dogeating as abjection, my intent is to foreground the colonized's view in locating and decentering colonial and neocolonial relations, amounting to a critique of the imperialist narrativization of history. I hope to show that the abject position did not always function to keep the people in their proper colonial place.

The practice of eating dogmeat has been part of the indigenous peoples' rituals, such as those of the Igorots in Northern Luzon. In time, however, eating dogmeat has come to be part of another ritual, as *pulutan* (picantes, dishes to go with drinks and drinking) to the *inuman* (drinking session). The inuman is a social act, a ritual of becoming "belonged" or affirming "belonging-ness" to a group or community. In traditional Philippine societies, the inuman blurs economic and political boundaries as the *datu* (chieftain) drinks from the same container used to pass liquor to the other members of the community. The inuman is also equitable—same amounts of liquor for everyone. Even when people are late to the session, they are allowed to catch up and have the same total amount of liquor the earlier group has already drunk. The most animated member acts as a *taga-tagay* (overseer of drinks) to ensure proper and equitable sequence of drinks and drinkers. Taga-tagays assume this functional position and, with the same skill, also act as *bangka*s ("vessels," carriers) of stories. Even in present times, the inuman is not only a drinking session but more of a session for storytelling, making sense of the narrative of daily survival.

Why do Filipinos drink? Cultural anthropologist Edilberto Alegre presents an explanation to Filipinos (note the pronoun *we*):

> Firstly, we are expected to. To drink is the rule, not to is the exception. At around fourteen or fifteen years of age, we begin to take our first gulps among our peers. There is no sanction to our drinking this early, so there is a secretiveness to it. We make sure our fathers do not know. It is not that we do it on the sly, for we do it openly within the barkada or even under the quiet, approving gaze of our older brothers. It is that as yet we have not yet achieved the status of those who drink publicly. Our fathers enunciate clearly the traditional sanction: *"Puede nang uminom kung marunong nang maghanap-buhay."* The social status is earned by a show of economic ability . . .
>
> Our drinking session is then a social act that involves role models and social expectations, and manifests definite stages from initiation and acceptance. In some places, there are gender distinctions: men drink, women should not. And yet in other places, it is "unisex."
>
> Secondly, it is an act/event separate and different from the quotidian flow of life. Our everyday life is defined by this:

we work daily. Those who keep office hours drink after office hours; the fishermen I know from Hagonoy (Bulacan) and Alaminos (Pangasinan) do it from lunchtime onwards. They return from the sea in the early dawn; they rest and sleep, and especially if they are not to go fishing that night, they drink.[9]

Focusing on the second point, Bakhtin's theory of the carnival provides an insight to understand the popular culture of inuman. Bakhtin provides the model of the carnival for transgressing, reversing, and erupting boundaries of life and death, good and bad, official and practical, legal and illegal among other binaries that structuralize the world. The inuman provides this carnival respite in being able to disrupt the homogenizing forces of daily economic production but, more significantly, as a renewal of the self in the society. The inuman disrupts the fixed narrativizing effects of everyday struggle with everyday life.

After all, this metanarrative of structuring everyday life in its proper place and time has been emplaced for as long as the colonial imperative has been experienced. Writing in 1573, Spanish adventurer Diego de Artieda observes the natives' obsession with drinking which is reflective, too, of the colonizer's obsession with (im)propriety of time and space of the colonizer/colonized dichotomy:

> The natives sustain life by eating little and drinking much—so heavily that it is a marvel if they are not drunk all the time, or at least from noon on. And the more important their position, the more intoxicated do they become, for they have more to spend for this purpose.[10]

As inscription of the proper takes place, so, too, is a building-up of the narrative of oppression and struggle in colonial history. The layers of categories add up through centuries of colonialism and neocolonialism, naturalizing the categories as well as the structures that support these. As colonial struggle has tended to be hyped on the national dimension of the 1898 Philippine revolution, most of the struggle, however, has been sustained on the everyday basis. The manifestation of this struggle is in the respite provided by the inuman, a carnival of sorts by which to struggle and survive the structuralizing and layering effects.

The pulutan acts as one of the agents of the carnival within the inuman. "Boredom is kept away by the pulutan—novel, seasonal—and the talk: a mixture of memory, dream, and reality . . . Pleasure comes from a multiplicity of causes: the drink, the pulutan, the company, the talk."[11] Even when taken from the colonizer's view, pulutan provides a carnival in neocolonial relations. Dogmeat as pulutan disrupts notions of civilized and savage, humane and inhumane, colonizer and colonized—tolerating the opposition the colonizer seeks to control, tolerated in the fascination of the practice.

How far can the colonizer tolerate? Tolerance is the cornerstone of Western liberal democracy that harps on plurality. Here are some ways of preparing and cooking dogmeat, excerpted from Alegre's book:

> Interview with Perdigon Vocalan (PV), owner-chef of Balaw-Balaw Restaurant:
> Interviewer 1: What's a different pulutan in Angono?
> PV: It's *kinubang aso* . . . a dog that you kill by bashing.
> Interviewer 2: Why do they do it? Does it taste any better?
> PV: Maybe. I've seen my grandfather kill a dog like that. It takes a while before the dog dies. You first have to bash here and there.
> I2: Isn't that cruelty to animals?
> PV: It is cruelty.
> I1: Maybe to make the meat more tender. So that it's easier to cook . . .
> PV: . . . If the dog dies, then it is skinned. After the dog has been cleaned thoroughly, until there's no more blood in the system, it is boiled with tamarind leaves. If the meat is soft, it is cooked with the same sauce for *lechon* (roasted pig) . . . .[12]

> I remember even when I was small, there was a cook for pulutan. Such skill is inherited. If someone overruns [*sic*] a dog, it is brought to this old man for cooking. Or if there is a baptism and a dog is to be cooked, they call on this old man. If it's a dog that needs cooking, the dog is brought to him. Tata Blas was his name . . .
> As if he had the only right when it comes to dogs .[13]

> Recipe for Roasted Dog: Starve the dog (no food) for two days. When the intestines have been cleaned out naturally, give the

dog a little *lugaw* (rice gruel) with salt. Butcher the dog, skewer
it, singe and scrape off its hair, then roast it over coals. After it is
cooked, remove the skin and make this into kinilaw. The innards
are removed intact ("pinag-aagawan ang lamang-loob," fighting
over innards), medium rare, and served with *sawsawan* (sauces).[14]

Michel Foucault's *Discipline and Punish* has provided a narrative
that has circumscribed the Western fascination with humanization,
which now has extended to affixing qualities of the human and humane
in domestic animals. The birth of the prison and the rise of the penal
system replaced public torture and spectacular punishment as modes of
disciplining the body and the body of people. This strategy is linked to
the enlightenment project of knowing, of realizing the "soul" through
the production of knowledge. Paradoxically, the body is entrapped as
the soul becomes the prison of the body.[15] As the modernist project
eventually takes up the place of enlightenment, moves toward the
greater "humanization" of the system only serves to further entrap
the "soul" to the body. The dual displacement of the Western body to
colonized bodies as well as through bodies of domesticated animals
equally intensifies the contradiction of the body/mind duality.

Thus, the West is both fascinated and disturbed by animal
violence. Discipline and punishment have extended to include domesticated animals; dogs prefigure the Western notion of humaneness
as dichotomized in home and animal shelter and pound emphasis.
"Humane-ness" signifies the attitude earmarked for dogs and other
pets as reworkings of the originary notion of humanity that never fully
transpired in the enlightenment project and which shifts tolerance
away from human issues of race, ethnic, gender, sexuality, and generational differences. It is not that dogs and the flora and fauna do not
figure in the environmental causes of the times. But most evidently in
the West, dogs have become surrogate other for some of the cleansing
of guilt of which the colonizer has chosen to absolve itself.

Humanity, integrated in Christianizing and capitalist ventures,
becomes the homogenizing frame that guides the civilized to place
a stake in the colonization of the uncivilized. The move toward
animal issues within the grid of humanity displaces the colonial
history of oppression as the West unabashedly shows no remorse in
its treatment of its colonized peoples. In 1846, Jean Mallat, a French
visitor to the Philippines writes:

The most inaccessible lairs of these wild mountains are
inhabited by a great number of small Negroes called "Negritoes"

... One of our friends owned one which he gave to us; he was called Panchote, was not lacking in intelligence and was most of all very mischievous.[16]

Slavery and genocide of races have always been the actual operations of colonialism. Such is the price of Western enlightenment the people from the colonies have had to pay. The colonized are still being continuously processed for integration to the First World developmentalism through transnationalization and the global division of labor. Women in the Philippines are circuited to the transnational set-up by functioning as mail-order brides, domestic helpers, and workers in transnational computer and garment factories. This is also the case for most Third World women.

The price of transnationalization is paid dearly by Third World people, especially women. The agent that pioneered the First World endeavor—women in food production—comes from the same bastion of those who now pay dearly its price. Women have been the main food producers in the Third World.

Food has also been the original intent of colonialism. Ferdinand Magellan's expedition goal was to look for the proverbial Spice Islands. With colonization, production of these agricultural crops and other cash crops was routinized and commercialized. Crop production was regionalized and monopolized in *encomienda* (rewards for participation in the conquest) and *hacienda* (pueblo or township) systems. In time, food has also been one of the myths perpetuated in neocolonialism. The mythology of panic over increasing global hunger due to increasing global population led to the selling of the Green Revolution. Most Third World nations were forced to switch from traditional rice strains to high-yielding varieties (HYVs) in order to increase yield of harvest. What was achieved was an agriculture heavily dependent on fertilizers and pesticides developed and produced mostly in the West. Global agriculture was achieved through the widespread commercial scope of the chemical industry, displacing traditional ways of life by integrating farmers from Third World countries to First World sites, including the more recent engineering and production of biotechnological crops.

Amid these burgeoning operations of Western homogenization, the colonized has experienced subjugation. But the experience of the everyday forestalls the completion of subjugation, making bare its operations and its own subversions. Dogeaters/dogeating as abjection is proof of this resilience.

3

Abdul R. JanMohamed explains the logic of colonialism which, for the most part, is still in place in neocolonialism:

> While the covert purpose is to exploit the colony's natural
> resources thoroughly and ruthlessly through the various
> imperialist material practices, the overt aim, as articulated by
> the colonialist discourse, is to "civilize" the savage, to introduce
> him [sic] to all the benefits of Western culture . . .[17]

The colonizer projects difference as wide and irreconcilable in order to indefinitely conquer the native. This way the native is dehistoricized and desocialized from having to achieve a sense of identity. This, however, is just one major operation of colonialism. The other might be one that purports identity in difference. As most natives are inscribed in a mass, there are, however, many unique communities within the (massified) colony. Herein lies a site for a collapse of hegemonic meanings and from which to recycle and restructure meanings of the native(s).

During the 1896 Philippine Revolution against Spanish colonial rule, two factions emerged that weakened the struggle for independence. The issue was the leadership of the Katipunan, the revolutionary organization. When Andres Bonifacio was elected as an official of the organization, the Magdalo faction questioned the qualification of an uneducated man. The Magdiwang faction supported the election but to no avail. This dichotomy was further emphasized during the American colonial rule when in the elections for the 1907 Philippine Assembly, only those who could read and speak English and Spanish were made qualified to vote. Bienvenido Lumbera and Cynthia Nograles Lumbera write about the origin of the dichotomy:

> The distinction went beyond indicating mere geographic
> origins and took on overtones of cultural snobbery as the effect
> of colonization seeped deeper into the consciousness of lowland
> Filipinos. In time, *taga-bayan* came to be a flattering term for
> the Hispanized and, therefore, "urbane and civilized," while
> the *taga-bukid/taga-bundok* was to mock the indio who had not
> learned the ways of the colonial masters and, therefore, among
> the *brutos salvages* (salvage brutes). In this way did the non-
> Christian Filipinos come to be regarded with condescension,
> if not outright contempt and suspicion, by lowlanders who

K
E
Y
W
O
R
D
S

soon began to think of themselves as more "genuine" Filipinos. Although it endowed town residents with a special status, colonialism constantly reminded them of their subjection to Spanish might. The name "Filipino," after all, was reserved for Spaniards born in the Philippines, and everybody else who had only native ancestors was an "Indian."[18]

Food heralded the distinction among Filipinos during the turn of the century, when Aguinaldo, head of the Magdalo faction, celebrated the first Philippine Republic with a French banquet:

- Hors' D'Oeuvre
- Huitres-Crevettes Roses-Beurre-
- Radis-Olives-Saucisson De Lyon-
- Sardines Aux Tomates-Saumon Hollandais
- Cocquilles de Crabes
- Vol-Au-Vent a la Financiere
- Abatis de Poulet a la Tagale
- Cotelettes de Mouton a la Papillote
- Pommes de Terre Paille
- Dinde Truffee a la Manilloise
- Filet a la Chateaubriand
- Haricots Verts
- Jambon Froid
- Asperges en branche
- Dessert
- Fromages-Fruits-Confitures
- Gelee De Fraises-Glaces
- Vins
- Bordeaux-Sauterne-Xerex-Champagne
- Liqueurs
- Chartreuse-Cognac
- Cafe-The [19]

Within the side of the colonized, there are a variety of positions that might be considered in order to demassify the native. The local elites have assimilated the culture of the colonial power that they seek to overthrow and replace. A penchant for the civilized's food marks their entry to the order of power. For these local elites, to prove one's readiness and appropriateness for independence, one must prove that one is already civilized, thus the reproach of Andres Bonifacio and Philippine cuisine. It also involved erasing dogmeat from the menu. Its absence marks the space of otherization within the Other.

Integration to the colonizer's domain is also a problematic strategy. In the first place, the colonizer's logic is to civilize. Recall President William McKinley's grueling decision to colonize the Philippines in the first U.S. experiment in colonial enterprise:

> I thought first we would take only Manila; then Luzon; then other islands, perhaps, also. I walked the floor of the White House night after night until midnight; and I am not ashamed to tell you, gentlemen, that I went down on my knees and prayed Almighty God for light and guidance more than one night. . . . And one night it came to me this way—I don't know how it was, but it came: one, that we could not give them back to Spain—that would be cowardly and dishonorable; two, that we could not turn them over to France or Germany—our commercial rivals in the Orient—that would be bad business and discreditable; three, that we could not leave them to themselves—they were unfit for self-government—and they would soon have anarchy and misrule over there worse than Spain's was; and four, that there was nothing left for us to do but to take them all, and to educate the Filipinos, and uplift and civilize and Christianize them, and by God's grace do the very best we could by them, as our fellow men for whom Christ also died. And then I went to bed, and went to sleep and slept soundly.[20]

The entire dogma of "Benevolent Assimilation," "White Man's Burden," and "Manifest Destiny" are made the rationale in this colonialist enterprise. And in the name of this enterprise, the carnage took its toll in the "little known war" of the U.S. ("the original Vietnam") with six hundred thousand Filipinos dead in Luzon alone.

The beckoning of native immigrants to the imperial center has yet to automatically open doors with neon greetings of "welcome." This road is equally paved in pain and sacrifice. Prior to 1935, before the formal declaration of the Philippine Commonwealth, there were no limitations to the number of Filipino immigrants to the U.S. Unsurprisingly, there were already eighty thousand Filipinos in the U.S. by 1929 in food production—asparagus picking in California, salmon fishing and canning in Alaska, and pineapple planting and harvesting in Hawaii. After 1935, however, when clear boundaries were delineated in Philippine-American relations that affirmed

KEYWORDS

power structural relations, the issue of unlimited immigration was dealt with. Franklin Roosevelt even appropriated USD 300,000 to pay for the fares of Filipinos who voluntarily returned to the Philippines. Anti-Filipino race riots, however, ensued in the late 1920s to early 1930s.[21] In Watsonville, California (January 1930), the charges made against the Filipinos in a resolution filed were as follows:

1. Economic. They accept, it is alleged, lower wages than the American standards allow. The new immigrants coming in each month increase the supply and hold wages down. *They live on fish and rice* [emphasis, mine] and a dozen may occupy one or two rooms only. The cost of living is very low, hence, Americans cannot compete with them.

2. Health. Some Filipinos bring in meningitis, and other dangerous diseases. Some live unhealthily. Sometimes fifteen or more sleep in one or two rooms.

3. Intermarriage. A few have married white girls. Others will. "If the present state of affairs continues there will be 40,000 half-breeds in California before ten years have passed."[22]

Filipinos even spearheaded unionization that demanded better working conditions and higher wages, further propping up the image that Filipinos were harder to deal with. All three concerns, however, are appeals to the sub-human categorization of Filipinos. The third concern is more significant in the discourse of racism. Filipinos, like many other "undesired" races, were prohibited by law to engage in interracial marriages with white persons. This is also the rationale of the anti-imperialist movement led by industrialists and other prominent figures, fearing that the American race will be tarnished by an inferior race, thereby producing sub-quality laborers. Considering the global expansionism undertaken by the U.S. during the period, this was not good.

Thus instead of the welcome sign, most establishments have altogether barred Filipinos. "POSITIVELY NO FILIPINOS ALLOWED." The Filipinos are abjected, abjection justified in economic-health-interracial imperatives; the discourse of food rides high as foregrounded in the colonialist predicament. In some signs—"NO DOGS AND FILIPINOS ALLOWED"—the subhuman is reduced to the category of the animal, bordered from the inside. From a distance, a fascination still holds that has come to tolerate the presence from the outside. By consigning the space of abjection to one that is within gazing distance, the abject is exoticized.

And if dogmeat is not to the colonizer's palate, how about the other exotic cuisine of the native?

> Group 1: The Rarest Pulutan: "In Paombong, Bulacan, newly-born mice are dipped in the strong local *nipa* vinegar. These go well with gin. In Cuenca, Batangas "bat and ball" are a favorite—sauteed bits and slices of the penis and testicles of goats. Monitor lizard (*bayawak*), cooked *adobo sa bawang*, *nilasing na palaka* (frogs soaked in gin or rum then fried) in Angono. *Kamaru* (mole crickets) fried crisp in Pampanga. Locusts *adobado* in Negros."
>
> Group 2: Barbecue perhaps: *Adidas* (chicken feet), IUD (chicken intestines), helmet (chicken head), walkman (pig ears), *bulaklak* ("flower," pig's small intestines).
>
> Group 3: Snack on the house: *Dinuguan* (pork meat with pig's blood in tamarind soup base), *tokwa't baboy* (fried tofu with boiled and diced meat from pig's head and ears) . . .[23]

For the West, the Philippines does not have its own cuisine in the tradition that the Chinese, Japanese, Thai, Indian, Indonesian, and other Asian countries have their culinary arts. The idea of Philippine cuisine has been erased in the politics of dogeaters/dogeating and other foods. The exotic is the gap by which the colonizer necessitates its function to the colony. Creativity is ignored, even in the metaphoricality of having "invented the yoyo, the moon buggy, and the fluorescent bulb." In the first place, are dogeaters capable of such creativity?

More food for thought. In time, however—similar to the dogs' becoming *man*'s best friend—Filipinos have come to be the U.S.'s staunchest ally in Asia. In the Philippines, *tuta* (puppy) has become the derogatory term for presidents and politicians who have continued to perpetuate U.S. dominance in the country. Food has also served to mediate two administrations in the Philippines. During the 1986 February Uprising, many fast food franchise holders, especially of American franchises, donated food to the military and people in revolt—a foregrounding of "business as usual" as Marcos fled to the U.S. and Aquino was installed to power. Foreign investments, along with foreign loans and aids, are contracts of reciprocity in Philippine and global politicking—"I scratch your back, you scratch mine."

In 1987, a few months after Aquino took over the presidency, she offered and partook of unrefrigerated Coke and hot *pandesal* (small bread roll) with the families of victims massacred by a military unit in Lupao. Food foreshadowed her administration's performance. No one has yet to be indicted for the massacre, nor for any human rights violation in the Philippines. Aquino's term ended in 1992, but the promise of substantial change remains unfulfilled. During her 1987 visit to Lupao, Aquino had a bad cold and could not taste anything.

For Third World countries, Western validation of food, culture, and politics is a necessary passport to prosperity. South Korea tried to duplicate Japan's performance by announcing its coming of industrial age via the hosting of the 1988 Olympics. The South Korean government wanted a sanitized image of its national culture, devoid of the persistence of eating dog meat. Some South Koreans believe that the consumption of dog meat boosts energy and improves sexual power. There was international pressure from media and animal rights group for the South Korean government to ban the practice. The First World validates the Third World as the Third World accepts the validation as a sign that it has become part of the First World.

4

In 1990, the novel *Dogeaters* was published by Filipino American Jessica Hagedorn. The novel caused a ripple in the American literary landscape, and was even nominated for the National Book Award. In the novel, Hagedorn reworks the notion of dogeaters/dogeating in more emancipatory aspects. The reviews, however, reduce the notion of dogeaters/dogeating back to its origin—addendum to the racist legacy of American neocolonialism.

Case I. "Philippine Dream Feast" by Blanche d'Alpuget.[24] Dogeating becomes the object of feast and as such, the dogeaters become the object of the West's spectacle. However, d'Alpuget qualifies: this is just a dream; as if only in dreamlike imaginary can one put the notion of abjection in safe distance. One may take "dream feast" as a sort of jouissance, to render the Western reader's symbolic and real in a flux. But one only does so in connivance with a counter-abjection (Philippine) of the abjected (*Dogeaters*, "dream feast"), thus neutralizing the possibility of an emancipatory position. In titling the review "Philippine Dream Feast," the reviewer postures not only with a knowledge of the novel but of a knowledge of a Philippine/ Philippine-ness. Philippine/Philippine-ness is reduced to an essential, the essential for neutralizing and disempowering the social and symbolic play of abjection.

Case II. "Sweet and Sour" by Katheryn Hughes[25]; coincidentally reviewed along with Amy Tan's *Kitchen God's Wife*—A penchant for creating meta-readings of food as abjection. In reviewing two novels about two different reworkings of women's place and practice (kitchen and cooking), Hughes dulls the emancipatory potentials of the novels. The reviewer categorizes as both sweet and sour the efforts of these women fictionists, commending yet positing the failure in the attempt as the review's centrality. In titling her review "Sweet and Sour," Hughes does not savor the combined tastes within the dish (both tastes complementing each other) but works to dichotomize the attempts (sweet) from the actual (sour). The sour taste becomes the highlight aftertaste: "fails to people it (the novel) with equal imagination," "no female equivalent of Mo or Rushdie."

There was more emphasis on "the qualification than on the innovation." Woman/Uncivilized becomes attached to the failure rather than the courage of the attempt, perennially relegated to attempts than to actual successes, becoming obscure appendages rather than the body that speaks and writes.

Man/the Civilized is the privileged operation by which neocolonialism is homogenized and woman/uncivilized is made absent. Colonialism has structured the colonizer's construction of the colonized, which guides "White Man's Burden," "Benevolent Assimilation," and "Manifest Destiny" to actualization. Neocolonialism has perpetuated the narrativization of its precursor, continuing genocides through military aid, right-wing paramilitary units, low-intensity conflict (LIC) or the U.S. surrogate war in areas with nationalist and revolutionary movements. Is this not to say that these genocides (spread through centuries of colonialism and neocolonialism) are very similar to the horror of the Holocaust? Kristeva marks the Holocaust as one of the greatest horrors of our time. Must horror be so encapsulated in a short period to become abjectionable, equally horrible? Kristeva implicates the Western mind so internalized in Judeo-Christian monotheism as the purveyor of the Holocaust. Is this not also the keepsake of neocolonialism? That by which willed the conversion, conquest, and translation of the colonized? That which has erased the histories of the colonized, the histories of women, and denying them enunciation?[26] This is the more frequent reading of the abject, one that operates in the more general sphere of neocolonial relations. As the neo/colonized needs to be demassified so as to constitute specificities of identity or flux of identities, one may need to look at other abjections like "abjection within abjection" or the layers of abjection to unravel its possible and real displacements; simply put, to expose the continuous otherization especially in the ranks of the Other. Clitoridectomy is one such layered abject position, putting the neocolonized in close complicity with abjection. As the neocolonized community constitutes itself through processes of exclusion and inclusion in foregrounding an identity and backgrounding its marginality, it too has sustained practices that are as repressive as its own neocolonial experiences. In clitoridectomy, women are abjected within the abjectionable form of neocolonialism.

Neocolonial pain and suffering are reproduced within the (re) productive bodies of women. Securing pleasure as the sole domain of men, clitoridectomy encapsulates another neocolonial experience—making women feel perennial pain in the sexual act, grounding the pain in men's right over women's bodies, making women nothing more than neo/colonized sexual machines.

It is in this fold that Le Doeuff's positive attibutions of humanism may prove emancipatory for the experiences of layered abjection. Le Doeuff explains two simultaneous aspects of humanism in realizing potentials for emancipation: generality ("humankind") and dispersal ("humankind is scattered in persons"). However, it is with the latter—"full distribution of humanity among individuals"— that Le Doeuff rethinks humanism in feminism which may very well apply to multiculturalism.[27]

Based on mutual respect and reciprocity, communities are far more able to construct notions of themselves both individually and collectively. Similarly in thinking of clitoridectomy, feminists are able to refigure the exclusion of the neo/colonized women, exposing the (male/patriarchal) culture that has victimized, silenced, and marginalized these women.

As neocolonialism grapples with the language of the uncivilized and woman, internalizing that which it seeks to create as an "exoticization of otherness," the uncivilized and the feminine resist this internalization, becoming sites of contention for meanings, sites for adventurous wanderings. The abject and abjection such as in dogeating/dogeaters intersect these sites, where a "burst of beauty" may overwhelm us,[28] surging forth new economies of meaning to arise and enabling other voices to speak. Here is one such retelling of a story.

1   Gayatri Spivak, "The Rani of Sirmur," *Europe and Its Other*, ed. Francis Barker et al. Vol. I (Cholchester: University of Essex, 1985).

2   Edward Said, "An Ideology of Difference," *Critical Inquiry* 12, no. 1 (Autumn 1985): 206.

3   Homi Bhabha, *The Location of Culture* (London: Routledge, 1994).

4   Renato Constantino, *Synthetic Culture and Development* (Quezon City: Foundation for Nationalist Studies, 1985), 10.

5   Julia Kristeva, *Powers of Horror: An Essay on Abjection* (New York: Columbia University, 1982), 135–36.

6   Ibid., 136.

7   Vicente Rafael, *Contracting Colonialism: Translation and Christian Conversion in Tagalog Society Under Early Spanish Rule* (Quezon City: Ateneo de Manila University Press, 1988), ix–x.

8   Michel de Certeau, *The Practice of Everyday Life*, trans. Steven Rendali (Berkeley: University of California Press, 1984), 174.

9   Edilberto N. Alegre, *Inumang Pinoy* (Metro Manila: Anvil Publishing, 1992), 200–201.

10   Ibid., 13.

11   Ibid., 203.

12   Ibid., 132–33.

13   Ibid., 152–53.

14   Ibid., 173.

15   Michel Foucault, *Discipline and Punish*, trans. Alan Sheridan (New York: Vintage Books, 1979), 30.

16   Jessica Hagedorn, *Dogeaters* (New York: Penguin Books, 1990), 41.

17   Abdul JanMohamed, "The Economy of Manichean Allegory: The Function of Racial Difference in Colonialist Literature," *Critical Inquiry* 12, no. 1 (Autumn 1985): 62.

18   Bienvenido Lumbera and Cynthia Nograles Lumbera, eds., *Philippine Literature: A History and Anthology* (Pasig City: Anvil Publishing, 2005), 31.

19   Renato Constantino and Letizia Constantino, *The Philippines: A Past Revisited* (Quezon City: Renato Constantino, 1974), 221.

20   President William McKinley, "Remarks to the Methodist Delegation," in *The Philippines Reader*, ed. Schirmer and Shalom (Quezon City: 1987), 22–23.

21   Emory S. Bogardus, "Anti-Filipino Race Riots," in *The Philippines Reader*, ed. Schirmer and Shalom (Quezon City: Ken, 1987), 59.

22   Ibid.

23   Alegre, *Inumang Pinoy*, 86.

24 Blanche d'Alpuget, "Philippine Dream Feast," *New York Times Book Review*, <u>79</u>
    25 Mar 1990, Sec. 7, p. 1.

25 Katheryn Hughes, "Sweet and Sour," *New Statesman & Society*, 12 Jul 1991.

26 Kristeva, *Powers of Horror*.

27 Michele Le Doeuff, *Hipparchia's Choice: An Essay Concerning Women, Philosophy, Etc.* (Cambridge: Blackwell, 1991).

28 Kristeva, *Powers of Horror*.

Geography

Popular Discourse of Vietnam in the Philippines

The collective effort of U.S. popular and political state apparatuses to deal with the Vietnam experience is an effort to construct an aspect of the American national heritage. The national heritage, in turn, rests on the privileged global hegemonic position of the U.S. Through these state apparatuses, tensions from contrary identities and geographies are necessarily diffused to construct this national heritage. Mainly through the strategy of conflating other identities and geographies, a refurbished history is perpetuated. The moment of conflation, in essence, is the "moment of the apocalypse," whereby the national heritage is salvaged—resituated and rehistoricized into a workable narrative. In what I will argue later, the apocalyptic moment renames the structure of beings and feelings to experience and to tell the narrative of the national heritage. The apocalyptic moment also becomes the site where contestation for other meanings is made possible, signifying alternative value systems and practices.

This essay analyzes the politics of the colonialist's strategy of conflating identities and geographies through war and film. Using the film *Apocalypse Now*[1] as a screen in the collective effort to deal with the Vietnam experience, I intend to present how newer historical memories of Vietnam are constructed; how these are spiritualized and made apocalyptic; and how these constructions can be problematized. These then lead to a space that marks the construction's own contradiction, setting sites from which new coalitions and practices arise, specifically in the politics of the Broadway musical *Miss Saigon*.[2] My own interest as a Filipino provides me with an agenda—to attach the Philippine colonial and neo-colonial experience in an analysis to recuperate the space and history of Filipinos in film and in history. There is a strong ground to do so. The first U.S. attempt at colonial enterprise started with its colonization of the Philippines. The U.S. bloody suppression of resistance by Filipinos, what has come to be known as the Philippine-American War, became a precursor to the Vietnam War, the U.S. using similar tactics and strategies in both cases.

I draw from Carlo Ginzburg's conjectural approach. The approach allows the deployment of seemingly disparate elements in constructing a discourse of historical memory of Vietnam and in interrogating how this memory becomes competitive for other social groups.[3] Similarly related to Bakhtin's dialogic, my own analysis, I hope, opens new relational aspects for remapping geographies and refiguring identities or simply for providing connections that do not seem to exist in the first place.[4] This last point, in turn, is related to the Foucauldian notion of abrupt discontinuities of consciousness—how disparate elements and disparate relations eventually open possibilities of looking into the construction and contestation of consciousness itself.

I also draw from the comment of Michael Frisch's Nigerian friend, unnamed in the article, for the significance of this project. The friend stresses the significance of history of those in the margins. "History is a giant stone that lies on top of us (the marginalized); history is something we have to struggle from under."[5] Foreshadowing one's politics and ethics is the weight placed on the historian from the margins. This can be seen ambivalently, but to take its positive side, the politics provides a distinct marking of a history "from under."

Dissecting the Horror

Kurtz' last words—"the Horror, the Horror!"—in Joseph Conrad's *Heart of Darkness*[6] and in Francis Coppola's *Apocalypse Now*, the film adaptation of the novel, interestingly frame the colonialist's own apocalypse. Like capital, the dying colonialist body abjects that which it has incorporated, then awaits to be reborn in some variant form. The old narrative fades, and new variations to an old theme resurface. However, for the colonized subject, it would be useful to frame the words differently, as an

> Ominous silence that utters archaic colonial 'otherness' that speaks in the riddles, obliterating proper names and proper places. . . . is a silence that turns imperial triumphalism into the testimony of colonial confusion and those who hear its echo lose their historic memories.[7]

The apocalyptic moment is thus reframed in a doubling, working well for and against the colonialist. This doubling, more so, marks for the colonized a certain empowerment to shatter the "historic memories" of the colonialist from which the colonized has been so entwined.

Apocalypse Now (1979) provides a journey toward this revelation. The film is a juncture for seemingly disparate elements—where Vietnam and the Philippines can be remapped; where Filipinos and Vietnamese can be refigured; where destruction, assimilation, and resistance come into the fold. The operations of the film and its making, as documented in *Hearts of Darkness: A Director's Apocalypse* (1991), refashion histories, geographies, and identities for the narrative of dealing with the Vietnam experience. It also opens other sites of contestation, as in *Platoon,*[8] another Vietnam film shot in the Philippines; and *Miss Saigon,* a Broadway production in Vietnam yet whose major roles are portrayed by non-Vietnamese actors (Welsh and a Filipina).

Shot on location in the Philippines to give "the appearance of battle-shattered Indo-China," the film tells of Willard's journey to "exterminate with extreme prejudice" the brilliant-turned-psychotic Colonel Kurtz.[9] Kurtz has turned against the military establishment, leading a group of natives who deify him. The journey has made Willard admire Kurtz, but, true to his duty, he kills Kurtz.

Though the film was not the first to deal with the Vietnam War—precedents include *Green Berets* (1968), *Limbo* (1974), *Rolling Thunder* (1977), *Heroes* (1977), *Coming Home* (1978), *The Boys of Company C* (1978), *Go Tell the Spartans* (1978), *The Deer Hunter* (1978), and *Hair* (1979)—the film set the Hollywood standard for the Vietnam picture.[10] Principal shooting started on 20 March 1976. What was believed to be a sixteen-week shooting in the Philippines ended a year later, on 21 March 1977. Filming snagged with the firing of Harvey Keitel (originally groomed to play Willard), the onslaught of typhoon Didang (Olga) that destroyed the sets, and the alleged heart attack of Martin Sheen dismissed, however, by United Artists "as heat exhaustion."[11] Originally budgeted for USD 12 million, the cost of the war epic escalated to USD 30 million.

As the standard by which to judge Vietnam films, *Apocalypse Now* is especially significant in many ways. It provides a way to explore the operations of an American collective confrontation with the Vietnam debacle. It also afforded the time and space for the creation of a truth narrative of this encounter. This confrontation, however, has resulted in the interchangeability of Vietnamese and Filipino identities, and of the landscapes of Vietnam and the Philippines. The "making-of" documentary, *Hearts of Darkness*, works in similar fashion. It reifies the colonial and neo-colonial structures with which the Philippines and the U.S are entwined.

My take-off point is the notion of Vietnam as trauma. The U.S. defeat in the Vietnam War created a new unwanted experience, that of trauma and of dealing with a trauma. I use the term "Vietnam" as an encapsulation of the traumatic Vietnam War experience. Thus, Vietnam films, in this essay, are specific to American films about the Vietnam War and the "Vietnam" experience. Vietnam films can be seen as the screen by which Foucault's notion of the confessional can be illustrated as "one of the main rituals for the production of truth." Though Foucault intended the notion as one of the "procedures for the individualization of power," the network of individuals produces a collective notion of a truth.[12] In this case, it is a truth of Vietnam.

In constructing the national heritage, as Michael Bommes and Patrick Wright point out, contradictions are abolished.[13] Though the point Bommes and Wright make overtly presents a totalizing perspective, abruptly impeding any resistance and liberation, it remains useful in that it emphasizes something that is overlooked— the hegemonic power structures at work. It is significant in locating a context for localized and diasporic efforts in contesting these structures.

Through *Apocalypse Now*, a mechanism related to penitence and the purgation of guilt, anxiety, and trauma of Vietnam take place, with the effect of constituting a truth of Vietnam as a component of the national heritage. Through individual participation in the screening of the Vietnam film, one is networked into the confrontation of the Vietnam experience, ready as Jane Fonda is (after seeing *Platoon*) "to put it behind us."[14] A Vietnam veteran who also served as coun-sellor at the San Francisco Veterans Center needed a community to watch the film with. Not wanting to see the film alone, the film for him, as noted in *The Hollywood Reporter*, "has stirred some rough memories."[15] Grounded in melodrama, whether in the vicarious or visceral experience, the film transforms the "good cry" into a senti-mental yet historical sojourn. Some twenty years after Vietnam, emotions are still sensitive to the experience. Vietnam films provide a process of coming to certain terms with the experience, as a desensi-tizing of the Vietnam sensitivity.

As individuals negotiate the memory of Vietnam, contact of this kind consequently forges a truth of Vietnam. Frisch, however, observes this truth as one of denial and disengagement. These reactions are emblematic as the invented category of "Post-Vietnam Syndrome."[16] This truth forged of Vietnam is reduced to its basic facticity: the use of the past tense is symptomatic of a "post-Vietnam" reading of the Vietnam experience, one in which historical impera-tives are collapsed for a workable present. Anne McClintock finds that the growing ritualism with "post" signals "a widespread, epochal crisis in the idea of linear, historical "progress." Specifically referring to the "post" in "post-colonialism," she writes that the prefix sets itself complicit with the "imperial idea of linear time," conferring upon "colonialism the prestige of history proper."[17]Similarly, the ramifications of the imperialist war with Vietnam and its still unre-solved closure remain as the privileged marker in the historicization of "post-Vietnam." More telling is the liberal politics of the apocalyp-tic moment of the "post-Vietnam" period: "Vietnam has ended. Get on with life. Time to move on." "Post-Vietnam" snags the historical connectedness of the present to the traumatic past.

The Vietnam film created a conditioned public sphere that localizes the actual war experience into the level of the individual. In the succeeding discussion, the notion of hegemony favors the reading along a frame of socio-political and economic references, constructed prior to the individual's encounter with the Vietnam film. The refer-ences evoke the collective trauma with the historical experience of the Vietnam War. With a shift to the focus of hegemony, attention is called from the means of force to the use of consensus in construct-ing notions of the community. In this case, actual war would be less preferred while popular cultural forms such as film would be idealized in explaining how people negotiated their lives within the power structures. However, force and consent provide simultaneous drives for the elaboration and critique of the power structures. War and film can then be rethought as useful frames in examining how power structures work and where the sites of resistance lie.

The making of the film gives valuable insights into hegemony and the relation of film and war. The filmmaking of *Apocalypse Now* is likened to a war within a war. From location hunting to precision detonation of explosions, to having Vietnam military advisors, *Apocalypse Now* and its making bear the stamp of authenticity of the war in its simulated war effort. As Coppola states, "It is not a film of Vietnam, it is Vietnam."[18]

Coppola constructs himself as colonialist master, acting in film-making as its field commander. He may have missed the war, but just the same, he wants to simulate the "authentic" experience of war both on and off screen. In location hunting, Coppola searched "exotic islands for the terrain that looked like what the U.S. forces had fought through along the Mekong Delta, in mountainous Cam Ranh, on Annam beaches and in the green hell of the Cambodian jungle."[19] This is interesting because Coppola, never having been in Vietnam, doubly simulates the geography of Vietnam. What he is basing his notions of the "authentic" terrain on are actually his own visions of the landscape of mainland Southeast Asia. These images of the landscape, in turn, were brought to him through newsreel and documentary war footages.

Coppola foreshadows a structure by which the spectator's viewing is partially or largely conditioned. Coppola's selection of shots, simulation of the images, erasure of peoples, destruction of geographies, among others, reify the structure by which the spectator then frames the Vietnam experience. What eventually gets conjured on screen represents a system of inclusion and exclusion, absence and representation, conflation and reification. It is primarily through a textual reading that I am able to operationalize hegemony in the film as one symptomatic of Vietnam's historical memorialization, and consequently, that of the Philippines. The process works in two ways—through the destruction of geography, and through the alienation of the individual body.

The opening scene sets the frame of reference for the film. The first shot is still of a Third World/underdeveloped landscape of a coconut farm taken from a helicopter. Soundless at first, a linear explosion occurs. The spectator then is made aware of the helicopters in an offensive action, not against an alien people (there are no bodies shown as a result of the offensive) but against a foreign landscape. The landscape is obliterated. Willard's face is then superimposed. Willard, either drunk or on drugs, stares for the most part, then

Fig. 1: Opening scene, *Apocalypse Now*

inflects a range of emotions—pain, fear, pity, alienation. The body is distanced from the mind. As an introduction to the narration, shots of the helicopter, the flames, and the dark smoke of the destroyed landscape and the alienated yet pained individual are juxtaposed. Such triangulation works again several times to frame segments leading to Willard's (and the spectator's) apocalypse.

The military establishment becomes the agent for the alienated white male individual to deal with his alien geography. The goal regarding the alien landscape is its destruction. Though the film would eventually include native bodies, this inclusion is only for the purpose of conjuring geographical decay, and hence calling for imperial intervention which comes into being through excess of military operations.

To authenticate the war film, cost was not spared to get the Vietnam/war effect—the simulation of destruction. For example, United Artists boasts of "more than 500 smoke bombs, 100 phosphorous sticks, 1,200 gallons of gas, 50 water explosions of 35 dynamite each, 2,000 rockets, flares, tracers and 5,000 feet of detonating cord are used in the 11/2 minute finale."[20] So grand was this recreation that the production notes brag of smoke filling the sky "until the sun was blotted out."[21] The spectator then becomes aware of the magnitude of the geography's destruction constructed as alien/foreign. However, this geography is forcibly linked to the magnitude of individual alienation constructed as a shared identity.

The Vietnam experience is authenticated by its triangulation. Military advisors were employed. The destruction approximated the bombing and other military operations in Vietnam. The white male individual, however, is more disjointed than the grittier image of Vietnam veterans as represented on television news during the actual war. The originary Vietnam image is recuperated later on in the film *Platoon.*

In *Apocalypse Now,* the white male individual—from Willard to Kurtz to the boat's crew—is portrayed as merely reactive to the geographical environment. The overreaction of the men to the Vietnamese on the boat represents America's overreaction to Vietnam and to the Vietnam experience thereafter. The overreaction is rationalized in two modes. First, it is exaggerated through the presentation of the landscape's death and decay, and second, through the presentation of the leadership and the bureaucracy as detached from the actual conditions of the men in battle. The white male body is then forced to mirror the geographical landscape. Not understanding the logic or the lack of it in the alien landscape, the body abjects that which it cannot incorporate. The body is machinized into the operation of war. The situation then reduces the men into machines, instrumentalizing their bodies to react to the geographic horrors. Atrocities are therefore made justifiable in the men's unenviable display of valor in battle.

It is the state of the mind, however, that provides a locus for the body. Drugs and alcohol in the film are made to stimulate the mental effect of Vietnam. *Hearts of Darkness* exposed the rampant use of drugs and alcohol on the set. Actor Sam Bottoms was hooked on amphetamines; actor Frederic Forrest also admitted taking drugs on the set. Dennis Hopper was captured as "stoned," arguing with Coppola about his lines. When Martin Sheen's alienatory opening sequence was filmed, he admitted being "so drunk [he] could barely stand up." The alienating effects are reproduced for the spectator, who is made to think of the film in terms of either a good or a bad trip, a good high or a downer, cathartically liberating or further alienating. In the construction of this Vietnam history, the spectator is positioned somewhat as a co-dependent in the trial of collective guilt. Through the "Vietnamization" (the imperial action justified as a reaction to the consequence of doomed geographies and detached leadership) of the logic, a naturalization occurs, displacing the guilt in less debilitating terms.

By equating the destruction of the self with the "natural" recourse in dealing with the alien space's destruction, one of two readings may result. First, the identification marks that there is no one to blame (all are innocent) or that both parties in the war are liable (all are guilty). Secondly, it also marks the identities and geographies outside the shared one as the final unburdening site of the collective guilt. The film provides a problematic reflexivity toward the margins as the end-in-sight of the Vietnam memory. The vanished colonies and the absent peoples become the dump site of the colonialist guilt. A paradox of history is reworked to the benefit of the colonial master. The colonialist is able to present a homeopathic solution to his psychological bind—that which had given him the problem provides the solution. As such, the figure of the colonized bears the weight of the transference, ending as the shock absorber of the colonialist. It should be emphasized, though, that in either case, a selective amnesia takes place.

History then is constituted through selected memory. In constructing the film (from the actual filmmaking process to its meta-construction through film criticism), the perspective of the hegemonic power is reified. According to Eleanor Coppola's account, the U.S. Department of Defense declined to assist in the filmmaking of *Apocalypse Now*.[22] Coppola sought the assistance of President Ferdinand Marcos to obtain military hardware (a major factor that made Coppola choose the Philippines as location) and "to simplify the complications of these particularly exotic areas."[23]

Gerald Sussman, who was one of few journalists allowed to cover the closed sets, doubts that there was no assistance from the U.S. Department of Defense. He believes that Coppola engaged in a "patron-client" relationship with the Department.

> The Pentagon's support included the use of important technical advisors, together with several hundred Clark Airbase and Subic Naval Station uniformed personnel in some of the key footage. . . . Coppola made specific script compromises in exchange for this assistance. In one major battle sequence, for example, Coppola substituted North Vietnamese (Democratic Republic of Vietnam) for the original (southern) Viet Cong flags over villages in the Mekong Delta south of Saigon and put North Vietnamese uniforms on the backs of the insurgents—in line with the Pentagon's "foreign (D.R.V.) invasion" justification for U.S. "allied" intervention of the war.[24]

The film then reflects this "official" history.

Criticism, on the other hand, supplemented the reification of "official" history. It works as an apologia for the dominant anti-war angling (devoid of actual historical past), which can be read, too, as the film's own "official" history. Marsha Kinder's[25] focus on the power of adaptation in *Apocalypse Now* foresees the dilemma. She writes, "Coppola adopts someone else's material or structure, absorbs and expands it by identifying it with his own experience, and thereby transforms it into his own uniquely powerful vision." The critic readily foregrounds the masculinist and colonialist rigor of Coppola's construction yet does not further raise issues to critique these points. The triumph of the rational is always foreseen and lauded, as in Willard's abdication of Kurtz's throne in the kingdom of natives. After his slaughter of Kurtz, the natives were only too willing to deify him, transferring the godliness of Kurtz to him. Not having any other rational choice, Kurtz chooses to reinforce the military institution. He agrees with Kurtz that the problem lies not with the structure but with the individuals running the structure.

In the textual reading of the film, supplemented by the instances of its production, one sees that the hegemonic structure of viewing the film or of experiencing the war equally reifies. Hegemony provides the context for analyzing sites of resistance. In this aspect of the project, I find that the Vietnam experience tends more to homogenize hegemony than to subvert it. It is thus useful to look for other Vietnam sites where resistance lies. I find this in *Miss Saigon*. This text reworks the Vietnam experience through the operation of conflation familiar in *Apocalypse Now*. However, the operation does not fully work as resistance evolved with the production of the text.

To go back to the film, hegemony also poses the problem of subalternity. Themselves a subaltern in the Philippine national landscape and identity, the Igorots who were cast as the natives in the film are further reconstituted in the place of the subaltern. The film totalizes the absence of identity of the Igorot people, reifying them as a transcultural native subject. This recalls the World Expositions at the turn of the century that brought Igorots and other indigenes to the West as transcultural native subjects for exhibition. The exhibition and viewing experience are made to highlight not the artifacts' ethnicities but the white race's supremacy. Similar operations work in the utilization of the Igorots in the film. In consideration of the authentic "feel," 230 Igorots, the indigenous people of Northern Luzon, were cast en masse as Kurtz's followers and brought to the southern part of Luzon where the film was shot. The film doubly erases them as an indigenous group. On one level, they are displaced by mythology, lumped together as the colonialist's subjects. On a second level, they are further displaced by a historicity, the film figuring them as indigenous to Cambodia, an act of utter disregard for the "real" indigenous peoples of Cambodia. The specific space of identity becomes immaterial to the Western feel; the indigene, however, is posited as the more authentic native body. What should also be emphasized is that this absence of a mark of collective identity is also (de)figured in the absence of any individual identity. Not one of Kurtz's followers speaks.

Furthermore, the rituals of the Igorots are also displaced, taken out of context for a suitable ending. Encountering an Igorot ritual that involved the slaughter of a water buffalo, Coppola decides to incorporate the scene in the ending over which he has so long agonized. Not having an idea for an ending, Coppola juxtaposes the slaughter of the buffalo with Willard's slaughter of Kurtz. Savagery is manifested and differentiated. While Willard's is forced upon him, the (displaced) Igorots' (uncontextualized) savagery is considered natural.

The construction of a workable history/memory of Vietnam excludes that which it cannot assimilate. What becomes memory is the somewhat coherent retelling of history as a space for nego-tiating everyday life. The national heritage is related to Benedict Anderson's notion of imagined communities (1991). Individuals imagine themselves as a community by forging a sense of commonal-ity with community ideals. An individual imagines one's belonging to a community through shared beliefs and practices. Reading a news essay or singing the national anthem becomes a ritual for the daily affirmation of this community. As in the screening of the Vietnam film, one imagines a community negotiating for a space of Vietnam's memory. This space, however, is "overdetermined" for the spectator by the operations of certain political and ideological state apparatus-es. What the spectator negotiates are one's relations to the Vietnam saga in the pre-defined space of mass culture. As mass culture defines the parameters of negotiation, contradictions are made to lie in the gaps and fissures. This then provides the space of resistance. I will go into this space in relation to the struggles in *Miss Saigon*.

Anderson suggests a strong affinity between nationalist and religious imageries.[26] The collective effort becomes a spiritualized experience. Filming the journey of war, then, becomes a journey into war. Filmmaking and the filmic text reflect each other's image. Coppola states, "I found that many of the ideas and images with which I was working as a film director began to coincide with my own life, and that I, like Captain Willard, was moving up a river in a far-away jungle, looking for answers and hoping for some kind of catharsis."[27] He goes on to mention that the effect was the same for all the "close collaborators," "no one was left unchanged."[28] After the filming, Coppola lost 60 pounds.

In *Apocalypse Now*, the river journey makes Willard question the order of the superiors. He is fascinated by Kurtz, his brilliant track record and his defiance of the entire military establishment. He begins to change his vision of the war and the world. This iden-tification with Kurtz is emphasized by his decision not to rescue a wounded Vietnamese who has been fired upon by the boat's crew. He shoots the latter dead to get him out of the way so he can concentrate on Kurtz. He remains fascinated when he meets Kurtz; nonetheless, he decides to kill him to preserve him rather than to see Kurtz die (to be placed on trial and sentenced to prison). Willard's wanting of a mission culminates in a moral dilemma when the mission is imple-mented. It then closes on a passive triumph of being able to play god or simply to use the rational, so fractured in a time of war instead. The symbolic landscape of the American national heritage is spiri-

Fig. 2: Climactic scene,
Apocalypse Now

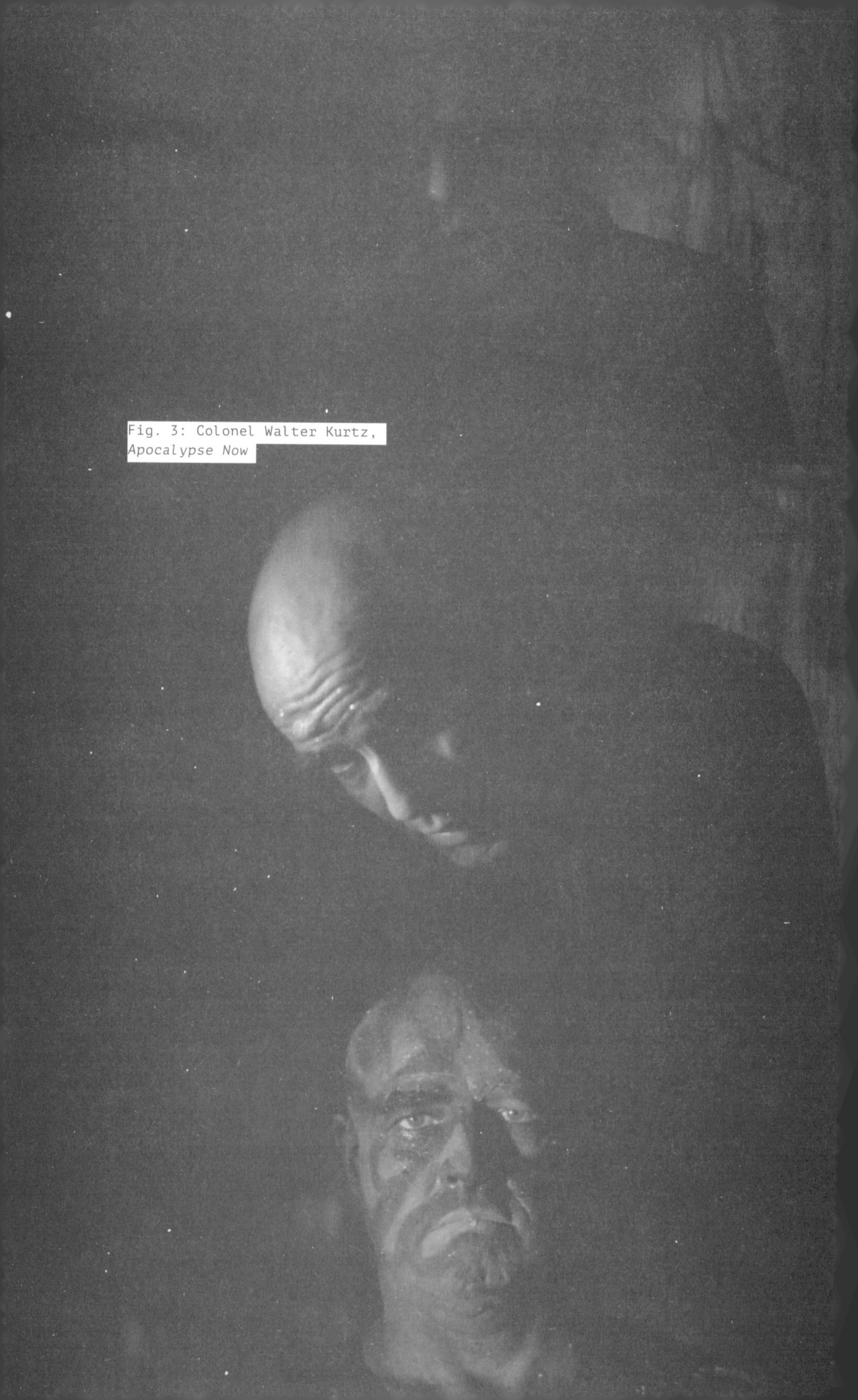

Fig. 3: Colonel Walter Kurtz,
Apocalypse Now

tualized. The national character is remythologized by the expected birth of "new Adam."[29]

By 1986, this "new Adam" had matured in *Platoon*. Playing on a similar structure of journey with the end-view of recognizing a loss, *Platoon* uses the same white male voice-over and makes greater claim to authenticity: the greater the authentic experience, the greater it transmutes into the spiritual. The genealogy of father to son, Martin to Charlie Sheen, is a continuance of the process of searching for Vietnam's meaning.[30]

Platoon is a discontinuance of the theatrical filming of Vietnam. Oliver Stone, representing himself as a participant in the Vietnam War, becomes the mid-1980s American informant of the war.[31] *Platoon* is an insider's point of view of the war through Stone's autobiographical account of his experience in the Vietnam War. This supposedly gave the Vietnam film a grittier realism. What can be more authentic than a filmmaker with actual combatant experience in the Vietnam War? Stone hired a military adviser to train the actors. He did not allow a transition between the 16-day training and the first day of shooting. The film was billed as a true-to-life Vietnam film and as a film based on a war Stone knew firsthand ("as a grunt with the 25th Infantry in 1967-68"). Another executive producer called the film "a movie that had to be made."[32] The claim to authenticity (which, in turn, draws on personal and historical claims) becomes a plea for the film's production and consumption.

Both films play on a loss. Coppola's Willard mourns this void. Stone's adolescent soldier (played by Charlie Sheen) mourns the loss of his innocence. These are symptomatic of the post-Vietnam mourning of the loss of empire. One distinct characteristic of "critical" Vietnam films such as *Apocalypse Now* and *Platoon* is this soft-porn melancholia "that long mourns the empires, and their grief always has a stagey quality to it."[33] The white male lead achieves a spiritual triumph in the film as the loss is acknowledged and displaced. The displacement is passed on to the colonized figure through a strategy of conflating these peoples' identities or of effacing their bodies on screen. The colonized body is destroyed, amassed, or effaced. The colonialist is fascinated with the colonized body as a way of recuperating his own loss of a body. Jameson refers to the disappearance of the bodies in relation to the First World "hysterical sublime": "the body is touching its limits, 'volatilized.' In the experience of images, to the point of being outside itself, or losing itself."[34] The film's destruction of bodies and landscapes has actual implications in the social sphere where effects of napalm bombs and torture, for example, remain. The white male is regenerated through the violation of the colonized's bodies and geographies.

Obscuring the Filipino Identity and Space

Anderson stresses, "All profound changes in consciousness, by their very nature, bring with them characteristic amnesias. Out of such oblivions, in specific historical circumstances, spring narratives."[35] This is the space to reframe the apocalypse.

In Baler, Quezon, one of the location sites for the film, the community's everyday routine was disrupted, as the locus of activity was shifted to the film site. The production induced food shortages and increased food prices. Taking advantage of the visitors, a culture of profiteering was instigated. Rents and transportation fees skyrocketed to the detriment of local consumers. A culture of excess was displayed as Coppola flew in food and alcohol from the U.S. to celebrate his birthday. In another instance, "200 'hostesses' were brought in from Metro Manila but made available only at Stateside prices."[36] The implications are equally serious on the national scale. In collaborating with Marcos, Coppola was contributing to the escalation of human rights violations in the Philippines. He entered into an agreement with Marcos to leave the mounted machine guns on the Hueys M-50 after the completion of the shooting. "The refurbished Hueys were used on a rotating basis between the film site and the real-life war against Muslim and communist-led New People's Army (N.P.A.) insurgents in the southern Philippines and other regions."[37] I should add to this magnitude the numerous civilians caught in the crossfire.

In the context of the effort to deal with the Vietnam experience, the Philippines becomes the uncanny. Such connections may seem thin. The only link the film has to the Philippines is through a superimposed shot of Kurtz's military background. The confidential typewritten report states that Kurtz obtained his master's degree from Harvard, with a thesis on the "Philippine Insurrection: American Foreign Policy in Southeast Asia, 1898-1905." The implications, however, are important. The term "insurrection," for one, has been pejoratively applied to the war engaged against the U.S., suggesting chaotic, isolated, and local instances of resistance.

The implications begin with U.S. interest in the Philippines at the turn of the century. On January 1890, Alfred J. Beveridge's first Senate speech emphasized the unlimited resources of the Philippines: "No land in America surpasses in fertility the plains and valleys of Luzon"; "The wood of the Philippines can supply the furniture of the world for a century to come"; "forty miles of Cebu's mountain chain are practically mountains of coal."[38] Just as Daniel Boone's account was a real estate promotion for Kentucky, Beveridge's speech was supporting U.S. colonization of the Philippines. In the terms of Henry Nash Smith, Beveridge perceived the Philippines as a "virgin land" waiting to be tapped. This originary space in which the U.S. projected the Philippines is linked to Foucault's heterotopia (whose contrary role is "to create a space that is other, another real space, as perfect, meticulous").[39] However, a year after his speech, U.S. military pacification drives took approximately six hundred thousand Filipino lives in Luzon alone. This information led an anonymous U.S. Representative to declare, "They never rebel in Luzon anymore because there isn't anybody left to rebel."[40] Genocide becomes the continuing strategy of conquering peoples and their geographies.

Forcing acceptance of colonial rule was the objective of conquering the Philippines. By militarizating and establishing democratic institutions, the U.S. was determined to affix its brand of colonial rule abroad. The ultimate goal of the West's conquest, after all, extended overseas to the Pacific. The U.S. conquest of the Philippines was a continuation of the myth of the frontier. The exotic space of the other has been transformed from virgin island to howling wilderness when resistance exists, and in time, to exoticized spaces of tourism and export-processing zones of multinational operations. The "other" space is networked into the imperial circuits for the various colonized functions of a source of raw materials and cheap labor to market for finished products.

William McKinley set the tone for enlightened colonization in 1898. In a remark to a Methodist Delegation, he pondered on the dilemma of colonizing the Philippines:

> I thought first that we would take Manila; then Luzon; then other islands, perhaps, also. I walked on the floor of the White House night after night until midnight; and I am not ashamed to tell you gentlemen, that I went down on my knees and prayed Almighty God for light and guidance more than one night. . . . And one night it came to me this way . . . there was nothing left for us to do but to take them all, educate the Filipinos, and uplift and civilize and Christianize them, and by God's grace do the very best we could by them, as our fellowmen for whom Christ

also died. And then I went to bed, and went to sleep and slept soundly, and the next morning I sent for the chief engineer of the War Department (our mapmaker), and I told him to put the Philippines on the map of the U.S.[41]

I quote McKinley at length to stress the earlier colonialist imperatives I have discussed in relation to *Apocalypse Now.* McKinley's apocalypse is reinforced in other racist notions of "benevolent assimilation," "white man's burden," and "manifest destiny." The colonialist discursive space, however, displaces the weight of the apocalyptic moment to actual peoples. This unnaturally affects the lives of the people as modernity is attempted and cultural imperialism is naturalized on them.

Thus, almost a century after, the Philippines continues to struggle toward notions of local, sectoral, and national communities. The discursive space is further layered in the institutions introduced and perpetuated by the U.S. in the Philippines. Government officials still come from the landed class, and therefore prioritize their own interests over those of others. A counterweight to these operations are the people's own initiatives. The mass movement, as an example, has provided a leverage for working class issues to be articulated in the public sphere. There remains communist insurgency in the countryside, waging a socialist war. Non-governmental organizations are initiating and complementing community-based programs. The struggle for a redefinition of identity and space continues.

The Convergence and Divergence in *Miss Saigon*

What have been discussed are some general terms of constructing a national community in the Vietnam experience and its corollary aspect, the difficulty of constructing an equivalent from a Filipino perspective. Filipino American critic, E. San Juan is cynical about this construction of the "homeland": "The authentic homeland doesn't exist except as a simulacrum of Hollywood, or as a nascent dream of jouissance still to be won by a national-democratic struggle."[42]

The stake, then, is constructing communities in diaspora at various possible levels. The text of *Miss Saigon* has constituted a temporal space of a community of Asian Americans. However, like *Apocalypse Now* and *Platoon,* *Miss Saigon* also draws from the colonialist operation of conflating identities and geographies. The resistance here provided a way for Asian American groups to forge an alliance whereby to sustain and expand notions of space and identities. The resistance and alliance-building are significant moves to create alternative and oppositional value systems and practices. The Asian American's own journey has been long, which is not to say that *Miss Saigon* provides the culmination of this journey. *Miss Saigon* is a phase in this Asian American journey.

After all, the Asian has been either lumped in a mass or conveniently ordered in a hierarchy of races. The massification begins with physical attributes—color, shape, size of the eyes, nose, face, and so on. Lack of knowledge of specific Asian groups is usually remedied through representations already constructed for other "minor" races. During the Philippine-American War, for example, editorial cartoons in the U.S. presented Filipinos as infants and savages—stereotype images of the peoples of Africa.

The positions of "minor" races were held in relation to the superiority of the white race. Composite facial pictures in "The Races of Men"[43] represented the centrality of the white race as personified by the noble woman, "in contrast with the swarthy males with eyes averted," and the classical Apollo figure.[44] Furthermore, groups were made to compete against each other for the favor of being privileged to be in proximity with the white race. Filipino farm laborers were welcomed to replace Japanese workers in Hawaii when the latter proved to be disconcerting for the plantation owners. Chinese coolies were tolerated during the building of railroads but were despised after the tracks were built. During World War II, the Chinese were preferred to the Japanese in the U.S. whose commitment to the Allied cause was always taken with suspicion. *Life Magazine*[45] came out with a physiognomic chart for the public to be able to distinguish Japanese from Chinese. Subtitled, "Angry Citizens Victimize Allies with Emotional Outburst at Enemy," the guide uses actual photos of male Chinese and Japanese Americans, noting for example, their "parchment" and "earthy" "yellow" complexions, more and less frequent "epicentric fold," higher noses and bridges that were supposed to be distinct in (though universalized within and among) the two ethnic peoples. While the Japanese in the U.S. were interned in camps during the war, the Germans were not treated equally harshly.

Miss Saigon emanates from this mold. The musical is Cameron Mackintosh's reworking of *Madama Butterfly* and Vietnam. The story is stereotypical, the taking of the Asian woman's own life for love of the white man. Ironically, David Henry Hwang who first reworked

Madama Butterfly into the gender bending *M. Butterfly* initiated the protest. The issue involved the hiring of non-Asian American actors to portray the Vietnamese leads in the musical. The Actor's Equity acceded at first, denying permission for non-American actors to come to the U.S. Charlton Heston resigned, saying, "I'm ashamed of my union."[46] When Mackintosh decided to cancel the show altogether, the Actor's Equity reversed its decision, realizing that Jonathan Pryce, a Welsh actor, was actually "a star of international stature," and Lea Salonga, a Filipino actor, actually had "unique ability." Consequently, the union's decision reaffirmed the insulting claim that there were no qualified Asian/Pacific actors to fill in the lead roles. There were also resignations on the side of Asian-Americans in protest of the ruling. Mackintosh, playing the colonialist overseer role in the debate, demanded the union first apologize before he reconsiders bringing his play to Broadway. This play, incidentally, had the biggest advance ticket sales at that time: USD 25 million. Also at stake were fifty jobs, thirty four of which were to actors of color. The protest landed on thin ice, and it was divisive, too. The female lead was also non-Asian American but nevertheless Filipino.

"Asian American actors have noted that they already have a hard time getting non-Asian roles as it is, and have even less opportunities to play Asian-specific roles," laments writer Johnny Ng. He ends on a positive note: "This is probably one thing that has galvanized the Asian American community across the nation. We are a diverse bunch and this is something we can all agree on."[47] Actor George Takei who portrayed "Mr. Sulu" in *Star Trek* is more cynical, "It's my firm belief that he's [Mackintosh] got an additional $25 million worth of free publicity."

The issues resulted in the unearthing of past and cultural anomalies. The use of white actors for Asian was standard practice even sixty years ago: Joel Grey in *Remo Williams*, Christopher Lee and Peter Sellers as Fu Man Chu, John Wayne as Genghis Khan in *The Conqueror*, Peter Ustinov as Charlie Chan. The earliest protest on this issue was in the 1970s, in the film adaptation of *Teahouse on August Moon*,[48] which cast Marlon Brando in an Asian role. More recent anomalies included Pryce's prosthetically altered eyelids and yellow facial make-up in portraying the Amerasian character.

Spearheaded by Asian American actors, a coalition was formed— the Asian Pacific Alliance for Creative Equality (APACE) in the West coast. Other groups that joined were the Asian American Journalist Association, the Asian American Legal Defense and Education Fund, Asian CineVision, and the Chinese Arts Council. Don Nakanichi,

Chair of the Asian American Studies program in UCLA, sent a letter to Actors Equity, exhorting the guild to stand pat on its original decision. In the East Coast, the issue brought about the alliance of the Asian Lesbians of the East Coast and the Gay Asian and Pacific Islander Men of New York. This alliance worked toward the issue of Asian American representation in the play, a divergence from the earlier position posited to the Actor's Equity. The issue cut across race as other groups joined the alliance—Brooklyn Women's Martial Arts, Gay Men of African Descent, Kambal sa Lusog, Las Buenas Amigas, Latino Gay Men of New York, Men of All Colors Together, Other Countries, Queer Nation, Salsa Soul Sisters, South Asian Lesbians and Gay Men, We Wah, and Bar Chee Ampe. A link with APACE was established, and a working relationship with other Asian and Pacific Islander groups was formed.

On the issue of *Miss Saigon*, alliance-building among and within Asian American individuals and groups eventually merged into a national network. Relations were evaluated, as new alliances were formed and old ones were cut. "Gray haired Japanese American wives and mothers and brash young white men from Queer Nation marched side-by-side" in a protest action.[49] The Lambda Legal Defense and Education Fund, a national law organization that champions lesbian and gay rights, however, chose to premiere the play despite protests from the Asian American community. Yoko Yoshikawa, one of the protesters, writes:

> At stake in *Miss Saigon* is how those who can control the means of representations and reproductions choose to define people of color and non-Western cultures, and to what ends. *Miss Saigon* rewrites the Vietnam War, pulling a sentimental love story from the carnage of carpet bombing, My Lai, and Agent Orange like a rabbit from a hat. Vietnam becomes just another exotic backdrop, good for a shot of nightclub sleaze and real live helicopter lift-off. Mackintosh and company spiced the racism of *Madame Butterfly*—a white man's wet dream—with the endorphin-pumping antics of Rambo and came up with a new version of an old story.[50]

In the Vietnam films discussed, in the opera *Madama Butterfly* and the musical *Miss Saigon*, the West inscribes death as natural to Asians. "The principal military advisor for *Apocalypse Now*— who spoke of the 'authenticity' of the film—General William Westmoreland, the U.S. wartime commander explained the

Vietnamese unremitting resistance to brutal imperialism as the Asian indifference to death."[51] This orientalist view reifies the structure of violence toward Asians and Asian Americans.

Bommes and Wright fail to forewarn of community-based consciousness outside the paradigm of the national heritage. Still working from within the myth of the model minority or the melting pot, the authors take community-based consciousness as liable only to the risk of appropriation by showcasing these contributions within the heritage of the nation.[52] However, where consciousness counters the national heritage, Bommes and Wright are silent.

In struggling with the *Miss Saigon* text, Asian Americans were remapping a space and refiguring an identity of their own, so to speak. The text has provided an opportunity for an imagining of an Asian American community, one that actively territorializes the space of hegemonic structures. This counter-memory comes by way of transference. Dominick LaCapra refers to transference as "a repetition-displacement of the past in the present as it necessarily bears upon the future." In stating that the desired objective is "not to blindly replicate the debilitating aspects of the past," LaCapra is calling for an ethics of writing history, one in which the "debilitating aspects" of the privileged position is problematized, allowing for histories within the margins to come in.[53]

Such transference works against the odds and against the grain. Identities and geographies remain contested. Its conflation only deepens the problem of reconstruction and reframing. I hope this is one such initiative in that direction.

Unfortunately, however, I have yet to acquire new information on how the alliance work has been since the efforts with *Miss Saigon*. Yoshikawa's own analysis of the lessons draws from the struggle toward creating a history and a space of collective identity. The point Yoshikawa raises may even be way ahead of what I have tried to outline in this essay.

Our coalition pointed the way to a possible future: where a complex identity is not only valued, but becomes a foundation for unity. We who occupy the interstices—whose very lives contain disparate selves—are, of necessity, at home among groups that know little of each other. We know what others do not in reconciling differences in our lives, and the mutable nature of borders. We have a deep hunger for a place in which we can be, at one and at the same time, whole, and part of something larger than ourselves. Our knowledge and desire may at times bring us to action: We push the parameters of existing communities wide and open, and cause the struggles of

different communities to overlap and meld. In the tangle, we may also
be midwives of vital coalitions.[54]

In 2000, however, *Miss Saigon* closed in Broadway and found a venue in the Philippines. The staging reified a self-orientalist value, which eroded the temporal gain of the alliance work against its Broadway opening. Alliance work needed to be transnationalized, especially when it came to cultural struggles. The play was staged in Manila's main cultural venue (the Cultural Center of the Philippines) with the full backing of politicians and big businesses only too willing to partake of this belated industrialized artifact. Resistance from various groups, led by the Concerned Artists of the Philippines, failed to prevent the massive financial and high-art support for the play. There was an amnesia of past political and cultural turmoil, caused by the very hegemony of global capitalists and culturati, willing to reinvent the past for present financial gain.

ENDNOTES

1   Francis Ford Coppola *Apocalypse Now*, 1979.

2   Claude-Michel Schonberg and Allan Boudil, *Miss Saigon*, 1989.

3   Carlo Ginzburg, *The Cheese and the Worms: The Cosmos of a 16th Century Miller*, trans. John and Anne Tedeschi (New York: Penguin Books, 1982).

4   M. M. Bakhtin, *The Dialogic Imagination* (Austin: University of Texas Press, 1981).

5   Michael Frisch, "The Memory of History," *A Shared Authority: Essays on the Craft and Meaning of Oral and Public History* (Albany: State University of New York Press, 1990), 20.

6   Heart of Darkness, Project Gutenberg Ebook, accessed 27 Jan 2015, http://www.gutenberg.org/files/219/219-h/219-h.htm.

7   Homi K. Bhabha, "Articulating the Archaic: Notes on Colonial Nonsense," *Literary Theory Today*, ed. Peter Collier and Helga Geyer-Ryan (Ithaca: Cornell University Press, 1990), 204.

8   Eleanor Coppola, *Hearts of Darkness: A Director's Apocalypse* (1991) and Oliver Stone, *Platoon* (1986).

9   Francis Ford Coppola, quoted in "Apocalypse Now," *Washington Afro-American*, 30 Oct 1979, 6 (hereafter cited as Production Notes 1981).

10 The range of early and contemporary Vietnam films of the 1970s ranged from big-budget studio that evoked hypermasculinity to melodrama that discussed the emasculinization of the soldiers. These included *Green Berets* (Rey Kellogg, John Wayne, Marvyn LeRoy, 1968), *Limbo* (John Sayles, 1974), *Rolling Thunder* (John Flynn, 1977), *Heroes* (Jeremy Kagan, 1977), *Coming Home* (Hal Ashby, 1978), *The Boys of Company C* (Sidney J. Furie, 1978), *Go*

Tell the Spartans (Ted Post, 1978), *The Deer Hunter* (Michael Cimino, 1978), and *Hair* (Milos Foreman, 1979).

11   sabdesi.net, "On-Set Stitches: 15 Films That Almost Killed Their Stars," accessed 14 Nov 2014, http://sabdesi.net/2013/09/on-set-stitches-15-movies-that-almost-killed-their-stars/ (hereafter cited as Program Brochure 1981).

12   Michel Foucault, *The History of Sexuality*, trans. Robert Hurley (New York: Vintage, 1990), 58–59.

13   Michael Bommes and Patrick Wright, "Charm of Residence: The Public and the Past," *Making Histories: Studies in History-Writing and Politics* (London: Hutchinson, 1982), 264.

14   Pat. H. Broeske, "After Seeing "Platoon," Fonda Wept," *Los Angeles Times*, 25 Jan 1987, accessed 13 Nov 2014, http://articles.latimes.com/1987-01-25/entertainment/ca-5554_1_jane-fonda.

15   "Platoon Troubles S.F. Vets," *The Hollywood Reporter*, 1987, 36.

16   Michael Frisch, "The Memory of History," *A Shared Authority: Essays on the Craft and Meaning of Oral and Public History* (Albany: State University of New York Press, 1990), 18.

17   Anne McClintock, "The Angel of Progress: Pitfalls of the Term 'Post Colonialism,'" *Social Text* 10, nos. 2 & 3 (1992): 85–86. She mentions that what seems to be the vogue of "post-ing" current cultures (as in "post-colonialism, post modernism, post-structuralism, post-cold war, post-marxism, post-apartheid, post-Soviet, post-Ford, post-feminism, post-national, post-historic, even post-contemporary") is problematic as it remains complicit to the imperatives of the privileged race-class-gender-ethnicity-sexual preference-etc.

18   Coppola, *Hearts of Darkness,* opening sequence.

19   Production Notes 1981, 2.

20   Program Notes 1981, 3.

21   Production Notes 1981, 2.

22   Eleanor Coppola, *Notes on the Making of Apocalypse Now* (New York: Limelight Editions, 2001).

23   Production Notes 1981, 4.

24   Gerald Sussman, "Bulls in the (Indo) China Shop," in *Journal of Popular Film and Television* 20, no. 1 (1992): 26. Sussman covered the filmmaking in a series of articles published in *Philippine Daily Express* in 1976–1977.

25   Coppola, *Notes on the Making of Apocalypse Now*, 1.

26   Ibid., 10.

27   Ibid., 1.

28   Ibid.

29   John Kellman, *American Myth and the Legacy of Vietnam* (New York: Colombia University Press, 1986), 206.

30 Charlie Sheen felt he wanted to be an actor after being with his father on location in the Philippines for *Apocalypse Now*.

31 The movie ad for *Platoon* features a picture of Oliver Stone (likely taken during the Vietnam War) and the text: "In 1967 a young man named Oliver Stone spent fifteen months in Vietnam as an infantry in the United States Army. He was wounded twice and received a bronze star gallantly in combat. . . . Stone has come a long way from Vietnam. But he has not left it behind. There were the men he knew and fought with in the country they could not win. The feelings of fear, comradeship, rage, and love. Feelings that won't go away for a lot of people. Especially the ones who lost pieces of their lives, or their bodies here. Oliver Stone was one of them and he still is. *Platoon* is his movie, and theirs."

32 Oliver Stone, quoted in Lawrence H. Saud, *Guts and Glory: The Making of the American Military Image in Film* (Lexington: University of Kentucky Press, 2002), 546.

33 Benedict Anderson, *Imagined Communities* (London: Verso, 1991), 111.

34 Andrew Stephanson, "Regarding Postmodernism—A Conversation with Fredric Jameson," *Universal Abandon*, ed. Andrew Ross (Minneapolis: University of Minnesota Press, 1988), 5.

35 Anderson, *Imagined Communities*, 204.

36 Sussman, "Bulls in the (Indo) China Shop," 26.

37 Ibid.

38 Alfred Beveridge, "Our Philippine Policy," *The Philippine Reader*, ed. Daniel Shirmer and Stephen Shalon (Quezon City: Ken, 1987), 25.

39 Quoted in Edward Soja, "History: Geography, Modernity," *The Cultural Studies Reader*, ed. Simon During (New York: Routledge, 1993), 146.

40 Quoted in Luzviminda Francisco, "The Philippine-American War," *The Philippine Reader* (Quezon City: Ken, 1987), 19.

41 William McKinley, "Remarks to a Methodist Delegation," *The Philippines Reader* (Quezon City: Ken, 1987), 25.

42 E. San Juan Jr., *Articulations of Power in Ethnic and Racial Studies in the United States* (New Jersey: Humanities Press, 1992), 122.

43 Published separately in *An Intermediate Geography* and *Physical Geography*, cited in Michael Hunt, *Ideology and U.S. Foreign Policy* (New Haven: Yale University Press, 1987), 48.

44 Hunt, *Ideology and U.S. Foreign Policy*, 51.

45 *Life Magazine*, Dec 1941.

46 Charlton Heston, "I'm Ashamed of My Union, Actor's Equity," *Los Angeles Times*, 13 Aug 13, 1990, F4.

47 Johnny Ng, "Bay Area Asian Actors Vow to Continue Fight," *Asia Week*, 24 Aug 1990, 3.

48   Guy Hamilton, *Remo Williams,* 1985; Don Sharp, *Fu Man Chu,* 1965; Dick Powell, *The Conqueror,* 1956; Clive Donner, *Charlie Chan and the Curse of the Dragon Queen,* 1981; and Daniel Mann, *Teahouse of the August Moon,* 1956.

49   Yoko Yoshikawa, "The Heat is On, Miss Saigon Coalition," *The State of Asian America: Activism and Resistance in the 1990s,* ed. Karin Aguilar-San Juan (Boston: Southend Press, 1994), 284.

50   Yoshikawa, *"Heat is On,"* 280.

51   Sussman, "Bulls in the (Indo) China Shop," 24.

52   Michael Bommes and Patrick Wright, "'Charm of Residence': The Public and the Past," in *Making Histories: Studies in History-Writing and Politics* (London: Hutchinson, 1982), 302.

53   Dominick LaCapra, *History and Criticism* (Ithaca: Cornell University Press, 1985), 72.

54   Yoshikawa, *"Heat is On,"* 293.

Primordiality

Japanese Cinema's Representation of the Philippines

F ilm historian Agustin L. Sotto recounts an anecdote told by Filipino director Manuel Conde of the Japanese Occupation during World War II:

> The Japanese demanded that every form of entertainment—
> movies as well as stage plays and vaudeville—carried some form
> of Japanese propaganda. Conde's problem was that there were
> no Japanese during the time of *Principe Teñoso*. How could you
> inject propaganda in a 19th century *corrido* [a romantic tale set
> in European kingdoms]? He finally solved it by stamping the
> glass of milk the princess was drinking with the trademark:
> Made in Japan.[1]

Conde's assimilative act marks the signifier of the instrument for incorporation. That the vessel used by a member of the national elite to drink the primordial liquid is "made in Japan" attests to the uncanny way Japan incorporates itself into bodies, beings, and geographies it seeks to penetrate and conquer. Both the authorship and stake are laid bare in the devolution of the vessel's source, the origin and imprint of authority. More so, the vessel itself contains the primordial liquid in the socialization of beings—milk as purveyor of the acutely liminal phase from plenitude to oral phase of the child.

How does Japan write itself as the authority in representing the other? What images are represented of others, particularly of the Philippines in Japanese cinema? In this essay, I investigate two historical moments of Japanese experience in the Philippines as rendered visible in Japanese cinema. The first moment is during World War II that produced, at least, two still available propaganda films on the Philippines by the Japanese Occupation. The second is during the 1990s that naturalized the Filipina domestic labor and character in postmodern Japanese geography. In the first moment, the images of Filipino infantile and wards are represented on screen; in the second, the images of the Filipina sex worker, whether as karaoke singer or mail-order bride, are projected on screen. What I intend to do in this essay is to map out the socio-political contours in which such historical moments and images are dialectically related. How is the Philippines represented, in whose interest is the Philippines represented, and what underscores such representations of the Philippines by Japan? I draw connections among seemingly disparate areas to draw a power matrix that circumscribes the relationship between the Philippines and Japan.

KEYWORDS

What underscores the historical Japanese influence-peddling is paranoia, a psychical disorder that presents delusions of both grandeur and persecution. Japan's megalomania—to incorporate Asia unto itself—finds a relational plane in the constant threat posed to destabilize such grandiose vision. On the one hand, high-profile crimes, for example, are made to constantly erupt for the nation-state to exercise its preeminence in managing destability. To a large extent, destabilization—or its *effective* management—becomes the nation's state of being. On the other hand, the comfort women issue is very much rendered, up to this date, invisible by the state apparatus, marking the reversal of the real: persecuting the imperial nation rather than the subjugated female national subjects of the imperialized nations.

Such paranoia, I contend, is not detached from Japan's calibration of its popular culture worldwide. More so, Japan's paranoia is also exported as the underscoring psychical ethos in the consumption of its popular culture. What then results is the fetishistic production and consumption of artifacts of paranoia. The consuming

I, threatened by guilt of grandiosity or martyred by persecution, purchases similar middle- and high-end products to sublimate the lack, that which has become the cause for being. As these products are anchored on infantile desires—Sanrio on young girl subculture, and anime on androgynous subculture—the compensation via consumerist spending spree becomes even more driven. Similar to Japan's production of destabilizing eruption—to render management of the state as natural and predominant—Japanese popular culture also performs a related drive: to render individual lack as imperative in the amassment and consumption of its artifacts. Through Japanese popular culture, state paranoia is internalized by individuals.

The paranoid state becomes the impetus for greater influence-peddling. Japan's earlier failure—to convince the rest of Asia of its co-prosperity sphere—did not deter future efforts by making other countries envy its economic development and proliferating popular culture of its dominance. For the rest of Asia, it has become the standard in which the modern nation is imagined. For Japan, cinema becomes one apparatus for imagining the rest of Asia. The case of Japanese cinema's representation of the Philippines becomes paradigmatic of how Japan has used and represented the other to continuously reinvent itself and its dominance.[2] What I find especially interesting in the representation of the Philippines is how such a case becomes integral to or illuminative of a global discourse. This is not to simply validate the historical persecution of the Philippines—a national imaginary of imperialist paranoia—but to historicize the rubric in which such persecution is generated: why and how is such imperialist paranoia emplaced in the national?

The experiences of Philippine cinema and diaspora are phenomena related to the experience of global colonialism and imperialism. The development of the film medium in the country began at the transitory period of a transfer of colonial power—from the aging colonial power represented by Spain to the emerging global power, the United States, with the Philippines as its first colonial venture outside the mainland. Such transition also marked a shift in the diaspora of Philippine nationals, one that was limited primarily to a small sector: local elites studying in Europe during late Spanish colonialism; the first wave of migrants, mainly composed of farm laborers, in the U.S. in the early phase of its colonial rule; and local elites—called *pensionados*—studying in various American universities. The struggle for a national cinema—a Philippine cinema—began with the shifting of the ownership of the production mode from colonial to local citizenry in the early 1900s. Such struggle involved the continuing domination of a colonial power. In its own imperialist venture during World War II, Japan maintained control of the Philippines and its cinema.

In the post-war era, the U.S. would still exercise neocolonial domination of Philippine politics and economics. Having fought with the U.S. against Japan in World War II, Filipino soldiers were allowed to migrate to the U.S. immediately after the war. In the 1960s, with immense need for skilled professionals in the U.S., Filipino doctors and nurses immigrated abroad, allowing for the brain drain to disenfranchise the local need in favor of the global impediment. Japan's emergence as a global economic power reverberates in the shifting of Philippine diasporic direction. During Ferdinand Marcos's dictatorship, Filipino migrant work was funneled to fuel the national economic development. The first wave of migration involved male workers doing blue-collar work in the oil-boom nations of the Middle East. The second wave involved female workers doing domestic work abroad—specifically nursing and health care in the Middle East, U.S., and Europe; domestic work in Europe, the Middle East, and the new Asian tiger economies of Hong Kong and Singapore; and entertainment work in Japan.

KEYWORDS

Philippine cinema, like the national experience in diaspora, is inextricably tied to the issue of nation. The substantiation of the "Philippine-ness," the material and imagined core idea of the nation, is constructed not only within the national parameters but also within the geopolitical sphere in which systematic diasporization has allowed Filipino nationals to find work and home outside the national space. So remarkable is the imprint of Philippine diaspora that foreign cinemas have represented images of the geopolitical national in various territories of Filipino labor, like U.S., Italy, Canada, Australia, and Japan. In this essay, I will investigate the specific case of Japanese cinema's representation of the Philippines and its geopolitical nationals. In another essay, I have already mapped out cinema during the beginnings of U.S. empire-building.[3] Films produced during this period involved short features—the beginning of the narrative feature film—popular at arcades and theater houses. It focused on U.S. military triumph in its colonization of the Philippines. Like the use of gender and sexuality in U.S. political and cinematic colonization of the Philippines, Japanese cinema's representation of the Philippines involved a shifting paradigm of sexual and gender relations, analogous to the ways Japan imagined itself to be a global power. Japan invoked its masculinity in its World War II venture, including the production of propaganda films glorifying its foray into imperialism in Asia. With the postwar turn to economic superpower status, Japan now invokes the rhetoric of femininity to represent its economic domination of former colonies in the World War II era now turned into recipients of its massive investments and overseas aid. The irony for these countries is predicated on being violently dominated militarily during World War II to enforced economic colonialism, now servicing the engines of the Japanese hyperindulgent national global economy.

Although the discourses of masculinity and femininity in Japanese cinema are not altogether separate entities, the reliance on one over the other in the war and post-war eras is quite historically poised. In this essay, I analyze the discourse of masculinity as mobilized in World War II propaganda films of Japan, one that lays out the grid of subsequent post-war dominance of Japan to other Asian countries, particularly the Philippines. Recently, however, the discourse of femininity is mobilized in Japanese cinema to interpolate non-Japanese nationals, particularly the female overseas contract workers and mail-order brides, within its cinematic and national landscapes. I also direct attention to a related imaging of Filipinos in overseas contract work in Philippine cinema, one that represents the actual and imagined feminization of the present migrant work as a parallel movement to the growing mobilization of femininity in the global and sexual division of labor.

Masculinity and Hysteria in *Dawn of Freedom* and *Victory Song of the Orient*

Two films, one feature and another documentary, provide the first historical moment of Japanese maneuvering within Asia.[4] However, Japan's military strategy started even earlier than its occupation of territories during World War II. As part of its cultural offensive, a Japanese propaganda machinery was already being emplaced in the Philippines by Japanese civilians even during the prewar era.[5] Japanese Occupation formalized and intensified such initiatives. *Dawn of Freedom* (1944) was part of the wartime propaganda machinery, with similar aims "to unmask the Americans as the real enemies and to eradicate their influences; to emphasize Japan's role as the leader of Asia; and, especially with regard to Filipinos, to recover the native character lost due to years of Occidental colonization."[6] Such aims can also be said about an earlier documentary effort, *Victory Song of the Orient* (1942), a film exhibited in the nearby Manila provinces, such as Laguna, Tarlac, and Nueva Ecija.

Even prior to World War II, there were already several films that tackled the war and Philippine relations with Japan. *Madaling Araw* (Dawn) featured how three brothers argued and got united in the struggle against a foreign nation; *Krisantemo* (Chrysanthemum) tackled the love story between a geisha and a Filipino athlete; and *Ararong Ginto* (Golden Plow) told the story of Japanese immigrants in Davao, suspected of being spies.[7] With the Japanese Occupation of the Philippines in 1942, facilities of film studios were confiscated. The Japanese established the Propaganda Corps that hired recognized professional and civilian Japanese. They oversaw the opening of movie houses through the establishment of the Central Booking Exchange. Only Hollywood and Filipino films, devoid of political and social messages, were shown. By 1943, German and Japanese films were imported and exhibited in the country.[8]

Prior to the establishment of a Philippine branch of the Nihon Eiga Haikyu Sha (Movie Distribution Company) in December 1942, news and documentary films were already being shown in the country.[9] The agency had exclusive control over importing foreign films, "mostly Japanese and German and later, Japanese war propaganda films for local consumption," and exhibition of all films in moviehouses.[10] To also curtail the dominance of Hollywood movies in the country, "the Japanese army immediately seized 1,238 American films and 1,638 short films."[11] The Japanese military press, after all, were impressed with Manila's many and big theaters, equipped with modern facilities that showed mostly Hollywood films.[12] Wartime propaganda films had to comply with the three aims that pushed for the goals of the Greater East Asia Co-Prosperity Sphere, an Asian geopolitical sphere under Japanese rule: "to unmask the Americans as the real enemies and to eradicate their influences; to emphasize Japan's role as the leader of Asia; and, especially with regard to Filipinos, to recover the native character lost due to years of Occidental colonization."[13]

Three Japanese propaganda films were shot and produced in the Philippines. Two are feature narrative films, *Ano Hata o ute* (Dawn of Freedom, 1944) and *San nin no Maria* (Tatlong Maria, or Three Marys, 1944), and one full-length documentary, *Toyo no Gaika* (Victory Song of the Orient, 1942).[14] Only two of the films—*Dawn of Freedom* and *Victory Song of the Orient*—are available for viewing. These films invoke a discourse of masculinity and hysteria that manifests the war effort of Japan in its grand scheme of Asian integration under its stewardship.

Dawn of Freedom (produced by Toho) forms part of three Southeast Asia war films, also comprised by *Singaporu Sokougeki* (All Out Attack on Singapore, produced by Daiei) and by *Biruma Sakusen* (Operation Burma, produced by Shochiku).[15] The film narrates the transnational contact through war between Filipino and Japanese men. Against the backdrop of the intensifying war in the Philippines, the Japanese effort against the American troops leads to Filipino acceptance. The fall of Bataan becomes the impetus for conversion. The film begins with the flight of American land troops fleeing the city. Captain Andres Gomez (played by Fernando Poe, Sr.) quickly drops by his home to prepare his belongings and to bid good-bye to his parents and loved ones. His mother gives him a traditional blessing. His young sibling Tony reiterates his request for an enemy's helmet as a *pasalubong* (returning souvenir) to his brother's colleague, Lieutenant Garcia (played by Leopoldo Salcedo). The film unfolds in the dual war spaces of the nation—in the home front, through Tony's contact with a caring and sensitive Japanese soldier; and in the battlefront, through Captain Gomez's contact with the Japanese troops.

Contact with the Japanese officers erases the demonized image of the "Japanese" as represented in the American-dominated and war-mongered local media. In his attempt to get a Japanese flier, Tony is side-swept by a speeding automobile, part of the fleeing American troops. He is paralyzed, and he gets the attention of a Japanese soldier who befriends his circle of playmates. The soldier brings Tony for examination by a Japanese doctor. The operation, however, only allows Tony to stand. Through the care of the Japanese soldier giving Tony regular massages, the boy attempts, but consistently fails, to walk again. When the Japanese soldier leaves with the troops, Tony watches with the other kids from the sidelines. He makes a courageous move to stand up from his wheelchair. With deep gratitude, Tony offers his regained ability to the departing soldier.

Captain Gomez, a West Point graduate, is captured by the Japanese troops. He is interrogated and is nonetheless humanely treated. There are scenes of abundant food rations, even scenes of bathing in the river, with a Japanese soldier lending his soap to the appreciative Captain Gomez. In another scene, another semi-naked Japanese soldier mends Captain Gomez's pants. These scenes are contrasted with Lieutenant Garcia's own contact with American officers. An American officer is singled out as a tyrant, demanding the already overworked Filipino troops to complete the construction of trenches. When Japanese balloons spread fliers and surrender cards to the battlefront, he demands those found with paraphernalia to be separated from the troops and be tried for desertion. No longer able to take the humiliation, a Filipino soldier escapes and is shot in the back. Lieutenant Garcia questions the decision of the American officer, but is rebuffed.

In a move to isolate Lieutenant Garcia, American officers commandeer him to a reconnaissance mission along enemy lines. He is set up for ambush by the abusive American officer. Lieutenant Garcia survives, wounded, and manages to escape. In his dying moment, he hears the voice of Captain Gomez blaring from the sound system, asking his colleagues to surrender as the only moral and patriotic option. As the war pushes on, Japanese troops ease the American and Filipino forces to Bataan. Captain Gomez is set free and discovers the dead body of Lieutenant Garcia. With the soldier is a helmet, with a message inscribed for Tony. It is the promised souvenir. The dual stories of the local characters end here. Another Captain Reyes (played by Angel Esmeralda) is shot by retreating American soldiers. As Reyes lays dying, he shoots the commander. The film ends with the triumph of the Japanese troops. The surrender scene involves a humiliated American contingent waving a white flag and requesting permission from the Japanese officers. Japanese officers look at their watches as they await the departure of the single vehicle that flees into the lonely countryside road while carrying the white and American flags. The final scene evokes Japanese gallantry and discipline as the lone commanding officer passionately addresses the phalanx of soldiers against the backdrop of smoke and ravage. The scene represents the triumph of Japanese soldiers and the commitment to rebuild from the ashes a new strategic landscape.

Dawn of Freedom is directed by Yutaka Abe, with the assistance of Gerardo de Leon, later considered a master of Philippine cinema, and features some of the biggest names in local cinema. The film narrates the coming of the Japanese in the Philippines and the shifting attitudes of captured soldiers, guerrillas, and civilian families toward the imminent Japanese Occupation, from the American-provoked resentment to enlightened acceptance. Three Filipino males become the locus of Japanese conversion: a twelve-year-old boy crippled by a speeding American truck and restored to health through the intercession of a Japanese officer; a West Point-trained Filipino officer captured yet humanely treated by the Japanese military; and a guerrilla who died finally confirming Japanese righteousness after a series of doubts. The only other convert is the child's grandmother who had earlier on resented the initiatives of the Japanese officer out of loyalty to her guerrilla son.

What gets represented in the film are images of the Philippines and Filipinos as wards of the Japanese military establishment. The boy is crippled for his blind loyalty to the Americans. He is slowly nursed back to health by the Japanese officer, who also intercedes on the boy's behalf with a Japanese doctor for his operation. There is even a scene in homoerotic gesture where the Japanese soldier massages the boy's legs. The Filipino officer is astounded by his captor's kindness. He is given a bar of soap to share in the bathing. His torn pants are sewn by a Japanese soldier. When he thanks the officers, they tell him that the Japanese soldier also makes a "good housewife." He becomes the local spokesman of Japanese imperialism, making a speech at the height of a battle between Japanese and Filipino soldiers: "I have returned to my origins after a senseless wandering."

Filipinos are infantilized as genuine love is only made possible through the doting care of the Japanese. As adults, Filipinos have never really experienced genuine love as their experience with the Americans have shown—they are harshly treated by officers, or run over by escaping troops. Their collective beings are deprived of genuine love. What gets to be unsaid in the process is the continued tutelage of Filipinos, from an oppressive colonizer to a caring one. By themselves, Filipinos are incapable of coming into being. The United States' enlightened colonialism that introduced institutions such as public education is eased out for its insensitivity to the Filipino soul. For the film, only an enlightened Asian colonialist experience can truly understand and catalyze the national being.

Though conversion is never complete, the process is idealized in the film.[16] The convert becomes a living testimony of Japanese benevolence, becoming a missionary for the Japanese cause. While local experience with past colonizers have introduced religion as part of the work ethic of colonial experience—e.g., Roman Catholicism for Spanish feudal colonialism and Protestantism for American capitalist colonialism—Japan introduced a Confucian work ethic that emphasized interior purity, obedience, and respect for hierarchy. Such passionate fervor of the convert of Japanese imperialism is unrepresented in past experiences. Only the coopted local elites get to mouth the colonizer's predicament. During the Japanese Occupation, the mimicry is selectively performed through the best beings or the potentials to become exemplary ones in the military establishment. Unlike American colonial experience where anyone skilled with education can move up the social hierarchy, the place of mobility in Japanese imperialism is reserved only for the best souls in the

Fig. 1: Kindness of invader, *Dawn of Freedom*

military establishment. The local officer survives while the guerrilla dies.

Thus, along with conversion comes a rescue narrative. Who, among the natives, is most worthy of redemption? By becoming an exemplar, the convert mimics the ethos of the Japanese soul. He becomes a member of the ruling military elite. But in the beginning, he has to be rescued. And prior to rescue, he must have optimized his skills. Such skills, as alluded to in the film, were American-generated—the officer's military training was from West Point, and the boy's optimism and social skills were learned from the American educational system. What is being optimized are the same skills generated by what is considered an equally worthy imperialist experience. More so, not all the natives were deemed capable of imbibing such American skills and Japanese soul. It is only through the hidden hand of both imperialists that the best Filipinos were engendered worthy of colonial substantiation.

Such colonial substantiation, however, is deemed only within a lowly placement in the global colonial hierarchy. The national being becomes an automaton for the Japanese military establishment. This foregrounds the future constitution of Filipinos in the Japanese sphere, from an automaton of the military establishment to an automaton of the entertainment-business complex. In both cases, however, the local automaton is made to serve the underbelly of the Japanese establishment. During World War II, the national being (he) was made to protect the terrain of Japanese interest in the Philippines. In the contemporary period, she was to serve in the entertainment-sexual need of Japanese state-business people inside Japanese territory. What also distinguishes the automaton is the enforced sexualization by the shifting historical thrusts of the Japanese establishment. It is infantile masculinity during World War II and feminized sexuality in more recent times.

While *Dawn of Freedom* fictionalizes the dual impact of Japanese occupation of the Philippines, *Victory Song of the Orient* heralds the Japanese triumph through documentary footage and realism. Both films relate to a specific time and space triumph of Japanese military forces—the trajectory that climaxes in the enclosure of American troops in the fall of Bataan and Corregidor. *Victory Song of the Orient*, however, is made for a Japanese audience. The opening titles are introduced through stills of Japanese military paraphernalia—boots, helmet, belt, and so on. The film begins with a map, locating the Philippines in the cultural imaginary of Japanese forces and audiences. It also showcases the Spanish and

Fig. 2: Japanese troops march to Manila, *Dawn of Freedom*

American influences on the Philippines, specifically highlighting the country's Westernization of culture through popular media, such as films, dance, and consumer culture. It then documents the saga of Japanese military operation in the Philippines. Using a map as a point of reference to locate the ensuing build-up and conquest of the Philippines, inching its way to triumph, the Japanese military forces are both humanized and idealized in the war operation. There is a scene where close-up faces of Japanese soldiers are flashed one after the other, ensuing to scenes of work and leisure in the battlefront. The film shows soldiers bathing and eating together, even performing theater to entertain the troops, smiling during their leisure breaks; it also depicts valor and perseverance in their guerrilla war effort.

Similar to Hitler's own war effort through film, *Victory Song of the Orient* pays homage to the Japanese troops and military might in its crucial war effort in the Philippines. After all, the Philippines provided the last bastion of rule by Allied forces in Asia. Its conquest spelled the triumph of Japanese rule in the region. The film aspires to a poetic rendering of Japanese victory, primarily over American troops in the Far East. There are shots of a deserted American camp in its ugly state, or nature shots before their destruction in war. It also depicts a simultaneity of conquest and rebuilding, as those who are wounded are treated, those captured are fed, evacuees are housed. The scene that renders the capture of American forces is interestingly framed. There is a montage scene that shifts from the medium shot of the American officers in dignified position in their individual quarters to the shots of their nameplate at the closing door. The portion leading to the final scene involves a similar quick-editing strategy. Marching Japanese soldiers are framed only through close-ups of their boots. The American flag is animated to shrivel and contract, creating the impression of Japanese soldiers trampling on the flag. A passionate voice-over provides the narration while marching band music, played by the Military Band stationed at the McKinley Barracks, accompanies the images.

The final scene is the victory parade involving the military and civilian forces at Luneta, the nation's premier park. After the images of superior Japanese artillery on parade, civilian groups—from Thai, Italian, and German expatriates, to Manila Department Store and Manila Hotel employees, to government employees—march alongside the Japanese. The image of the Japanese flag hovers to tie in the dual impact of the parade—showcasing Japanese military might, and the across-the-board spectacle of local acceptance of Japanese occupation. The last shot again harps on the introductory image—it is the

PRIMORDIALITY

map of the Philippines, now triumphantly cohered by the Japanese military might, zooming out to a newly redefined placement in the global schema under Japanese dominion, or at least the Asian component of the global schema of imperialists.

Historians Renato Constantino and Letizia Constantino believe "Japan was a late comer among imperialist states," having "developed her capitalism in a world already dominated by Western imperialism."[17] Thus, Japan's state was provided a paramount role in negotiating its imperialist mediation in the global order. They further clarify that Japan's "imperialist career" was also motivated by a "domestic pressure . . . in order to solve internal contradictions."[18] Thus, the state provided for both an "instrument for the repression of the masses" and "mediator of the [ruling class'] own differences."[19] Together with military conquest, education and cultural formation became instruments of colonial control, so much attuned to the nationalistic ideals of Japan's own national and transnational development trajectory.

The two films provide a belated pedagogical tool for socialization within the Japanese global schema. It involves the process of colonialism via military conquest, and as justified by the "policy of attraction," providing for Philippine independence so long as the country agrees to be part of the Co-Prosperity Sphere.[20] This policy of attraction necessitated the creation of spectacles, transmitted familiarly through a pastime introduced and propagated during the American colonial rule: movie-going. Given the historical brutality of the Japanese occupation, against the mix of filmic war spectacle, local characters' epiphany of a justifiable Japanese rule, sensitive portrayal of Japanese troops, and the support mechanism for displacement, it was difficult to shift attitudes and values justifying such rule. By 1944, Japanese defeat was already imminent. The film's use value did not evoke a commensurable exchange value. This was also the period of intensified guerrilla resistance in the countryside.

Resistance, however, was deemed improper given the nature of Japanese colonial enlightenment and military might. For how can one imagine oneself free, with Western colonialism well entrenched in the Filipino way of life? Such contradictions were smoothed over by the very belatedness of the film. It involved stretching the symbolic value of the Fall of Bataan, the event that temporally castrated American presence in the country. It made Japanese conquest, and acceptance of its colonial rule, inevitable. Within the film, elements of production yielded its own course. For one, "real prisoners of war were drafted as actors—a violation of the Articles of War."[21] A production staff member also reported that there was difficulty "recruiting

Filipino actors since at that time Japanese defeat was more or less just a matter of time."[22]

Victory Song of the Orient attempted to memorialize Japan's triumph in defeating the American troops in the Philippines. The film has four parts (Bataan Campaign, Corregidor Attack, Rebuilding of Manila, and the Grand Celebration of the Fall of Bataan and Corregidor), each leading to the final episode. The film, produced by eighteen Japanese crewmen and sixteen Filipino staff members, had a massive screening in various provinces prior to its premiere in Manila. While *Dawn of Freedom* provided a belated discourse on the Japanese occupation, *Victory Song of the Orient* gave a timely outlook. The two films, however, utilize a discourse of masculinity to stress their point of justifiable Japanese occupation. Revolving around the racialized supremacy of the Japanese phallus, inferior Filipino male conversion was inevitable. Filipinos were less Asian for their acceptance of American colonial rule. The film invokes a dual discourse on masculinity. As represented by the adult male characters, realization of their own masculinity is filtered through the screen of the conquering colonial masculinity. Captain Garcia's own conversion was through a rational acceptance of an Asiatic rule rather than what he had already imbibed, American domination. As represented by the young male character, it involves an infantilized masculinity—one that needed the literal and figurative operation of Japanese war and male technology in order to salvage the debilitating effects of American rule. Tony's grappling with his own masculinity involves a shifting process—from a paralyzing state enforced by escaping American troops to a recuperative act voluntarily undertaken under Japanese tutelage. It was only after allowing himself to be examined and healed by Japanese military technology that Tony was able to walk again. But this only occurred after his Japanese patriarch had already left. What becomes of Tony's masculinity is the allowing of one's own body to be redefined and resubstantiated by Japanese colonial rule, in order to excavate that which is Filipino.

The narrative trajectory of the documentary *Victory Song of the Orient* underscores the conquest and acceptance of Japanese rule in the Philippines. The film is generally made up of war footage of Japanese operations, including its capture of American soldiers. The final scene is a local parade honoring the Japanese colonial order, with various sectors and organizations in procession. The film restored the peaceful coexistence of imperialists and natives it had earlier set up. The film's beginning sequence showed the peaceful acceptance of American cultural influences in Manila. Thus, the masculinist trade-off during World War II among imperialists repeats the Spanish and American dealings at the turn of the twentieth century. The Philippines is once again fetishistically infantilized and feminized in the renarrativization of imperialist penetration.

Both masculinities involve tutelage and enlightenment. After all, Captain Garcia's West Point background and Tony's ability to speak English already invoke an economic and cultural capital found in only a select margin of Filipinos. It is no historical accident that only Captain Garcia, among his company that included Lieutenant Garcia and Captain Reyes, had the successful conversion. The film was addressing a rational audience, capable of dually understanding a pro-Japanese, anti-American rule that can propagate the Filipino's own self-rule. What Japan was undertaking is to emplace Philippine masculinity and nation into the matrix of its colonial domination. What is unique about Japan's imperialist proposal is the promise of postcolonial rule to Filipinos even in its Japanese colonial state. Such toilet retraining needed a new schema of tutelage and coming-into-being. After all, toilet training involves a simultaneity of experience in incorporation and disavowal. This retraining in film is part of a larger cultural re-orientation, primarily operationalized through education. Movies and education legitimize the ethos and praxis of Japanese occupation of the Philippines.

Japan's educational policy in the Philippines was embodied in Military Order No. 2, dated 17 February 1942, and had the following basic points: the propagation of Filipino culture; disseminating the principle of the Greater East Asia Co-Prosperity Sphere; the spiritual rejuvenation of the Filipinos; the teaching and propagation of Nippongo; the diffusion of vocational and elementary education; and promoting love of labor.[23] As historians Teodoro Agoncillo and Milagros Guerrero explain, "The motive behind this educational policy was not only to create an atmosphere friendly to Japanese intentions and war aims, but also to erase the Western cultural influences, particularly British and American, on Filipino life and culture."[24]

Filmic and education narratives of an egalitarian yet racially pure nation under the tutelage of Japan provided its own internal contradiction. In *Dawn of Freedom*, what purports to be a historical drama did not materialize fully. There was no return to the domestic fold as a way of smoothing out historical contradictions. The non-return provides a depersonalized view of the political perspective of war and occupation. The local men were merely left to their own freedoms as Japanese men were extolled for their continuing commitment to

Fig. 3: Montage scene, *Victory Song of the Orient*

the war struggle. The final scene where the Japanese commander speaks to his troops provides a pedagogical closure in the ways the film is to be understood, but only from the Japanese side. From the Filipino side, such belated historical retelling, precisely because it uses the conventions of a narrative film, does not provide a way of being sutured into the historical discourse. The belatedness provides a gap between the perceived realities—already experienced and articulated through trauma—and the imagined rationale of occupation— one that does not justify the inhumane experience of a lingering war. In *Victory Song of the Orient*, what remains as strong pro-American sentiments delayed the installment of Japanese sympathy to the war cause. The victory parade that provided closure to the documentary narrative's trajectory was belied by a Filipino journalist invited to the premiere: "That victory parade was participated in by us Filipinos out of obligation, and not willingly."[25] What proved to be a stronger resistance to the pedagogical reorientation toward Japanese rule was the performance of pro-American sentiment precisely at this period when enforced Japanese triumph inversely articulated impending American victory.

K
E
Y
W
O
R
D
S

The education apparatus also realized the pedagogical failure of justifying Japanese occupation. As Agoncillo and Guerrero state, "There was not much enthusiasm in returning to schools, first, because the Filipinos as a whole were suspicious of Japanese intention, and second, because the children found more enjoyment and money in selling anything or in helping their parents tide over the difficult times."[26] By 1943, only a third of elementary school children and a third of secondary school students were in school.[27] Historical experience with war provided for the gap that negated the positivizing pedagogy of education and film. With martial rule in war, threats of air bombing, and curfew, evening screenings were cancelled. Strict production and reception controls also reduced the potential of film to effectively propagandize the Japanese occupation.

Japanese colonialism and its enforcement of masculinity, on the one hand, infringe on Filipinos' historical claims of the Filipinos toward national sovereignty, and on the other hand, are internally flawed to inflict total hegemony. Though not dispensing with the real epistemic and literal violence inflicted and experienced during the Japanese occupation, Philippine political and cultural struggle can be critiqued for only providing an occupational resistance that hinges on America's return. It did not surmount and transform its anti-Japanese campaign to an anti-colonial struggle. In the movies, for example, pre-war Filipino films that suspiciously critiqued growing Japanese presence were echoed with familiar racist narratives of anti-Japanese campaign in post-war cinema. Euphoria replaced pessimism in film narratives and moviegoing in general.[28]

Even the actors that embodied a feminized masculinity during the Japanese occupation—in *Dawn of Freedom*, Poe, Sr., Esmeralda, and Salcedo, for example—would continue to extensively work in the film requirements of the post-war movement, one that valorized both local and American heroism. The duplicity of actors' productive life—business as usual—remains artificially constructed. During the war, enforced portrayal by the Japanese military in film can easily be misconstrued as pro-Japanese propaganda by the audience. Their performance provided a political risk. Like bodies of convicts, the actors were doubly marked. As Tony Bennett states of convicts in his configuration of discipline, surveillance, and spectacle, and which can be said of actors during the Japanese occupation, "In schemes to use convict labor in public contexts, it was envisaged that the convict would repay society twice: once by the labor he provided, and a second time by the signs he produced, a focus of both profit and signification in serving as a never-present reminder of the connection between crime and punishment."[29] Actors performed similar dual functions as they are held hostage by the ideological apparatuses of the Japanese occupation. However, during post-war productions, these actors flowed with the reinvigoration of capital, thus assuming another feminized position—their labor and existence are overdetermined by the infusion of new capital. Similarly, their masculinities are signified by their performative bodies on screen, and off-screen by the continuation of their performance of screen bodies.

On the other side, post-war Japanese reconstruction hinged on the consolidation and reinvention of the *zaibatsu* (financial cliques), and the massive marketing of electric appliances. Domestication of capital through technology provided for the growing consumer demand that fueled the Japanese boom of the postwar period. Emasculated by their postwar U.S.-sponsored Constitution, the zaibatsu expansion in all aspects of the economy eventually found a wide market in home appliances and technology. Initially, up until the 1960s, it involved the "assimilation of rural Japan into a national metropolitan culture."[30] In recent years, it involved the assimilation of developing countries into its national metropolitan culture. Thus, Japan's masculinity is regained in its effort to cosmopolitanize and metropolitanize its national culture for a new global market.

What becomes the experience of Japanese colonialism remains in the uneven implementation of its rationality, especially heightened by the impetus of an intensifying global imperialist war. Japan's bullying strategy inevitably proved to be of no match to the U.S.'s own bullying during World War II and postwar geopolitical reconstruction. Postwar reconstruction castrated Japan, harping on its near-success in dominating Asia under its paternal wing. However, Japan's own imagined temporal and masculinized greatness also imagined its conquered nations as children and wards. In *Dawn of Freedom*, the Japanese officer reads a folktale moralizing about ideal colonial virtues. In another scene, the Filipino soldier confesses his epiphany to the Japanese officer, "Makes me feel I have come back after aimless wandering." Japan's rational is mimicked in film, pedagogically inscribing the colonial trajectory of its occupation of Asian nations. As infantilized colonial subjects, Filipinos on screen readily awakened to the logic of Japanese rule. The films acknowledged resistance but only from U.S. perpetuation of its non-Asian dominance in the Philippines. But once U.S. defeat was ensured, Filipinos readily accepted Japanese rule. Films then represented the narrative of Japanese colonial rule, a fantasy-ideal as only the medium of film can doubly articulate. First, film's staging of events is based on the aesthetics of realism, positivizing reality to affirm beauty and its triumph. Ideology, unless overtly visualized, is made nominal to the issue of representing the unrepresentable in beauty. Second, the very construction of film is negated to represent a seamless artifact, devoid of any mode of industrial production. What ensues in the very experience of film infantilizes the audience, bringing their present consciousness in an impasse in order to use filmic reality to filter the unconscious. The unconscious, in psychoanalysis, derives its wellspring from infant to childhood experiences.

In its own emasculated state, Japan can only speak of its phallic greatness in retrospect, as nostalgia for an era never to arise either in the present or in the future, a nostalgia built on an idealized fascistic past. Film again becomes an idiom to talk about nostalgia, marking a return to the early moments of subject-formation. Such moments are idealized even as the real experience never achieved ideal status. The past is memorialized in its greatness, becoming the absent organizing signifier of the present.

Femininity in the Female OCW Films

Post-war reconstruction gave Japan global power not derived from military might but from economic dominance. However, unlike other superpower nations, Japan was relegated to the sidelines of world politics. Forced to accept a post-war anti-militarization constitution by the U.S., Japan focused its energies on generating greater national economic kineticism. So successful is Japan's economic boom that hatred generated by nations colonized in the experience of World War II was now turned into ambivalence. With the tide of Japanese investment and overseas aid that now flows into the same Asian nations, the new reaction is that of love. However, for most Southeast Asian countries victimized by Japan during World War II, even with investments beginning to pour in, many still assumed a cold stance toward Japan. The Philippines still retained a memory of war trauma from Japan way into the 1960s. Thus very little popular cultural exchange occurred between Japan and the rest of Asia, except for samurai films and television series, reiterating Japan's militaristic legacy. Japan surpassed most of Southeast Asia's former colonizer's investments and overseas development assistance in the 1970s and onwards. This resulted in a shift in attitude, which was also propelled by a shift in popular culture direction, from cultural products of former colonizers to those of Japan. Nora Aunor, the Philippines' leading movie personality then, would do a touristic movie set in Japan, *Winter Wonderland*, showing scenes of snow and other exoticized First World Asian images. Such exchange in the 1970s proved to be relenting of national trauma in favor of national envy for Japan's historic transnational economic development.

What also marked late twentieth century economic and political kineticism was the migration of people, specifically overseas contract workers. This newer identity seeks to sell their labor outside the nation-space for bigger economic reward. Not only does Japan generate a negativizing truth of its dominance—one that does not fully confront its violent past, such as the issue of comfort women and the amnesia of the war period's atrocities in its history textbooks—it also realized this in such a way that the geopolitical body of the overseas contract worker (OCW) is dominated from within its national borders. This was foregrounded in Japan's World War II efforts when it conscripted Koreans and Taiwanese nationals into working for its war machinery, forcing foreign nationals to become slaves for its war effort. Relative individual agency is now emplaced in the systematic recruitment of foreign labor to perform menial domestic work in Japan and elsewhere. However, enforced recruitment remains a material basis for foreign laborers coming into Japan as these nationals have very limited choice and destination to perform their specialized "lowly" labor.

Some fifty years after World War II, the Philippines further exchanges national bodies with Japan. There are some fifty thousand Filipina overseas contract workers in Japan, believed primarily to perform "entertainment" work. These Filipina workers partly comprise the four million overseas contract workers, remitting roughly USD 7 billion to the Philippine economy annually. In contemporary history, such remittances sustained the national economy, especially in times of crisis. The Philippines is considered to be one of the world's largest labor exporter. Filipinas in Japan form part of overseas contract work pigeonholed in certain domestic services, domestic work in Hong Kong, Taiwan, Malaysia, and Singapore; nurses in the United States; construction work in the Middle East; and seamen with various shipping companies.

So glaring is the reality of Filipinas in Japan that films have proliferated their image as part of Japanese national life's natural geography in the 1990s, whether as entertainment workers in urban centers or as mail-order brides in rural areas. An offshoot of such contact are 4,630 Japanese-Filipino children (popularly known as "Japinos" or "anak ng Hapon," children of Japanese) in 1992, and 5,551 children in 1996.[31] These children are increasing in rate every year as more and more Filipinas account for the largest single group of foreign women marrying Japanese men.[32]

In 2000, there were 175,033 Filipinos in Japan, 59,626 of whom have received permanent status, while 99,038 are classified as temporary and 16,369 are irregular.[33] More and more Filipinos are recruited into the service of Japanese economy. 38,930 Filipinos were deployed in 1998, 46,851 in 1999, 63,041 in 2000, and 74,093 in 2001, making Japan the third most popular OCW destination, after Saudi Arabia and Hong Kong.[34] Japan ranks the Philippines as the fourth largest source of foreign nationals, after Korea, China, and Brazil.[35] What is not said in these statistics is the predominantly female background of the migrant worker in Japan doing entertainment work.

What is happening in Japan is not isolated from the general Philippine trend in overseas contract work. The town of Pozorrubio, for example, "has the dubious distinction of having the most number of women workers abroad among Pangasinan's 48 towns."[36] Journalist Luz Rimban further writes, "In this stretch of plains near the gateway to the Cordillera mountains, a six-year-old census counts 3,500 overseas workers—nearly all of them women—out of a population of 49,000. About 500 of these workers are maids in Hong Kong, while the rest are spread out in Singapore, Malaysia, Taiwan, London, the Middle East, and Europe."[37]

The general trend in the Philippines reflects the growing number of women working abroad, "actually outnumbering men since 1992."[38] Statistics from the Philippine Overseas Employment Administration (POEA) reveal "that not only are there more women workers abroad, there also appears to be a steady decline in the number of men leaving the Philippines."[39] Rimban cites further statistics representing the feminine trend in overseas contract work:

> POEA figures on worker deployment show that out of the 260,588 OCWs who left the country in 1992, about 51 percent (132,131) were women. The following year, there was a drop in the total number of OCWs deployed—256,197—with a corresponding decline in the number of male OCWs at 115,533. But the number of women workers deployed overseas grew to 140,664.
>
> By 1994, almost 60 percent of the 258,984 OCWs who left the country were female. In the first quarter of 1995 alone, there were more women among the 114,566 newly hired OCWs. Of that total, 69,435 or 60 percent were female while only 45,131 were male.[40]

Thus the figure of the female overseas contract worker embodies the major Philippine trend in diasporic movement. The female OCW figure becomes emblematic of the discourse of nation, even in the transnational sphere. I have argued elsewhere that the suffering woman, denoted in social melodrama films, the nation's ethos as she embodies the discourse of the *inang bayan* (mother-nation).[41] The suffering woman represents the "national condition," analogous to her own suffering, redemption, and containment in the narrative of nation. The female OCW film is similarly poised in the social drama mode, embodying the national ethos of having to be physically there (hostland) instead of here (homeland), while emotionally conflating the two geopolitical spaces. For the choice, in most cases, had been made. Torn between the perils of the homeland's incapacity to provide for her and her family and the hostland's oftentimes violent and apathetic terrain, she claims the fate of being physically in the hostland yet emotionally attached to the homeland.

The imperfect fit is symptomized in Japanese cinema by the figure of Ruby Moreno, an actual overseas contract worker who later became a major movie star in Japan in the 1980s. In film and television, she represents the generic geopolitical body of the overseas contract worker and mail-order bride. At the time of her popularity, most roles representing the laboring alien figure was cast in her mold, characterized as female, Filipina, young and sexual, and, thus, desirable. Such qualities become the requisites of Philippine overseas contract work—using the very conditions of poverty and corrupt bureaucracy that substantiated nationality as inimical to generating laboring bodies and transnational income. Moreno cornered all the Filipina characters in Japanese films in the 1990s, even becoming the first foreigner to win the female performance award from the Japanese film academy for her role as an entertainer in *Tsuki wa dotchi ni dete iru* (All Under the Moon; Yoichi Sai, director, 1993).[42] She has also co-starred in such films as *Afureru Atsui Namida* (Swimming in Tears; Hirotaka Tashiro, director, 1991), *Tokyo Deluxe*, and *I Love Nippon*. She was cast as the Filipina OCW in Japan in *All Under the Moon* and as the mail-order bride in *Swimming with Tears*. Though there were other Moreno/Filipina migrant films, these films were chosen for analysis to provide representational stakes on the stereotypization of Filipinas or Third World women as contractual entertainer or mail-order bride.

These films were received with critical acclaim, catapulting their directors to national and international recognition. *Swimming in Tears* was screened at the New York's New Director/New Films Festival, the San Francisco International Film Festival, London International Film Festival, and Berlin International Film Festival. The film also won numerous awards in Japan and the New Director Award at the Osaka Film Festival. *All Under the Moon* swept Japan's film awards, including best actress award for Moreno. It was also shown in various international festivals. Based on a comic book, the film was directed by a second-generation Korean Japanese, the leading director of this heritage.

All Under the Moon tells the dual stories of Connie, a Filipina karaoke singer, and Chung Nam, a Korean Japanese taxi driver, in their quest for a place and fit in the underbelly of Japan's economy. I stated elsewhere that the Filipina's position, on the one hand, remains supportive of Japan's ten-trillion-yen-a-year sex industry.[43] As a foreign worker, Connie at first has legal status with her initial contract, but later became of illegal status with the Philippines' burdensome requirement of renewing her contract every six months. Connie's status is predicated on both her capacity to support the Japanese sex industry at a menial price and on her incapacity to achieve constant legal status within the Japanese nation-state. This is the site of the Filipina OCW figure's suffering. Torn between her menial task in the underbelly of a national sex industry and

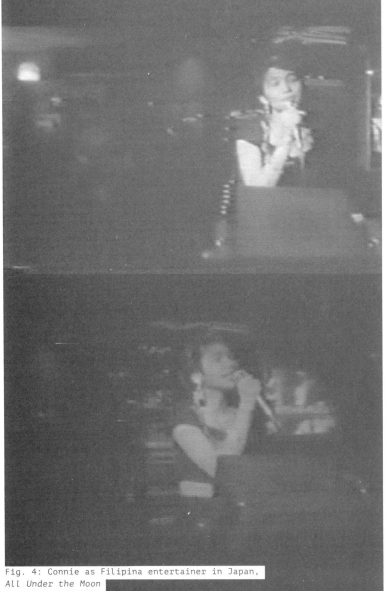

Fig. 4: Connie as Filipina entertainer in Japan,
All Under the Moon

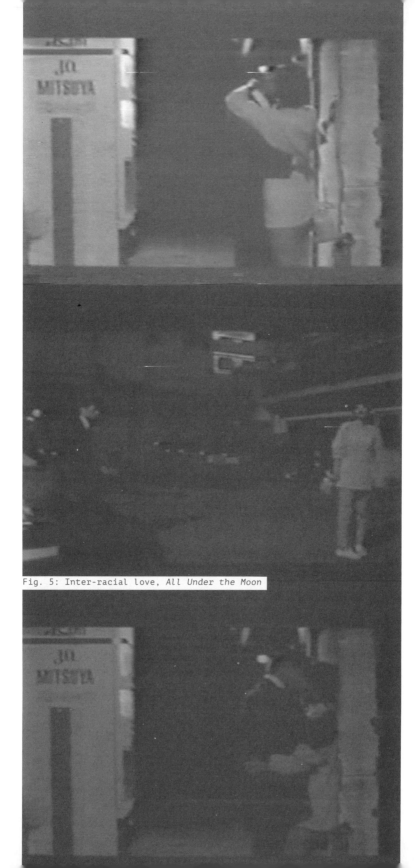

Fig. 5: Inter-racial love, *All Under the Moon*

her boundedness by her incapacity to transcend her posting, she is perplexed to accept and negotiate her position.

On the other hand, Connie is paired off with Chung Nam. Both performing intermittent natures of work—to wait on people, provide personal service of the hourly kind, to make the paying customer's lives better—Chung Nam and Connie seem to be different peas of the same pod. However, Connie is relegated to the lower position (feminine) position, awaiting both promise of domestic closure with Chung Nam and a return to the homeland. She is a romantic and nostalgic at heart. Her positionality is much worse than Chung Nam—she is illegally staying in Japan, performing her part in the sex industry. "There is an empowerment-cum-disempowerment mechanism at work in the Filipina character: the marginality of her position, in general, already places her in the 'seamy underbelly of Japanese nightlife'; but more important, given the spatial allotment in the film, her subaltern body is made visible by performing and being re-regulated within another sexual economic substratum—that of the Korean Japanese ethnic group."[44]

Though the film attempts to portray a sympathetic image of subaltern groups in Japan, it, however, does so at the expense of the figure of the Filipina OCW whose position is constructed as lowly even in the hierarchy of subaltern groups. The Filipina OCW is doubly feminized in the film—using her feminine attributes, she, at first, is able to land a job in the underbelly of the Japanese sex industry, then to be an alien of illegal status in the country; and using the same attributes, she aspires for domestic closure in her quest for a relationship with Chung Nam in Japan. While Chung Nam is at least a legal resident of Japan, Connie is an alien entity whose illegal status is forever etched in her body. If she decides to return to the Philippines, she can only be readmitted into Japan under another identity, albeit with extreme danger and difficulty, with the constant probability of being apprehended, detained, and criminalized; if she decides to stay, she cannot return to the Philippines. Though Chung Nam's Korean background is also etched in a translocal national-ity—he can only be a Korean Japanese within acceptable sites and positions in Japan—he can still materialize mobile travel outside his host nation. Connie is trapped in the black hole of existing as a non-existent identity.

Moreno portrays another nominalized geopolitical figure—the mail-order bride—in the film *Swimming with Tears*. This figure finds affinity with the illegal alien status of overstaying OCW in Japan—harping on encased complex legalities about stay and return, and imminent arrest, conviction or deportation, and of course, isolation, loneliness, and despair, and the dream and materiality of escape to the homeland and its bind. The film begins with her as a mail-order bride to a Japanese farmer in an isolated and cold place in Japan. She escapes this fate, moves to the city and tries to locate a fellow national contact. Her friend has already left the noodle restaurant. The owner pities her and allows her to work. The film chronicles her fate in the city, imbricated in her own quest for regularization of everyday life and her implication in other people's complicated lives. She decides to return to the Philippines. With unfulfilled promise of economic rewards, she laments her lost opportunity. Like a knight in shining armor, her husband returns to mend things with her. The film ends with both of them distantly facing each other in a busy low-end residential street. Their emotional faces reconnect their domestic relation amidst the tumultuous surroundings of poverty.

The film ironically poses the issue of return. In Japan, Moreno's character dreams of returning to the Philippines. In a montage sequence, she writes to or receives imaginary letters from her mother, explaining their abject conditions and the possibility of redemption with her stay in Japan. In the Philippines, however, given the abject conditions she tried to escape from by staying on in Japan, she dreams of a figurative return to the hostland. She is lonely to be cut off from familial social relations in Japan. Equally, she is also lonely in the Philippines, severed from the economic bounty of Japan. What return is there to speak of? The film cites the impossibility of a return, its being a nostalgic ideal in a neither here nor there predicament.

In *Swimming in Tears*, Moreno portrays a mail-order bride character who escapes from her husband in an isolated countryside. In one scene, she asks, "Why do Japanese look down on Filipinos? Look down on Asia? Because the gods are different? I never hated people. But I can feel I am gradually changing. I get a feeling that the Japanese prefer to hate than to love. The Japanese only think of themselves." In the film, Moreno's character is always sobbing. Tears signify her catharsis and purgation, and the cycle of pain and anguish. For Filipino melodrama, tears are plentiful. In real life, tears are an outlet for the individual's pain and suffering. These also signify the temporal breakdown of order. In recent years, certain mental disorders have been found to be common with newly-acquired overseas work. Several cases of bipolar disorder have been diagnosed in Filipina workers in Japan. Bipolar disorder entails disabling manic and depressive episodes in the patient. Unlike other mental

Fig. 6: Quiet meal between Filipina mail-order bride and Japanese husband, *Swimming in Tears*

Fig. 7: Home and farm life, *Swimming in Tears*

disorders, the patient goes back to the original level of a functioning individual after the disability. Because of guest-relations and entertainment work, the Filipina worker sustains a performative histrionic that further gets complicated, in more recent times, with substance dependency. In such a case, tears no longer provide catharsis: it means a total breakdown of the functioning self. As long as the self swims in tears, a lingering push-and-pull of survival and decay are at play.

Tears abound in the film as the ethos of return is discursively elaborated. Such a flow of tears in the film, a marker of the melodrama genre, provides the affect of isolation and anxiety experienced by the OCW figure and the overseas contract returnee. Loneliness and desperation are valued empathies of the OCW. In these, the OCW continues the grind, making her human amidst her inhumane conditions. This distinguishes the OCW from the alienating effect of machineries to laborers. The OCW realizes her suffering, the laborer accepts and learns to forget his. The OCW, at least those represented in film, is interrogated daily neither to fully accept nor to forget her fate. She is constantly terrorized by her everyday condition of "unbelonging" to the hostland, thus constantly reminding her of her fate or predicament. Her memory of home keeps her from altogether being alienated. Her idealized home becomes the impetus to stay on. As she stays on, she continues to remember, continues to become this diasporic cyborg human entity.

However, what seems to be a lose-lose situation is redeemed in the film via the classical Hollywood mode. The improbable is made possible, the return is realized and idealized. Twice, the Japanese male redeems her from her abject identity and environment, promises to return her to the First World, and even to indulge her with patriarchal love. The suffering tears realized throughout the film is now exchanged for the happy tears of domestic closure. She swims out of the waters of her own tears, rescued by the Japanese man. Such closure underscores a First World patriarchal fantasy of rescuing and redeeming the Third World woman. The First World man scouts for a Third World partner as their own women have chosen to empower themselves with other possibilities. He chooses from the mail-order bride catalog—or is matched through institutionalized means such as the intervention of the local council—and brings the woman to the First World site. Because of constraints from First World immigration laws, the Third World woman must hang on to her condition in the domain of the emasculated First World man. She performs domestic work, auditioning to the First World man in order

Fig. 8: Happy ending, *Swimming in Tears*

to obtain the legal papers. But when she chooses to escape, as the character in the film does, she becomes of illegal status. She breaks her contract to attain legal status via marriage. Thus, the narrative of rescue is further emphasized in the First World man's decision to redeem her and again from her abject Third World reality. What the film seems to obscure is that "Third Worldly-ness" is an essential part of the figure of the Filipina OCW. Her tears have not moved her to the exclusivity of the First World domain. Their constant flow has only signified her essential Third World predicament—that which seeks to remind her that her return is never complete, whether it be to the hostland or homeland, always neither here nor there.

Moreno portrays the mob member's girlfriend in *Tokyo Deluxe* and the "little girl lost" in *I Love Nippon*, where her character performs *hara-kiri* (suicide) for the love of her man. More often than not, she is the archetypal Third World woman sacrificing and dying for her lover. Her "typical" Third World features, raw or organic acting style, her waif body type, and her perennially young-looking facial features provide the constant stereotype. She is doubly marginalized as a woman and a Third World woman at that.

Another documentary film, *My Wife Is a Filipina*, reconstitutes the Third World woman as site of First World rescue. While the documentary stresses the complications of interracial marriage from both Japanese and Filipina backgrounds, it does so reifying, at least from the Filipina's point of view, the fantasy of transnational social mobility. While it is not the filmmaker's fault that such reinforcement is generated, the film also poses the constant positioning of threats and genuine love that underscores the relationship. With the constant shift of preference and realities in postmodern Japan and as implicated in the Philippines, the viewer, like the characters of the documentary, can only hope for the best as such shifts do provide material and figurative threats to their already tension-filled relationship.

Filipinas in Japan cannot return to the Philippines without the markers of economic success. Even Moreno has her own temporal success story in Japan. Coming from the ranks of Filipina overseas contract workers in Japan, she is heralded as the emblematic star for all the needed Filipina characters for film and television. She single-handedly represented the related and divergent Filipina bodies in Japan. Her own body naturalized Filipinas in media representations. At the moment, with tensions from her manager and dwindling interest in Filipina characters, she has yet to star in another big-budgeted Japanese film. That the Filipinas were the model minority at one time, "the flavor of the month" ethnic group, provided both for a temporal space for recognizing her invisible work and altogether rendering her invisible again. Filipinas are redeemed until the next model minority is heralded by Japanese national hegemony. But Moreno has also succumbed to the resolution most Filipinas choose despite or in lieu of a return: marrying a Japanese.

Such constant changing of interest and consumer preferences are attuned to the postmodern consumerist societies. There is no loyalty to any single product, probably only to brand names like Sanrio or foreign labels. And because of the very marginality of their work that renders them quasi-invisible, Filipinas do not render brand registers. They become products of their labor in postmodern consumerist societies, bearing portions of the weight of the masculinist business and state subcultures. They provide entertainment, and in the process become part of the literal machinery that is made to entertain business and state personnel. These personnel are no longer content with just karaoke but also with attached female bodies in the performance of their leisure time.

After all, Japanese popular culture means good business worldwide, necessitating constant reinvention of products and product lines. Japanese animation, for example, is a global commodity whose consumption generates some USD 15 billion business. Sanrio's fifteen thousand products earn USD 2.86 billion annually. Preferences are made stable as long as possible; loyalty is derived through constant harping of nostalgia for ideal childhood. The nation-state that contains eruptions of destability has consequently produced a terrain of destability management as the nation's state of affairs. This means that eruption is no longer the stable construct; it is now the destability that has become the staple of everyday life. The nation has erupted paranoia as the nation's own state of mind.

This means that business primarily draws on the state's exercise of national paranoia to generate products that sublimate the national anxiety. Animation and Sanrio products attune the anxious national minds to a longing for idealized childhood. To a large extent, the very make-up of Moreno as a waif-like Third World beauty plays along the national paranoia. What is obfuscated is the discussion of non-ideal childhood pasts, especially those that underscore its not-so-ideal history. Moreno signifies a continuum in the narrative of postmodern consumerist choice in post-industrial societies.[45] It is interesting to consider that comfort women signify a breakdown of the narrative, heralding the real in their action to be rendered visible in history. Their retro-action leaves little for support, especially when history is deemed at its end in postmodern societies.

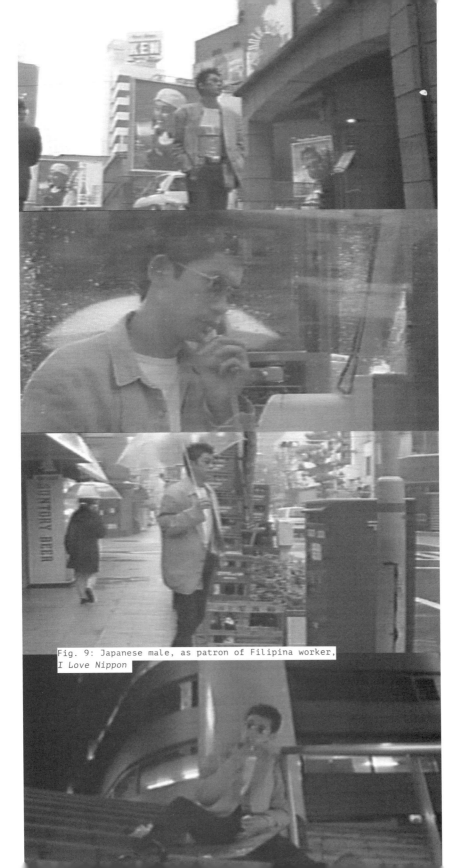

Fig. 9: Japanese male, as patron of Filipina worker, *I Love Nippon*

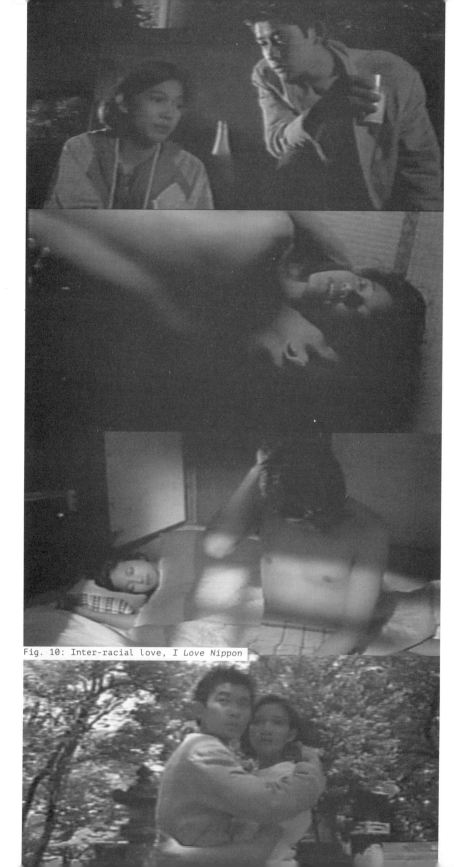

Fig. 10: Inter-racial love, *I Love Nippon*

In its own emasculated state, Japan can only speak of its phallic greatness in retrospect, as nostalgia to an era never to arise either in the present or future, a nostalgia built on an idealized fascistic past. Film again becomes an idiom to talk about nostalgia, marking a return to the early moments of subject-formation. Such moments are idealized even as the real experience never achieved ideal status. The past is memorialized in its greatness, becoming the absent organizing signifier of the present.

What I had intended to do in this essay is to map out the representations of the Philippines in Japanese cinema—how the primordial liquid and vessel are transfused to infantile wards. In so doing, I also mapped out the various socio-historical shifts in Japanese and Philippine interests. Japanese representations of the Philippines can be used to analyze representations of the Asia Pacific. Images and representations "made in Japan" need to be contested and dialogued with various national critiques. With Japan becoming the Philippines' and Southeast Asia's primary paternal developer, patterns of preference are remolded. From its experience of trauma and violence during World War II with Japan, the Philippines has deemed this country friendlier and benevolent in more recent times. Thanks to capital and pop culture influx, the Philippines sees Japan in a more positive light. Even as its media does not reflect this at the moment, Japan becomes more benevolent as younger generations are reared by popular culture with amnesia of the World War II past.

With its insular society, peoples of Asia Pacific are nonetheless also being represented in Japanese cinema. In such films as *I Love Nippon*, *World Apartment House Horror*, *Swallowtail Butterfly*, *Ai ni Tsuite Tokyo*, *Junk Food*, *Nanmin Road*, *Sleeping Man*, *Beijing Watermelon*, *Betonam No Da-cham*, *We Are Not Alone*, *Umi Hoozooki*, *Night in Hong Kong*, *Ramen Taishi*, *Gonin I and II*, and *Hong Kong Night Club*, Asia Pacific nationals are represented, implicating at times Japanese involvement in the various nations. Japanese documentary also has a long legacy of involvement in the Asia Pacific.

In the first period of the Philippines' experience of Japanese transnationalism in World War II, propaganda war films marked the assertion of Japanese masculinity as prism to examine Filipino ideals deemed corrupted by American colonialism. To assert Japanese military masculinity is to dominate and feminize local masculinity. In the second period, the post-war economic development of Japan was experienced at a price—the castration of its former source of dominance, military might. The boom period emplaced the figure of the Filipina migrant as the nexus of popular representation of the inevitable influx of migrant labor to Japan, which in turn has become a major node of transnational capital. Feminized herself, Japan now mobilizes femininity as the fetish to assert its displaced masculinity. Thus, the Filipina in Japanese films—weighed heavily on Moreno's shoulders who cornered the market—is either the lowly Third World female entertainer or the mail-order bride of the emasculated Japanese male. The OCW figure is also a newly actualized popular identity in Philippine cinema. However, her suffering in the hostland is mythologized through an elaboration of the suffering in the homeland, oftentimes overtly implicating the predicament of the emasculated and feminized nation who can neither safeguard nor provide for her citizens.

Feminized in Japanese and Philippine cinemas, the Filipina OCW figure becomes central to the discourse of transnationalism as experienced either by a First or by a Third World nation. Domestic issues hound the Filipina OCW, making her remember her humanity and social relations, be it in their nostalgic or in their real worth. In the repetition of Filipina OCW's visibility in film, she becomes a historical figure in the epochal moment of global and sexual division of labor. In contrast, masculinity was mobilized to dually mark the colonialist's superiority and the native's domination in Japanese propaganda films of World War II. In the imperialist projects— global domination in World War II then and transnationalism now— sexuality is mobilized to stress the play of power. The language of imperialism is expounded through the vernacular of sexuality. Films mobilize this discourse of sexuality in transnationalism, positioning femininity as integral in the substantiation and configuration of the Filipina OCWs. In turn, such femininity is reconstructed by real and filmic Filipina OCWs to make sense of their lives—remembering their bodies as sites of unending geopolitical struggle, their retooling of femininity becomes important in deciphering the operations of imperialism. In reinstrumentalizing their femininity, imperialism can also be reformed—albeit ideal, while awaiting its overthrow—to make it accountable for the insurmountable suffering it has caused. Through Philippine diaspora, a virtual and real map of collective bondedness may be drawn.

KEYWORDS

ENDNOTES

I am thankful to the following people who generously helped source materials for this research, and who unselfishly shared their time and ideas on the matter: Monma Takashi of the Yamagata Documentary Film Festival, Hayashi Kanako of the Kawakita Film Institute, Kenji Ishizaka and Reiko Ogawa of Japan Foundation, Aaron Gerow, Miki Adachi, Mitsuyo Wada-Marciano,

Terada Takefumi, Yomota Gorky Inuhiko, and Farah Trofeo. Funding for this research was provided by the Sumitomo Foundation.

1   Agustin L. Sotto, "War and the Aftermath in Philippine Cinema," *Panahon ng Hapon: Sining sa Digmaan, Digmaan sa Sining*, ed. Gina Barte (Manila: Cultural Center of the Philippines, 1992), 172.

2   I have discussed a similar move by Japan in two essays. One is "Global/Local Nation and Hysteria: Japanese Children's Television in the Philippines," *Image and Reality: Philippine-Japan Relations Towards the 21st Century*, ed. Rolando S. Dela Cruz (Quezon City: Institute of International Legal Studies, U.P., 1997), 239–62. In this essay, I point out how the discourse of Japanese animation is localized in a similar disenfranchising use of children by businesses. The other essay is "Japanese Legal Culture, Animation Studies, Security and Sovereignty," unpublished manuscript, 1999, which draws connections between the hyperactive use of female sexuality in Japanese animation and its erasure in Filipino comfort women.

3   See Rolando B. Tolentino, "Film in the Age of Empire: Cinema, Gender and Sexuality in the U.S. Colonization of the Philippines," *Bulawan: Journal of Philippine Arts and Culture* (Manila: National Commission for Culture and the Arts, 2001), 68–79.

4   A third film, *Tatlong Maria* (based on the novel by Jose Esperanza Cruz), a feature, was also produced after the success of *Dawn of Freedom*. However, no print of the film has been presently located.

5   This point is stressed by Motoe Terami-Wada, "Strategy in Culture: Cultural Policy and Propaganda in the Philippines, 1942–1945," *Panahon ng Hapon: Sining sa Digmaan, Digmaan sa Sining*, ed. Gina Barte (Manila: Cultural Center of the Philippines, 1992), 23–33. An even earlier foundation setting of Japanese influence in the Philippines is discussed by Lydia N. Yu-Jose, *Japan Views the Philippines 1900–1944* (Quezon City: Ateneo de Manila University Press, 1992).

6   Ricardo Jose, "*The Dawn of Freedom* and the Japanese Wartime Propaganda," quoted in Sotto, 172.

7   I am thankful to Geraldine G. Genrozala who pointed out these films in her study "*Dawn of Freedom*: Transnasyonalismo sa Pelikulang Propaganda," unpublished, n.d. Such points are culled from Agustin Sotto, "War and Its Aftermath in Philippine Cinema," *Diamond Anniversary of Philippine Cinema* (1994), 26–27.

8   Again, I am grateful to Genrozala for the points on the Propaganda Corps and Central Booking Exchange. She reconstructs the points by incorporating research by Motoe Terami Wada, "The Cultural Front in the Philippines" (Ph.D. dissertation, U.P., 1984); Teodoro Agoncillo and Milagros Guerrero, *History of the Filipino People* (Quezon City: Malaya Books, 1970).

9   Motoe Terami-Wada, "The Cultural Front in the Philippines, 1942–1945: Japanese Propaganda and Filipino Resistance in Mass Media" (Ph.D. dissertation submitted to the University of the Philippines, unpublished, October 1984), 208.

10 Agustin L. Sotto, "War and the Aftermath in Philippine Cinema," *Panahon ng Hapon: Sining sa Digmaan, Digmaan sa Sining* (Manila: Cultural Center of the Philippines, 1992), 172.

11 "Dawn of Freedom Notes," *Imperial Japan at the Movies* (Yamagata: Yamagata International Documentary Film Festival, 1997), 36. *Dawn of Freedom* was premiered in Tokyo on 5 Feb 1944. Originally entitled *Mito Sakusen* (Philippine Operation), it was changed to *Anno Hatte O Utte* or literally "Tear Down the Stars and Stripes." For the Philippines, it was decided to use *The Dawn of Freedom* or "Liwayway ng Kalayaan." The Philippine premier was set for 5 Mar 1944 but was moved to the 7th. It was hailed as an outstanding achievement by those who were present: "Minister of Interior Teofilo Sison, Camilo Osias of the KALIBAPI, Vicente Madrigal of the Philippine Red Cross and First Secretary Shintaro Fukushima of the Japanese Embassy" (Sotto, "War and the Aftermath.")

12 "Dawn of Freedom Notes," 32.

13 Ricardo Jose, quoted in Sotto, "War and the Aftermath," 172.

14 For an account of the production and exhibition of the three films, see Terami-Wada, "Strategy in Culture" and "Cultural Front," 215–26 (these are succeeding sections) and Sotto, "War and the Aftermath," 172–75.

15 "Dawn of Freedom Notes," 32.

16 For a discussion on the intricacies of conversion, see Vicente Rafael, *Contracting Colonialism: Translation and Christian Conversion in Tagalog Society Under Early Spanish Rule* (Quezon City: Ateneo de Manila University Press, 1995).

17 Renato Constantino and Letizia R. Constantino, *The Philippines: The Continuing Past* (Quezon City: Foundation for Nationalist Studies, 1978), 31.

18 Ibid.

19 Ibid.

20 R. Constantino and L. Constantino, "Philippines," 60.

21 Sotto, "War and the Aftermath," 172.

22 Quoted in Terami-Wada, "Cultural Front," 220.

23 Quoted in Teodoro A. Agoncillo and Milagros C. Guerrero, *History of the Filipino People* (Quezon City: R.P. Garcia Publishing Co., 1977), 411.

24 Ibid.

25 Quoted in Terami-Wada, "Cultural Front," 217.

26 Agoncillo and Guerrero, "Filipino People," 411.

27 R. Constantino and L. Constantino, "Philippines," 69.

28 For a discussion of film themes during prewar and postwar Philippine movies, again see Sotto, "War and the Aftermath."

29 Tony Bennett, "The Exhibitionary Complex," *Culture/Power/History: A Reader in Contemporary Social Theory* (Princeton: New Jersey, 1994), 127.

30   See William W. Kelly, "Finding a Place in Metropolitan Japan: Ideologies, Institutions, and Everyday Life" and Marilyn Ivy, "Formations of Mass Culture," *Postwar Japan as History* (Berkeley: University of California Press, 1993), 189–238 and 239–58 respectively.

31   These statistics are culled from Elena L. Samonte, "Japanese Nationality Law and Japanese-Filipino Children," manuscript, 1998, 1.

32   Quoted in Samonte, "Japanese Nationality Law," 1.

33   See "Stock Estimates on Overseas Filipinos," http://www.poea.gov.ph/Stats/ st_stock2000.html, as appended in Mamoru Tsuda, *Filipino Diaspora in Asia: Social and Personal Networks, Organizing, Empowerment, Ethnicity, and Culture* (Osaka: Report submitted to the Japan Academy for the Promotion of Sciences, 2002), v.

34   See "Deployment of OFWs, 1998–2001, by Top Ten Destinations," http:// www.poea.gov.ph/Stats/deployment2001.html, as appended in Tsuda, vi.

35   In Tsuda, "Deployment of OFWs," 5.

36   Luz Rimban, "Filipina Diaspora," *Her Stories: Investigative Reports on Filipino Women in the 1990s*, ed. Cecile C. A. Balgos (Quezon City: PCIJ, 1999), 127.

37   Ibid.

38   Ibid.

39   Ibid.

40   Quoted in Rimban, "Filipina Diaspora," 128.

41   See Rolando B. Tolentino, "'Inangbayan' in Lino Brocka's *Bayan Ko: Kapit sa Patalim* (1985) and *Orapronobis* (1989)," *National/Transnational: Subject Formation and Media in and on the Philippines* (Quezon City: Ateneo de Manila University Press, 2001), 25–50.

42   I have discussed the transnational links between the Philippines, Korean Japanese, and Japan in "Subcontracting Imagination and Imageries of Bodies and Nations: The Philippines in Contemporary Transnational Asia Pacific Cinemas," *Sites/Sights of Contestation: Localism, Globalism and Cultural Production,* ed. Kwok-kan Tam (Hong Kong: Chinese University Press, 2002.

43   I have analyzed this film in "Subcontracting Imagination and Imageries of Bodies and Nations," *National/Transnational*, see pages 162–67.

44   Ibid., 163. The phrase is from a flier for the 1994 Japan Today Film Festival.

45   The figure of the Filipina OCW is also a newly minted identity in Philippine cinema. She has been imaged in such works as a nurse in the U.S. in *Merika* in the 1980s, a domestic helper in the Middle East in the film biography of the abused heroine Sarah Balabagan, or the "Japayuki" or Filipina OCW in Japan, Maricris Sioson, murdered in the host country, the latter both in the 1990s. However, the more recent three "Flor Contemplacion" film versions stand out as a manifesto of the interest in the travails and not-so-isolated fate of the Filipina OCW. Flor Contemplacion, a domestic helper in Singapore,

was accused of and sentenced to death for the murder of a child and a Filipina co-worker. Massive protests ensued during and after her execution, as many Filipinos found the sentence unjust and even abusive.

The most popular version of the three films is *The Flor Contemplacion Story* (Joel Lamangan, director, 1995) which starred the Philippines' most popular actress, Nora Aunor, whose own life story emulates the struggle of the Filipina OCW figure in their quest for a better life. The film till then was the biggest box-office draw in the nation's history. The film dizzily chronicles Contemplacion's saga before and during her execution. What is made integral in the film narrative is the story of mass protest against her execution by various cause-oriented groups. Here, the real and filmic reality further merges as what is experienced in Moreno's own individual saga. Her actual background becomes the wellspring of her filmic identity. In *Flor Contemplacion,* it is the foreknowledge of real people and events that makes the filmic reality all the more evocative of the sentiments and aspirations of OCWs and their families.

The Filipina OCW in *Flor Contemplacion* is made analogous to the fate of the mother-nation. On the one hand, she embodies the suffering of her fellow country people, thus sharing their abjected fate and aspiration for a better future. On the other hand, her suffering is so intensive that it is up to those outside her to liberate her. She is already condemned to her fate—her predicament rebounds to a shameful closure, sentenced to die in the hostland, the worst fate for an OCW—and is powerless to change it. Mass protests gave her a figurative liberation, making her death not just a statistical one but also an aesthetically pleasing and pleasurable one— in the service of the nationalist project. Through her doomed body and beautiful death, other OCW bodies were made visible. Her individual body represented the collective existence and condition of the OCW, especially the Filipina OCW. The project, I think, succeeded in using her femininity to tie it up with individual and collective suffering, aspiration, and struggle. As the discourse of the mother-nation gravitized in her body through the nationalist project, so, too, did she become the temporal release from the intensifying oppressiveness of the national condition. That the nation-state is not able to provide for the needs of its citizens here and abroad is crystallized in Contemplacion's real and filmic (after-life, posthumous, postbody) existence.

The national condition was too heavy to carry. Contemplacion called attention to this condition. She provided the relief to the very condition in which her life was directed by the actions of the citizenry and the state. Her femininity was instrumental in the self-reflexive gesture and in providing the closure, albeit temporal, in which to steer the nation to move on. The ambassador to Singapore was recalled; the president accepted the resignation of the secretary of the Department of Labor and Employment. These entities were the extended-affects (after-life) of Contemplacion and the collective tears, raising the possibility of tears being able to move molehills and mountains. That Contemplacion's postmortem body was also able to curtail the career lives of bureaucratic officials proves the temporal and relative power of the (dead) Filipina OCW to redirect energies—from pathos into action, from a collective position of injustice to quasi-judicial treatment of individual officials.

Flor Contemplacion's success rests on the in-mixing of historical and filmic realities. It is a grand political project to emplace the Filipina OCW in a historical position, a testament to the collective travails and aspiration of the nation. Another film tackles the tragic everyday reality of the Filipina OCW. *Anak* (Child; Rory Quintos, director, 2000) mobilizes another superstar in Philippine cinema, Vilma Santos, who is played in media as Aunor's rival, to retell the generic story of anxiety and aspiration of the Filipina OCW. Santos portrays the role of a domestic worker in Hong Kong, though much of the film focuses on the time of her break from a contract. Back in the Philippines, her family is in disarray as she is not attended to affectionately by her children, especially her eldest daughter who is experiencing her own confusion through drugs and promiscuous sex. Verbal confrontations between mother and daughter are loud and mercilessly brutal. What I was especially interested in the film was its providing of an "open-ended" closure, one that mitigates her life choice as OCW to go on despite domestic travails. The Filipina OCW/mother really has no choice but to keep on contractually working overseas. One of the final scenes is the quick but tearfully abundant farewell scene between the mother and her children at the airport. Anyone who has been to Manila's airport in Manila will know that it is really no place to create an emotional scene. as escorting family members can only pay their farewells respects behind steel partitions that separate them from the departing family member at the airport's exterior areas. Tears are not allowed to flow freely, abruptly cut in the cringing voices of family members and departing OCWs.

She suddenly and repeatedly leaves her family. The claustrophobic feel of the airport scene is followed by the final scene, an extreme long shot of her, now back in Hong Kong. On her day-off, she moves as one with the other numerous Filipina OCWs that have reterritorialized the commercial space of Hong Kong's business district. She disappears among the crowd of Filipina OCWs, creating familial bonds in their free time, familiar and alienated national bodies huddled together on a periodic basis. What the film successfully says is that domestic closure is insufficient to provide for the material existence of daily life. The domestic is still to be negotiated in the interfacing of the national and transnational. The film character embodies the pathos of the Filipina OCW—conscious that the family's domestic travails and national aspirations are interfaced with her own travail as a transnational geobody.

Hysteria

Japanese Children's Television in the Philippines

G rowing up in Mandaluyong, I was bombarded by Japanese children's shows. My earliest memory was excitedly anticipating every Sunday evening's showing of *Shintaro the Samurai*, a black-and-white, live, action-packed adventure series about a renegade warrior. My excitement was almost always thwarted due to being required to attend Catholic evening masses with the rest of the family. During the Marcos dictatorship, like millions of other children, I would come home before five in the afternoon to tune in to Japanese animated cartoons on television, the most popular of which was *Voltes V*. Aired every Friday, the show was about five air fighters, bolted together to form a robot-warrior. The Voltes V toy, which came with the laser sword, was a precious commodity signifying membership into the upper-class. Because of complaints from parents, the show was banned in 1979, by no less than then-President Marcos. During the People's Uprising in 1986 that eventually toppled the Marcos government, the generation of activists who scorned the presidential move joked, "Kaya kasi napatalsik dahil binan ang *Voltes V* (He was deposed for having banned *Voltes V*)."

In my early 30s, Japanese children's shows were making a comeback. Unlike the recent wave of Mexican telenovelas initiated by the Marimar series, Japanese children's shows are sustaining their popularity and dominance of transcultural translated programming. I find my enthusiasm for and consumption of the earlier Japanese shows reproduced in my young nephews and nieces. Moreover, there is more aggressive marketing of the television shows, as merchandise—from toys, games, clothes, school supplies to food and watches are displayed and sold in stores nationwide.

This immense soft-selling of Japanese popular culture in the Philippines comes at an opportune historical juncture when the nation is experiencing sustained economic take-off and flight. But more importantly, Japanese children's shows in the Philippines produce new cultural relations, embodying recent socio-economic and political developments. Children are positioned in the historical juncture both as intended audience and as embodiment of the new cultural and social relations, as spaces in which to locate the nation. This essay investigates the contending and dialoging forces that shape the national fascination with Japanese popular culture. In the increasing acceptance of the on-going globalization of Japanese popular culture, the Philippines translates this aspect of global culture locally, albeit anxiously. What, then, are the stakes poised in such resurgence of profit and interest in Japanese popular culture in the Philippines?

KEYWORDS

In this essay, I read Japanese popular culture as an agent of globalization, how globalization is experienced from within the national urban space. As the nation moves forward economically, there is a growing hysteria simultaneously being generated, as seen in the middle-class discourse on children as embodiment of the local experience with modernity. This local hysteria is connected to the larger hysteria embodied in Japanese children's shows. Supposedly culturally odorless, the shows erase both Japan's failed, and thus traumatic, attempt at enforcing a global hegemony in World War II and its current attempt to reposition itself globally. In other words, by erasing Japanese history, the shows provide a slide board, or more extremely, a tabula rasa, on which to reencode the national ethos in countries that now receive these shows rather well. This is attuned to the global localization thrust of the Japanese popular culture industry, in which newer social relations and interests are being nationally redefined and redifferentiated through the filter of Japanese global culture.

I begin the essay by investigating the erasure of Japan's national trauma in the projects of global, if not regional, dominance through the shows' production of a national hysteria over the absence of history. I then analyze its cultural translation, transnationalization, and localization in the Philippines, expounding on the relationship of Japanese children's television and the local experience of modernity. In both analyses, I focus my attention on the growing use of children's bodies as signifiers of the desire to globalize and localize national experience on the one hand, and the attempt to erase and place national hysteria over history on the other. In the case of Japan, it is its violent trauma over World War II that is nominalized; in the Philippines, it is its history of being the sick man of Asia, or its neverending war against poverty. Both instances of national hysteria are targeted to project affluence, but such experience with the modern and postmodern are done differentially, with children positioned as the cultural idiom of national trauma, hysteria, and these modern and postmodern experiences.

"Losing One's Head": Hysteria, Japan, and Children's Television

On 24 May 1997, Jun Hase, an eleven-year-old with a learning disability, disappeared, supposedly to visit his grandfather who lived near his home. His body was found three days later on a hill. He had been strangled before being decapitated. Pieces of paper were stuffed in his mouth. Patched together, a note had the killer issuing a threat, "[T]his is just the beginning." Shock and fear immediately rose in Kobe where, two years ago, an earthquake had killed some 6,300 people. A letter-writer claimed responsibility for the brutal death of the schoolboy that sent Japan, "a nation unaccustomed to violent crime," into panic.[1]

A national hysteria over the brutal slaying of the child ensued. Newspapers screamed headlines of the crime, and morning talk shows descanted on the same. Prime Minister Ryutaro Hashimoto even took "the unusual step of personally instructing police and government officials to do everything in their capacity to solve the case."[2] More than five hundred police officers knocked on people's doors in Kobe to search for evidence. Kobe's Board of Education issued letters warning parents who, in turn, took steps to keep children within sight and reach.

Such hysteria over the beheading of a child parallels Japan's own hysteria over the loss of its own head. Hysteria, after all, provides the hysteric with a "feel[ing of] an intense pleasure, an improper pleasure, that cannot properly speaking be allowed into experience"; in other words, hysteria is "a story of turning away from, an avoidance of, another story."[3] To "lose one's head," is to lose one's rationality, one's ego-ideal; it is a temporal experience of psychic instability. Anxiety, in the constant feed of crisis, especially through children, becomes the nation's new constant state. On the one hand, the nation, after all, has been regularly bombarded with related brutal slayings of children: in early spring alone, one child was violently attacked with a knife, and another ten-year-old was bludgeoned to death. The letter claimant's threat had only fueled the nation into further hysteria. Children's victimization in postmodern Japan is always handled through hysterization. The more recent phenomenon of child prostitution, serviced by persons who grew up in the 1980s, is nurtured by the desire for "money, brand names, materialism."[4] On the other hand, national hysteria is also felt in the national and children's experience of the postmodern. *Tamagotchi* (virtual pets) for example, are celebrated as an embodiment of postmodern Japan, and of the postmodern experience in general.

The victimization of children provides a double layering to the hysteria. That children are easy prey to heinous criminals threatens the experience, both present and future, of modernity and the modern civil society and state. As for the nation's past, it has already created a national amnesia over Japan's role in World War II. Like the present effect of hysteria on the nation, the national amnesia is channeled through paranoia, continuously feeding through the fear of the possible disturbance, if not loss, of affluence. But unlike the present hysteria, the paranoia is never fully open for public scrutiny, a historical Pandora's box left unopened.

Two related developments further complicate the crime on Hase. First, the letter claimant blamed the harsh educational system for producing an entity like himself: "I am not forgetting revenge for the compulsory education that has produced me as an invisible existence and on the society that has produced this compulsory education."[5] He adds that a friend of his friend, "the only other invisible person in the world," told him that by murdering children, he would be able to "create a new world."[6] Education, the state's primary apparatus for the socialization of children, is positioned as the ultimate threat to society. Even as critics have already pointed out the complicity of the educational system in the abuse and endless labor of children, the Japanese state has yet to yield to this reality.[7] Moreover, the harshness of the educational system provides the necessary socialization for the perpetuation of individual and commercial affluence. In a 1990 survey of grammar school children nationwide, it was discovered that 63.2 percent were suffering from high blood cholesterol, 36.2 percent from ulcers, 22.2 percent from high blood pressure, and 21.4 percent from diabetes.[8] Not only is the child's body made prone to disease, it is also regimented through endless work and abuse:

> Children attend cram schools from a routine of rushing home
> after school, grabbing dinners packed by their mothers,
> exchanging schoolbooks for cram school books, spending from
> 5 to 9 p.m. at the cram school (or going to more than one extra
> school if their mothers have chosen to have them specialize),
> perhaps staying on for private lessons until 11, and, when
> entrance exams are around the corner, getting home after
> midnight to tackle school homework, topped off with a touch of
> video game playing before going to sleep around 2 a.m.[9]

The second issue that aggravates the already nervous state is related to the confession of a fourteen-year-old suspect. That the crime was committed on a child by a child leaves the nation in a quandary, but this fact, too, is also traced to the educational system. Both student, through bullying, and teachers, through infliction of corporal punishment, are complicit perpetrators of violence. What results, then, is the "normalization of dysfunction," or a state of reversal where "children are stripped of their innocence and adults of their authority."[10] Furthermore, this dysfunctional state is "usually attributed to individual deficiencies, whether on the part of the family (especially the mother) or the child him/herself."[11] Violent cases, such as Hase's beheading, then herald the return of the repressed, the normal. In this condition, the state is exculpated. Thus, the nation experiences hysteria that provides for both the community's complicity with and critique of the state. The criminalization of the state, a temporal and nervous condition, becomes possible only through the incidence of a crime that can be connected to the state. This critique, however, is easily obscured by the perpetration of paranoia that inhibits the further expansion of the critical public sphere. Through further paranoia, the state implores the people to resolve their individual inner tensions of being, but never to collectively actualize systemic transformation. Hase's beheading is, instead, transformed into a discourse of disturbance against civil society, "Until the killer is caught, neither will the rest of Japan [forget Hase]."[12] The fact that violent crimes on children continue, almost regularly, breaking the normality of the dysfunctional nation, has made the tensions always present. Therefore, as the state has never been fully subverted, so has the state never fully contained the inherent tensions coming from the preparation and use of children for nation-building. The result is the memorialization of the child victim, including the promise "never to forget the victim," as classmates of Hase publicly talked about during his funeral.[13] What is erased are the social tensions generated from childrearing for national development.

"To lose one's head" is to lose one's location in a perceived trajectory. As Japan's materiality and virtuality have been triggered by increasing affluence, so has it turned to this trajectory of wealth in place of its experience of the modern and postmodern predicament. The disruption of the dysfunctional state, symptomized by the crime against Hase, provides a juncture to analyze the national hysteria in Japanese children's shows. I believe that the same kind of production of hysteria and paranoia is triggered by the desire to maintain wealth unabashedly in both violent crimes against children and Japanese children's shows. Both use hysteria in the display of social tensions, then use paranoia to contain the hysteria, producing another hysteria on children and nation-building.

Considered culturally odorless in Japan's bid to export its popular culture, Japanese children's shows are conduits for the dissemination of paranoia to contain national hysteria. While the odorless quality of the cultural products seems necessary to allow identification for various cultures, my thinking, however, is that the product is never totally culturally odorless. Traces of guilt from its World War II leadership and continuing affluence are negotiated and determined. While their Japanese origins are consciously effaced by culture industries, the very conventions of Japanese children's shows undeniably lead to an exploration of anxieties over the nation's past and present. The production of meanings on hysteria within the texts is supported by a related production of consumer-related products, equally hysterically consumed through individual, group, and national production of excess meanings attached by audiences.

Thus, hysteria can be seen on two levels: within the texts themselves, and in the production and consumption of these shows and show-related products. Japanese animation series embody child and child-like superheroes. These characters lead double lives. But unlike

American superheroes (such as those of DC Comics), what resonates in the characters is the technological transformations of the child body. The body parts and gender characteristics are transformed into instruments for the technological defense of a given moral good. The superhero is also part of a group, instead of a tandem. In *Sailor Moon*, for example, the girls are collectively transformed into superwoman heroes in sailor uniforms. They use tiaras and several magical weapons, such as magic wands, to pull off their battles. The homosocial environment of the superheroes' community is replete with innocent homoeroticism. In some cases, as in *Ranma 1/2*, the lead character is transformed into a female subject every time he is doused with water. There is a constant blurring of gender and sexual identification.

Though imbued with superpowers and technologized bodies, the characters act their mental age. They regularly break into temperamental outbursts, commit childish errors, get entangled in adult-related scenarios, and so on. Yet these superheroes carry on with their missions, from saving the planet to winning a basketball championship. In the process of pursuing these missions, the superheroes are always in frenetic action—this depicted through multiple action shots within a single frame. The profusion of energy and movement direct to the climactic saga of each episode. This profusion, in turn, also points to the management of hysteria via the dissemination of paranoia. In the first place, the shows abound in hysteria, imagined disjuncture of mind-body, and self-other relations. The frenetic action, inability to fully resolve the saga, recurrence of weaknesses, and unreliability of even superpowers, among others, bring about both disgust and pleasure. But there is also the need to contain hysteria through the management of paranoia, since the saga never completely ends in a single episode. Enemies may return recharged, alliances may be broken, and new enemies are always forthcoming.

The hysterization of the nation is represented through children's bodies. The national condition is replete with kineticism of the child superhero, like dusting off a foreign entity in one's body. Freud related hysteria with a continuity dualism, the conversion of psychical into somatic conflict. Monique David-Menard, however, contends an epistemological break.[14] The proliferation of movement in Japanese children's shows becomes the symptom of the suspension of national jouissance, and channel to savor affluence and the legacy of World War II without guilt. The suspension, however, is temporal. As such, hysteria evokes both disgust and pleasure. However, such jouissance is "radically heterogeneous" and irreducible into a single order of

Fig. 1: *Ranma 1/2*

experience.[15] Having suspended jouissance, the national condition is contained through paranoia. The specter of otherness—a "foreign body"—continues to haunt the subject until the hysteric is poised in a libidinal economy of ungratified desire; as Lacan asks, "Why sustain her desire only as an unsatisfied desire?"[16]

Lacan suggests that the hysteric is always female; hysteria, therefore, is a feminized position. As Japanese animation places hysteria in children's bodies, the national condition is doubly hystericized—not only feminized, but also infantilized. In other words, the doubly othered is represented as the pivot of the national hysteric's disgust and pleasure, the other spoken for as she speaks of the national condition. Affluence, after all, has been embodied in the female body, signifying the nouveau shift in lifestyle; so also has it been embodied in such political figures as Evita Peron and Imelda Marcos to signify excess and conspicuous consumption. Read allegorically, Japan has been femininely positioned after its World War II defeat, gelded of its militaristic power. The training of women into modernity also alludes to the rearing of children into the project. While children need to be protected en route to modernity, they also need to continuously signify the national condition in its various stages. Ian Buruma suggests that the "infantilism of postwar Japanese culture" results from managing trauma of World War II defeat through a fetish for childhood.[17] This signifies an evasion of responsibility which the nation consistently negotiates with, including popular representations; it is an evasion clearly sought but never fully materialized in the linkage of present affluence with past trauma.

"As Asia [and the world] advances, Japan's experience may have a special resonance."[18] Japanese children's shows are a USD 15 billion business, larger than conglomerates. *Dragonball Z* and *Sailor Moon* are two of the most popular series. Outside Hollywood, only Latin American telenovelas and Japanese animated series have become viable television-export projects. The world has consumed these shows with gusto. *Dragonball Z* has consistently rated number one in Asia and Europe. It is also Japan's best-rated cartoon show, with an 82 percent audience share. All indications lead to the hysterical production and reception of Japanese animated series, ensuring a constant, if not excessive, supply to meet equally increasing demands by audiences. Though this development can readily be explained by multinationalism and postmodernism, what can also be generated from the upsurge interest in Japanese popular culture is the growing interest in children as embodiment of a new innocence against which newer and harsher social relations are being developed.

The transnational condition has allowed the proliferation of other centers and peripheries, constantly defining newer social relations in the global and sexual division of labor. Japan's new export has created the nation as a new global center for popular culture. This development has reinforced old relations, even as it creates new ones. The production of meanings in the reception of Japanese animation can be dealt with more closely in the analysis of global localization, a by-word in Japanese culture industry that speaks of localizing the global need for products and experiences. The Philippines repre-sents a related hysteria with Japan. On the one hand, it is disgusted by its Japanese legacy, belittling Japan's abrupt take-over and defeat in its conquest during World War II. Japan is represented popularly by parody; images of overweight sumo wrestlers and kimono-clad women abound in media. On the other hand, it is also enamored with Japan's economic and cultural ascendancy, and its penetration of the local landscape of capital and aid. Given a choice, Japan comes close to the United States as local students' preferred country to live in. The present neocolonial attraction and love provide an interest-ing habitat for the analysis of cultural and technological boundary crossing and translation.

K
E
Y
W
O
R
D
S

"Dreaming Modernity": Global Localization, the Philippines, and Japanese Children's Shows

Global localization is a concept and practice coined by the Japanese culture industry to operationalize technological dominance in the media market, including those devices used in the domestic sphere. While Hollywood may churn out and dominate global film production, for example, its further dissemination is dominated by Japanese technology, e.g., video cassette recorders, laser discs and players, video and computer games, and so on. While new technological innovations are introduced to bring comfort to homes, new products and peripherals are required to operate these innovations. Thus, instead of producing films that directly compete with local industries, the Japanese culture industry simply produces newer technologies to localize trade and domestic consumption. What results is newer social relations so unlike the dominance of Hollywood in domestic film markets that directly perpetuate United States representations of global cultural hegemony. Thus, Japanese cultural products may be culturally odorless, but they nonetheless have the uncanny smell of Japanese-ness.

Because of newer economic developments taking place in the Philippines, the markers of modernity are evoking Japanese technological innovations. Three million Filipino overseas contract workers in 125 countries and territories bring in USD 4 billion annually. This amount benefits nineteen million Filipinos, whether directly or indirectly. Overseas contract work has consistently been the Philippines' number one export. Part of the enigma of overseas work involves two issues: the transformation of the body, and the transmutation of signifiers of modernity into the national sphere, both of which entail dreaming modernity and the issue of domesticity.

Dreaming modernity involves a national development that focuses on middle-classification of people's way of life, services, and products. The national aspiration is toward gentrification of the historically disenfranchised, a fact that altogether makes the dream within reach, yet ungraspable to many individuals. Dreaming modernity entails the issue of the modern and cosmopolitan. While modernism imbibes a consciousness toward the liberal-pluralist subject, cosmopolitanism involves a practice of embodying the liberal subject through markers of modernity. For Filipinos, the markers of modernity have always been signified from the playing field of the United States' cosmopolitan centers, the architect of the Philippines' present political and economic systems. Japanese popular culture has been massively disseminated in the country only since the late 1970s, with the influx of Filipina migrant workers to Japan. Japan's capital investment and aid to the Philippines further the high regard for Japanese-ness. Fantasy preoccupies much of dreaming modernity's operation. For fantasy sanitizes the unreachable, making the object of desire psychically within reach. But the reality is always based on desire never being fully consummated. Thus, fantasy, like hysteria, is based on a sado-masochistic relation of self-other formation that never fully swings toward one pole of the binary. The libidinal economy requires constant struggle amidst the odds of ever fully realizing modernity's dream. For when the signifiers are achieved, the markers are made higher in the constant engagement between psychical libidinal and material political economies.

What transpires, then, for most Filipinos doing overseas work is the issue of domesticity. The national body is transformed for domestic-related transnational work, like electronics, garments, entertainment, medicine, and so on that uses nimble fingers, perfect eyesight, and sexualized labor—all informing the further feminization of migrant work.[19] And indeed, the larger percentage of persons working or seeking work abroad has increasingly been female. Furthermore, the necessity of transmuting signifiers of modernity into the national space invokes domesticity. The body and the home become figures of female work space, where the signifiers of modernity are to be encased. Female-work cycle begins and ends in the home. The cycle begins with home-related work overseas, and ends with the return in the homeland with the purchase and display of the markers of modernity.

The transformation of the body is evoked in the influx of some 220,000 Filipinos in Japan. These are mostly women, working as entertainers, and comprising the biggest single international minority inside Japan. The female body type is objectified: young, able bodies performing entertainment and sex-related work, willing to be of service to Japanese male professionals. A more recent phenomenon is the exodus of transgendered individuals, and male entertainers. On the one hand, the national body for export is readied through social conditioning in the homeland. With some eight hundred thousand college graduates annually, there is no place else to find work but abroad. Lacking technological skills for advancement, the body is used for home-related work. Sex and home work, tourism and entertainment provide hospitable spaces for Filipino migrant work. Filipina domestic helpers keep middle-class and affluent Singapore and Hong Kong residences intact. The Asian hotel circuit is filled with Filipino bands, mimicking in perfect diction and rhythm American popular music. In the 1970s, Japanese male tourists went to Manila and Bangkok for sex tours; now the service is provided in pockets of Japan's metropolis, with Filipinas comprising two-thirds of *Japayukis*.[20] On the other hand, the demand for exportable bodies is precisely made for domestic work, caused by the instantaneous vacation of women in advanced economies where they are also encouraged to do professional work. The national body, therefore, supports the growing economies of advanced countries. In Japan, male professionals regularly visit entertainment clubs where Filipinas perform work, in order to relieve themselves of work-related tensions. Filipina bodies are used to unwind the Japanese male professionals; male leisure translates as more work for othered women.

Migrant work is seductive because it offers the possibility of getting what one wants. "What one wants" is the marker of modern and cosmopolitan life, the acquisition of which becomes more likely

working abroad than working in the homeland. For most Filipinas working in Japan, the signifiers of modernity include a large-screen colored television, video cassette recorder, handy video camera, jewelry, stuffed toys, trendy fashion, education diplomas for loved ones, refrigerator, stove, and so on. These signifiers technologize the domestic sphere; and so, the body that is technologized for domestic work becomes the body that generates new technologies for the domestic sphere. The economic and social terrains become conducive to Japanese imports. And it is this bombardment of technological innovations that is played up in the global localization of Japanese popular culture in the Philippines.

Local reception of Japanese children's shows involves a reworking on two levels: the level of corporate production, which includes the transformation of shows that are dubbed in colloquial Filipino, the national language, and the marketing of show-related products; and the level of individual reception, which includes the production of newer localized meanings that are negotiated and that may or may not be attuned to corporate hegemony. The interfacing of the individual with local and global business allows for newer social relations to develop and unfold. For the most part, the production of meanings is centered on profit, mass consumption, and audience compliance. This leaves very little room for individual agency, especially as to how children are positioned in the social hierarchy.

The succeeding section will focus on the elaboration of corporate meanings as in dialogue with the larger production of social and cultural hegemony. There are four types of Japanese children's shows in the Philippines. The most popular exhibit high production and technological values, and combine mythical and contemporary locations. Others are *Dragonball Z, Zenki, Ranma 1/2, Sailor Moon*, and *Power Rangers*. It also includes shows such as *Super Boink, Dragon Quest, The Slayers, Ghost Fighter, Magic Knight Rayearth* and *Jiban*. These are fast-paced shows that use a greater number of animation cell drawings for quick, smooth movements, and harness stylized editing and overall production. There are also shows that combine live action with animation, with Caucasian actors playing heroes in the live segments: *Bioman, Maskman, VR Troopers*, and *Jetman*. There are also shows loosely adapted from literature: the *Little Women* series, *Koseidon, Zorro, Ang Mahiwagang Kwintas* (The Enchanted Necklace), *Time Quest*, and *Mga Munting Pangarap ni Romeo* (Romeo's Little Dreams). Lastly, there are the shows that deal with contemporary concerns of the young, such as basketball in *Slam Dunk*.

The first two types of shows invoke the construction of fantasy in the technologization of children's working bodies. The constant exposure of superheroes to conflict, action, near defeat, eventual triumph, and more, suggests the unending and unyielding system of movement and labor by children. Considered morally but not psycho- logically mature, these children never cease in their work to defend their society at all costs. Such costs include the wanton destruction of nature and public property. Tensions do arise from two orchestrated temporal events in children's televisual lives: the incompatibility to work with the labor collective, and the misplaced prioritization of personal rather than professional life. Their primary assets are not their superpowers, but their willingness to work in a group and their genuine sincerity to defend their social value system. Their enemies are represented as adult-looking creatures who have lost their innocence, and who thus are either jaded or childish.

Children's bodies are represented with endless movement and action, engaged in a continuous work program. Their personal lives, which include studying, friendship, heterosexual and family relations, are abruptly abridged in favor of performing their larger social mission. They are at the beck and call of hegemonic society. In the semi-animated shows, the children-heroes in the live segment are distinguished from their peers by their semblance of normality. In contrast, their colleagues are nerds, bullies, and other marginals.

Fig. 3: *Little Women*

Regular bodies are retechnologized by having them clothed in sleek, flashy colored costumes, and imbuing them with strength, super-powers, and skill. In their transformation, the faces are hidden under masks; their bodies' significance is known only through their specific superpower and function in the collective's schema of defense strategy and tactics, and through color-coded costumes. Their task is always to defend their social universe, represented by a moral value system that paves the way to their eventual triumph. They are guided by a moral and technological higher spirit. In *Power Rangers*, the heroes are guided by a luminous face inside a giant tube; the spirit brings the variation to the mission in perspective.

In the series, their enemies are a family of apocalyptic-looking creatures. The group always triumphs in the end, for enemies lack the moral foresight, collective effort, and genuine sincerity in their desire to conquer the world. The threat comes from foreign bodies, from extraneous geographies. Worldly threats are considered minimal and manageable; the real threat to society comes from its peripheries. Their mission, therefore, involves a clear demarcation of proper spaces: containment of peripheries to protect the center. The intrusion of foreign bodies requires a flushing out operation that maintains the status quo protected, a situation nostalgic of Cold War rhetoric and strategies. The paradox, however, is clearly poised: such containment is never complete as foreign bodies continue to intrude and pervade the center's space, leaving ample room for another round of missions for succeeding shows. The sado-masochist relation is apparent in the manichean ethics of the Japanese popular animation series. The struggle never ceases; the moral triumph is never fully attained; the heroes, as well as the villains, continually work.

The semi-animated, semi-live format represents a clear-cut negotiation of at least two realities: the domestic and the profes-sional. The popular animated series, however, blurs the realities, invoking simultaneity in the experience of personal and professional missions. What the literary-based shows do is to invoke education as the primary socialization mechanism for children. In these shows, the children are always lectured by adults for their misplaced adven-turism, ignorance, ineptness, and so on. Education becomes a peda-gogical apparatus for preparing children to have adult behavior and the social environment. Shows dealing with the contemporary youth's life evoke a similar pedagogical imperative. *Slam Dunk*, for example, teaches sportsmanship and racial tolerance. What is also normalized is access to education in the learning of such ideology. There exists in the series a group of young and affluent street thugs, visually represented with long hair, black fashion, and motorcycles, and deemed never to succeed in social contradictions that involve the moral good. Such moral perspectives can only be learned through integration in the social institutions. What is more insidious in these shows is the use of dubbing that places the national in the service of the transnational. Modernity's syntax and language are nationalized through the dubbing of shows that exhibit the modern and postmodern experience.

Paranoia over the loss of the child's organic body is produced in the shows. Panic is constantly produced and disseminated through a moral conflict and the battle for the moral good. The normal child disappears, to be replaced by the technologized body of the working child. What is produced in the shows is a hysteria over movement and containment: Who has access to its enforcement? How, and for how long? Paranoia over the loss of the organic child is used to flush out foreign elements into their properly segregated places. Losing the proper place of the organic child's body is tolerated for the advancement of the moral experience. This experience with the moral good is likened to the modern and postmodern experience— with spiritual, technological, and affluent experiences come a social goof, acculturating individuals toward hard work and perseverance that push forward social life itself, promising unimaginable mobility and wealth within everyone's reach.

Filipinos' attraction to Japanese cartoon superheroes is perpetuated at the historical juncture when the Philippine economy takes off and flies, albeit still poorly compared to its Southeast Asian counterparts. Children's bodies are used as vectors of this economic gain, especially as the Philippines-as-basket case was represented by the "sick man of Asia" image. With the economic upsurge, the sick man image is dissolved in favor of vigor and vibrancy represented by children's bodies. In the 1996 Asia Pacific Economic Council (APEC) meeting in Manila, the government-produced television trailer involves a music video of the locally-recorded APEC tune, sung by a child from an affluent political family and interspersed with images of the president's trips abroad, young children, assembly line workers, and economic zones. It also includes Lea Salonga's triumph in the Tony awards, and international fashion model Anna Bayle. The proliferation of the presidential body's presence in the company of international political luminaries invokes a body in constant movement. And indeed, President Fidel Ramos is the most widely traveled Philippine president, having some thirty foreign trips to his record aimed at generating more foreign investments in the country. Some of the audio-visual representations of Ramos's development thrusts are the words "Philippines 2000" painted on roofs of new school buildings, the notable thumbs up sign also flashed by celebrity endorsers, and its reiteration in political speeches given throughout the country. Young children represent the promise of affluence being generated by assembly line workers in booming economic zones. Salonga and Bayle become the quintessential Philippine export of bodies—Salonga victorious in the multinational casting of *Miss Saigon* in London and New York theaters, and Bayle as a fashion model to haute couture designers. Salonga also started as a child actor in repertory productions before making it big in the multi-million-dollar theater production.

Japanese animation superheroes become condensed signifiers of the present national predicament. Their figures allow for the varied inscription of newer social relations, representing idealized bodies that configure the promise of affluence and transnationality, even as the economic boom exacts a heavier price from the historically marginalized individuals and sectors. Japan becomes the imagined model of economic and technological national transformation in its endless use of technological power to protect the present economic environment. Technology has proliferated in the national system that demands the infusion of newer and better forms for transnational operations. In the process, the domestic sphere is also being technologized; but domesticating technology, ironically, only produces the need to generate greater technology. With newer transformations being worked out in the national system, technology becomes an apparatus of individual and social oppression and liberation. For the historically disenfranchised, more technology means more work for and greater requirements on their already oppressed bodies. For the ruling class, more technology means less work, more leisure.

The fascination with Japanese animated series is further inflected by the middle-class desire to imbibe ideology in the further acquisition of its material embodiment. The proliferation and successful dissemination of show-related products produce a further global localization of modern desire. *Dragonball Z* has even commissioned a musical concert to honor the television series. These products, after all, deal with all aspects of modern childhood existence—film, fashion, school supplies, toys, food, game shows, music, and television segments. The inaccessibility of these products produces a temporal lack in the organic being of modern children. The children's bodies learn to dream modernity early on, using their bodies to signify the modern shift. As the child's body becomes a

KEYWORDS

symptom of modernity, so, too, does it become a receptacle of modernity's symptoms. On the one hand, the children's bodily development signifies a turn to modern science, technology, and consumerism. On the other hand, the children's bodies also embody the markers of modernity—brand-name fashion, peripherals, lotion, cologne, jewelry, and so on.

This is the middle-class fantasy for Filipino children. Plagued with malnutrition, common diseases, and poor living conditions, Filipino children, like overseas contract workers, are socially conditioned to idealize such a middle-class fantasy of modernity. But unlike the overseas contract workers, the children have no agency in buying themselves into the business of modernity. What then is aimed by the simulacra of modernity in Japanese animated shows is children's socialization toward the ideology and praxis of modernity. Regardless of whether children are gifted with show-related products, they are always already acculturalized to think, feel, and act modern. What can also be generated from children's socialization into modernity is their future readiness to be exported as part of the overseas contract work trade. The link is uncanny. However, when realized through the participation of the Philippines and Filipinos in the global and sexual division of labor, such a link is altogether crucial in the economic survival and take-off of the nation.

Children, as poised by no less than national hero, Jose P. Rizal, are "the hope of the nation." Such a saying has become part of the national popular culture. I believe that such a positioning of children has inspired a middle-class reaction of concern for the safety and wellbeing of children, a reaction that continues to precipitate in the present cultural discourse of philanthropy. "Bantay Bata" (Safeguard the Children), an initiative of the nation's largest media conglomerate, ABS-CBN Foundation, seeks to uphold children's rights and welfare. One of the trailers produced for this purpose is a collage of children, from various socio-cultural and ethnic backgrounds, each child enunciating the various international rights of children. Another project includes a 24-hour hotline to report cases of child abuse. Bantay Bata also has projects for the benefit of street children, children of *lahar*-ravaged sites, and victims of sexual abuse. It also sets up day-care centers. What Bantay Bata effects is not the safeguarding of children but the surveillance of the discourse on children. ABS-CBN also actively promotes of children's educational shows in the Philippines, and advocates similar programming in Southeast Asia. While being pedagogical in nature, these shows, however, highlight the liberal agenda for nation-building—glorification of the nation's historical and imagined past, in the context of the centennial of Philippine independence, and its heroes. All these developments are somewhat attuned to the present direction of liberal nation-building, of Ramos's Philippines 2000 that seeks global competitiveness for local industries and products, the liberalization, privatization, and commercialization of public services. The family that owns ABS-CBN has taken serious participation in these new government offerings.

The discourse of children is supported by the discourse of philanthropy. It is intended to eradicate refuse in the channels of capital. The management of street children reflects the desire of business to contain, at least from public view, the condition that development is not for all. Like most Third World nations, the Philippines' uneven development has taken its toll on women and children. The constant movement of rural people into cities and global sites has generated an army of surplus bodies. Children suffer the most because they are forced into selling their labor cheaply, or even work for free. In other words, the social condition has already acculturated children into work, as child labor goes unabated in the country. Street children, therefore, do not fit into the category of working children. They represent the future threat to business, as the present rise of kidnapping, carnapping, murder, rape, extortion and other criminal cases would indicate. The support for street children presents a demarcation of proper places and behavior, attuned to the missions undertaken by child superheroes in Japanese animated shows. Street children also represent the failure of a liberal state to care for its wards. What then is being undertaken in the philanthropy to children, especially to street children, is the eradication of potential perpetrators of crime, the potential eradication of proper sites and behavior. Because of the failure of the family set-up, the philanthropic institution introduces street children into the notion of citizenship for nation-building by giving temporal access to its rewards: food, education, shelter, clothing, and so on. In other words, the philanthropic institution has taken on the state function, devoid of civil interests; what is being privileged here is private interest as disseminated, expectedly, through media. The language of philanthropy, therefore, is not spoken without a corresponding visual object.

The present management of children redounds to the future management of the nation. Hegemony's desire to control "wayward" children posits a desire for greater movement, a sustenance of pursuit and accomplishment of dreams of modernity. In Japan, as Hase's case shows, the violent crimes committed on children disturb the national status quo, and destabilize the accumulation of wealth. In

the Philippines, the caretaking of "wayward" children becomes itself
the agent of disturbance; as a country so unused to easily acquired
sustained wealth begins to consider dreams of modernity, harboring
desires for continuous flight and take-off. As nothing comes in the
way of capital, the management of children becomes an imperative, if
not of the state, then of business. Children become both the object of
modern desire and its abjection.

In an episode of *Ang Mahiwagang Kwintas*, John is locked up
inside a cabin in a submarine. He does not know what he and his
girlfriend are doing there. They explore the submarine for possible
answers, but to no avail. In the process, they endanger the crew and
passengers of the submarine. The submarine remains submerged
at the bottom of the sea, avoiding an enemy ship. In the ending, the
submarine surfaces, and John's airplane appears. A woman, dressed
like a mother, instructs them how to land on an island borne by the
aircraft. The children leave the submarine.

The child learns the discipline to manage, on an individual level,
hysteria. Though made the overriding principle in Japanese popular
culture, hysteria is considered subversive; excessive pleasure and
disgust need to be managed. Paranoia seeps in, allowing for the reverberation of national hysteria in the individual. Both hysteria and its
disciplining mechanism, paranoia, are embodied in children. Both
Japan and the Philippines place much weight on children's socialization via education, albeit differentially. In Japan, the child is educated
to be prepared to take over the management of a wealthy economy.
Any disturbance upsets the ecological shape of business. In the
Philippines, the child is educated precisely to get them off the street.
Without assurance that it could carry on the sustained economic
growth, business and the state cover all possible grounds within their
limited reach to manage the nation's future.

Children are made to embody the nation's future, where the
global and the local are interfaced to sustain dreams and realities of
affluence. Japan, for the Philippines, becomes the model of realizing
the dream of modernity. But even as the Philippines begins to feel its
sustained development, its conversion of the dream is held and felt
differently, one that places a high moral premium on the surveillance
of children for work. "Wayward" children, then, are hysterically
poised in society, needing liberal love and attention.

Japanese children's shows in the Philippines become objects of
identification, not only for children, but also for the liberal state. For
in these shows, the heroes ride high, travel far and wide; the heroes
always triumph; the heroes never totally fall. Devoid of historicity, the

shows perplex business and the state into dreams of modernity, like the sudden sustained economic take-off and development, in ways unimaginably attainable by all. Still part of the fantasy package, the nation hopes that such unimaginability and unattainability will eventually redound not to the present generation but to the future generation, more acculturalized and socialized toward becoming recipients of the dream. Both in the present and future generations, children are already being positioned to harbor and realize the eventual, real economic flight.

Thus, any move to uplift the status of children needs to consider positions whereby children embody themselves. By this, I refer to two considerations: a critique of orthodoxy of the discourse on children, and a consideration of agency among children. The positioning of children and the discourse on children needs to be challenged, posing the ideological stake in such emplacement of children—for whom? As the analysis of Japanese children's shows and other integral children's programs have shown, the primacy of vested state and private businesses dominates the discourse. Children's rights and welfare, while proving vital to the cause of children, need to be reconceptualized to consider agency among children. Children are not only to be gifted with rights and welfare by social institutions, they also need to be considered for their capacity to substantially contribute to the shaping and substantiation of society.

The dominant ideology of children is interested to perpetuate children and childhood as phases toward some idealized maturity. Like the related discourse on censorship and national development, children are oftentimes positioned as wards waiting to be socialized into the adult business of national development. The seemingly forward-looking agenda, however, remains passive and static, as children remain integral to the perpetuation of conservative and timeless national ideals.

Herein lies the hegemonic desire to place children in the service of someone else's interests. Children need to embody themselves. This means that they realize their childhood in creative and critical ways that underscore their rights and welfare. Realizing their childhood needs to be undertaken in the present tense, in the now, and not in some unmapped past or unmappable future. To paraphrase the national hero, "Children *are* the nation."

KEYWORDS

Research for this essay was made possible through a fellowship from the Institute of International Legal Relations, College of Law, University of the Philippines. I am grateful to Rolando de la Cruz, Rommel Rodriguez, and Miki Adachi for their support and assistance.

1   Associated Press, "Kobe Nightmare: Letter-Writer Lays Claim to Beheading," *Philippine Daily Inquirer*, 7 Jun 1997, 12.

2   Reuters, "Japan Teener Confesses to Beheading of Schoolboy," *Philippine Daily Inquirer*, 39 Jun 1997, 12.

3   Ned Lukacher, "The Epistemology of Disgust," *Hysteria from Freud to Lacan: Body and Language in Psychoanalysis,* ed. David Menard (Ithaca: Cornell University Press, 1989), vii.

4   Setsuko Inoue, quoted in Jeffrey Bartholet, "Innocence for Sale," *Newsweek*, 23 Dec 1996, 15.

5   Associated Press, "Kobe Nightmare," 12.

6   Ibid.

7   See Norma Field, "The Child as Laborer and Consumer: The Disappearance of Childhood in Contemporary Japan," *Children and the Politics of Culture* (Princeton: Princeton University Press, 1995), 51–78, and Arita Michio and Yamaoka Shunsuke, "The 'Over-Worthy Child' Syndrome," *Asahi Journal*, 20 Mar 1992, 11–16.

8   Arita and Yamaoka, cited in Field, "Child as Laborer and Consumer," 53.

9   Ibid., 54.

10 Field, "Child as Laborer and Consumer," 60.

11 Ibid.

12 Kay Itoi, "The Game of Horror," *Newsweek*, 9 Jun 1977, 16.

13 Ibid.

14 Monique David-Menard, *Hysteria from Freud to Lacan* (Ithaca: Cornell University Press, 1989).

15 Lukacher, "Epistemology of Disgust," xi.

16 Jacques Lacan, quoted in Lukacher, "Epistemology of Disgust," vii.

17 Ian Buruma, quoted in Jose Manuel Tesoro, "Asia Says Japan is Top of the Pops," *Asiaweek*, 5 Jan 1996, 37.

18 Tesoro, "Japan is Top of the Pops," 37.

19 I talk about female migrant domestic work in "Bodies, Letters, Catalogs: Filipinas in Transnational Space," *Diliman Review* 45, no. 1 (1997): 51–67.

20 *Japayuki* is a euphemism for a foreign female sex worker in Japan.

Sovereignty
Japanese Animation
and Filipina
Comfort Women

I n 1992, when *Lola* Rosa Henson publicly announced that she was a comfort woman, unsympathetic people questioned her motives. One woman journalist interpreted the act as a publicity stunt to earn money; neighbors teased her granddaughter about her prowess to "service battalions of soldiers."[1] Even the head of the body tasked by the Presidential Commission on Human Rights to look into the case issued a report stating that he sees "no large-scale forced prostitution by the Japanese during the Second World War."[2] This conclusion he based on "interviews and research on diaries, official documents and guerilla newspapers."[3] Such insensitivity, though not in all cases, is institutionally grounded. After all, why would anyone desire the need to construct a residual identity, especially enmeshed in trauma, patriarchy, and militarism? Why would one attempt to out oneself to an identity relegated to, if not obscured in, the margins of history? Why would one need to articulate the trauma from an "I" point of view, as Lola Rosa does of her account of incarceration in a Japanese comfort zone? She says:

I lay on the bed with my knees up and my feet on the mat, as if I were giving birth. Whenever the soldiers did not feel satisfied, they vented their anger on me. Every day, there were incidents of violence and humiliation. When the soldiers raped me, I felt like a pig. Sometimes they tied up my right leg with a waist band or a belt and hung it on a nail in the walls as they violated me.[4]

Lola Rosa's hideous past was something new to the public, but the novelty wore off as more elderly women told similar tales—the horrors, secrecy, the political and personal need to come out in the open. The identity is openly displayed only to be relegated once more to the margins as nations and institutions fail to recognize such an identity. In the first place, why is there a need to come out?

The Filipino comfort women's struggle for identity presents a counter-model to the kind of transformative identity and subjectivity narrativized in Japanese animation. While characters in Japanese animation draw their power precisely from transformations of identity—the otherwise ordinary youth are transformed into brightly-costumed superheroes in *Mighty Morphin Power Rangers*, for example—comfort women are debilitated by the prolonged institutional maneuvers to "yet-to-transform" or delay their already marked identity. What is common between comfort women and Japanese animation characters is the use of sexuality to mobilize and demobilize identity formation. Though there is an attempt to neutralize or blur gender distinction in Japanese animation, such attempts get nominalized in the sexual division of superpower labor. In *Mighty Morphin Power Rangers*, male and female characters are color-coded and distinguished by the kind of masculine and feminine superpowers in the collective set-up. Japanese animation characters, therefore, are sexualized in order for power to bequeath identity unto them. Meanwhile, Filipino comfort women are withdrawn of sexual identity, and thus, they lose the power to articulate other forms of identity in their quest for remembrance and justice. Media representations of comfort women, after all, present a paradox of disbelief. For how can these women, now aged, claim to service as many as thirty Japanese soldiers? Lying with the institutional discourse of aging, the aged Filipinas are supposed to be devoid of any sexuality. What is generated in the media, then, is a double othering of Filipino comfort women based on their sexuality, or lack of it, in media texts. These media representations are signified by a betrayal of past history and present physiology. Firstly, their ghastly experience during World War II is now a historical relic annihilated by Japanese capital's newer significance in the country. In other words, the by-phrase right now is capital-sex configuration as represented by the fifty thousand Filipino contract workers in Japan doing entertainment work. Secondly, their present physiology of aging bodies contradict the cultural consciousness of asexuality, wisdom, and respect.

Such kinds of representation filter into popular and intellectual consciousness. As abominable subjects, the figure of the comfort woman is the historical and social accident, imminent in, yet marginal to, the narratives of World War II and postwar eras. Their historical and physiological dislocation from the materiality of their conditions provides a disjuncture of misrecognition in both popular and intellectual cultures. Earlier on, they are transformed into isolated objects of humor in unsaid popular consciousness, while becoming negligible objects of history in intellectual consciousness. But the emerging figure of the comfort woman in the public sphere within the last six years entails a claim to great historical consciousness. The comfort woman represents a block claim to history similar to Filipino World War II veterans or *manong* (male) immigrants to the U.S.

In this essay, I posit the notion of sovereign nations as an unequivalence of sovereign subjects. The nation may be constructed as sovereign, and so are its ideal subjects, the citizens. However, the emergence of newer identities, such as the figure of the comfort woman, belie the national project of identity formation. As not all of us fit well into the model of the citizen, the emergence of newer identities presents us with historically and institutionally marginalized and disempowered experience. Thus, newer subjectivities attempt to grapple with non-institutional experiences, such as displacement, oppression, diaspora, exile, residual, and emergent experiences, which in turn present counter-models of community and nation formation.

I discuss first the notion of subjectivity as especially distinguished from the national project of citizenship. I proceed to show how subjectivity via sexuality is pedagogically constructed in Japanese animation, especially in the show *Ranma ½*. The last section discusses the counter-construction of newer identities by discussing the figure of the Filipino comfort woman and her institutional lack of sexuality. The on-going court case in Tokyo, based on the class suit filed by Filipino comfort women, attests to the national legal culture that arbitrarily heralds and shuns sexuality as embodiment of historical identity and reality. The essay is intended to draw connections between seemingly unrelated entities, as a way of prefiguring the debates surrounding the present national and communitarian cultures on identity and subject formation. It is only through the thinking of disjunctive and conjectural relations that institutional and counter-institutional forces are deconstructed, made into understandable realities that seem to hold sway of our past, present, and future individual and national lives.

Subjects, Subjectivation, and Subjectification

Scholarship on subjectivity has focused primarily on macro-notions of state security and sovereignty.[5] Though such discussions are apt and useful, I veer toward a micro discussion of sovereignty, though one grounded in history, geography, and modernity. Only when the individual is constituted as sovereign will the issue of security be dually an issue and a non-issue. On the one hand, it becomes an issue insofar as the material conditions for the sovereign subject are democratized and, therefore, made attainable to the greatest number of people. The quest for sovereignty of subjects is anchored in realizing the materiality that brings forth the sovereign subjects. Issues are therefore poised as either threat or contribution to the subjects' materiality. On the other hand, it becomes a non-issue when both the subjects' sovereignty and materiality are no longer threatened. Security becomes a non-issue. Before we can talk of security, we must first examine the notion of sovereignty.

The subjects are the individuals constituted by the forces of history, geography, and modernity. They are transformed by such forces even as they transform those forces. When pedagogical forces successfully shape and substantiate the subjects, they become citizens, the ideal subjects of the nation. When the subjects transform themselves into some identities other than the ego-ideal of the subjects of the nation, they become contrary subjects. Though still enmeshed in the hegemonic forces, they nonetheless renegotiate an alternative subjectivity. These subjects, however, warrant newer ways toward citizenship, a position that is bestowed by the nation-state's recognition and concern for welfare. On the one hand, newer identities are historically constructed. On the other hand, new alternative identities are also constituted in the process.

Subjection or subjugation refers to the modes by which the forces of the nation-state impose their will through force and consent on its subjects. It refers to the institutional as well as historical forces and practices in which the ideals of the nation-state's subject are produced. While subjection refers to the hegemonic forces that shape and substantiate the subjects, subjectivation refers to the coming-into-being of the subjects—how the subjects produce themselves in spite of and despite the influence or control of the hegemonic forces. Subjectivation is the process by which the terms and resulting subjectivity are interpellated by repressive and ideological state apparatuses. Subjectivation is always in dialogue with and contrary to the larger forces that produce it. The subjects choose an image and substance either more attuned to the hegemonic or contrary notions of the citizens. Subjectivity and citizenship are positions always in a flux, even as the historical, geographical, and modern forces are already foregrounded in their formation.

It is notable that subjection's effects are always uneven. Patronage politics in the Philippines interpolates the majority—the historically disenfranchised—into citizenry largely through elections as voting subjects. For the most part, the masses are disenfranchised into citizenship. No other presidency in recent history has more overtly and unjustifiably used the masses than Joseph "Erap" Estrada's in the campaign for and maintenance of the Philippine presidency. With the largest winning margin in postwar national elections, Estrada campaigned with a personalistic pro-people agenda. In power, however, more favors have been dispensed to big businesses and former Marcos cronies than to the masses who are still evicted out of their shanty homes and who bear the brunt of the economic crisis. Citizenship in the Philippines is a highly classed, sexualized, genderized, and politicized issue.

Thus, other modes of citizenship through newer subjectivities need to be sought. Subjectivation is the ongoing negotiation between the hegemonic forces that produce the ideal citizen and the initiatives from below that recodify and renegotiate such hegemonic processes. It refers to both how the codes of the ideal citizen are retransformed, and how newer subjectivities emerge in these negotiations.

Ranma ½ and the Mobilization of Sexuality in Citizenship

Japanese animation provides a vocabulary to articulate the historical, social, and modern forces that shape the present time's kinds of consciousness.[6] First, it has reached global proportions. Japanese animation is a global commodity whose consumption generates a USD 15 billion business. Together with portable appliances, pop music, software games, and various branded products with popular characters (such as those of Sanrio's), animation has helped to globalize or glocalize Japan and Japanese-ness in the world market.[7] As Koichi Iwabuchi theorized about Japanese glocalization, animation, like other Japanese popular cultural products, is poised as culturally odor free, allowing for various national cultures to divergently and locally reinterpret and rework the product.[8] Japanese animation, like Japanese hegemony, has been globalized locally. From this statement, we can decipher two things: first, like individual subjectivity, Japanese animation is renegotiated by the various local cultures even as this is forced upon them; second, like national identity, animation is an allegory of or at the very least provides a fantasy scenario to present Japanese culture.

The second significance of Japanese animation is that it provides an analogue to the postmodern predicament in two ways. First, Japan becomes the model of cultural formation based on economic prosperity. With most of Asia still working at economic prosperity, Japan's excess national wealth, despite the ongoing crisis, is still to be envied, not unlike the Freudian penis envy. Japan still yields the largest capital surplus, which, for most nations, remains a fantasy ideal in national economic management. And in the present discourse of the economic crisis, all hopes are pinned on Japan's relenting of its surplus to rescue the region, if not the world, from its present dismal situation. Japan's generally national postmodernism is, for the most part, Asia's fantasy of modernism. Developing countries in Asia have limited access to a middle-class spending culture. The production of scarce sovereign subjects also yields a threat to the stability of the rest of society who have reaped the capital surplus. What is then produced locally, as in the Philippines, are pockets of postmodern sites like Makati and Ortigas, pockmarked by contradictions of surplus capital not fully grounded. The proliferation of First World entertainment and service sector establishments coexists with the Third World army of informal sector and services. With the increasing economic significance of Japan to the Philippines, Japan becomes a model of economic and cultural development—what the Philippines aspires itself to be. Given the nature of Filipino pride, the Philippines only looks up to the United States in terms of patronage and ideals.

Second, the narrative content of Japanese animation builds on the images of postmodern development. The characters of *shonen* (for boys), *shoujo* (for girls), and *tokusatsu* (live action with heavy special effects) animation genres have at least dual social identities. Even as normal persons, the characters in the mentioned animation

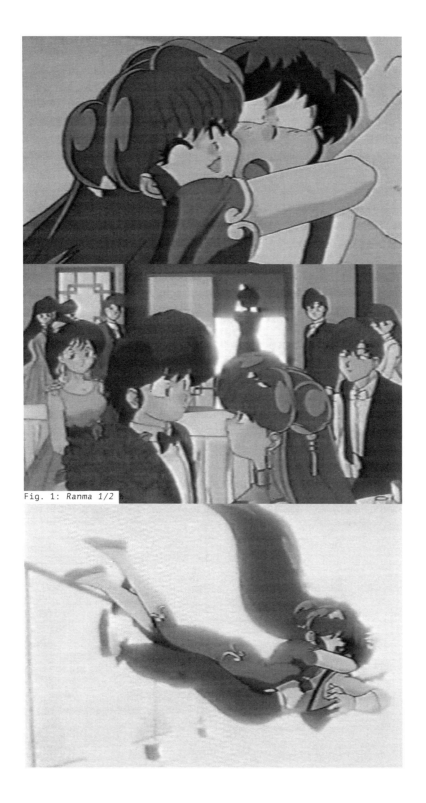

Fig. 1: *Ranma 1/2*

genres have two sets of people to deal with, and consequently two modes of behavior—first, within the social group of superheroes they belong to, and second, the community outside the group. As superheroes, the characters have even tougher, logistically speaking, existences—for they contend with secret identities, costumes, super-powers, and the fight against evil forces that threaten the community and nation. Unlike American comic heroes, specifically those of DC Comics, most Japanese characters work within a rigidly defined social hierarchy that involves a high command of superior wisdom and segmentation of power and roles. The sum power is greater than combined individual powers.

Such characters dwell on insurmountable kineticism. They move across vast spaces at very minimal time; they are on call twenty-four hours a day; they exhibit, even as their normal selves, the qualities of a superhero; they willingly transform their individual mistakes into assets for the glory of the group, despite all odds. These character-istics of Japanese superheroes are emblematic of the postmodern era—where identity is no longer monolithic but always produced in relation to other social beings, and where the subject's kinetic energy prefigures the equally insurmountable movement of capital, goods, and people.

What is interesting in this kind of postmodernism is its diver-gence from Western paradigms of postmodernism. While the West optimistically celebrates, pessimistically withholds sanction, or critically engages in the entry of and diversity in postmodernism, Japanese postmodernism, as represented in its animation, remains highly moralistic and legalistic. What differentiates the normal self from the superhero self of the character is access to a greater military arsenal. What unites both selves is the recurring theme of moral and legal good in the fight against the evil threat. In other words, in this postmodern era where evil can strike anywhere, anytime, the char-acter's cause-for-being remains deeply grounded on the institutional forces such as the government, as represented by the superior being that guides the team, and community, as represented by the team work.

This is the reason why I think that Japanese animation is a peda-gogical tool for national identity formation. For one thing, animations meant to cater to children have reached audiences far beyond the intended age group. For another, what is being generated in Japanese animation is a continuity of traditions even in the present postmodern time, a desire for the reconstitution of the moral and legal fiber even in an age where these are easily trampled on the kineticism of capital.

K
E
Y
W
O
R
D
S

However, using this classical paradigm, Japanese animation renarrativizes modes of national identity formation. These modes valorize the historical and institutional forces that make the world a better place for everyone. Somewhere in these modes is the use of sexuality as a mobilizing and demobilizing agent of identity formation, even in transhistorical times and transcultural settings.

Ranma ½ is an animated adaptation of the original comic series by Rumiko Takahashi. The series features the travails of the title character, Ranma, who endures a Chinese curse that transforms him into a woman whenever he is doused with cold water. In order to change back into a male, Ranma must be doused with hot water. Sexuality is mobilized to create the dominant and marginal figures of the superhero. In the OAV[9] episode "Desperately Seeking Shampoo" (1997),[10] Shampoo, a Chinese woman, openly displays affection for the normal Ranma, the masculine self. Ranma disavows the affections, but changes his mind when Shampoo suddenly and more aggressively disowns him. What caused Shampoo's sudden rejection of Ranma, the man she has been chasing all this time?

Cologne, Shampoo's great-grandmother, is cleaning her personal jewelry collection, when Shampoo walks in on her. Cologne tells Shampoo to take any piece of jewelry she wants. Shampoo decides to take a brooch. Only when Shampoo becomes possessed by the brooch does Cologne realize that it is the cursed Reversal Jewel. The brooch is powerful in two ways—in its upright position, it reinforces genuine unconditional love, but inverted, it heightens hatred for the other. Eager to see Shampoo marry, Cologne conspires to use the Reversal Jewel's powers in order to make Ranma chase after Shampoo. Despite his efforts to woo Shampoo, Ranma is overshadowed by the possessed woman's power. He fears the loss of power over women. In an accident where Shampoo's brooch is displaced, Ranma is caught in a compromising position with Shampoo. The crowd thinks that Ranma forced himself on Shampoo. Believing that love is a battle, Ranma decides to finally declare his love for Shampoo in the hope of winning the sex war. Shampoo realizes the brooch's power, and decides to be quiet right when Ranma is about to confess to her. Witnesses hide under the table, in a bid to catch Ranma's pronouncement. Ranma then realizes his genuine love for Akane, his fiancée. Right before Ranma confesses to Shampoo, Akane shows up and declares she loves Ranma. This is due to the Reversal Jewel, which was placed on Akane by a Chinese man named Mousse (who is childhood friends with, and also in love with Shampoo) in order to foil Ranma's plan. Cologne notices the Reversal Jewel on Akane's head, and removes it

184

from Akane right when Ranma makes a comment about how Akane is cute under her tomboy exterior. Akane, no longer possessed by the Reversal Jewel, is insulted by Ranma's comment, and punches Ranma out of a window. As Ranma wonders what happened, he gets clobbered by jealous male antagonists. The last scene takes place in the hospital where Ranma is plastered from head to foot, and the members visit him to affirm his place in the community.

Ranma's male sexuality dominates female sexuality. Both sexualities possess the same ability to change genders, and the only things codified to distinguish the male and female sexualities are Ranma's height, hips, waist, stature, voice pitch, hair color, and the addition of breasts, which are repeatedly panned in close-up shots in the animation. Ranma's clothes are also often depicted as larger and looser in his female state. However, Ranma's normal state is his male self. The episode represents the construction and reification of male sexuality. Precisely because it is threatened by a doubly marginal figure (the Chinese woman), male sexuality is mobilized to wage war on the sex issue, reconstituting Ranma's place in the community of elderly men, young women, and male antagonists.

Ranma, in his male state, is already distinguished as his normal self. The aberrant figure of female sexuality that temporally dislocates and dominates his identity is confined to scenes with female friends, who make fun of Ranma's nominal identity. The containment of female sexuality, whether within Ranma's dual self, in Shampoo, or in other women characters, becomes the moral and legal cause. This shows the privileging of male sexuality as the moral and legal norm. Any intrusion into this moral and legal domain becomes the rationale that justifies the ensuing battle. Ranma reinforces his identity only through subjugating other identities, those posed as threats to his own. Such a threat is represented by female sexuality, presented as an external curse in *Ranma ½*. The presence of non-Japanese characters in Japanese media remains unusual, despite the position of Japan in the transnational world. Moreover, Japan remains a highly insular place, with a small expatriate population compared to its sizable domestic population. Thus, when non-Japanese characters are represented, Chinese characters, for example, are depicted as gushing over Japanese masculinity. Furthermore, Shampoo's great-grandmother, Cologne, represents the barbarity of non-Japanese ways—using magic to trap a Japanese man to marry a non-Japanese woman.

Like Hong Kong movies that are characterized by gender-bending depictions of maleness and femaleness, Japanese animation also provides a blurring of sexual and gender constructs. However,

Japanese animation provides a more rigid reconstitution of sexual and gender divides, generally through a reinforcement of patriarchal forces. What is being emplaced in *Ranma ½* is the superiority of Japanese masculinity that necessitates a subplot of depicting national and foreign female sexuality as abnormal and needing containment. Ranma's male sexuality becomes the primordial marker of his superhero life. It is only this sexuality that actually mobilizes the logistics of militarism to contain the threat against the status quo. In the figure of Ranma, the privileging of male sexuality necessarily involves the containment of female sexuality. Furthermore, Ranma's male sexuality also distinguishes him from the threat of dominance by other races.

Hegemonic subjectivity involves the dual move of inscription and erasure. The inscription of hegemonic subjectivity entails the erasure of other subjectivities deemed as threats. Yet such threats are necessary in identity formation. The quest for selfhood involves an othering in two moves. Since the other is always signified as an object of disavowal and fascination, the self needs to marginalize and not obliterate the other in order to be subjectivized. The presence of a contained other within the control and surveillance of the self continually reinforces the subjectivity of the privileged self.

Contrary Subjectivity and Citizenship in Filipina Comfort Women

The emergence of the sovereign subject in hegemony does not dispel the simultaneous or belated emergence of contrary subjectivities. In the first place, such contrary subjects are only heralded through the same mechanism that produces the hegemonic subject. How is it possible to produce contrary subjectivities despite hegemony's maneuver to flatten, ignore, or celebrate difference? Let us make a distinction. Subjectivity of newer identities, such as the Filipino comfort woman, may emerge simultaneously with the national production of ideal subjects. However, the nation-state's recognition of various subjectivities, especially contrary subjectivities, remains the privileged mode in acquiring the benefits of citizenship. The case of the TNT (*tago nang tago*, illegal immigrant) or overseas contract workers always connotes secondary citizenship because of the host nation-state's selective recognition of such subjectivities. Thus, contrary subjectivities are always in transit to being, always in exile from a self, and therefore, constituted in diaspora. Contrary subjectivities are also always historically and materially constructed. They do not pop out of nowhere into our consciousness; their encounter with our consciousness is overdetermined by historical and material conditions that the nation is engaged in, willfully or not.

Since Lola Rosa openly declared her past on 18 September 1992, some forty women have gone public about their traumas in Japanese comfort camps. Some eighteen comfort sites have been placed, generating more historical data on the condition of comfort women during World War II. While kineticism seems to signal Japanese animation characters' coming of age, the slow grind marks the national culture's continuing erasure of comfort women subjectivity despite its emplacement already in the open. Michel Foucault's conceptualization of the dual nature of power elaborates on the continuous kind of erasure being generated to make invisible the figure of the comfort woman. The juridical function of power, as manifested in the law, is based on negation—prohibition, control, regulation, limitation, and so on.[11] It is precisely in the national legal culture that disallowed the entry of the comfort woman figure into the institutions of the nation-state. Yet Korean and Filipina comfort women have entered this gate-keeping arena, filing class suits to force the nation-state to acknowledge its experience in institutionally containing foreign female sexuality in the service of its forces during World War II. The entry into the legal battle makes clear the interrelatedness of Japanese legal culture with internationally accepted laws. The arguments of the class suit by comfort women rest on international law, such as the Hague Convention, Genocide Treaty, and the Anti-Apartheid Treaty. What the class suits have done is to put the Japanese legal institution and culture in a position where these are forced to take cognizance of laws and cultures beyond its own national territory, especially at a time when Japan has made itself believe its major role, at least, in global culture. Such gain from legal culture eventually permeates other cultural spheres such as education. In seven junior high school textbooks, there is token mention of comfort women and how these women were "treated harmfully," but there is absolutely no mention of Filipina comfort women.[12]

The other function of power is productive, wherein "subjects are themselves constructed, defined as particular kinds of subjects, and particular identities."[13] The productive function of power allows for the emergence of contrary identities that, among other things, continue to keep Japan haunted by its World War II past. In this function, power is negotiated, allowing for contrary subjects

to call into question some of the terms being forced into the negotiating table. The subjectification of comfort women allows for the
emergence of their subjectivities despite hegemonic measures to
erase such identities and national past. Along this function, newer
tactics toward identity formation are taking place, bringing the figure
of the comfort woman into the foreground.

The international network established by the Japanese military
forces in World War II is recircuited to generate solidarity among
women from the same nations in the struggle for historical and
judicial justice. The continuing advocacy of groups such as the Asian
Women Human Rights Council and LILA Pilipina also redefines
the terms of making the women's coming out institutional. These
groups have mobilized individual senators and representatives, even
city councils, to declare support for the cause of Filipina comfort
women.[14] What these tactics attempt to rework lie in the very core
of institutions and historical forces that have disenfranchised and
allowed, though belatedly, the contrary subjects to emerge. The
tactics have reworked both the juridical and the productive functions
of power to quite constructive means.

What is interesting for me is the kind of self-representation
generated by the surfacing of the comfort woman's image and subjectivity. Obliterated by history and intellectuals, the comfort woman
used her own narrative to make visible her identity. This results in
testimonial literatures, characterized by the individual's recounting of the traumatic past, her active engagement to force hegemonic
history to take cognition of such past, and her historical block claim.
The two books published on the subject of comfort women are
wholly or partly testimonial literature.[15] Not since the underground
movement has testimonial literature been similarly and productively
mobilized.

This kind of rewitnessing of history circumvents the ways in
which history has been generated. This is unique because the very
marginal forces that were taught to be subservient and nominal are
now able to acquire a speaking voice to pose counter-claims to the
institutions that have subjugated their locations. The historical
accident that generated the courage to speak always speaks from
a doubly estranged voice—estranged by fifty years of history, and
estranged by the kind of war instrumentalization (sex slavery) forced
upon the subject. The accident also generates the unique place in
which the speaking female subject reconstructs her personal, social,
historical, and gendered past. Though estranged and erased in

history, she is able to rearticulate history in some negotiable terms where she has active agency, and where the terms of history are called into question.

When one speaks using the first-person point of view, one assumes the voice of the speaking subject. Culturally, the dominant mode is to speak through the third-person. To speak through this point of view is to assume one's self in an other. To speak through the first person is to territorialize the self as a distinguished entity from other selves and others. The "I" becomes the subject of the narrative, and the retelling of history through the "I" is the emplacement of the erased subject in history. The testimonial produced is not only a recounting of the subject's past but also a re-accounting of the forces of the past, always already rearticulated in the present forces that produced the subject's invisibility.

When one speaks through the "I," one already has generated enough courage to place the trauma in some manageable, non-threatening terms. The testimonials of comfort women use a tactic condensing the traumatic past. Nine months, for example, would only occupy a paragraph of the account or a section of the book. The graphic sexual details remain, continually assaulting the reader's senses even as the account of the period of incarceration and institutional rape become, after some time, conventional. What is generated in such testimonials is a transference of subjectivity, for no reader can deny the existence of brutality and courage in the written text. What is also generated is an appeal to the national construction of identity formation. For how can the nation construct ideal citizenry when it has not grappled with its oppressive and repressive historical past? What is then being posited is a call to a common nationalism based on shared traumatic experiences. In this country, trauma is a way of life, as popular culture continually gets assaulted by the national culture.[16]

Trauma recovery becomes the life choice in the testimonials. The trauma that produced repression, even death-like acceptance of such reality, is now reworked toward its own recovery. The catalyst that produced the recovery stage is the process not only of coming out by the comfort women but the very creation of a critical public sphere produced by their outing. For if we follow the analogy of transference in testimonials, what is being posed is not only the recovery of individuals, but also the nation. What is being challenged is the very premise on which sovereign subjects have been constructed through postwar national history that negate the narratives from below. For the very acceptance of the premise, for national culture, is to assume a historical and social linkage of young Filipina identities continually being generated by Japan only through sex work—from slavery to paid sex work.

For the masculinized projection of national culture tensely negates feminization, especially one posited from the outside. Some four centuries of colonial and neocolonial rule, have already dampened the operation of national culture. National culture is always projected as masculine, and therefore can turn a blind eye to the feminization of its Filipino and Filipina workers in the global and sexual division of labor. By employing women in sex and sex-related work in Japan, or domestic work in Hong Kong and Singapore, the masculine imago of national culture is continually being emplaced. As such, the nation itself acts as a pimp by allowing migrant work, especially female and feminine, to support the national economy's recurring plight. However, the Filipino comfort woman and sex-related worker are never placed in the same category, even though both figures represent the image of the sacrificial lamb. For to allow such a continuity is mind-breaking for national culture, which prides itself on narratives of heroism and valor.

Thus the figure of the comfort woman, represented through her own testimonial, breaks the very construction of national culture. For how can national culture stand proudly when continuing victimage and struggle for justice remain unfavorably unresolved? This is why national culture, upon the surfacing of the comfort woman figure, deemed the narrative a historical relic. The attempt not to link past trauma with present cause becomes the gap that provides the nonrecognition of comfort women's claims to citizenship. Without the nation-state's acknowledgment of identity status, comfort women remain contrary subjects.

The JPY 2 million cash lump sum compensation, channeled through a private fund, and a personal letter of apology from Prime Minister Ryutaro Hashimoto fail to recognize the comfort women's struggle for forms of citizenship precisely because of the acts' nonrecognition of historical accountability. What is being generated is an acknowledgment of the present predicament of comfort women but not the historical process that produced such identities. As such, the plight of comfort women, much like their figures in contemporary representation, is considered a historical aberration. The continued denial of national subjectivity or presence in the nation's historical materiality and consciousness is a denial tied up with Japan's own denial of its aggression during World War II.

Female sexuality, as in *Ranma ½,* is like a historical curse needing proper emplacement and containment in Japanese national culture. Unlike the women of *Ranma ½,* however, comfort women's sexuality hinges on historical trauma, not on a jouissance of female youthfulness. Comfort women's present sexuality is erased, attuned to the discourse of aging. Yet sexuality—specifically, its violation—is really the rationale for reconstituting contrary subjectivity in comfort women. This same sexuality, however, is denied when the issue of claim to citizenship is brought up.

Female sexuality is further echoed in the divergence of positioning between Japanese animation and Filipina comfort women. On the one hand, Japanese animation basks in kineticism that transforms identities and sexualities instantaneously. On the other hand, Filipina comfort women struggle with the kind of static energy imposed on them by media representations, stereotypically pegged in coming out and death coverage, and in the limiting discourses of aging, patriarchy, profit, and militarism. Testimonials, however, recodify evidence of truth-claims by presenting photographs of comfort women as evidence to historical claims. There is a desire for the organic historical body in the self-representation of comfort women. Furthermore, the two local books on comfort women are also replete with illustrations, much like animation, drawn by the women themselves. What is being undertaken in these representations is a reworking of the kind of passive energy encoded for these women, primarily by media and legal culture. In the illustrations, there is a desire for emphasis and movement, a kind of generic maneuver to represent all comfort women, divergent from the iconic authenticity posed by photographs.

The testimonial is resignified by the illustrations and photographs accompanying the written text. This kind of constructionism, accounting for both the narrative and media text, is an attempt to grapple with newer technologies. Just as the women construct their own narratives, so do the media text provide a layered signification field in which the narratives permeate. Such reworking of technology presents a kind of bonding between the figure of the comfort woman and available technology. This is already prefigured in the transformative bonding generated by comfort women from various Asian sites in the present times. It also foregrounds the affinity of the comfort women with other females involved in war and nationalism, the women raped in Bosnia and Indonesia, for example.

Death and Subjectivity

Lola Rosa passed away in 1996. Of the 169 documented Filipina "comfort women," twenty-three of the women have died since April 1998.[17] Death, however, does not cease the process of identity formation. The quest has already generated a liminal historical moment—of recognition, non-recognition, and misrecognition of historical identities and accountability. This moment has already generated the mechanism toward a heroic kind of memorialization. That even in death, the subjectivity of comfort women has already surfaced even as it remains unanchored in institutional acceptance.

Unlike the identities of some Filipina mail-order brides that are divulged only through their violent deaths, usually in the hands of their foreign spouses, the comfort women's identities have surfaced through an overt historical block claim. Because of the tendency to hide their identities against public scrutiny, Filipina mail-order brides are only memorialized after their deaths, and individually, not through a collective identity. With the commencement of publicly coming out, even belatedly, the collective and historical identities and conditions of comfort women have filtered into the national culture. National culture's inability to fully grapple with such identities already marks a cohesion of the comfort women's effort at institutional recognition. They have become the scars that have yet to heal, the curse that has yet to be dispelled.

Though the comfort women's memorialization fits well in the discourse of aging and dying, it has also started shifting attitudes within Japanese legal and popular culture. In an opinion poll taken in 1992, "25 percent supported humanitarian measures for former 'comfort women' and 36 percent stood for clear-cut apology and compensation, whereas only 10 percent held 'no apology and compensation.'"[18]

As a nation continually justifies its sovereignty, so do its subjects, whether idealized or contrary, vie for sovereignty. If, in legal culture, contrary subjects are negated, then other productive engagements with power need to be established. If claims to citizenship remain an uncodifiable domain for contrary subjects, then, in the issue of human rights and justice, citizenship ought to be rethought. For how can the nation be sovereign and secure if its subjects are not?

I am grateful to Ma. Lourdes A. Sereno, director of the Institute of International Legal Studies, and Rolando S. de la Cruz, project director of "Law and Security in Japan." I am also thankful to Professor Jonathan Chua for editing and providing comments on this essay.

1   Maria Rosa Henson, *Comfort Woman: Slave of Destiny* (Pasig: Philippine Center for Investigative Journalism, 1996), 141.

2   Quoted in "Advocacy Activities on the Filipino 'Comfort Women,'" *War Crimes on Asian Women: Military Sexual Slavery by Japan During World War II, The Case of the Filipino Comfort Women Part II* (Quezon City: Task Force on Filipino Comfort Women-Asian Women Human Rights Council, 1998), 147.

3   "Advocacy Activities," *War Crimes on Asian Women*, 147.

4   Henson, "Comfort Woman," 65.

5   I, however, draw on Thomas J. Biersteker and Cynthia Weber, "The Social Construction of State Sovereignty," for the conceptualization of state sovereignty. Published in *State Sovereignty as a Social Construct*, ed. Thomas Biersteker and Cynthia Weber (Cambridge: Cambridge University Press, 1996), 1–21.

6   I had earlier worked on the topic of Japanese animation in "Local/Global Hysteria: Japanese Children's Television in the Philippines," *Image and Reality: Philippine-Japan Relations Towards the 21st Century* (Quezon City: Institute of International Legal Relations, University of the Philippines-Diliman, 1997), 239–62.

7   Koichi Iwabuchi has written various studies on Japanese global popular culture. See "Genius for 'Glocalisation' or the Sweet Scent of Asian Modernity: Japanese Cultural Export to Asia," manuscript, 1997; "Return to Asia? Japan in the Global Audiovisual Market," *Media International Australia* 77 (Aug 1995), 94–106; and "Complicit Exoticism: Japan and its Other," *Continuum* 8, no. 2 (1994): 49–82.

8   Iwabuchi, "Return to Asia," *Media International Australia*, 99–100.

9   OAVs are often direct-to-video movies that are not broadcasted on TV. Thus, this is not considered an episode of the original TV series, but its own release.

10   In the US, "Desperately Seeking Shampoo" is the title listed for the English dubbed version by VIZ Media. It originally goes by the Japanese title "Shampoo *Hyōhen! Hanten Hōju no Wazawai*" (Shampoo's Sudden Switch! The Curse of the Contrary Jewel).

11   Discussed in Roxanne Lynn Doty, "Sovereignty and the Nation: Constructing the Boundaries of National Identity," *State Sovereignty*, 129.

12   Nippon Shoseki, quoted in "Descriptions About 'The Forced Comfort Women' In All the Seven Junior High School Textbooks in Japan," *War Crimes on Asian Women*, 281.

KEYWORDS

13 Ibid., 129.

14 See "Section 3: Movement for Redress" for a thorough documentation of the support and linkages established by advocacy groups for the Filipino comfort women, *War Crimes on Asian Women*, 127–292.

15 See Henson, "Comfort Woman," and AWHRC, *War Crimes on Asian Women*.

16 I have written about trauma and disaster management as normalizing policies of the national culture in "Pagbagsak ng Flight 387 at Edad Ozone: Mga Sangandaang Isyu ng Kulturang Popular, Syensyang Panlipunan at Pangkulturang Pag-aaral," paper read for the Round-Table Discussion on the Social Sciences, the Humanities and the Arts, Philippine Social Science Center, 18 Feb 1998.

17 See "Another Filipino 'Comfort Woman' Dies as LILA Pilipina Lolas Still Wait Verdict in Compensation Suit vs. Japan," *War Crimes on Asian Women*, 214–15.

18. Quoted in "Restore Justice," *War Crimes in Asian Women*, 138.

Fatherland

Nationalist Films
and Modernity
in South Korea,
Taiwan, and the
Philippines

D istance along Philippine national highways is measured by monuments. Every kilometer stretch of the national highway is indicated by yard-high landmarks, the designs of which are a microcosm of national politics. Imelda Marcos had theirs made resembling coconuts, with a hollow in the center originally conceived to hold coconut oil with which to light them. During Corazon Aquino's term, these markers were replaced with yellow tombstone-like monuments. Fidel Ramos opted for pebble-wash tombstone markers. The periodic revision of these distance markers is part of the larger project of transforming and reinventing the nation. Imelda Marcos's "Filipino" design was part of then-President Ferdinand Marcos's agenda of coming up with symbols to meet cosmopolitan ideals of the *Bagong Lipunan* (New Society), the official utopia of the nation. Aquino used the color yellow, from the song "Tie a Yellow Ribbon," an anthem for her assassinated husband, oppositional leader Ninoy Aquino. This song also became the anthem of the middle-class protest movement that would eventually topple the Marcos dictatorship in 1986. Ramos

prized global competitiveness, and the design he preferred reflected a rejuvenated and functional subsystem that in turn suggests an
equally hardworking presidency.

Why the effort to reinvent landmarks and highways? The
meagerness, in number and scope, of Philippine highways has not
dampened the official energies to transform them from simple paths
of transport to imagined superhighways in the mobile exchange
of people, goods, and capital. And because of uneven development, aggravated by the archipelagic national space, all roads lead
to the various centers of national and regional trade and commerce.
Highways now mark the envisioned smooth flow and exchange of
produce to the centers. The landmarking of highways measures
proximity to these centers, as the centers become both the emergent
and the residual sites of global capital as it accumulates and pene-
trates the national space. However, the highway landmarks point
not only to the centrality of economic and political centers but also
to the originary national historical moment of a single monument.
The monument of Jose Rizal, the official national hero, in the nation's
premier park, is point 0 in the highway system. Every other place is
measured from this point. Thus, a landmark bearing the number "25,"
for example, means that it is twenty-five kilometers away from Rizal's
monument in Manila. Just as all highway landmarks bear the spatial
relational distance to this privileged national monument, so also do
the landmarks and highway system bear the weight of the relations to
the significance of the monument.

The significance of Rizal in the construction of the Philippine
nation is not to be understated. Historians and government officials
have handcrafted a mythology of Rizal as purveyor of enlightened
nationalist ideals—from his nationalist novels up to his martyrdom
in death—that eventually pushed elite nationalist leaders to declare
Philippine independence, and as such, as Asia's first republic. As
the nation has also become the emblem of modernity, Rizal's figure
has also become the national symbol of Philippine modernity. After
all, Rizal's significance has been an American colonial handiwork.
Chosen to represent the ideals of enlightened colonialism, Rizal
prevailed over other heroes of the revolution against Spain, the
colonizer before the U.S. came in. His significance materialized
when he was officially designated as the national hero by colonial
administrators, and his meaning and materiality were mythologi-
cally disseminated. All towns in the country have at least one Rizal
monument and one major street named after the national hero. Rizal
was invoked for emulation by the U.S. to prepare the local citizenry

for its own national independence. Nationalist historians, however, antedate the modeling of the nation by already imagining the Philippines as a republic even prior to the coming of the U.S. Rizal's position was already concretized through a dialectical opposition and relation with another hero: Andres Bonifacio, the unofficial national hero, mythologized as a plebian revolutionary. For lack of available archival materials, Bonifacio is spoken about with a tight relation to Rizal who had premonitions of greatness. Rizal had a propensity to save personal possessions, reflect on all things, and build an artillery of sources of his intellectual prowess. For even in the postcolonial era, Rizal is the locus and impetus for the formation and transformation of the nation. The centennial of Rizal's death jumpstarted the celebration of the centennial of Philippine independence. Rizal is the condensed originary national signifier of the Philippine nation. To speak of the nation and its experience with modernity, one has to go where the highway landmarks lead—to Rizal.

Indeed, for the celebration of the centennial of Philippine independence to culminate this year (1998), there are at least three big-budgeted films in production. *Rizal in Dapitan* (Tikoy Aguiluz, 1997), produced last year, provides a model for these nationalist historical films. The film is highly pedagogical, and centered on the male figure as originator and purveyor of larger nationalist struggles and ideals. However, to insert an anticlimactic note, the paper is not focused on the genre of nationalist historical films. My interest is rather on the convergence of issues of nationalism and modernity that bring about first, the resurgent overt preoccupation of the dominant institutions in nation-formation, and second, the counter-hegemonic practices in the travails of modernity that the majority of the nation has yet to thoroughly figure out. Such travails of modernity result from emergent social relations formed in a liberalized market economy, in which new forms of pain and suffering are generated for and experienced by those historically poised in the margins. I present a cognitive map of the affects brought about by historical processes that attempt to deal with past national traumas amid present and sustained economic national flight. How does it feel to be a modern postcolonial citizen that is both traumatized by the past and gentrified by the present cultural and economic geography? In the construction of the nation's past, present, and future, the colonial and imperial historical moments are at play, together with the nation's own invented nationalism. How has the affect that allowed a tasting of the postmodern future provide a dialogue with recent economic woes and beings in some nations in the Asia Pacific?

My hypothesis is that the experience of modernity is interconnected with the experience of the nation. As the nation is never organically whole, so the experience with modernity is never complete. The nation that is imagined to experience growth and stability is at once interrogated by the uneven penetration of the experience with modernity. The further division and feminization of global labor are not only symptomatic of the modern penetration; the division and feminization are crucial in perpetuating the modern as the ideal for national economic, political, and cultural transformations. I use nationalist films to trace the trajectory of nation-formation in the light of more recent economic national developments that have transformed (at least, up to now) Asia Pacific nations with newly-acquired wealth. The nationalist films I choose to examine come at a time when the various nations in Asia Pacific are experiencing sustained economic growth, and can now, therefore, engage with certain past national traumas using the grid of Western liberal democracy and the nation's own invented nationalism. The historical distance provides both a safeguard and a means for subversive penetration into the present cultural geography that, with increasing gentrification, erases the trace of possibilities of political social transformation. By nationalist films, I am referring to those films that provide a historical reenactment of an originary moment, usually posed as a national trauma, in the construction of the nation's present being. There is a consensus in the significance of the particular national past as the "nation thing"—as a hinge that both holds against and provides the impetus to greater national mobility. Like the authority figure in psychical socialization, the fatherland figure in nationalist films provides the libidinal drive that seeks to dominate the narrative of the postcolonial nation—instantaneously mobilizing and immobilizing the national past in order for the nation to move onwards. For if the language for articulating the nation's past is through the present experience with liberal democracy, then the nation's own invented nationalism becomes the parole to articulate these historical processes from which a concept of the modern postcolonial nation emerges.

I begin the paper with a discussion of state and civil society in a postcolonial nation, looking into their workings and limits in the South Korean film *A Single Spark* (Park Kwang-su, 1996). I proceed with an elaboration of the effects of the state and civil society in issues of citizenship, especially those living in the city, in the Taiwanese film *Super Citizen Ko* (Wan Jen, 1995). I then look into the transformation of the national into a transnational state and civil society in the

Philippine film *Eskapo* (Chito Roño, 1995). While providing a relational perspective into the experience of modernity in South Korea, Taiwan, and the Philippines, the paper also intends to present, in a general sense, a continuing narrative of modernity's transformation of the postcolonial nation.

State, Civil Society, and Fatality in *A Single Spark*

The 1980s were marked by the historical shift of political power from dictatorial rule to popular presidencies in the Asia Pacific. Oppositional leaders have taken the rein of government. At the same time, the move to democratize the nation also comes at a time when the nation has already been economically liberalized and is reaping the rewards of economic liberalization, when it has already been well placed in the global economic network, whether as an enclave of global capital or as a terrain for the global division of labor; when there is no position to speak outside the global economy. But the economic integration is not the only process by which capital survives and flourishes in developing nations. For if capital is allowed to penetrate the national economy, the state—the coercive institution of the nation—has to rely more and more on consensus building, or to "represent [the state's] own interests as those of society as a whole."[1] As David McLellan writes of Antonio Gramsci's idea, "The concept of hegemony was thus the answer to the puzzle of capitalism's ability to survive in the bourgeois democracies of the West."[2] The state is able to reinvent itself through civil society, which for Gramsci is the domain of the private that allows for a discussion of the everyday practices in which the nation-state is to be perceived. It now seems remote to think of newly-found wealth only among the cronies and *compradors* of the state. Economic liberalization has democratized the acquisition of wealth, trickling it down to individuals and sectors that generate and consolidate the middle class. It has made real estate prices soar so high that landed farmers can now own capital. Political liberalization also comes into play in the transformation of the economy. States are only too eager to transform past atrocities into present workable "win-win" situations in the name of national peace and harmony. Commissions of truth and good government—fact-finding committees to look into the excesses of past dictatorships especially in cases of human rights violations and corruption—are formed by national governments wanting to deal with their traumatic past, an undoing of the state's doing. The objective is not to try personalities but to present a collective truth about the past, both as national closure and birthing of eras.

But the project is never complete, as it is at once interrogated by the disjuncture of national crises of ending and beginning. As Gramsci stated, "The crisis consists precisely in the fact that the old is dying and the new cannot be born; in this interregnum a great variety of morbid symptoms appear."[3] Yet the crisis has been naturalized in everyday life. Through civil society, the crisis is normalized as the nation's state of being. Hegemony is also manifested in the same morbidity that characterizes its working-project nature, never complete and always in the process of formation. The workings and limits of civil society are thus ambivalent—at once representing a break in the purely coercive state but also limited by the language through which such a break can be articulated, and that is, the discourse of the state's own civil society. Homi Bhabha calls this doubling "the nervous state," allowing for a self-reflexive instance of articulating, for our purpose, both the temporal breakdown of the state and resurgence of civil society functions.[4]

This doubling allows us to speak of *A Single Spark* (1995), a film biography of the political awakening and self-immolation of labor union martyr Chon Tae-il. Park's directorial focus is to present the fetish of the state for surveillance and discipline, and how activists are able to circumvent the state operations. By the continuing existence of a network of activists and protest actions within the very network in which the state interrogates these people and actions, state power is never complete. However, the civil society that allows for the existence of emergent protest activism is only articulated through the language of state crisis. The film depicts such pervasive state surveillance and discipline in sweatshop factories that self-immolation becomes an instant reprieve from civil society's indifference to the workers' plight. Chon's self-immolation becomes the morbid symptom in the crisis, a way to temporally break state hegemony in civil society. In doubling a crisis within a crisis, Chon provides a punctuation to the workings of the state. This punctuation, however, also points to its very limit, becoming the single last action of political dissent. Park reworks this life in the larger course of directing the formation of the recent civil society in South Korea that allowed, for example, for the election of a former political dissident, Kim Dae Jung, into the presidential office in 1998.

The film begins with documentary footage borrowed from the Korean People's Photographers Association of a more recent mass

Fig. 1: Mass action,
A *Single Spark*

we inherit the desire

protest involving youths and students. This event is the result of the trajectory of Chon's awakening and martyrdom. The film is poised in the interregnum of a shift from past political oppression to present-day politics of civil society that allows for such films to be made and to take a critical stand. The state somehow manages to distance itself from its own history. Thus, while Chon's self-immolation presents the doubling in the filmic text, the film itself represents the doubling of the state, forecasting the interrogation of its nature and the limit of such an interrogation. While allowing room for discussion of new dimensions of recent civil society, the film is readily available to sanction state hegemony. It is precisely in the very dissidence allowed within the language of the state that the film is able to articulate its protest. Such protest is twice removed—historically, the film deals with the nation's official past, and depicts state coercion; discursively, the film is made using the "alien" language of the state in which the past is articulated and that, in turn, has displaced the life of Chon. Moreover, the film becomes part of the continuum of recent civil society that allows for such film to be produced and released in the present time. While interrogating the state, the trajectory in which the film has poised Chon's story is made within the grid that has resulted in the recent civil society. The availability of Chon's story only in the present is precisely allowed by the marginal existence of a civil society in the 1970s. Chon's story opened up this civil society to what it is today. This recent civil society allows for the retelling of Chon's story because it fits within its own narrative of developmental democracy.

Any move to articulate a counterhegemonic language, at the very least, invariably implicates the hegemonic language it seeks to subvert. As Michael Taussig states, "No writing is above the reality it realizes, and this is especially the case with the State, arbiter of reason in an unreasonable world."[5] Any critique of the state happens within a paradox: it has an ability to articulate an inside/outside position whereby to speak of one is to implicate the other; thereby, the workings of the state are exposed, but only to the extent that both the state and critique have come to their limits. In the succeeding section, I elaborate on this failure in terms of Chon's self-immolation, and in terms of the labor conditions in which such action took place.

In the film, prior to Chon's own self-immolation, he lights up a black book containing the labor code. Chon's symbolical gesture marks the state's failure to implement its own laws on the safety and just compensation of its workers. His own immolation, depicted in slow motion, repetitive shots of black-and-white and colored

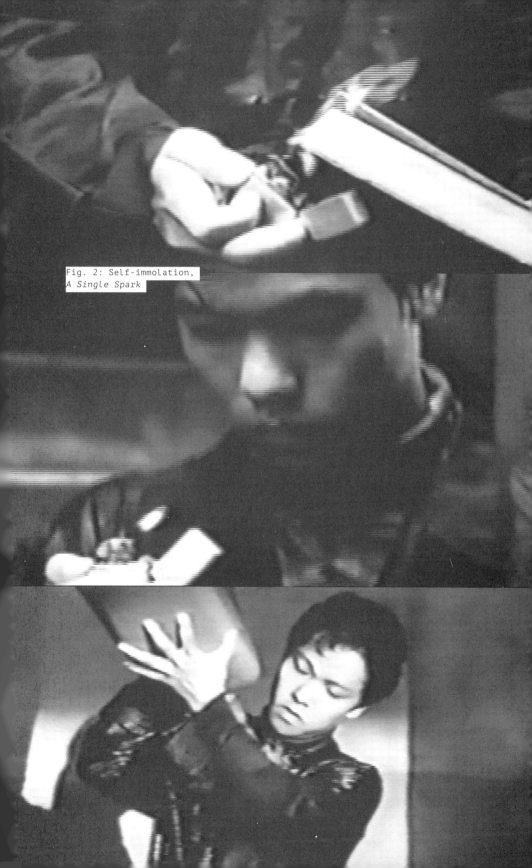

Fig. 2: Self-immolation,
A Single Spark

intercuts of fire engulfing his body, marks the double failure of the state. The state did not provide for adequate protection of its youth laborer-citizen; neither did the state oppress Chon enough for him to accept the conditions of the sweatshop. However, as Chungmoo Choi has pointed out with the series of self-immolations in South Korea in 1991, "The symbolic power of the powerless thus cashes in on the vested social faith to seduce the masses into their romantic venture . . . the line of criticism is directed at the romantic nature of the *minjung* movement and its failure to embrace a larger populace, a charge of exclusionism."[6] Such sublime death and its cinematic depiction in *A Single Spark* allow for very little room to examine the politics in which the sublimity is to be contextualized as a political action. The analysis is similar to Gayatri Spivak's own interrogation of the *sati* or wife-burning after the husband's death.[7] The sublime death, though it defies some textual codification, does not do justice to the woman subject.

Benedict Anderson, however, puts the idea of fatality in another light, as vital to the project of imagining the nation. He states, "The idea of the ultimate sacrifice comes only with an idea of purity, through fatality."[8] This purity comes with the disinterestedness of individuals for the nation, a kind of pure primordial love that allows the nation to extol human sacrifice among its citizens. Anderson also places the "interplay between fatality, technology and capitalism" as the "essential thing" in the formation of the nation.[9] Though Anderson uses the notion in language in relation to the territorialization of the nation, such a notion can also be used to establish the connection between the nationalist movement's self-immolation and contrary state formation as a way of reconceiving a new form of imagined community. Chon's self-immolation marks the fatality of the language of the state. When fire starts to engulf his body, cameras begin flashing, capturing this moment of pure self-sacrifice. The body that commanded the attention of workers in the sweatshop district will attract a larger number of workers in tomorrow's newspapers. This identification with the burned body by unknown, nameless, and faceless workers throughout South Korea provides the network to imagine a contrary notion of nation, other than that espoused officially.

Such a fatality, as technologized originally by the burning body and then reproduced by the media, only seeks to mark the limits of media dissemination. Chon's earlier initiative to bring his case to the media yielded an initial positive feedback from the state's labor apparatus. It then became a matter of procedure within this state apparatus that such positive response was undertaken only to prolong the energies as well as anxieties over the poor labor conditions. Chon's death provides a knee-jerk response from the state, though he is now marked for secular nationalist martyrdom. In a flashforward scene, Chon's biography becomes a standard reading for the new generation of workers in the area. The capital operations that instigated Chon's search for reprieve remain ever present. Ironically, it is through the gentrification of the national economy that labor standards are upgraded by the state and businesses. After all, Nike's working condition and pay in Indonesia, for example, will not do for South Koreans performing the same work load. It is a matter of keen transnational business sense that South Korean enterprises and the state give to workers their due wages in order for greater products to be purchased from the same wages paid to them. With the greater role emphasized by capital in the interplay of the imagination of the nation, Chon's fatality and the technology in which this is disseminated gravely restricts the potential for subversion and liberation. Such a fatality simply punctuates the hegemonic language, unable to move the terms in which grammar and syntax of nation-formation, for example, are to be used for counter-hegemonic purposes.

The state still hovers as the large entity that prefigures the inscription of the nation and modernity in nationalist films. In the process of seeking redress for ill practices and conditions of the sweatshop where Chon works, labor officials would connect these conditions with the patriotic mission of Korean workers. The state rationalizes the poor conditions and unjust practices in the sweatshop factory as part of the trajectory of the national project for economic development. With sustained growth of the Asian economies until the crisis of 1997, the standards operative in the 1970s working conditions are either minimized or transported to other less-developed transnational sites. This does not mean that state and capitalist oppressions are eradicated; it means that these are displaced elsewhere or newer oppressive relations are established with recent movement of capital. By focusing on the life of the martyr Chon and connecting such sacrifice to recent protest actions by youth and students, *A Single Spark* missed out on other pertinent connections, especially as these relate to newer social relations with the more recent movement of capital and the restructuring of labor. Recent International Monetary Bank prescription for bail-out money to be flushed into South Korea's saddled economy required the liberalization of hiring and firing of workers. The production of critical texts should include the production of a range of contexts in which such texts can be read. Rather than maintain allegiance to the official trajectory of the recent civil society, nationalist films should equally elaborate on further broadening the connections between the past national trauma with present conditions of gentrification and newer exploitative relations with capital, especially as it concerns a collaborative project of consciousness-raising.

The paradox of critique of the state speaks of a politics that engages in Bhabha's notion of doubling. What I want to briefly explore further is the direction in which emergent critiques of the state can be channeled, directions that provide for self-reflexive, dialectical, and perspectival approaches and, in turn, raise, at the very least, ethical issues of empowerment. Because of the interchangeability of positions, Bhabha's doubling easily sidetracks the ethical issue of "for whom?" What is negated in the process are the very limits of exposing the state, marginalizing the issue of literal violence that comes with the epistemic violence inflicted on already traditionally marginalized individuals and communities. How then to empower the margins?

The margins and social movements have survived even with or without the theoretical sophistication of the academe. Though the academe has enriched the various groups' experience, it has done so largely in terms of enriching the articulation of the experience. Choi states, "Resistance or struggle has real-life consequences beyond intellectual imagination. How we read what is not written needs to involve these practical considerations."[10] What then do these practical considerations entail? *A Single Spark*'s unique contribution to a model of politicized commercial filmmaking is the creation of a counter public sphere that engages the participation of various sympathetic individuals to the production of the film. As Kyung Hyun Kim points out, "Through grassroots fundraising, more than 7,000 individuals helped to finance this project, raising about half the cost of film production."[11] Such participation calls to mind the political nature of filmmaking in "Third Cinema," a collaborative nature of making do with the given resources to interrogate not only the issues of cinema but also the contextual issues that produce such a cinema.

This counter public sphere moves forward Third World directors' earlier attempts to produce political films. What comes to my mind is Filipino director Lino Brocka whose political films provide a counter-register of images and issues to those disseminated by the Marcoses and Aquino. Though he did not engage in direct grassroots organizing in filmmaking, his films were directly poised against official hegemony. What can be learned from Brocka is a more timely response, quite historically-poised films that undermine the very contexts in which the films are produced, including entanglement with censorship, judiciary, and the military. From Park's film, what can be productively added is a kind of grassroots organizing that broadens the participation in political filmmaking. The more than seven thousand names acknowledged in the final titles provide both material and symbolic meaning to *A Single Spark*. Such filmic tactics from Brocka and Park produce a model for engaging in a political kind of filmmaking at a time when the overtly political is being interrogated to give way to the micropolitics of cultural identities and everyday life.

Citizenship and the City in *Super Citizen Ko*

Super Citizen Ko tells the story of an aging Ko's investigation of a colleague's fate. Ko has been forced to report the colleague to the police to escape further torture during the Kuomintang's "White Terror" campaign in the 1950s. The film shows the shifts in Ko's national identity—from being a soldier of the imperial army when Taiwan was colonized by Japan, to an intellectual imprisoned for allegations of working for Taiwanese independence during Chang Kai Shek's era, to an aging citizen in present Taiwan. Ko's quest is undertaken at a time when Taiwan is undergoing a national election, choosing between pro-unification and pro-independence political parties, where issues are openly raised, issues which could have cost someone's life fifty years ago. Ko is lost in the politics, time, and space of modern Taiwan.

Ko's search for a colleague's fate is an analog of his own search for national identity; it is a search that marks the pain and limits of national identity formation. He is lost in the newness of Taiwan's politics, time, and space, after he was imprisoned for sixteen years and chose to isolate himself for eighteen more. When he can no longer bear the haunting imagined memory of his friend's execution, Ko begins his search. This search is predicated not on success but on the symbolic resolution of individual national identity. In the film, this is exemplified in the scene at the end of the film where Ko lights candles in the isolated graves of the victims of Taiwan's forgotten period. For how can the search anchored in Taiwan's forgotten history be made to materialize in the 1990s, when such national memory has already been invoked in the everyday politics? How can a repressed memory be dealt with when it has now surfaced? How

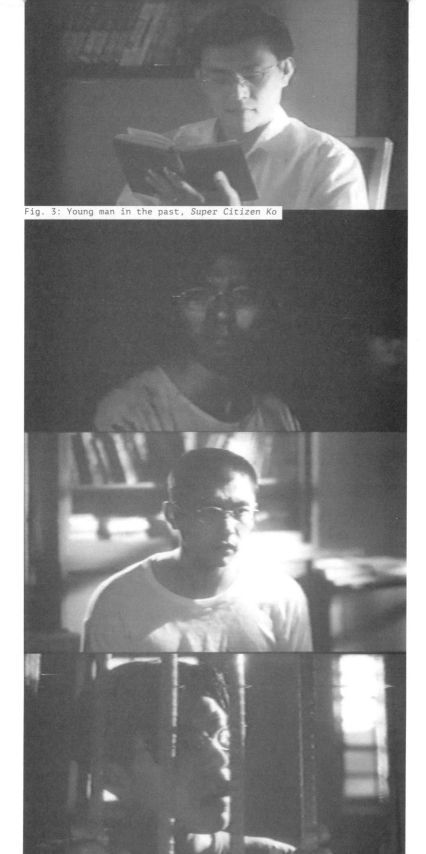

Fig. 3: Young man in the past, *Super Citizen Ko*

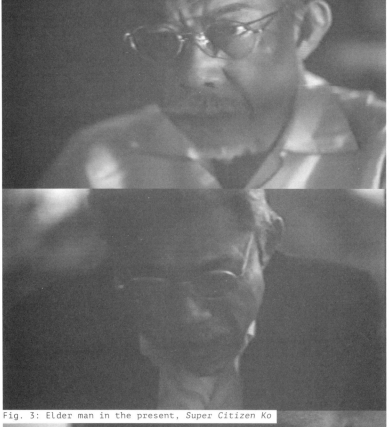

Fig. 3: Elder man in the present, *Super Citizen Ko*

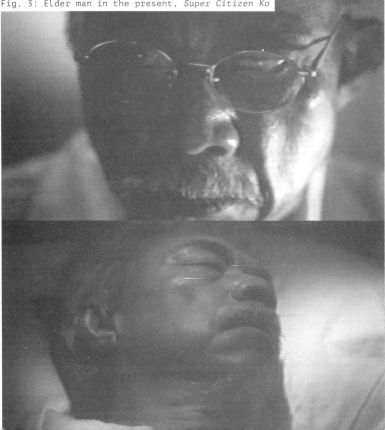

can one begin to talk about a traumatic past in an age when the past has been symbolically and materially obliterated, when the signifiers of the past trauma have already been transformed into nodes of the post-Fordist service sector? In the film, the building of the Bureau of Public Security that supervised surveillance, torture, and summary execution in the 1950s now houses the Lion Forest Department Store; the military tribunal office is now a five-star hotel; the execution site is now called Youth Park. Like Ko's citizenship, the city is a signifier without a signified.

Citizenship is posed as an arbitrary construction of hegemony and individual agency. Because of various historical shifts in Taiwan, institutions are continuously introduced, and new social practices are continuously redefined and enforced. Modern Taiwanese politics have been set and dominated by mainlanders. Individuals are not as quick to reinvent themselves. How individuals invoke their relationship to the shifting identities of the state is foregrounded in the issue of citizenship. Individuals who immediately grapple with their relational identities—becoming full-fledged citizens, like Ko—are the first to be troubled by succeeding impositions of new orders and identity requirements. When he is determined to make his own claim to identity—to become a Taiwanese citizen—it is too late because the rigidity of past identity claims has now become liberal electoral issues. The nation now votes on the kind of national identity it wants to perform every four years.

Civil society has now taken root in Taiwan after decades of authoritarian rule that has overseen the national economic growth. Unlike the recent past in *A Single Spark* that fits in the continuum of civil society's maturity, recent civil society in *Super Citizen Ko* comes

Fig. 5: Picture for posterity, *Super Citizen Ko*

as a blast of the present, devoid of any historical blocks. The existence of civil society comes to Ko as an alienation, forging distance to any material subject formation. All his accumulated signifieds cease to have any signification in the modern period. He is a floating absent signifier. He becomes one of the latest fashion victims, the retrenched workers who have failed to reskill themselves with the latest of machine or service sector technology, the latest political scapegoat. When an open civil society somehow manages to surface in the state, Ko's accumulated identities become unaccustomed to present-day dispensing of power. Since Ko's generation represents pre-boom Taiwan, this open civil society becomes a by-product of sustained economic growth. This realization further isolates Ko and the history he represents—where have all his generation's pain and suffering led to?

Super Citizen Ko becomes part of the spectacle involved in the resolution of the 28 February 1947 incident that marked native Taiwanese resentment of Kuomintang rule. It also unleashed a backlash on Taiwanese as an estimated eight thousand people were killed in the rectification campaign. As Ping-hui Liao states, "While the 8,000 certainly included not only members of the Taiwanese elite, large numbers of local intellectuals were killed or imprisoned, which put an end to civil society that was beginning to take shape."[12] What was at stake then—civil society—becomes more and more a natural aspect of the postwar and, now, the postindustrial state. The recent civil society is not god-sent; it is also emplaced in national and transnational survival. How can the modern state mobilize its people and the global community for continued economic growth, at a time when its nationality is continually being besieged by mainland China's desire for a return of the prodigal son, a la Hong Kong? So highly maintained is the overseeing of the national economy that Taiwan is one of the few countries in the Asia-Pacific that has escaped the crisis affecting the region. Its sustained economic boom becomes its primary political weapon to thwart any move to reunify with China. Thus, the originary island and Japanese coloniality are invoked in national identity formation to expunge a purely mainland China identity.

The unravelling of the national trauma on the 28 February 1947 incident becomes a national spectacle, with a zealous production of incident information artefacts:

The Historical Research Commission of Taiwan Province (1991) then started work on an official history of the Incident, which

was published in November 1991. Even earlier, however, especially after 1986, many articles and books about the uprising had
begun to appear. Drawing on oral history and historiography
similar to the subaltern studies in India, writers used interviews to compile biographies of the victims and to describe and
analyze the Incident within its historical context. And a major
event in this process was the summer 1989 production of *The
City of Sadness*, a film directed by Hou Hsiao-hsien that won an
award at the Venice Film Festival because of its political subject
matter.[13]

Super Citizen Ko also produces an effect that, as Liao mentions,
is part of "a tendency . . . to see 'martyrs' as precursors of the Taiwan
Independent Movement or as victims of political persecution."[14]
This martyrdom is interestingly poised in the depiction of Ko's
alienation from the urban space. In one scene, Ko blankly stares at
people marching for various political parties in an upcoming national
election. The ground level alienation is further intensified by an
overview detachment to the city's new transformations. In the scene
where Ko goes to a Taipei tower, the breathtaking view of modern
city buildings and open greenery is given a warped perspective by his
dystopic voice-over narration of how the city, as an analog of national
politics, has been gentrified. Ko's own trauma of the past—intercut
black-and-white footage of his colleague's execution—further isolates
the modern city. What the city does to Ko is to present the new signifying field in which transformations of identity are to be filtered. In
the process, Ko realizes his loss; he becomes a signifier unable to
adapt to newer hegemonic signifying practices.

Ko is not citified, as more recent national governments would
have encouraged it. His body does not bear the marks of a highly
cosmopolitan and modernized city. His dated fashion, detachment
from his daughter's modern family life, alienation from cityscapes,
and displacement in national politics and civil society become
symptoms of a loss of subjectivity. He is melancholic not from
longing for an originary national identity but from a sense of family
coherence as he imagines the family of his early years in black-and-
white footage. The break-up of the family was predicated by the state,
upon his incarceration for a crime against said state. Surprised by
his decision to divorce, his wife decides to end her life. His daughter
grows up alone, persecuted by teachers for having a traitor for a
father. With recent amenities of technologizing family coherence in
modern Taiwan, the family readily becomes the symptom of national

growth and unity. Having lost his family—Ko's primordial source of identity—to the state, he is unable to fully deal with newer shifts in state and civil society.

The city becomes emblematic of the tensions arising from loss and the inability to deal with this loss. The city is indifferent to multiple identities, even as its civil society advocates a plurality of tolerable politics. Claims toward identity in the highly modernized city become extremely limited. From Ko's own quest for claims of national identity, the problem, as posed by the city, is that the national has given way to the transnational claims of Taiwanese and Taiwanese-ness. The city becomes unsympathetic to national claims, as its present politics only seeks to reaffirm the intransitivity of national claims. Taiwanese identity is to be sorted transnationally, as Ko's ocular view of the city suggests. For the city becomes the quicksand of history, new structures that arise become devoid of historicity and historical block claims. As Saskia Sassen states, "The denationalizing of urban space and the formation of new claims centered in transnational actors and involving contestation, raise the question—whose city is it?"[15]

For urban planners, the city is a model of economic efficiency and modern living. For those who "walk the city" to use Michel de Certeau's contrary image, the city is experienced in its rawness and how people make do with urban reality.[16] But Ko's own experience with the city negates both models, for the city has moved beyond being purveyor of everyday existence. Even the perception of the everyday is mediated through popular ideal images, from ghetto basketball to liberal democracy. Ko looks at the city as highly urbanized and liberalized. It is precisely these characteristics of the city that alienate Ko. The modes of surveillance and discipline such as the blackout city or curfew siren that used to haunt the city have been transformed by highly segregated lines of economic and political transformation. Pain is not just a mental state; it is the material state of the city. Where, then, to stake Ko's claim on the city?

To stake specific claims on the city amid globalization follows through what Nicholas Garnham proposes, the "universal rationality as a cultural principle."[17] Garnham sees no other option but to take a universalist position in the debates of globalization, one that attempts to "democratize the globe and the role of an increasingly globalized media system."[18] Thus he claims that "while globalization calls for the development of a parallel concept of global citizenship and representative global political structures, at this time the only effective political structures we have are nation-states, and our actual

Fig. 6: Mapping the city, *Super Citizen Ko*

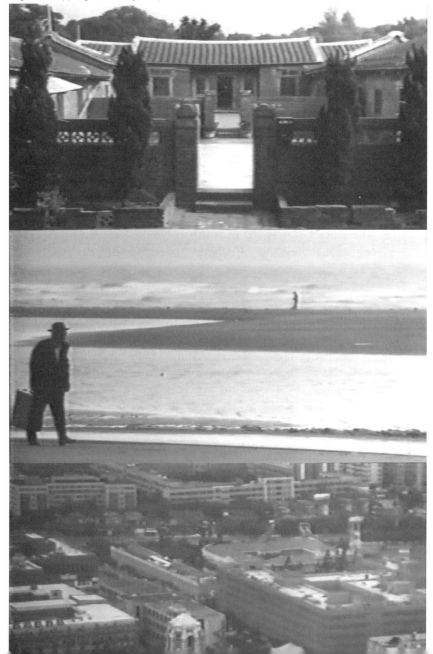

citizenship identities are national."[19] Garnham's idea seeks to liberalize the modern public sphere, but does very little to question the
very tenets in which liberal democracy may obliquely fit in various
nation-states. How can a new discursive strategy—one that purports
to be as global as the most recent economic drive of capital—be
applied when the very implementation of capital has not been evenly
developed and globalized? In *Super Citizen Ko*, the city becomes the
organizing geography for Ko's search. As the city has lost its historicity and the nation has trivialized its past, what the film implies is the
transnational movement of national identity formation. Sassen gives
due consideration to marginal identities, such as immigrants making
claims of citizenship on a denationalized city.

However, in the film, while civil society has allowed for at least
two political positions, Ko's own historical background leaves little
room for accommodation. Ko shows the limits not only of recent
civil society but also of the very politics that have institutionalized
this civil society. In this new city and civil society, Ko cannot make
claims to citizenship, as his being is so anchored on Taiwan's past,
a history nominalized in modern politics. Modern politics have
allowed such views to proliferate, yet do not really invest power
on the state to negotiate such terms—on whether to become independent, or to return to mainland China. Taiwan, like Ko, becomes
a signifier without a signified. But unlike Ko, Taiwan's in-between
identity is poised as a postmodern postindustrial dominant organizer
of Taiwanese reality. Ko has already lost touch with both the organicity of the past and the simulacrum of the present. *Super Citizen
Ko* is a pessimistic look at citizenship within the national space.
Such a national identity, as the film suggests, can only be genuinely
generated transnationally.

The point that the film makes is a critique of recent Taiwanese
civil society, one that has failed to substantiate Ko's being. This point,
I think, posits the continued strength of the state to organize and
define Taiwanese modernity and nation. The state may have liberalized, but only in relation to absorbing alternative politics and history
that support its own survival as a quasi-nation internally, and a trans-
nation externally. Ko's own obsession with what really happened only
presents the futility of unearthing historical truths. Like Ko's own
quest and discovery, such truths have long been buried in isolated
grave sites, and all one can do is to memorialize the memory.

Citizens, as Ko embodies, are signifiers looking for a signified.
Even when the signifying field has been set up by the state and civil
society, bodies would always be looking for alternative claims. Thus,

Ko's citizenship is one of becoming a super citizen, as the film's title suggests—searching for a non-existent yet basic signified in identity formation. His citizenship, like those of most Taiwanese, is poised neither nationally or transnationally. Citizenship, then, becomes a floating essential signifier, transforming as divergent needs and claims call upon it. However, citizenship does not bear the promise of delivery, nor of return, should one be unsatisfied with it. Citizenship is relational. Like Ko's nostalgic view of family organicity, citizenship depends on the company one imagines to keep. Such a utopic view, however, is imbricated by the trauma one individual or nation will never wholly resolve, even if it attempts to deal with the trauma fully. Yet for Ko, the meaning or the lack of meaning of citizenship can only be resolved in the quest, in the struggle to come up with a workable truth of being and nation. Unlike *A Single Spark*'s overtly political mode of filmmaking, *Super Citizen Ko* presents a new-wave return to the political. The visuality presented in the film, especially as to how Ko relates to the city, mimics the camera. The film foregrounds and critiques the media for the institutionalization of dominant claims that alienate historical block claims such as Ko.

Privatized and Transnational Civil Society in *Eskapo*

In *Super Citizen Ko*, the transnational link was suggested to be the purveyor of present-day civil society and identity formation. In *Eskapo*, however, the connection is more embarrassingly overt, using nationalism in the service of big business and traditional oligarchs. The film narrates the heroic escape from Marcos's maximum security prison by two members of affluent Filipino families. One of them is Genny Lopez, scion to a political dynasty and business empire which includes: the monopolistic franchise of an electric company, the nation's largest television and media conglomerate, and, formerly, a leading newspaper. The other is Sergio Osmeña III, also a scion to a political and business dynasty in Cebu. Upon declaration of martial law in 1972, they were imprisoned for allegedly plotting to overthrow Marcos. The film explains that Marcos used them as hostages to quell political and economic opposition. When all else failed, after five years in prison, they decide to escape from the military camp and fly out of the country via private plane.

Funded by Lopez's own film company, *Eskapo* presents a nationalist project that is tied up with business and traditional

political interests. Disenfranchised during the Marcos dictatorship but re-enfranchised during Aquino's takeover of the presidency twenty-five years later, the rich have never seen better times. Most families saw the return of their properties, businesses, and political power, having already earned profit and mileage. The film tackles a trauma shared by nation—the Marcos dictatorship—that provides the impetus for greater endeavor in business and politics among the traditional rich. In the film's ending intertitles, updates on the careers and pursuits of Lopez and Osmeña are presented—the political activities they engaged in during their exile in the U.S., the return of their sequestered businesses, and the further enlargement of business and political interests. So unabashed is the film in acclaiming the two personalities that the film even utilized the country's two leading dramatic actors to portray the characters. The film legitimizes big business and traditional politics, especially as to how these were repressed, liberated, and transformed.

What I find interesting in the film is the posing of transnational links, especially as to how the U.S. figures in the whole project of bringing in recent civil society. For if in *Super Citizen Ko*, the transnational link is nameless, in *Eskapo*, it is the continuation of the benevolent link between the U.S. and the Philippines that discusses notions of civil society and citizenship. U.S. coloniality is invoked through a massive continuation of the hegemonic narrative that binds the U.S. and the Philippines. Articulated in the highly disseminated language of William McKinley's benevolent assimilation, U.S. domination of Philippine politics has continued to evoke conflicting and dialoging nationalist responses.[20] For the mass movements, it was no less than a quest for a genuinely independent Philippines. For the traditional politicians, such a nation can evolve through links with nations more experienced in the task of self-governance and economic prosperity. Because of the enlightened colonial project, the U.S. to this day remains the single most important purveyor of economic, political, and popular culture in the country.

What McKinley stated in the halls of the White House, on the night he decided on the colonization of the Philippines, reverberates in the way the film depicts the U.S. In the film, the U.S. is the safe haven for families disenfranchised during the Marcos dictatorship. The fathers of both Lopez and Osmeña have chosen to become political refugees in the U.S. to flee from Marcos. What is implied is the U.S. as an embodiment of the ideals of the liberal state and a working civil society. It is a model for the clans' own vision of a workable political system, one that tolerates dissent and acknowledges populism. For the film itself, as well as the fact that *A Single Spark* was allowed public exhibition, is a testament to truth-claims about the medium, freedom of speech, rationality, and other libertarian ideals. The showing of the film marks the opening of a civil society that not only tolerates past dissent, but more importantly represents present maneuvers to sustain this civil society. What is also being invoked is the authorship of recent civil society by the traditional rich who thus have legitimate moral and judicial truth-claims. Underneath this local authorship is the invocation of the U.S. as staunch model of liberal democracy.

What is not said about the two prominent people's escape to the U.S. is the unavailability of such an option for most of the people repressed under the Marcos dictatorship. Their escape involved the hiring of a private plane. Most oppositionists that sought refuge in the U.S. were already part of the elite politics in the Philippines that were disenfranchised during the Marcos dictatorship. In addition, 1960 immigration pattern had allowed only for the migration of highly-skilled professionals. As the greater number of people who comprised the oppositional mass movement met neither criteria, the site of struggle was mostly undertaken within the national space. The national space became the privileged domain of nationalist struggle. Consequently, in order for exiled oppositionists to maintain their political and economic clout, there ensued a reverse migration, when

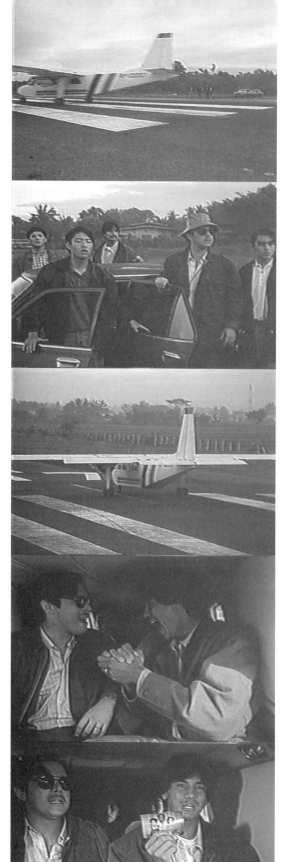

Fig. 8: Male repre-
sentatives of
Philippine elite flee
the Marcos dictator-
ship, *Eskapo*

international pressure on Marcos's human rights violations was beginning to swell.

What is squeamishly uncomfortable about the set-up is the way nationalist films have been invoked in the service of big business and traditional politics. In the refashioning of nationalism for the maintenance of hegemony, big business and traditional politics have set the agenda in redefining the terrain of engagement. Traditional politics have helped usher in laws banning child labor, the inclusion of marital rape as a crime, stringent protection of the environment, and other politically correct state measures. In the same light, traditional politics have also aggressively rubberstamped laws maintaining ongoing capitalist principles of liberalization, privatization, and globalization. On the one hand, forest parks are declared national monuments free from illegal logging. On the other hand, and in the same vein, the Omnibus Investment Code is ratified, guaranteeing preferential treatment of big transnational capitalists. The Mining Act also allows the speculative exploitation of all land resources. Whereas, in the past, the state's propaganda films disseminated official viewpoints and representational images, the task, like most governmental functions, has been taken on by big businesses. Now, more than any other time in the history of Philippine businesses, is the era wherein corporations are keenly interested in social issues and alternative practices as part of good business sense. Atlas Consolidated Mining Corporation is involved with a shoemaking project for Abaca, a *sitio* within the mine's parameters; Central Azucarera Don Pedro gave loans to housewives and dependents of employees to start up an industrial rags project; Negros Navigation has set up Bangko Sang Barangay (The Poor Man's Bank); San Miguel Agribusiness Division and Pilipinas Kao have opened cooperative projects; Phelps Dodge and Ramcar are involved in various livelihood projects.[21]

The state function is being privatized in tension-filled ways. Like Michel Foucault's notion of power, state power—i.e., political power—is made prolific rather than amassed by institutions. State power is being delegated to businesses. On the one hand, political power is filtered through the active participation of business. In the coming Philippine national elections, for example, business loyalty to presidential candidates has already been made clear earlier on by contending business interests. On the other hand, while the nation-state is being continually interrogated and redefined by multinational corporations, it has also moved into directions that befit an enlightened liberal community. The military is modernized; the police professionalized; more infrastructures are being built by business participation through build-own-transfer contracts, deals that allow businesses to establish and to own priority infrastructures for at least twenty-five years before these are turned over to the government. In addition, water and power distribution has already been privatized. Specialized hospitals and the prison system are also on their way toward privatization. What is perceived to be a better, more efficient delivery of basic services is now placed in the hands of business by government perennially riddled with a bloated and corrupt bureaucracy. In short, business is setting a major bulk of the agenda of nation-building and, consequently, on national identity formation.

Civil society is being privatized in ways that are circuited toward transnational objectives. Transnational objectives of good government have been set by traditional politicians and big businesses to mimic the U.S. model. This is where the U.S. shows its tenacity in maintaining its colonial and imperial legacy. While Japanese popular culture has started to infiltrate the national cultural domain, the model of political and economic governance has always been the U.S. The link is subtly generated in the film. For one, as the film shows, human rights are a democratic issue. Even, or because, the Lopezes and the Osmeñas have also suffered human rights violations under an authoritarian regime, their claim to political power is as legitimate as that of the marginal figures who were tortured or who have died under the dictatorship. Marcos's legacy becomes a democratic leveling mechanism to perpetuate claims of victimage and political power. This power is being vigorously redefined in two ways. Osmeña continues in his endeavor of traditional politics, while the Lopez clan pursues greater political reach through good business sense. Osmeña's political power, like that of traditional politics, has already been made to serve business interests.

Another point generated are the working subjects, able to reclaim and enlarge the meager resources that are nonetheless theirs. The final intertitles show the professional work ethics of the scions to claim what is rightfully theirs. The working subject is poised as the model for preserving civil society. By continually working to generate surplus, the individual achieves power of a liberal kind. Political power as imbibed in the working subject is generated as an economic by-product. By generating economic surplus, political power is also generated to liberate other less privileged working bodies. Power is democratized through political gentrification. Civil society gradually becomes a pursuit of big business for it yields a power mimicking state power.

Business undertakes the financing of the dissemination of laissez faire and human rights as prevailing social interests in *Eskapo*. Being a media mogul, Lopez doubles as both break and continuity in the democratic tradition of media to provide a public sphere for articulating dissent and consent. His story of victimage and rescue appearing on film seemingly poses the possibility of media to constitute and transform the public sphere. However, his authoring of the film biography—both as film subject and as producer—represents a narcissistic relation not only to oneself but also to one's claims. *Eskapo's* public service becomes self-service. Lopez, who should know the trauma of losing the media to the dictatorship, indirectly stresses class interest as purveyor of public interest. Nothing is neutral, not even those that seem to provide sympathy to trauma management. What the film becomes is a pedagogical tool for management of the public sphere, clearly demarcating the models and interests of civil society that produces this sphere.

Nation and Modernity in the Presence of the Fatherland

Nationalist films in Asia Pacific cinema embody both the ideal way of dealing with a past national trauma—what contexts are to be used to generate meaning over the trauma—and the operations of hegemonic and counterhegemonic realities—how the past is made usable for present contending interests. More importantly, nationalist film interrogates the absence and rise of recent civil society, precisely because they deal with social trauma. The figure of the fatherland, the masculine allegorical authority of the narrativization of the nation, provides the map to read the past trauma and present predicament. The fatherland, however, is to be distinguished from the motherland: the motherland provides the spiritual inspiration in the formation of the nation and national identity, while the fatherland provides the material mapping of the formation and elaboration of the nation.[22] The social mapping of the nation is invoked through the discourse of civil society and the state. The fatherland embodies the organization of civil society, marking its absence, birth, and recent maturity through the enlistment of effects both on the male individual figure—some micro-collectivity—and the nation.

The elaboration of the national experience in South Korean, Taiwanese, and Philippine cinemas also expounds on the nation's experience with modernity. On the one hand, the nation is continually being interrogated and defined by contending and dialoging forces nationally and transnationally that produce oblique relations of power and national formation. This disjuncture in being and power almost always materializes through the experience of pain and suffering. On the other hand, the formation of nation and national identity, and modernity prevail under the most trying circumstances. The nation is already spoken for in the experience of modernity, and vice-versa. One can therefore speculate that the nation is an enlightenment construct that interfaces with the more universal experience of modernity. The local experience of nation-formation is the parole in the language of modernity.

Thus there exists a relational mode in which nation-formation and modernity implicate each other in Asia Pacific cinema. Such self-reflexivity can also be seen in the meta-filmic quality of nationalist films. Because it documents a nation's past and present, nationalist films elaborate on the film's own relationship both with filmmaking, media, and society. Each analyzed film presents contending views about film and the media, both how one uses and is used by film and the media to visualize and audiolize the nation's past and present. While the film narrative provides certain trajectories of nation-formation and the experience with modernity, the self-reflexive meta-film provides commentaries on the very relationship of the film to its media.

There is another counter that is being disseminated to mark the countdown toward the actual centennial day of the proclamation of independence. The originary counter that marks the remaining number of days until the centennial of Philippine independence is located in Freedom Park fronting Malacañang Palace, which is home to the presidency. There was so much media hype during its one hundred day launch. Because of the massive infrastructure build-up, Metro Manila's traffic was further rerouted to accommodate the expected and largely required attendance of schoolchildren. Such a counter is technologically less calibrated than the digital clock displayed in Tiananmen Square, which counted how much time was left before Hong Kong returned to China. The official centennial counter, however, is being disseminated to various national and local offices. It is basically a day calendar whose pages one can tear off, working back from one hundred to one. The originary and mass-disseminated counters represent the maneuvering of time and, hence, history to meet present hegemonic needs for the most intense project of nation-formation. Time is made into a trajectory of itself, devoid of other factors in the ascendancy of hegemonic truth-claims to national history. It becomes a signifier with a sole signified, and thus constricts the parameters of allowable play of meanings. Time is reversed instead of projected forward. The centennial of Philippine independence now owes authorship to the power behind this reversal of history. Though it may be considered trivial, the reversal of history remains vital to the authoring of the most recent and intense project of nation-formation. It sets up the authority in the management of history, the centennial celebration, nation, national identity, and citizenship, and more importantly, the succeeding hundred years of national transformation. In other words, the national future is already marked by a reversal to the originary past. It is precisely because the gesture is symbolic that it yields to contending signifying practices—good and bad nationalisms, hegemony and counter-hegemony, nationhood and colonialism, nationalism and imperialism, localism and globalism.

This discussion of nationalist films in the experience of nation-formation and modernity allows the critique of such emplacement of the public sphere in civil society. If the terms for engagement are already being set forth by the state and its hegemony, then one of two things can be undertaken by those in which such hegemony is being emplaced—a critique of the state becomes necessary to illuminate both the workings and the limits of civil society, and the new ways of both challenging this civil society and moving toward the institutionalization of a counter-public sphere within the state-owned civil society.

ENDNOTES

I am grateful to Professors Esther Yau and Jonathan Chua for the suggestions on improving the essay.

1   David McLellan, "Gramsci," *Marxism After Marx* (Boston: Houghton Mifflin, 1979), 186.

2   Ibid.

3   Antonio Gramsci, *Selections from the Prison Notebooks* (New York: International Publishers, 1971), 276. He also clarifies the notion of hegemony in a footnote: "The 'normal' exercise of hegemony on the now classical terrain of the parliamentary regime is characterized by the combination of force and consent, which balance each other reciprocally, without force predominating excessively over consent. Indeed, the attempt is always made to ensure that force will appear to be based on the consent of the majority, expressed by the so-called organs of opinion—newspapers and associations—which, therefore, in certain situations, are artificially multiplied" (ibid., 80).

4   Homi Bhabha, "Anxious Nations, Nervous States," *Supposing the Subject*, ed.
     Joan Copjec (London: Verso, 1994), 201–17.

5   Michael Taussig, "The Magic of the State," *Public Culture* 5, no. 1 (Fall 1992):
     65.

6   Chungmoo Choi, "The Discourse of Decolonization and Popular Memory:
     South Korea," *positions* 1, no. 1 (1993): 99. The Minjung movement, according
     to Choi, "began in the wake of the popular April 19 Revolution in 1960 and
     developed into an anticolonial national unification movement by the end of
     the 1980s. Its proponents considered it an extension of Korea's long tradition
     of popular nationalist movements, from the 1894 Tonghak Peasant War and
     the 1919 March First Independence Movement to the April 19 Revolution,
     which toppled the U.S.-sponsored Syngman Rhee regime (1948–1960)" (ibid.,
     90).

7   Gayatri Spivak, "Can the Subaltern Speak?" *Marxism and the Interpretation
     of Culture*, ed. Cary Nelson and Larry Grossberg (Chicago: University of
     Illinois Press, 1988), 271–313.

8   Benedict Anderson, *Imagined Communities* (London: Verso, 1991), 144.

9   Ibid., 42.

10   Ibid., 99.

11   Kyung Hyun Kim, "Notes on *A Single Spark*," *Post-Colonial Classics of Korean
     Cinema 1948–1998 Souvenir Program* (1998), 17.

12   Ping-hui Liao, "Rewriting Taiwanese National History: The February 28
     Incident as Spectacle," *Public Culture* 5 (1993): 287.

13   Ibid.

14   Ibid.

15   Saskia Sassen, "Whose City Is It? Globalization and the Formation of New
     Claims," *Public Culture* 8 (1996): 206.

16   See Michel de Certeau, "Walking the City," in *The Practice of Everyday Life*
     (Berkeley: University of California Press, 1984), 91–110.

17   Nicholas Garnham, "The Mass Media, Cultural Identity, and the Public
     Sphere in the Modern World," *Public Culture* 5 (1993): 251–65.

18   Ibid., 251. Garnham cites three reasons for making a universalist claim on
     the debate on globalization: "First one can conceive of the problem of a na-
     tional or local culture being threatened by a globalising process only from
     a universalist position. . . . Second, the very phenomenon under discussion,
     globalization, is a universal phenomenon based on a universal symbol of
     value, the system of money. Third, a debate is only possible if the partici-
     pants share some common set of values within which they can say meaning-
     fully that they understand each other's positions and either agree or disagree
     and why. And finally, and perhaps most important, because the participants
     in the global cultural market itself show every sign of happily accepting at
     least that minimum universals on which any shared cultural space depends"
     (ibid., 258–59).

19   Ibid., 259.

20   In President William McKinley's remarks to a Methodist delegation, he narrates how he decided on the U.S. colonization of the Philippines: "I walked the floor of the White House night after night until midnight; and I am not ashamed to tell you, gentlemen, that I went down on my knees and prayed Almighty God for light and guidance more than one night. And one night late it came to me this way—I don't know how it was, but it came: 1) That we would not give them (Filipinos) back to Spain—that would be cowardly and dishonorable; 2) that we would not turn them over to France and Germany—our commercial rivals in the Orient—that would be bad business and discreditable; 3) that we would not leave them to themselves—they were unfit for self-government—and they would soon have anarchy and misrule over there worse than Spain's was; and 4) that there was nothing left for us to do but to take them all, and to educate the Filipinos, and uplift and civilize and Christianize them, and by God's grace do the very best we could by them, as our fellow-men for whom Christ also died." This was quoted from "Remarks to Methodist Delegation," *The Philippines Reader*, ed. Daniel B. Schirmer and Stephen Rosskamm Shalom (Quezon City: Ken, 1987), 22–23.

21   See Juan Miguel Luz and Teodoro Y. Montelibano, *Corporations and Communities in a Developing Country, Case Studies: Philippines* (Manila: Philippine Business for Social Progress and Center for Corporate Citizenship, 1993).

22   See Partha Chatterjee's gendered distinction of nation-formation in "The Nation and Its Women," *The Nation and Its Fragments: Colonial and Postcolonial Histories* (Princeton: Princeton University Press, 1993). I have also talked about the mother-nation in "*Inangbayan*, mother-nation, in Lino Brocka's *Bayan Ko: Kapit sa Patalim* and *Orapronobis*," *Screen* 37, no. 4 (Winter 1996): 368–88.

KEYWORDS

Masses

Power and Gangsterism in the Films of Joseph "Erap" Estrada

J oseph Estrada, an action hero for four decades, was elected thirteenth president of the Philippines in 1998. He won with the biggest margin in presidential election history, garnering 39.9 percent of the votes cast in a field of eleven candidates. He cornered 38 percent of the 71 percent available votes from class D.[1] Estrada won big by using the *masa* (masses) as a cornerstone of his presidential campaign and governance. Despite his affluent background, he succeeded to project himself as one of the masses thanks to his star system. Estrada came out of the local action film genre, the *aksyon* film or the *bakbakan*, "films that focuses [*sic*] mainly on physical conflict."[2] His action films depicted characters in solidarity with, and providing leadership for, the masses. So successful is his filmic career that his double excess, more than the usual excess attributed to aspiring politicians,[3] was pardonable, even as the foibles of other candidates and politicians were not.[4] His campaign slogan *"Erap para sa Mahirap"* (Erap for the poor; Erap, his pet name, is an anagram of *pare*, meaning "bosom buddy") was not so much based on genuine pro-masses politics as it was just a mnemonically and rhetorically effective device mobilized in his campaign. That a "defender of the masses" (in film) used a pro-masses slogan through a political party called The Laban ng Makabayang Masang Pilipino (Fight of the Nationalist Filipino Masses) spelled some redundant certainty of victory.[5]

The masses in Estrada's films are massified, i.e., individuals forced by circumstance to bond together and search for a liberator. In politics, such a representation remains sublimely real. Estrada coached the masses to posit him as their ally and salvation. And the masses, which comprised the huge voting population, gave him the ultimate chance to serve them. In this essay, I am interested in assessing how Estrada's films and politics have mobilized the masses. This is a cultural analysis of the discursive construction and use of the masses. How do individuals bond together for a political purpose without having to realize their class interest? How do the masses remain a massified entity inside and outside Erap's filmic and political machine? How are the masses extolled in entertainment industries and yet marginalized in actual social politics? How are the Filipino masses metropolitanized in recent imperialist globalization?

K
E
Y
W
O
R
D
S

The first section of the paper deals with the two dominant modes of constructing the Filipino masses—one based on nationalist historiography and alternative nation-building, the other on the cultural capitalist agenda of homogenizing audience, as in the films of Estrada. What historical block claims are made for the masses? How are the masses massified and demassified using speech, gender, and commodification? The second section discusses the notion of power, as specifically manifested in gangsterism and as culled by Estrada. What historical moment heralded Estrada into power, and how does his kind of gangsterism fragilely cohere the nation? An incipient violence underscores the use of gangsterism and the masses, one that represents alienation, a Third World metropolitanization of the citizen-subject, and masochism.

Masses and the Films of Estrada

The modern meaning of the masses revolves around a binary opposition. As Raymond Williams explains, "[One] is the modern word for many-headed multitude or mob: low, ignorant, unstable; and [two] is a description of the same people but now seen as a positive or potentially positive social force."[6] The first category connotes a dystopic classist remark on the masses; the second category connotes a class utopia. It is in the second category that the masses serve as a possibility for social transformation, according to how they are generated and mobilized for certain collective ideals.

Etienne Balibar explains the dialectics of class and masses as "the continuous transformation of historically heterogeneous masses or populations into a working class, or the successive avatars of the working class, together with a corresponding development in the forms of 'massification' specific to class situation."[7] However, while the masses have been generated by the culture industries—mass consumption, mass culture, mass communication—class has been elided in this modernist project. Though claiming to access the widest reach, the masses have not accessed their potential as a socially transformative entity. On the one hand, some films about the masses may signify the utopia of social transformation, of highly politicized masses transformed into politically mediated and sustained proletariats, environmentalists, feminists, gay activists, and so on. On the other hand, real experience suggests a high degree of defiance of the masses to such transformation; the masses have yet to become political entities other than pawns mobilized for electoral politics. Though certainly accounts of the masses successfully transformed into critical masses abound, the masses have yet to be transformed into a massive class entity. By this, I refer to a kind of class over determination that can prove antithetical to the prevailing order and chaos of imperialist globalization. The masses are especially significant in class and class-related issues, providing the impetus in the transformation of the masses into a class issue. As Gilles Deleuze and Félix Guattari state, "Beneath the self reproduction of classes there is always a variable map of masses."[8] The masses provide the basis of class mobilization, as class becomes the impetus for the masses' transformation.

As a consequence of the negation of class in the possibility of the masses, culture industries are looked upon as the dominant mode by which individuals, unknown to each other, bond and redefine themselves as critical entities or resultant communities. Such acceptance of right-wing hegemony of the culture industries toward the masses implies two further consequences. First, a contrary macropolitical analysis is purged, for the cultural dominance under imperialist globalization is poised as infallible. Second, cultural analysis therefore focuses on locating sites of resistance—usually in the interstices—within the dominant cultural and economic matrix. Class is further negated as inappropriate in analysis specific to culture and culture industries. It is also deemed a given, a fixed undertaking devoid of questioning, and therefore the need to simply move on, in how people make do and make sense of their classless realities.

The economic reductionism of class is triggered by the wide-ranging influence of imperialist globalization in all spheres of daily social experience. Imperialist globalization has successfully and kinetically moved capital that now redefines ways of sensing and experiencing reality. An ideal of imperialist globalization is the middle-classification of the masses, the attainability of a democratic standard of living for the majority of the population. The masses' gentrification is looked upon as a way of easing the political in issues that might tend to be political. In so doing, the political is eventually made to echo conservative and liberal politics. Class issues then give way to monitoring and distribution of government funds to projects, public accountability, electoral reforms and so on. What is particularly insidious in this class-less schema is the wholesale buy-in of postcolonial nations to middle classification as a national ideal.

The social imaginary of being middle class involves rationalization and substantiation. Culture industries are mobilized to reinforce and centralize themes of individual toward the fantasized ideals of national mobility. In the Philippines, there have been two divergent reactions to the fantasizing of the nation and its masses. The first one is provided by an oppositional nationalist historiography in which the masses are poised as central in history-making and nation-building. The second one is provided by movies as culture industry, in which stars, specifically action stars, are made spectacularized entities of the possible in politics. Because of the nature of the Filipino aksyon genre, the lead actor's fetishistic physical contact with the forces of the anti-hero and the masses brings into play a familiar fantasy in the aspiration for politics. A proof of this is that the stars catapulted into local and national politics are male leads from aksyon films.[9]

Colonialism brought in a colonial historiography that valorized and justified the influences of colonial rule. It played up the gains of great men and events in nation-building both symbolically and materially. On the other hand, nationalist historiography provides a case in point in how the masses were reclaimed as agents of history. Historian Renato Constantino states in his highly influential rewriting of national history that "[the] rich tradition of struggle has become a motive force of Philippine history. Participation in mass actions raises the level of consciousness of the masses. The more conscious they are, the more they become active and the more telling their contribution to the changing of society and the changing of their attitudes, until they come to realize that struggle is their histori-

cal right and it alone can make them free."[10] The masses' participation in the struggle to be free becomes the defining concept in
national history. The activization of the masses is the agent of being
in Philippine history. The pedagogical function of envisioning nationalism in the masses becomes the imperative of rewriting national
history. Constantino continues, "The only way a history of the
Philippines can be Filipino is to write on the basis of the struggles of
the people, for in these struggles the Filipino emerged."[11] The masses,
who accept a dormant emplacement in colonial historiography, are
awakened in nationalist historiography, made active subjects of the
nation.

The nationalist moment of class betrayal of the masses is
embodied in the Tejeros Convention of 1897. What was intended to
consolidate the revolutionary forces of the Katipunan emerged as the
occasion for its fragmentation into two camps: the Magdalo and the
Magdiwang factions. The former embodied the elite class dominance
of the affairs of the revolution; and the latter, its mass interest. Emilio
Aguinaldo of the Magdalo faction secured the presidency while the
plebeian leader Andres Bonifacio was elected the Director of Interior.
A member of the Magdalo faction protested Bonifacio's election,
"saying that the post should not be occupied by a person without a
lawyer's diploma."[12] Bonifacio was outmaneuvered, and eventually
ordered executed under Aguinaldo's command. This historical class
betrayal is documented and renarrativized in another nationalist
historian's work, *The Revolt of the Masses: The Story of Bonifacio and
the Katipunan* by Teodoro Agoncillo.[13] The book maps Bonifacio's life
against the backdrop of the revolutionary movement, pedagogically
positioning Bonifacio's consciousness against the larger wellspring of
the masses' own fermenting nationalist consciousness.

Such a betrayal becomes the defining moment of a Philippine
mass nationalism, one that seeks to position itself as distinct from the
classist variant of local intranationalisms. To a large extent, the cause
for the continuing nationalist struggle is the assertion of Bonifacio's
(and the masses') own disavowal by elite nationalism—that the
majority of the people remains under an oppressive national system
that only benefits a few. Bonifacio becomes the condensed signifier
of the mass nationalist legacy, continuing mass struggle, and future
utopia of mass control of the mode of production. He becomes the
signifier of the nation's past, present, and future. He embodies the
experience and the promise of securing the class interest of the
masses. Subsequent interrogation of official and elite nationalisms by
mass nationalist movements centers on the politicized image of the

mass subject. The assertion of a nationalist culture—including arts and literature, media and culture—is predicated on the emancipation and liberation of the masses.[14] Thus, to mobilize the concept of the masses involves the mobilization of a continuing political mass nationalism.

A contrast to the conceptualization and mobilization of the masses comes from mainstream cinema that seeks to propel actors into star images.[15] Culture industry plays a pivotal role in the breeding and orchestration of actors into stars, whose signification field extends beyond the celluloid texts.[16] Estrada, for example, mobilized his star system to yield gains in personal politics. His affinity with nationalist historiography is his filmic capacity to mobilize the masses and herald himself as their leader, to project himself as coming from one of their ranks. There is no overt betrayal of the masses; he remains the messianic figure embodying the mass condition and aspiration.[17] His films allow the mass audience to suture in dreams of mass nationalism actively at work in various local contexts. I analyze three Estrada films to illustrate the trajectory of Erap's mobilization of the masses. In *Geron Busabos* (Geron the Bum, 1964), the representatives of the underprivileged masses exist in the postwar boom years. In *Diligin Mo ng Hamog ang Uhaw na Lupa* (Sprinkle the Arid Earth with Dew, 1975), issues of land reform and continuing feudal oppression plague the landless peasants. In *Sa Kuko ng Agila* (In the Eagle's Claws, 1988), the presence of United States military bases in the country allows for a coalition of political masses. What seems to be a political trajectory of the masses—from gangs to political coalitions—is crucial to Estrada's presidential campaign and management.

Geron Busabos narrates the life of Geron (Estrada), a young intermittent laborer and leader of a homeless group of beggars, sex workers, and other laborers. Geron could have joined a protection racket syndicate, yet he chose to earn a living by working as a hand in the market. Even with his measly income, Geron does not succumb to the lures of easy money. A friend who robs a Caucasian to get cash for the treatment of the sick child and who uses Geron's name to extort money from stall owners is twice disavowed by Geron. By conniving with the syndicate, this person frames Geron for killing an underworld character. The film ends in a chase. Geron is wounded but proves his innocence and determination.

Geron becomes the locus of relations just as Quiapo, Manila's old district, becomes the nexus of commercial relations in the film. Quiapo's cityscape provides a matrix of institutions and institutional practices—the Catholic church whose patron, the Nazarene,

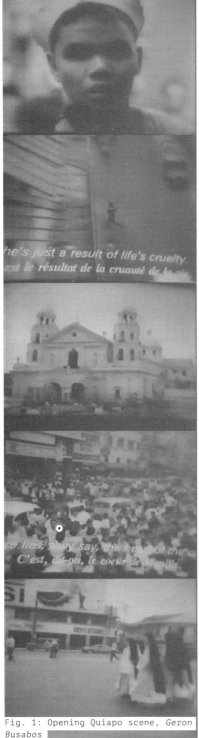

Fig. 1: Opening Quiapo scene, *Geron Busabos*

Fig. 2: Confused encounter with a foreign woman, *Geron Busabos*

extols tolerance of pain and suffering; the marketplace, where rural produce is retailed in urban space; and the country's first underpass, the marker of modern urban transformation. Geron is the Christian subject who re-enacts Christ's pain and liberation, the proto-laborer subject of the postwar economy, and the citizen-subject of the nation. He embodies the necessity for economic and modern transformation of bodies and cities. The surrounding masses provide the contradictions to this transformation. Geron is surrounded by other intermittent workers—*sampaguita* lei vendors, beggars, syndicate members, street musicians, part-time laborers—each of whom is ill-equipped to manage the economic and political transformation of the postwar economy. It is Geron's brute force, his manual labor, and his puritan value system that sustain him as a model citizen-subject. His common sense, drawn from survival tactics in street living, becomes the substance that determines his being. As Geron himself states, he believes in institutions but not in the corrupt men running the institutions.

Like Geron, Estrada's own coming into national being has been mythologized in two narratives. The first is his defense of a Filipino classmate against an American bully, which caused his expulsion from an elite boys' school, and his disenchantment with formal education as forbearer of human and social knowledges. The second is his petition and subsequent move to demolish the wall partitioning doctors and lowly workers in a cafeteria at a mental institution, which claimed the attention of both his doctor wife-to-be and his fellow workers. Such narratives play on the liminality of domains. Here is a man who could afford exclusive education but gave it up in defense of the abused Filipino. Here is a man who acts to change an unjust structural hierarchy. Estrada's politics afford him the liminality to mediate between two vested-interest realities. Such liminality of Estrada's power lies also in the perpetuation of "Erap jokes," classist jokes playing on Estrada's lack of intelligence, education, breeding, and fine being. Spread predominantly through high technology—the internet and text messaging, newer forms of orality—by the disenchanted middle and upper class, Erap jokes only reinforce Estrada's position as one of the masses. The attacks on Estrada are an assault on the class interest of the poor. What is especially interesting in the fabrication and dissemination of Erap jokes is the way class issues are brought into the foreground, when Estrada deems it necessary, as to evoke from the masses a real and reactionary disenchantment with the rich.

The battle is drawn along class lines in an ongoing class war orchestrated by Estrada. When an anti-Estrada rally led by Cardinal Sin and former president Corazon Aquino was mounted, Estrada was quick to pick up the class issue. Pitting against the anti-government elitist forces was his own participation in the predated birthday party celebration of Brother Mike Velarde, who leads a flock of millions. Cardinal Sin's rally, held in Makati, the country's financial district, represents elite interests while that of Brother Mike, a fundamentalist preacher with massive following in the D and E classes, and who played a decisive role in Estrada's election victory, is represented at a mass rally, held in Luneta, known as the "people's park."

The masses in Estrada's films are embodied for a double lack—miss on both physical and moral constituency and common-sense substance. The two other figures who provide Geron with a contrapuntal challenge are the female sex worker and the aging good cop. Because she is a sex worker, she is not able to fully experience romantic love with Geron, for he chooses to engage in love with the innocent sampaguita vendor. Because he is unaware of the politics surrounding police promotion, the aging good cop is not able to catch up with Geron's kineticism and moral righteousness. In one scene, Geron feels more privileged than the cop. Geron has graduated from being a street kid to a semi-skilled laborer while the cop remains a sergeant after almost two decades of fine service. The twice-disavowed character is morally wanting, but not wholly, as he asks for Geron's forgiveness before dying. So massive is Geron's hold on people that even the bad guys are influenced to do good. Geron becomes the master signifier of the masses' own movement in the modernization of and maintenance of tradition in the nation.

In *Diligin Mo ng Hamog ang Uhaw na Lupa*, David (Estrada) enjoins the masses to make him serve as their leader when the older leader is killed by the landlord's forces. The landlord plans to transform the land into a subdivision to be able to take up the challenge of the booming nation. The landlord orders the murder of the older leader to punish him for not working enough to convince the tenants to vote for his (landlord's) brother, who is running for governorship. The landlord orders the tenants' houses bulldozed, and the leader killed. Filmed like Moses' exodus, the tenants desert their land with David leading them. Despite persistent harassment from the landlord's forces, they continue to clear the grass land, work on irrigation, and construct new dwellings. David consummates his love for the slain elder's daughter. When the landlord's men destroy

Fig. 3: Hailing of a leader from the peasant ranks, *Diligin Mo ng Hamog ang Uhaw na Lupa*

the dam, they consolidate their forces to fight off new dangers and to rebuild their source of livelihood.

David's religious figure is uncanny. He is David, battler of giants or the wise young leader; Moses, leader of the exodus and postwar reconstruction; and Jesus, sufferer and liberator. The masses are thrown to him to be led. When they pack their things to escape further harassment from the landlord, the woman brings in David to lead them. Being a woman, she is unable to fully carry the weight of the masses' leadership. David rescues her from this anxious position. The masses also provide the backdrop for his epiphanies. When David and the woman make love, the masses sing the theme song, thereby fusing the issue of land reform and sexual consummation. The interior scene of lovemaking is intercut with the exterior scene of the masses singing around the bonfire.

Yet the film also shows another mass, contrapuntal to the dominance of the feudal lords. The armed mass movement provides swift justice when a farmer's daughter is gang-raped and murdered by the landlord's peasant. However, so incongruous is the political in the mass movement that David's brother, a member of the armed movement, unilaterally decides and orders the burning of David's hut because of David's disavowal of revolutionary principles and his questioning of the movement's moral righteousness. David shoots down the possibility of revolutionary mass change. Calling its leaders cowards, he challenges them to engage with the government in a dialogue. When he becomes the tenants' chosen leader, he involves the masses not in an armed struggle but in a contrary agrarian practice, one characterized by collectivity and land ownership. What is being poised in the film is the need for land reform.

The film was made at the height of Marcos's martial rule, whose cornerstone was land reform. Marcos's own iconography for the land reform involved him heartily smiling while planting rice seedlings in muddy fields. Marcos knew that land was the cause of massive discontent with the various national governments. Though his program was limited to rice and corn farms, he sought to liberate millions of farmers from agrarian bondage. What resulted, however, was dismal—a privileging of landed oligarchs and new cronies in agricultural businesses. Marcos's grand national vision was transformed for the interest of his few favored close subjects.

Estrada's own venture into politics was heralded through a close liaison with the Marcoses. Becoming mayor of a suburban town, he dwelled on greater benefits for the police while extolling them to greater professionalism, and built a public market and a public high school. Such architectonics recall Geron's Quiapo and the aspiration for the modern and traditional. The two leaders were involved in parallel modernization of the nation.

The masses in Marcos's realm become politicized only when they are massified for public spectacles—e.g., lining the streets, awaiting the arrival of international figures, paid to be mobilized for Marcos's rallies, or to participate in historical parades instantly climaxing in the Marcos's regime. Estrada's masses in *Diligin Mo ng Hamog . . .* are no different, becoming the units that form the spectacle in the mass exodus and the agents of transformation of the barren into productive lands. It is the pronounced self-effacement of David that eventually lingers in the film. The silent type that produces results, David relies little on public speeches but more on working side-by-side with the masses. He takes on much of the burden of the newer feudal harassment. In so doing, the self-effacement becomes self-valorization, the righteous member becomes finally recognized and signified as mass leader.

In *Sa Kuko ng Agila*, Tonio is a jeepney driver who witnesses the daily atrocities engineered by the presence of a United States military base in Olongapo, the biggest outside the mainland—a fisherfolk friend is killed when fishing in sea territory marked by the bases as restricted, a sex worker friend is jailed for killing a serviceman during a rape attempt, a ward is raped by an American, and so on. Without intending to, he shoots two hatchet men in self-defense. He flees and hides, only to resurface to clear his name. He falls for the journalist (played by now Senator Nikki Coseteng) who exposes the rape of his ward. The gang lord-aspirant mayor is exonerated by the courts. In the end, Tonio is cheered by the people, chanting his name while marching in the streets with the various enlightened sectors of the anti-bases coalition.

Olongapo is an allegory of the Philippines sieged by the literal and epistemic dominance of U.S. imperialism. As an allegory, the conditions of oppression and liberation in the film's location become the mediated experience in which Estrada is heralded as a national figure, a defender of the national masses. His filmic experience in politicizing the various sectors (except the women and female sex workers, a task taken up by the journalist) becomes a mode in which he propagandizes his national aspiration for Filipinos. Sure enough, such strong nationalist sentiments produced alliances between Estrada and the mass movement in the Aquino and Ramos adminis-trations, and produced his now-realized presidential ambition. The masses are represented by communities of the fisherfolk, the already enlightened student activists (led by the character portrayed by his son, Jinggoy Estrada), and the informal sector of female sex workers. The swelling of sympathizers and concerned people enlarges the mass. In the final scene, the slow-motion action of Tonio leading the mass action, with red flags and streamers waving, call into force the affinity with the nationalist mass movement.

Estrada is able to reinvent himself from a close Marcos ally to a staunch nationalist politician in the subsequent presidential administrations. Estrada's own temporal isolation from local politics during the Marcoses' exile led to an ingenious maneuver—that is, his resurrection as a nationalist, understanding of yet still disenchanted with the transformations of the Aquino and Ramos administrations. From a *comprador* of special administrative favors from Marcos that ensured efficient delivery of civic dole-outs, Estrada becomes a nationalist citizen-subject in the subsequent administrations, a move which opened up the possibility of staging the national through a nationalist rhetoric and performance. The masses in *Sa Kuko ng Agila* provided for him the paradigmatic shift to nationalist politics, a strategy for political longevity and viability. The politicized masses, however, remain enmeshed in personality politics, chanting Tonio's name instead of militant slogans. The significance of sound in the last slow-motion scene becomes uncanny, providing the impetus of the personality of the traditional politician in the coming wave of a new and more militant politics.

The masses are central to Estrada's filmic and political star systems. However, there remains a conscious representation of Estrada as iconographic of the "defender of the masses." His ordinary fashion (dirtied and even tattered shirts, denim jackets and pants, Converse rubber shoes), pomaded hair, lean moustache, angry-young-man look, hefty weight, and black wristband are markers of his working class yet masculine affinity. His characters are usually outsiders either in terms of origin or in terms of class relations, yet maintaining great virtue and patience.[18] He is the protector of the marginal. Thus, violence is never gratuitous, and opposite sex relations favor the virtuous woman. The hero is to be differentiated from the antagonist, represented as fashion savvy, mestizo, Spanish-speaking, weightier, wearing a necktie or scarf, with a cohesive family, and inhumane. And similar to Estrada's own weighty signification, the film's location in actual places of squalor or the mise en scene in general further confuses relations between the real, symbolic, and ideal. Estrada of the real and filmic politics is enmeshed in liminality to draw linkages between the ideals of both spheres that amounted, in Estrada's experience, to a maximized political and filmic mileage.

The aksyon hero is paralleled to the hero of the epic poems.[19] The epic is bearer of the social narrative of origin and conditions of specific communities in the Philippines. Proof of the mnemonic prowess of the epic is its sustainability even in the present day, and the absence of an epic in the Tagalog region, the most heavily colonized ethnic group in the country. While diverging from the notion of the epic as bearer of pure indigenous knowledge, I am proposing an analysis of the cultural politics of origin in the epic hero and nationalism. Land signifies the location of action in the epic and nation. It is the issue of transcendence and coming back. To talk of the land issue is to see the letter arriving at its destination, of the angst or absent signifier that coheres Philippine nationalism. The quest for sovereign territory, after all, is the motivation for the continuing nationalist struggle and movement. In *Geron Busabos*, the absence of land allows the contained movement of Geron and his pack. They experience the absence of land in the kind of work and speech they are entrusted to. Geron works only on days and hours when jobs are available. He engages in double-talk of love and hate with women. He is able to do so because of his landlessness, his ability to move from one destination to another, and his inability to move in permanently. In *Diligin Mo ng Hamog . . .*, the issue of land is mythologized in biblical terms, depicting land reform as central to any community and human development. On the one hand, the tenants are already landless in the enforced feudal relations of working in the fields of absentee landlords. They do not own the land they till, and the owners are not there to personally enforce feudal agreements. On the other hand, the masses' seeking of paradise devoid of economic determination becomes an unrealized utopia. The state owns the land of their utopia. What happens is a material and symbolic landlessness. The film's insistence on Marcosian land reform further aggravates the issue as history has shown its dismal performance, and the shifting to landlord-sanctioned cooperatives and stock corporations during Aquino's era, remains in place even in the Estrada administration. In *Sa Kuko ng Agila*, the quest for sovereignty is overtly positioned. Who really owns Philippine land? What becomes of the land issue in the trajectory of the three films is a greater transparency at pedagogy in which the films tackle the land issue. From an absent signifier in *Geron Busabos*, the land becomes mythologized for the purpose of propagandizing land reform in *Diligin Mo ng Hamog . . .* and allegorized through overt discussions of issues in *Sa Kuko ng Agila*. The land then becomes the signifier of the primal scene of national terror that organizes modern-day mobilization of national imaginaries. The masses become the landscape in which the land issue is narrativized.

Fig. 4: Righteous husband, *Diligin mo ng Hamog ang Uhaw na Lupa*

In Estrada's films, however, the masses do not speak or they speak only in unison. The masses never articulate the land issue. Given what Lacan has said, "that concepts take on their full meaning only when orientated in a field of language, only when ordered in relation to the function of speech," the masses are devoid of speech and organization of the real.[20] Therefore, the articulation is possible only in the unconscious, where the discourse of the other is possibly settled. What I think is being preserved in the unconscious of the masses in Estrada's films is the continuity of the mass nationalist project, a desire to free the mass subject. If Estrada's "desire finds its meaning in the desire of the other" (masses), on how crucial the masses become to Estrada's subjectivity, then "the first object of desire is to be recognized by the other."[21] Thus, the prominence of Estrada's character in films embodies a desire for ultimate and undeniable recognition—Estrada's character is Estrada as defender of the poor. What Estrada has done in film is to create, as what Lacan has suggested, "a function of language" not to inform but to evoke.[22] His evocation is garnered through a consequential response, a desired action to be specific, from the masses that constitute Estrada as the chosen leader. Prior to this evocation is Estrada's own disappearance in the masses, that his narrative is no different from the metanarrative of mass oppression and salvation. This evocative function finds affinity in the muted masses. How do they evoke their collective desire? By being silenced, they resist Estrada's language system, the machination of the ideal citizen-subject that massifies their existence and nullifies their speech. For in the end, Estrada will not survive in his own domination of the language system and must be able to evoke another sphere of seduction with the masses.

Estrada's filmic epiphany rests on the masses hailing him as their interpellated signifier of being. But Estrada's epiphany also rests in the domain of control of seductive women. In *Geron Busabos*, the drunk Caucasian woman in the exclusive club seduces and abjects Geron, repeatedly telling him that the club is not a place for him. The Caucasian woman brings Geron to his proper site of contest, into the city side streets where he could effect some social change. In *Diligin Mo ng Hamog*... the slain elder's daughter Perla recaps for David the choice he has to make. Perla gazes at the people in the caravan, using the masses as collateral to David's choice and destiny. Before the first sex scene in the film, Perla and David engage in sexual and national double-talk:

> Perla: *Ako ay lupa, matagal na naghintay sa patak ng ulan.* [I am the earth who has waited a long time for rain.]

> David: *Pagyayamanin ko ang lupa. At sa bawat halaman na itatanim ko ay didiligin ng hamog upang manatiling sariwa.* [I will enrich the earth. And every plant I sow will be watered by dew to keep it fresh.]

Through Perla's seduction, David realizes his proper and improper places. The land becomes the site of oppression, love, and struggle. He becomes the tiller and defender of lands and the masses' lives.

Diligin Mo ng Hamog . . . shows another sex scene in which David's roles as defender and nurturer are solidified. The sex scene involves an attempted gang-rape of Perla by the river. Such a scene, as in the gang-rape of a farmer's daughter in the rice paddies, calls attention to the tolerated sexuality during the early part of Marcos's martial rule. Marcos played up the proliferation of the *bomba* film, the soft porn genre, during the pre-martial law years to justify his declaration of martial rule. When it was declared, the bomba that featured mestiza bodies permutated into the wet-look film which used idealized Filipina brown bodies—petite body, oval face, and long hair—nationalized in Marcos's New Society, his utopia of "authoritarian democracy."[23] Perla was portrayed by Gloria Diaz, a Miss Universe beauty-title holder. The films were called the "wet-look" because the private parts of women were not exposed but displayed only through the veneer of white wet clothes. David comes to the defense of Perla, and realizes the need to protect and nurture Perla, who signifies, according to the film's dialogue, the land.

Fig. 5: Exodus and rebuilding, *Diligin mo ng Hamog ang Uhaw na Lupa*

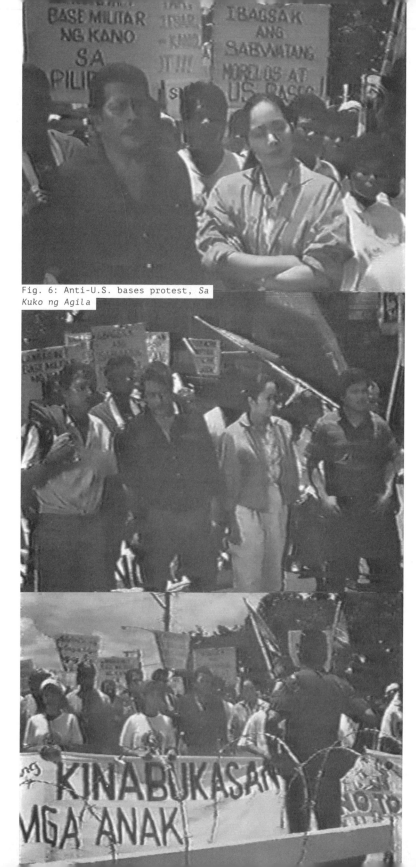

Fig. 6: Anti-U.S. bases protest, *Sa Kuko ng Agila*

In *Sa Kuko ng Agila*, though Tonio is already personally critical of American atrocities, he becomes publicly critical of it through a female lawyer-turned-journalist. This female character is typical of the strong women representation in Estrada's films—they humble him only to the extent he realizes his godly mission; then they become accessories in the male struggle. When Tonio is unable to fully articulate his feelings for the female character, the journalist asks, *"Nagdadalawang-isip ka ba dahil mas mataas ako sa iyo o dahil mas mababa ang tingin mo sa sarili mo?"* (Are you doubting because I am more privileged than you or because you think so lowly of yourself?) Once affirmed, Tonio is able to grapple with his ego-ideal, made synonymous with that of the masses.

By alienating class in the masses, the films doom individuals into a single commodity.[24] Marx stated in his definition of commodity as a "mysterious thing [. . .] because the relation of the producers to the sum total of their own labor is presented to them as a social relation, existing not between themselves, but between the products of their labor."[25] When individuals are constructed as a mass, the social relations between individuals are established only in relation to their production of the mass entity. The individual labor is negated in favor of a collective input that is never attributable to a single individual. Paradoxically, individuals will never have the chance to see the mass commodity, and therefore can never attribute their individual participation as something substantial in the mass. Individuals are always already alienated in the mass, never fully integrated and substantiated into the mass. Individuals, however, can only evoke the mass. This means that the individual can feel a certain nostalgia for the mass, for being part and parcel of the mass, but can never define with certainty what the mass is or was all about. Individuals can only speak of the mass in retrospect. The individuals bonding to form the mass become receptacle and symptoms of the mass—they embody the mass, they are the mass themselves but they are also infinite units of the mass and, therefore, negligible and manageable.

As a commodity, the mass is subject to fetishism. Politics and culture industries are the primary arena in the fetishism of the mass. The mass is made inseparable to the very production of Philippine politics. The massive vote-buying in elections, for example, is predicated on the mass being circulated, being demanded and sold. Culture industries also buy and sell the mass in the kinds of representation of mass in popular products, being made reflective of mass conditions and experiences on the one hand, and being targeted for consumption in mass capitalist culture on the other. What becomes of the mass, therefore, is a double fetishism of both consumption and production, becoming the very producer and consumer of products of the culture industries—what you produce you consume, what you consume you also produce. The mass becomes a kind of public private property of politicians and culture industries, which claim it as their own.

Marx has stated that alienation is based on private property.[26] The mass when proletariatized, as Marx stated, is "compelled to abolish [private property]."[27] In so doing, the proletariat mass becomes substantiated. For when the proletariats do not pursue their historical claim, they "feel destroyed in this alienation, seeing in it its own impotence and the reality of an inhuman existence."[28] Like the possibility of finding class in mass, the proletariat becomes one only through the private property, specifically its negation. Estrada unleashes his own alienation in film—he is always an outsider—to connote power. The masses, however, are alienated to thwart the possibility of an exit against the helplessness of their condition. What the task, therefore, presents is to raise the masses into a proletariat consciousness, one in which "this poverty [is] conscious of its own spiritual and physical poverty, this dehumanization which is conscious of itself as a dehumanization and hence abolish itself."[29] A critical perspective allows not for the production of self-reflexivity of the masses in texts—for how can one take over culture industries— but a kind of way of engineering the political in the understand-

Fig. 7: Reaction after verdict, *Sa Kuko ng Agila*

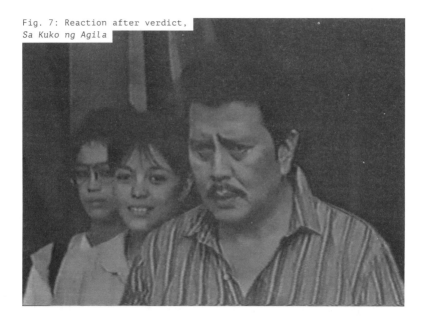

ing of possibilities in the transformation of the masses into some other entity—this entity called proletariat. As reported in Estrada's biography, such was the scene immediately after his inaugural address:

> Just after the President had driven off to his new official resi-
> dence, Malacañang Palace, long queues of humanity with ap-
> petites whetted like Batangas knives stormed the various food
> stations [housing the donated 5,000 roasted pigs and 20,000
> roasted chickens]. When food began to be given out, pandemo-
> nium broke loose as hordes of the masses rushed like swarms
> of starving locusts toward the stations, jostling one another and
> running off with whatever food pieces they could grab as their
> prize.[30]

Power and Gangsterism in Estrada

At another amassment of people, a stampede occurred. People had been queuing outside the presidential palace gate for application forms for possible jobs. The stampede killed at least one person and injured dozens. The positivizing intercourse of people's hopes and government promises causes the damage inflicted on the whole so-cial order of massification. On the one hand, the stampede disrupts such a given order; on the other hand, it also extols damage and life, usually of a member of the mass. As Balibar reminds us, "No one can be liberated or emancipated by others, although no one can liber-ate himself without others."[31] Estrada's power presents an insidious violence inflicted among the ranks of the historically disempowered mass.

In his films, this kind of covert violence is penetrated through his inner circle, a gang-like culture where he is central as the gang lord.[32] Though the literal violence is inflicted on the anti-hero and his gang, giving the aksyon film its fetishistic physicalization of violence, the covert violence is inflicted on the members of the inner circle. By sucking the subjectivity of its members, the gang lord positions himself as the central dispenser of meaning and practices. Individuals become dispensable, their subjectivity not integral to their being. Their existence as individuals is predicated on their being at the beck and call of the gang lord. As such, they do not need subjectiv-ity; the gang lord forecloses any possibility for the individual to gain subjectivity.

Gangsterism in Estrada's films takes on a parallel dimension in his politics. Gangsterism refers to a clique illicitly running the affairs of the nation. Presented suggestively as an underworld, the gangster's realm is ruled by the gang lord, the utmost representation of totalitarian control. What Estrada has done in politics is to wed the above and underworlds, by using underworld tactics to manage the affairs of the above world or the nation-state. Such gangster tactics readily opens up the possibility of Estrada being labeled as a totalitarian figure. His political ambition, after all, was realized and nurtured at the height of the Marcos dictatorship. He embodies the Marcosian trace, reinstalling the Marcoses and their cronies to a mass degree of public acceptance.[33] By "Marcosian trace," I play on the idea of Freud on repression and rupture, "[The] common character of the mildest as well as the severest cases, to which the faulty and chance actions contribute, lies in the ability to refer the phenomena to unwelcome, repressed, psychic material, which, though pushed away from consciousness, is nevertheless not robbed of all capacity to express itself."[34] The post-Marcos era left a vacuum of supremacy in the gang which some two decades later Estrada would fill up. Though invisible in public coverage of Imelda Marcos's affairs—e.g., her acceptance of an exemplary mother award at Malacañang Palace or her lavish birthday celebration in 2009—Estrada remains complicit with any Marcos affair as with any Marcos-related political discourse. It is precisely in his invisibility that the gang lord sustains control over gang members and their spheres of influence.

Marcos cronyism and its permutation in the Estrada administration are back big-time. Eduardo Cojuangco Jr. resumes control of the beer-and-food conglomerate San Miguel Corporation. Another presidential friend, Mark Jimenez, mediated the country's biggest business deals. He remains in the country fighting an extradition case filed by the U.S. government. What is especially exacerbating about the cronyism of the Estrada administration is the built-in informality of decision-making, "There's too much reliance on informal processes. That creates unpredictability."[35] There is also an accommodating attitude toward every member worth maintaining. As *Asiaweek* cites as an example, "He split the agriculture department to provide jobs for two presidential advisers—agriculture secretary Angara [Estrada's losing vice-president running mate] and food security czar William Dar."[36]

Gangsterism also rests on the proliferation of gambling and other get-rich-quick plans. Though scorned by the characters Estrada portrays in his films, these practices proliferate in his administration.

There is no other time in Philippine history when legalized gambling is so widespread—jai-alai betting and on-line bingo has joined the lotto and casino. The two contending noontime shows have undergone quick reformatting, giving away huge sums of money and prizes to winners of game segments. The prize is usually higher than the average annual income of Filipinos. As a consequence of this tele-visual psychosis, people fall in line for months, just to be able to have a chance to participate in the contests. Behind this cultural phenom-enon, based on the popularization of gambling as a vehicle for social mobility, is a social helplessness, masses of individuals waiting for a material redemption of their plights. It also underscores the fact that the symbolic imagery of Estrada is no longer enough to bolster the masses; the masses are already awaiting real remuneration for their participation in the Estrada machine.

However, the process whereby the masses actively take on the material issue is slow to grind. A newspaper reported of Estrada's inaugural address: "[He sounded] just like the champion of the masses in the movies he used to make—he threatened the crooks and criminals, revered the elderly and heroes of the past, promised deliv-erance for the poor and oppressed."[37] What such a report underscores is the brevity of power of Estrada's signifier, that every text and act become a reverberation of his star system ideal. Such a report perpe-tuates Estrada's myth and negates the violence, both epistemic and literal, it inflicts on the masses.

Anthropologist Jean-Paul Dumont, referring to the violence of Japanese atrocities in Siquijor which can be referred to Estrada's own kind of infliction of violence on the masses, states, "The expe-rience of violence had structured the ideology of the experience in such a way that the ideology, in turn, structured the experience."[38] Violence circulates through Estrada's masses relying on the ideology of Estrada—as signifier of defender of the poor—as much as this ideology relies on the experience of an Estrada violence. A way to deal with such violence is through dereliction, primarily signified by the elite-class interest in Erap jokes. For the masses, the acceptance of their powerlessness perpetuates violence—i.e., internalizing, project-ing, and materializing violence in the high incidence of crimes among the already marginalized, including members of family. The masses' stance of ridiculing the icon—as in a protesting teacher demanding full release of back pay at the presidential palace, mimics Estrada's macho stance—connotes a sacrilegious or profane act, punishable for being disrespectful to authority.

Such profane acts, however, are individualized and localized reactions, almost improbable to imagine can cohere into a mass action. If what Raul Pertierra states of the cause and effect of Philippine violence is true—

> [The] lack of complementarity between the ideological structures within the jurisdiction of the state but outside its control, and the material-economic resources outside its jurisdiction but within its control, needed for its reproduction, points to the absence of a direct reflection of class relations in the Philippine polity. As a result, the practical consciousness of many Filipinos is embedded in routines derived from notions of kinship, locality, and association that generally lie outside the formal structures of the state, even if substantially coterminous with it.[39]

then class again becomes an elided category in which social relations are experienced. The perceived lack of complementarity might indicate the specificity in which class relations in the Philippines are developed and perpetuated by national and local politics. For how can practical consciousness be without the regimentation of the state's national consciousness? Where then to claim the social signification of the masses?

In the next section, I am interested in fleshing out the extent of Estrada's "supreme violence," the paradox of which being that it "is no longer experienced as violence."[40] That Estrada is seen as productive or neutral only seeks to perpetuate the invisibility of the material violence. In laying bare the implications of Estrada's violence, I intend to "render visible the violence that maintains the very neutral, 'non-violent' framework that is subsequently perturbed by the eruptions of (empirical) violence."

Jose Lacaba writes of the *bakya* (wooden clogs) crowd, referring to the lowly crowd, the *masa*, as another class-related issue, reflecting "[the elite's] alienation from the mass of Filipinos who make up the bakya crowd."[41] His suggestion furthers the violence, the alienation of class in mass, and mass in class. What this implies is that intensification and nullification of class in mass, and mass in class. Estrada's own pretension at mass—mass background, mass work, mass aspiration—invokes a desire to be in at least two positions, locations, and subject positions. His identification with Bonifacio as hero falls contradictory as his inauguration was designed after Aguinaldo's own. This is consistent with the laying bare of his own class interest—on the one hand, he presides over Southeast Asia's fastest-growing gross development product; on the other hand, "Estrada is the first president not to succumb to worker's pressures to raise wages."[42] In wanting to become the master signifier, Estrada mobilized the contradictions of class interest generated between his overwhelming popularity with the people, and the business-as-usual attitude of the elite. In a poll taken in June 1999, 28 percent of business executives said Estrada failed to deliver his promises; also during that period, Estrada received a 74 percent approval rating from the people.[43] In playing up class, Estrada is alienating the mass of Filipinos from each other. In playing up mass, he is alienating real class issues in the discussion of mass. As Balibar points out, "Social relations are not established between hermetically closed classes or alternatively that class struggle takes place within classes themselves."[44]

Another manifestation of violence is the metropolitanization, instead of proletarianization, of the mass especially in the era of imperialist globalization. Metropolitanization involves the transformation of bodies, geographies, and economies in the name of attracting greater capital, mostly from international sources. It seeks compliance with global standards of, at least, middle-class living, even when actual material resources remain limited. Such metropolitanization involves the nation and its masses' minuscule role in the global and sexual division of labor. Subcontractualization, six-month contracting of labor, is fast becoming the norm of employment. Masses of Filipinos perform overseas contract work. Some five million workers remitted USD 9 billion in 1999.[45] In Estrada's films, Quiapo, rural areas and the hub of American militarism, for example, become the organizing geography in which other sites, such as bodies and sexualities, are made to conform. The masses are made to redevelop based on their substrata role in the global penetration of capital in the national. With perceived gentrification, the metropolitanized masses are caught up in a sado-masochistic libidinal economy, experiencing pain and suffering for the promise of middle-class redemption. It is in the emplacement of the masses into the economic sphere, devoid of class, that they remain politically inchoate, an ideal of Third World subject-citizen formation. They are connected to the illusory markers of being middle class; they are conjugated from their class interests.[46] These continuities and stoppages mark the uneven embodiment of capital penetration among the masses.

Finally, masochism is another manifestation of violence, the experience of "corporeal pleasure in pain."[47] Moral masochism, as Kaja Silverman explains, involves a stronger psychic entity for the ego to be pushed to the last extremity.[48] This psychic entity refers to the thoroughness with which "the subject has been subordinated to prohibition and denial."[49] Estrada can be read as this psychic entity that has caused a moral masochism in the masses. In his films, he becomes part and parcel of the available cluster of images from which the masses see themselves as they want others to see them (Silverman's imaginary introjection), and in his state function, he is the Law in which subjectivities of the subject-citizen are to be generated (Silverman's symbolic introjection).[50] While the imaginary introjection allows for a certain room for individual agency, Estrada's four-decade posturing as master signifier of "defender of the masses" presents him as a veritable image of subjectivity in which subject-audiences and subject-citizens are heralded. Taking off from Zizek's formulation of democracy and totalitarianism, the Estrada subject *knows very well* that Estrada is unreal, not really the defender of the masses, *but just the same* he/she acts as if Estrada's mystique was possible.[51]Estrada's fetishism with the masses, however, belies total control. For he, too, introjects the masses as the other's master signifier from which his own subjectivity is to be generated. Estrada and the masses love each other as much as they want to annihilate each other.

The erosion of class category in Estrada's masses gives way to an economic development model of identity and nation-formation. The middle-classification of the masses has already reorganized major aspects of our social experience. Laws, for example, have been legislated to favor privatization, liberalization, and commercialization. Such acts of the state and commerce eventually reorganize spheres of experiencing emotions, education, culture, media, religion, political parties, and so on. Where then to claim the politicized signification of the masses?[52] The etymology of *bakbakan* films connotes a slow erosion or decay, as in how termites might be able to interiorize the wooden structures. On the one hand, Estrada could very well embody the masses, staging for them in films and politics how one of them can succeed. There is an ongoing reversal of moral accountability, with Estrada putting pressure on the masses to strive even harder. As he has said in *Geron Busabos*, "It is men, not the system, that is the problem." Thus, Estrada has used the masses for politicking, not for politicization. On the other hand, the masses could be that entity that has already interiorized the master signifier. Many criminals have and will enjoy immortality via the film biographies produced out of the aksyon films. The analysis of masses has shown that their general silencing negates forms of intersubjectivity whereby communication and solidarity can be rendered possible. How might the model of the master signification, one that serves only Estrada and preempts the subjectivity of individuals comprising the mass, be interrogated to allow for individuals to look into each other for models of bonding and active subject-formation?

The political needs to be made integral into attempts at newer modeling of subject-formation. What have been presented thus far in this essay are the modes in which subjection of the masses are fantasized and materialized in Estrada's films and politics. What needs to be further theorized and materialized is how subjectivation of marginally emplaced individuals realizing subjectivity might be realized.[53]

ENDNOTES

1   From the Social Weather Stations exit poll, quoted in Isabelo T. Crisostomo, *President Joseph Ejercito Estrada: From Stardom to History* (Quezon City: J. Kriz Publishing, 1999), 314.

2   Joel David and Lynn Pareja, "Aksyon," in *CCP Encyclopedia of Philippine Art: Volume VIII Philippine Film* (Manila: CCP, 1994), 82–83. The local aksyon genre developed as a reaction to big-budgeted Hollywood films.

3   Being a gambler, womanizer, and alcoholic.

4   Estrada's film background is not discussed without a feature of his political career. See Emmie Velarde, "Joseph Estrada," *All Star Cast* (Manila: Cine Gang Publications, 1981), 30–39; Quijano de Manila, "Erap in a New Role," *Joseph Estrada and Other Sketches* (Manila: National Bookstore, 1977), 1–43; and Ricky Lo, "Joseph Estrada, Era ni Erap," *Star-Studded* (Makati: Virtusio Books, Inc., 1995), 68–73.

5   The literal use of *masa* is perpetuated up to Estrada's first year of office with "Ulat sa Masa" (Report to the Masses) and "Paradang Masa Laban sa Kahirapan" (Parade of the Masses Against Poverty). The socioeconomic implications of Estrada's first year is succinctly elaborated by Antonio Tujan Jr., "Sizing Up Erap," *Perspectives* 1, no. 13 (19 Jul 1999): 4–9. For a historical development of masa, see Corazon L. Santos, "Ang Politisasyon ng Masa at ang nobelang *Sa mga Kuko ng Liwanag* ni Edgardo M. Reyes," (unpublished manuscript, 1999).

6   Raymond Williams, "Masses," *Keywords* (New York: Oxford University Press, 1983), 195.

7　Etienne Balibar, "From Class Struggle to Classless Struggle?" *Race, Nation, Class: Ambiguous Identities* with Immanuel Wallerstein (London: Verso, 1991), 162–63.

8　Gilles Deleuze and Felix Guattari, *A Thousand Plateaus: Capitalism and Schizophrenia* (Minneapolis: University of Minnesota Press, 1987), 221.

9　A partial list of the more prominent aksyon stars becoming politicians are: Senator Ramon Revilla; his son, Bong Revilla, the governor of Cavite; and Lito Lapid, governor of Pampanga; Rey Malonzo, mayor of Kalookan City; and Estrada's own son, Jinggoy, mayor of San Juan.

10　Renato Constantino, *The Philippines: A Past Revisited (Pre-Spanish-1941)* (Manila: Constantino, 1975), 10–11.

11　Ibid., 11.

12　Ibid., 184–85.

13　Teodoro Agoncillo, *The Revolt of the Masses: The Story of Bonifacio and the Katipunan* (Quezon City: University of the Philippines Press, 1996).

14　For a problematization of literature and national consciousness, see Caroline Hau's critical essay "Literature, Nationalism and the Problem of Consciousness," *Diliman Review* 46, nos. 3–4 (1998): 3–24.

15　The notion of masses has an affinity with crowds in film, as discussed in Martin Rubin, "The Crowd, the Collective, and the Chorus: Busby Berkeley and the New Deal," in *Movies and Mass Culture* (London: Athlone, 1996), 59–92.

16　For a discussion of culture industries, see Herbert Marcuse, "Some Social Implications of Modern Technology," *The Essential Frankfurt School Reader* (New York: Continuum, 1993), 138–62. Also, for the use of mass technology, see Claude Lefort, "Outline of the Genesis of Ideology in Modern Society," *The Political Forms of Modern Society: Bureaucracy, Democracy, Totalitarianism* (Cambridge: MIT Press, 1986), 181–236. Both essays deal with totalitarian regimes.

17　The notion of sacrifice and messianic mission can also find parallelism in the notion of abjection. See Julia Kristeva, *Powers of Horror: An Essay on Abjection* (New York: Columbia University Press, 1982).

18　For a list of characteristics of the action hero, see Agustin Sotto, "Christ Figures in Troubled Land," *Unang Pagtingin sa Pelikulang Bakbakan*, monograph (Manila: Cultural Center of the Philippines, 1989), 8–9.

19　See, for example, Zeus A. Salazar, "Ang Kulturang Pilipino sa harap ng mga Institusyong Panlipunan sa Pelikulang Bakbakan," and Prospero R. Covar, "Paniniwala, Pananampalataya, at Paninindigan sa Pelikulang Bakbakan," *Unang Pagtingin sa Pelikulang Bakbakan*. Also see Isagani Cruz, "Si Lamang, si Fernando Poe Jr., at si Aquino: Ilang Kurokuro Tungkol sa Epikong Pilipino," in *Kritisismo: Mga Teorya at Antolohiya para sa Epektibong Pagtuturong Panitikan* (Manila: Anvil, 1992).

20　Jacques Lacan, *Escrits: A Selection* (New York: W.W. Norton & Company, 1977), 39.

21   I am adapting Lacan's statement on self and other, Ibid., 58.

22   Ibid., 86.

23   I discuss the various permutations of the bomba genre in "Mattering National Bodies and Sexualities," and "Articulations of the Nation-Space: Cinema, Cultural Politics and Transnationalism in the Philippines," dissertation (University of Southern California, 1996).

24   For a discussion of the relationship of money and subjectivity, see Slavoj Zizek, "'I or He or It (the Thing) Which Thinks'," *Tarrying With the Negative* (Durham: Duke University Press, 1993), 27–29.

25   Karl Marx, "Capital, Volume One," *The Marx-Engels Reader* (New York: W.W. Norton & Company, 1978), 320.

26   Karl Marx, "Alienation and Social Classes," *The Marx-Engels Reader*, 133–35.

27   Ibid., 133.

28   Ibid.

29   Ibid., 134.

30   Crisostomo, *President Joseph Ejercito Estrada*, 315.

31   Etienne Balibar, "Subjection and Subjectivation," *Supposing the Subject* (London: Verso, 1994), 12.

32   For an elaboration of violence in other bakbakan films, see Joel David, "Men and Myths" and "Ma(so?)chismo," *Fields of Vision: Critical Applications in Recent Philippine Cinema* (Quezon City: Ateneo de Manila University Press, 1995), 80–84.

33   The high-profile birthday celebration of Imelda Marcos was featured in the *Philippine Daily Inquirer,* 3 Jul 1999, 1. Photos by Dennis Sabangan include the Marcos children dancing, or greetings by American actor George Hamilton.

34   Sigmund Freud, *Psychopathology of Everyday Life* (New York: Mentor Books, 1964), 159

35   Alex Magno, quoted in "Better Than Expected," 19.

36   Ibid.

37   Quoted in Crisostomo, *President Joseph Ejercito Estrada,* 314.

38   Jean-Paul Dumont, "Ideas on Philippine Violence: Assertions, Negations and Narrations," *Discrepant Histories: Translocal Essays on Filipino Cultures* (Philadelphia: Temple University Press, 1995), 266.

39   Raul Pertierra, "Political Consciousness Versus Cultural Identity," *Philippine Localities and Global Perspectives* (Quezon City: Ateneo de Manila University Press, 1995), 16.

40   Slavoj Zizek, "Appendix Taking Sides: A Self-Interview," *The Metastases of Enjoyment* (London: Verso, 1994), 204.

41   Jose F. Lacaba, "Movies, Critics, and the Bakya Crowd," *Readings in Philippine Cinema* (Manila: Experimental Cinema of the Philippines, 1983), 177.

42   Todd Crowell and Antonio Lopez, "Better Than Expected," *Asiaweek*, 2 Jul 1999, 18; quoted by Roberto Romulo also in Crowell and Lopez, "Better Than Expected," 19.

43   Quoted in Gil C. Cabacungan Jr. and Elena R. Torrijos, "Poll Shows More Execs Unhappy Over Economy," *Philippine Daily Inquirer*, 1 Jul 1999, 1; and Martin P. Marfil, "Estrada Vows to Liberate Poor," *Philippine Daily Inquirer*, 8 Jul 1999, 1.

44   Balibar, "From Class Struggle to Classless Society," 171.

45   Doris Dumlao, "$8B in OFW money seen to prop up RP economy," *Philippine Daily Inquirer*, 1 Oct 1999, B1.

46   Deleuze and Guattari define connection as "[indicating] the way in which decoded and deterritorialized flows boost one another, accelerate their shared escape, and augment or stroke their quanta" while conjugation as "[indicating] their relative stoppage, like a point of accumulation that plugs or seals the lines of flight, performs a general reterritorialization, and brings the flows under the dominance of a single flow capable of overcoding them" (220).

47   Kaja Silverman, "Masochism and Male Subjectivity," *Male Trouble* (Minneapolis: University of Minnesota Press, 1993), 36.

48   Ibid., 39.

49   Ibid.

50   Ibid., 40.

51   Slavoj Zizek, *Looking Awry: An Introduction to Jacques Lacan through Popular Culture* (London: MIT Press, 1993), 168.

52   In film, this has been explored by Petronilo Bn. Daroy, "Social Significance and the Filipino Film," *Readings in Philippine Cinema*, 95–108; and Patrick Flores, "Plotting the People Out," *Pelikula* 1, no. 1 (Sept 1999): 10–13.

53   See Etienne Balibar, "Subjection and Subjectivation," *Supposing the Subject*, 1–15.

Judiciary

Lack and Excess in the Representations of Justice

P hilippine cinema primarily represents the judicial and legal systems as externally inaccessible to those who seek redress from it. In the rare times they become accessible, they are deemed the harsh implementation of either an inhumane or an inutile system—inhumane because they seek to implement a rectification process that does not consider the melodrama of the human condition, and inutile because they are unable to resolve that which it is supposed to do due to larger impositions of transnational military treaties or local corruption. This essay seeks to investigate the representations of justice in contemporary Philippine cinema—firstly, the conventions of the legal scene in film; secondly, how these images typify a politicized imagination of the judicial system; and lastly, the stakes in cultural politics involved in such representations.

What seems to be a judicial lack is predetermined by a simultaneous experience of excess. The primordial lack of justice cohabits the space of the excessive effort to sustain and project the lack in some other ego-ideal or the naturalization of trauma. The massive condition of poverty—a figuration of excess or, in fact, an excess of lack—provides the void that reinforces the construction and deconstruction of judicial lack and excess. The Philippines' poverty rate is the highest in Southeast Asia at 40 percent, which means that some 15.3 million Filipinos (half of the poor population) live below abject poverty.[1] In turn, this national lack leads to an easy maneuvering of abusing power, constituted to disenfranchise the historically marginalized. Poverty bespeaks a lack, including the lack of judicial access. Poverty also constitutes the excessive abuse of power, including the excess of containment via the law and its exile and displacement of the historically marginalized. This dialectic of lack and excess of poverty, disenfranchisement, power, and the judiciary is what propels the cultural politics of how law and justice are represented in Philippine cinema.

Legal films—centered on court battle scenes, providing an impression of the judiciary's dysfunctional nature—are very rare in Philippine cinema. Court scenes, however, remain plentiful in at least three genres. In action films, one finds the action hero or his loved one falsely convicted, or the guilty powerful figure as innocent. In sex movies, we see the female lead star accused of a crime which was done for a moral right. In melodrama, however, the court scene becomes a dramatic narrative convention. This is the space where suffering seems endless or the heroine is exonerated of a false accusation. In the domestic melodrama *Adultery: Aida Macaraeg*,[2] the pregnant heroine is torn between her forced marriage to a convicted drug pusher and her new life as the other woman of a rich married man. The court scene becomes the crux of the emotional upheaval as her husband is suddenly paroled and her present partner, a "respectable" man, decides to take custody of their son until the case is settled. The court scenes are calculated to show her sure defeat in the legal case. She kneels in front of her husband, begging him to release her from her duties as his wife. Aida believes that the only person she can claim as her own is her son. Just when the decision is to be handed down, the husband disrupts the proceedings by withdrawing his case against Aida. The denouement shows Aida in the breakwater of a park, when the son suddenly comes running to her, accompanied by her husband. The husband confesses that he and her partner have already resolved the case—the partner will release Aida's son and the husband will relocate, leaving them in peace.

The film ingenuously weaves the culture of domestic disarray by intercutting a radio melodrama with the aggravation of Aida's familial predicament. Aida works as a Chinese restaurant recep-

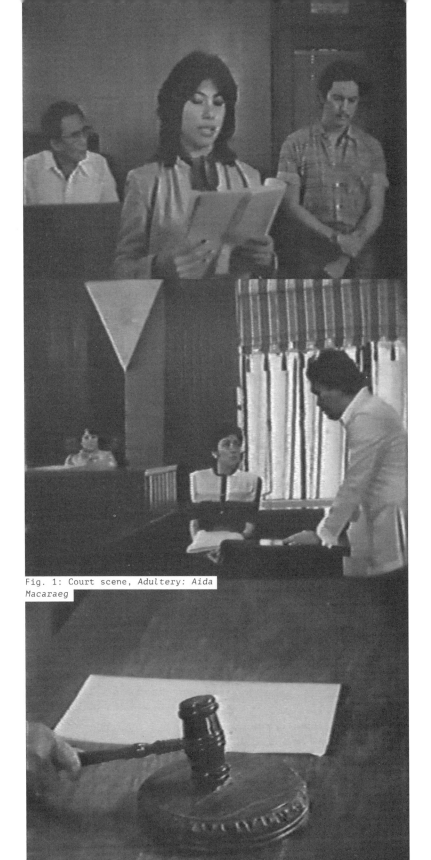

Fig. 1: Court scene, Adultery: *Aida Macaraeg*

tionist. Her meager salary supports her father's medical needs, her sister's education, her brother's young family, and her mother. She represents the *mater dolorosa* (suffering mother), iconic of the pained Virgin Mary symbol in Catholic-dominant Philippine society. The last straw in her family saga is the unexpected revelation that her unemployed brother's wife was expecting a second child. She decides to move in with her boyfriend but chooses not to marry. Her religiously devoted mother disowns her, like her younger sister who chose to become the mistress of a rich man. Her mother's move to declare her as immoral posits her as a trespassing deviant, marking her moral downfall and aggravating her ethical turbulence.

Court scenes in Philippine films are deemed uncinematic because of the actual location's materiality. Halls of justice are not known for their architectural innovation, much less for sensitive interior designs. These have been sites known to be fire-traps and security-risk areas—sections or buildings have burned in separate incidents due to faulty wiring, low ceilings, and congested and enclosed interiors. There have also been continual reports of stolen evidence in various court depositories, and of convicts attempting— and succeeding—to escape through the court building. The court scene usually takes place in a big, oftentimes dilapidated room that serves as a trial court. The judge sits on a raised wooden podium for older court scenes, or simply at a study table with a gavel in recent scenes. An oversized Philippine flag is draped as the judge's backdrop. On the walls are big pictures of the incumbent president and notices of silence. Because of the courts' general lack of space, they also serve as storage, with gray filing cabinets lining the walls. Legal scenes are depicted in film only through this site, or through lawyers' offices.

There are three horizontal axes of action, with only one vertical axis that connects the judge to the others. The judge is the center of the action, who often remains silent in the scenes. Actors who play the role of the judge sit in front of the nation's most important signifier—the national flag which represents their national mandate to dispense justice to those who seek it. The role of judge is usually portrayed by honorable and senior-looking actors. In earlier films, actors did not wear robes. Robes became mandated costumes when they were instituted as a requirement for all judges. The second axis is the witness stand, which takes up much of the scene. This is the axis where witnesses and suspects are forcefully interrogated by opposing lawyers. The third axis is the accused's family or friends, or the complainant in the audience row. This is the familiar site of reaction shots—usually a close-up shot of worried looks—as the character in the witness stand tries to grapple with the questions. The vertical axis, however, emanates directly from the judge, dispensing a ruling, stating a recess, or ordering the witness.

Aida asks her husband a final question at the end of the film: *"Ano ang nangyari sa atin?"* (What happened to us?) The moment of domestic bliss has become a nostalgic experience—it never existed but nonetheless is now idealized. The husband answers, with possible reference to the accessibility of the nation's judicial system, *"Huwag mo nang itanong, baka mas masakit kung malaman natin ang sagot."* (Don't ask, it might be more painful to know the answer.) The husband's new position, however, is exemplary of the triumph of the prison system and its power to reform and rehabilitate criminals. Even when not functioning to its fullest potential, the judicial system is idealized in a conscious repression. This essay attempts to foreground the repressed answers, painful as this may seem. The renarrativization of the trauma underscores the cultural politics in locating the newer imaginary of blissful ignorance in repression.

Political Disenfranchisement and Postcolonial Condition

The judiciary system is perceived to be inutile, only seeking to validate those in power in the Philippines. In social melodramas such as *Minsa'y Isang Gamu-Gamo*[3] and *Sa Kuko ng Aguila*,[4] films that tackled the U.S. bases in the Philippines, the narratives are poised in the anti-climactic closure offered by local courts being inutile to dispense justice to the disenfranchised characters. The star system driving the films—Nora Aunor, the brown Cinderella in *Minsa'y*; Joseph Estrada, the defender of the masses in *Sa Kuko*, and an actor who would later become president—evokes the ordinary citizen's quest for justice in the judiciary system or recourse to quasi-judicial means when the system becomes unavailable. The mass audience is made to identify with icons typifying ordinary people's quests for social justice. On the one hand, this identification makes justice a doubly imagined fantasy, circulated in the fantasy production of film-viewing and in the casting of icons being deprived of illusory justice. On the other hand, the lack of justice in film produces another form of identification in the real, as icons strive to expand on their star status by joining politics. Estrada is the most celebrated and infamous case: he reached the highest position in 2000, and was deposed in 2001. He now is entangled in his own quest for justice, as he evades prosecution of his corruption cases, his fans remaining steadfast in their support.

The legal system in the Philippines has been mostly based on the colonial masters' systems—Spain (family and property laws, and absence of jury trial) and the U.S. (trade and commerce, labor relations, taxation, banking and currency). The failure of the legal system in the Philippines is emphasized in recent history, from the Marcos period (1965–1986) to the present. Marcos compromised the legal system by reconstituting the Supreme Court with appointees beholden to his presidency. There are only some thirty thousand lawyers practicing in the Philippines, one-third of whom are based in Manila. A court study found that "even if the judges were to work 50 percent faster, it would take them 476 years to catch up [with the volume of cases filed]."[5]

Minsa'y Isang Gamu-Gamo tells the intertwined narratives of two lovers from lower-middle-class families in Pampanga, the site of the Clark Air Force Base, the biggest American air base outside the mainland.[6] Corazon has just been accepted as a trainee nurse in Michigan, and goes through the process of finalizing her papers at the U.S. Embassy in Manila. Bonifacio dreams of entering the U.S. Navy in the immediate future. Their American dream begins to shatter as Bonifacio's mother, Yolanda, a worker in the base's commissary, is interrogated and humiliated by a Filipina merchandise officer. She gets ordered to go to an enclosed cubicle, is strip-searched for illegal goods and, when told to leave, has her panties confiscated by the officer. The officer playfully toys with the panties hanging on the tip of her pen, waving it at the crowd, twitching her nose in disdain at the soiled underwear's smell. Bonifacio and Yolanda decide to file a complaint, despite the mother already showing early signs of hesitation, given the scenario painted by the lawyer. The lawyer decides to file a criminal complaint for slander against the merchandise control guard, and sends a letter of protest to the American base commander. The mother asks Bonifacio, "*Tama kaya ang ginagawa natin? Paano tayo lalaban sa Amerikano?*" (Are we doing the right thing? How can we fight the Americans?) The periodic enunciation of rhetorical questions emphasizes the anxious psychical state in the social melodrama. The oscillation of will and choice—to fight for justice or to negotiate with the bigger power—becomes the nexus of aggravating circumstances for the lead characters to decide their fate in the film's ending.

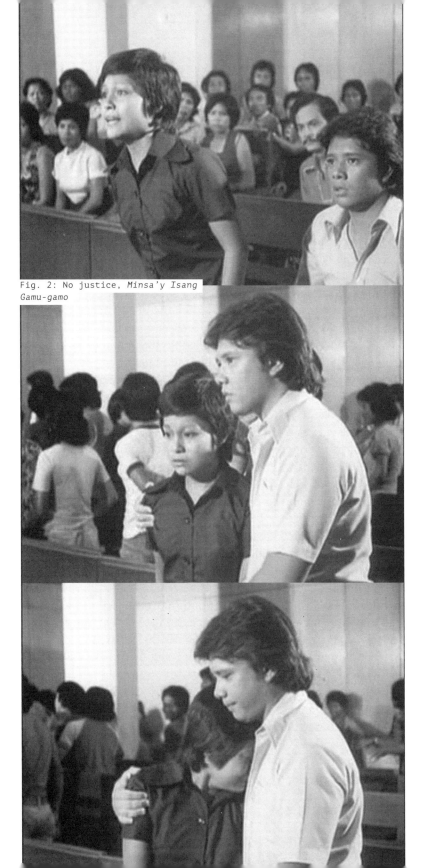

Fig. 2: No justice, *Minsa'y Isang Gamu-gamo*

In retaliation to her complaint, the guard, backed by two American service personnel, raids Yolanda's PX (American goods) store, confiscating all items. Yolanda is caught off-guard and, when once again offered an "amicable settlement," decides to take it against Bonifacio's protestations. Her goods are returned, but Bonifacio decides to relinquish his plans to join the navy, much to Corazon's disappointment. During her farewell party, her younger brother is neglected because of the preparations. Her brother decides to accept the invitation of his friends to scavenge in the bases' restricted dumpsite areas. He is shot dead by a bored American serviceman. Upon seeing the dead body transported to their gates, Corazon is shocked and tries to resuscitate the bloodied body. She takes control of cleaning the body, and seats herself at the back of the coffin. When an American negotiating team comes to console the family and deliver their generous donation for the dead's kin, Corazon is outraged when they explain that her brother was mistaken for a wild boar. She blurts out the film's memorable line, *"Ang kapatid ko ay hindi baboy!"* (My brother is not a pig!) Corazon's hysterical scene is the climax of the film's melodramatic saga, connoting both realization of disenfranchisement and empowerment. From hereon, the anxious state is turned to anger and resolve to fight for justice.

They decide to file a criminal case despite the hesitation of the lawyer, the same one chosen by Yolanda and Bonifacio. The lawyer is frank when he says that the case is hopeless. Yolanda is stunned, and says *"Pero ito ang Pilipinas, Attorney. Kung nasa ibang bansa kami baka nga wala kaming laban. Pero tayo ang Pilipino. Ito ang Pilipinas. Sila ang mga dayuhan."* (But this is the Philippines, Attorney. If we were in another country, we may not have a chance. We are Filipinos. This is the Philippines. They are the foreigners.) During the first and only hearing of the case, the lawyer representing the U.S. bases stands up and notifies the court that the case cannot be heard, showing a certificate that "Corporal John S. Smith has returned to the United States as his tour of duty has been terminated." The lawyer then declares, "The case cannot proceed until the accused is returned to the Philippines." The judge concurs and sends the case to be archived.

All judicial recourse is shut down for Corazon. In obvious frustration, she shouts to the court, *"Sino ang mananagot sa aking kapatid?"* (Who will take responsibility for the crime committed against my brother?) Bonifacio comforts her in an embrace. Walking down the stairs, Corazon is stopped by the base lawyer who attempts to forward an envelope containing dollars for her brother. The lawyer repeats the apology and the case of mistaken identity. Corazon pulls out a photo of her brother from her wallet and says, *"Masdan mong maigi ang kapatid ko. Sabihin mo sa kanila, hindi siya mukhang baboy ramo."* (Look closely at my brother. Tell them that he does not, in any way, look like a wild boar.) Outside the court, a commotion is caused by a motorcycle driver's skidding accident. The driver's helmet is taken off by somebody else from the crowd. Corazon's lawyer tells the crowd to let her in, since she is a nurse. The film ends with a shot of Corazon staring down at the Caucasian driver.

Minsa'y Isang Gamu-gamo is credited as "the first important film to tackle the subject of [. . .] American presence [in the Philippines] and its consequences. It showed another face of the so-called special relations between the Philippines and the United States."[7] Such a relationship, enforced through a military treaty between the two nations—although transacted when the Philippines was a U.S. colony—provides the black hole that makes all civil and criminal cases against the U.S. military personnel and bases unaccountable to the local and national courts. This source of the primordial judicial lack—the transnational military treaty—negates the possibility of justice being enforced and the legal system being duly operational. What results then are paralegal settlements that suture acceptance of lack and excess of power. Yolanda divulges this realization to her cousin in accepting the settlement, noting, *"Wala pang asunto laban sa mga Amerikano ang hindi nauwi sa* amicable settlement." (There has yet to be a complaint against the Americans that will not be resolved through amicable settlement.) Her cousin presents her own strategy of containment of the issue: *"Mababait naman ang mga Amerikano. Kung hindi sila bumalik noong panahon ng Hapon, nasira na ako."* (The Americans are kind of nice. If they had not returned during the Japanese occupation, I would have been dead.)

The legal issue is centered on territoriality—where can one claim justice? The film frequently echoes this thrust. The young brother's shooting takes place inside the military base's scavenging section. Earlier, three boys were shot inside the same location. What becomes of Filipinos who, therefore, are trespassing subjects in their homeland? U.S. claim on national territory is further echoed in the father's sensitive remark regarding Nixon's state visit to the Philippines and Apollo 11's satellite-televised landing on the moon: *"Sa kanila na rin ba ang buwan?"* (Has the moon become American territory?) Historically, the bloody conquest of the Philippines provided the U.S. with its first colonial-building experience outside the mainland. Poised to claim its sovereignty after proclaiming its independence from Spain, the Philippines realized its maintenance of colonial status under U.S. tutelage. Corazon's training in an American hospital is a postcolonial issue, as some fifty thousand Filipina nurses have migrated to work in the U.S. With the liberalization of U.S. immigration law and the continuing shortage of nurses in western countries, the Philippines is the largest exporter of registered nurses to foreign countries, with some two hundred fifty thousand nurses working abroad.[8]

Bonifacio's dream to join the U.S. Navy is also a historically determined option. Since 1952, an agreement between the Philippines and the U.S. governments allowed no more than one thousand male Philippine citizens to enlist in the U.S. Navy.[9] The agreement was modified in 1954, setting the recruitment ceiling to two thousand Filipino personnel.[10] As of 1989, there were 19,251 Filipino enlisted personnel and 588 Filipino officers in the Navy.[11] As seafarers, "Filipinos used to comprise the largest number of seamen in international shipping lines" as there are some four hundred thousand registered seamen employed in international vessels.[12] The gendered emplacement—of Filipinos in defense and seafaring, and Filipinas in the health care sector—is historically determined through colonial and neocolonial ties between the Philippines and western nations, specifically the U.S. This is the reason E. San Juan Jr. implores Filipino-Americans "to confront [their] own singular destiny as a 'transported' (in more ways than one), displaced, and dis-integrated people."[13]

The military power relations—in ways that propelled Philippine colonial and neocolonial relations with the U.S.—overdetermine the territoriality issue and consequential issue of autonomous nations, independent states, and sovereign bodies. The U.S. military bases issue, after all, is also a territorial issue. These bases were first established in support of the Spanish-American war to develop U.S. markets overseas. When the U.S. granted independence to the Philippines in 1946, it made sure it had access to some twenty military and naval bases, with the Clark Air Field and Subic Naval Base as the biggest and most important ones.[14] It costs U.S. taxpayers USD 200 million annually to maintain these bases, and has made the U.S. government the Philippines' second largest employer, second only to the national government. The Philippine military "has also received unprecedented financial support" from the U.S. military presence.[15] Between 1972 and 1983, its size has more than tripled, growing from 54,000 to 213,000, the reserves increasing from 17,000 to 118,000.[16] The fast-track development of the military became the

KEYWORDS

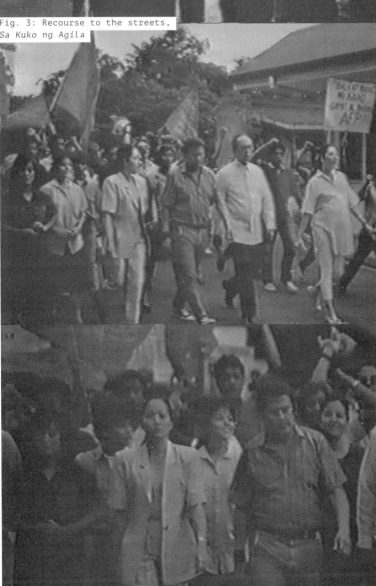

Fig. 3: Recourse to the streets,
Sa Kuko ng Agila

J
U
D
I
C
I
A
R
Y

bulwark of defense under the Marcos dictatorship. In turn, the U.S. military bases propelled the Marcos dictatorship. The military and defense sector's pampered statuses become the recurring logic of subsequent presidencies, and the cause of human rights' lingering dismal state in the country. With historical, economic, political, and cultural ties, the Philippine state has yet to cease being a U.S. neocolonial territory.

Another film that deals with the presence of, and abuse in, the U.S. bases is *Sa Kuko ng Aguila*. The film's story propels an ordinary man—a just jeepney driver, the most popular mode of transport in the Philippines—into a leadership role against the abuses and presence of the U.S. military base in Olongapo, site of the Subic Naval Base. The climax of the film begins with the court scene that exonerates the wealthy politician. Outside the court, the driver and crime victim are awaited by the crowd, holding protest signs and streamers. As the politician comes out, he is intimidated by the angry masses' protests. The politician evades the crowd, quickly escaping through his car. The driver is catapulted into the leadership of the protest movement. They take their cause into the streets. The final slow-motion shot dramatizes the driver, his girlfriend, the victims, and close associates marching in front of the mass of protestors and the righteousness of their struggle.

Cinematically, the flow of meaning foregrounding the dialectic of excess and lack is circulated through the star system. Stars, after all, also bear the weight of the dialectic—through the spectacularization of their bodies in excess, and the drawing from the primal economic and psychical lack of fans and moviegoers. In *Minsa'y Isang Gamu-Gamo*, the superstar of Philippine cinema, Nora Aunor, represents the lower-middle-class legal debacle with the U.S. bases. Aunor became famous during the Marcos dictatorship, which sought to emulate a modern nationalism. This nationalism typified the brown body, as well as features that Aunor had which contrasted against the dominant Caucasian or mestiza beauties of the time. She also mythologized the formula of hard work and luck—Horatio Algers of sorts—to perpetuate the fantasy of social mobility in Philippine society. Before her fame, she used to sell drinking water in a train station in the most depressed region of Luzon. She persevered, joining and winning singing contests. She became a singing sensation. She later moved on to acting, winning box-office fame. She started out as a teeny-bopper star until she finally became an actress of superb caliber. Because she represented the myth of mobility, the Marcos dictatorship utilized her as an accessory to the nation-building project, enlisting her to campaign for the presidential couple and their programs.

In *Sa Kuko ng Aguila*, the ordinary but just driver is portrayed by Joseph Estrada, whose iconography represented the leadership in solidarity and in the struggle of the masses. Such beginnings would pave the road for his ascent to politics. He began as mayor of a Metro Manila suburban municipality and close ally of the Marcoses. Later, he became a senator, proving his worth when he campaigned to abrogate the military bases treaty as vice president in 1992, and as president in 1998. Because of massive corruption and immoral acts, he was deposed in 2000, becoming the second president to be forced out of office. Estrada is crucial in the military discourse because of his vacillating position—from an anti-bases supporter in 1992, the year the bases treaty was abrogated, to masterminding the approval of the Visiting Forces Agreement (VFA) in 1999 which brought back American troops to the country.[17] The VFA was designed as part of the network of military treaties and laws supported by the U.S. in its global antiterrorist war. With the abrogation of the 1992 treaty, the territorial space of the two most important bases was transformed into economic zones, housing factories, and offices of multinational companies. These zones remain predicated on the enforcement of U.S. military exercises to denote a secure and stable economic regime.

What is being foregrounded historically in the legal entanglement—and simultaneously foregrounded in the star system—is the issue of social justice. The machination of politics creates new directional flows that negate even the impediment of the biggest stars representing the national dilemma in the U.S. bases. While star and political alliances have shifted, the vacuum of social justice remains unattended. While military bases have transformed into economic zones, these sites remain magnets for sex work and the continuing disenfranchisement of children and environmental concerns. The Philippines is said to be fourth among nine nations with the most child sex workers, with some sixty thousand to one hundred thousand children involved.[18] Estimates of the total number of women and children involved in sex work vary from three hundred thousand to five hundred thousand.[19] The number of sex workers is said to be about the size of the nation's manufacturing workforce.[20] The military exercises under the VFA are expected to bring in about ten thousand U.S. military servicemen to twenty-two docking ports all over the country, which, according to the Coalition Against Trafficking of Women-Asia Pacific (CATW-AP), "will result in an increase in the number of prostituted women and children."[21] Poverty remains the primordial lack that makes disenfranchised healthy bodies enter sex and entertainment work inside and outside the Philippines. Seventy-five thousand Filipinas comprise half of all foreign female sex workers in Japan.[22] There remain some fifty thousand Amerasian children in the country, and most have become "underprivileged and targets of the flesh trade because of their looks."[23]

Abandoned because of Mount Pinatubo's eruption in 1992, portions of the Clark Air Base remain highly toxic, poisoning one area's water supply and resulting in massive cancer disease among its residents, especially the children.[24] The discursive flow of the military treaty remains in place, along with the lingering issues of social justice and its negation. What is also negated, as San Juan points out for Filipino Americans, which can also be generally said of Filipinos, is that "the reality of U.S. colonial subjugation and its profound enduring effects [....] distinguish the Filipino national-ity from the Chinese, Japanese, Koreans, and other cohorts from the Asian mainland."[25]

Jon Mills writes of Lacan's idea of paranoiac knowledge—how the production of knowledge is enmeshed in paranoia—that "Knowledge is paranoiac because it is acquired through our imaginary relation to the other as a primordial misidentification or illusory self-recognition of autonomy, control, and mastery, thus leading to persecutory anxiety and self-alienation."[26] Philippine cinema's representation of justice and the legal system pose the inac-cessibility of these ideals of liberal democracy through perpetuating paranoia in producing knowledge about the judicial system. There exists a primordial misidentification—the victim seeking redress in a system that is already predicated on upholding the transnational treaty—or an illusory self-recognition of autonomy. Defeated in the film, the victim nonetheless achieves moral redemption and victory, as the audience identifies with the correctness of the stance. In *Sa Kuko ng Aguila*, it is the taking on of struggle for social justice to the people; in *Minsa'y Isang Gamu-Gamo*, it is white hate, the looking down (in the censored version) or the turning away of Corazon from the scene of the accident involving the injured Caucasian driver as an act of retribution.

Reproduction and Subjectivation

Louis Althusser posits the crucial point of reproducing the condi-tions of production in hegemony.[27] The role of the Repressive State Apparatus "consists of securing by force (physical or otherwise)

the political conditions of the reproduction of relations of production which are the last resort relations of exploitation."[28] With this
emphasized, the "intermediation" of the ruling ideology ensures
an enforced harmony between the Repressive and Ideological State
Apparatuses. What ensues is an ideology that is a "representation of
the imaginary relationship of individuals to their real conditions of
existence."[29] This ideology interpellates the concrete subject. This
section marks the ideology of the prison system as interpellative of
the concrete subject of the disenfranchised citizen. Subjectivation
becomes the process of concretizing the subject, how the repressive
and ideological state apparatuses hail—simultaneously disenfranchising and empowering—the subjugated subject. In *Adultery: Aida
Macaraeg*, the husband who goes through the prison system, which
emphasizes manual labor as redemptive of the human subject, eventually transposes this subjectivity to comprehend and forgive the
heroine.

The central theme in the two films is the experience of prison to
articulate the success, albeit partial, of the judicial system. The prison
is the deterrent to the characters' lives becoming wholly unproduc-
tive. The shooting of these scenes in actual prison sites—related to the
effect of shots taken in actual squatter's communities—provides the
grit and squalor that make possible the abjection of such subhuman
experience. If, in squatter's communities, the effect is to gentrify the
experience of poverty, then in prison scenes, the effect is to render
the invisibility of an abject subhuman experience. What results is a
pedagogical construction of ordinary people's access to citizenship—
via a paranoia of the prison system and the tolerance of an ineffective
judicial system.

Bulaklak ng City Jail (Flowers of the City Jail, 1984, directed by
Mario O'Hara) narrates the story of a singer in a low-end beer pub
who is jailed for a murder attempt. Angela defended herself from the
wife of the man she was having an affair with, and in the process, she
accidentally plunged the knife into the wife's body. She cannot afford
the PhP 5,000 bail, and endures the daily grind of the city jail's female
section. The beginning scene, which brings her to the jail's section,
captures the fear of a first-time offender. When she is locked up in
the cell, she gets her initiation from the inmates—she is assaulted,
undressed, and verbally abused. In the morning, she is naked, lying
on sheets of newspapers on the floor, and begins her orientation to
life as an inmate. She discovers the hierarchy of power inside the
city jail. Within the women's section, there is Breaker, the *bastonera*
(enforcer of rules, peace, and order), the *mayora* (an inmate supervi-

Fig. 4: Deplorable prison condition, *Bulaklak ng City Jail*

sor), Paquito (the male guard who has a pick of women in exchange for small favors of leniency), the female warden, and the city jail warden. Being a first-time inmate, she is at the bottom of the penal food chain, reeking of prostitution, drugs, and abuse.

Her life is regimented by the discipline of the city jail system. There are no utensils or non-breakable dishes allowed. Feeding is done by roll-call of individuals by cell. She eats her first meal in a small water container with her hands. She has to obey the orders of those above her—including Breaker's instruction to give in to Paquito's desire to have her for the night. When she declines, she is brutally punished by Breaker. She is only tolerated when inmates find out about her pregnancy. As her pregnancy progresses, she fears being separated from her child. A fellow inmate, Viring, is forcefully separated from her young daughter who lived with her inside the cell since she was first jailed. Angela grows wary during her stay. She is inspired by the successful escape of a fellow inmate, Juliet. Juliet lures the guard to have sex with her while awaiting her trial in court. The guard brings Juliet to the cemetery and, while unaware, is hand-cuffed by Juliet. She steals his gun and escapes. The knowledge of the escape causes a euphoria inside the women's section. Inmates clap their utensils together and jeer inside their cells. Angela also fears the city jail because of its periodic rumbles and gang clashes. In one scene, bodies of dead male inmates are taken out in the open space area for collection.

Angela, however, decides to attempt to escape. On her first try, she is caught by the guard. She is punished by Breaker and placed in the isolation cell. On her second attempt, she decides to fake her child's delivery. In the hospital, she asks the guard for permission to go to the toilet, and successfully escapes from there. The following shot depicts the euphoria of her fellow inmates, celebrating her successful escape. After all, the defense lawyer assigned to her by the court instructed her to admit her crime, get reprieve for said crime, and endure her term in jail. This arrangement, according to the lawyer, may even be shorter than proceeding with the trial. The evidence and circumstance are glaringly against her favor—the assault weapon was found, and the wife she defended herself against is the aggrieved party in the case. During the court plea proceedings, however, she maintains her innocence despite her lawyer's obvious frustration. When the court's clerk asks for Angela's stance, she looks back at the lawyer. The dramatic silence is broken when she reiterates her plea of innocence.

Angela searches for a private lawyer to take on her case. A jailed inmate's mother agrees to take on Angela's case, in exchange for providing information on her own daughter's mysterious death in the city jail. The official reason of escape was the version given by Breaker, who was present when Paquito was having sex with the new inmate. In one of her errands, Angela is followed by guards who recognized her in the crowd. She attempts to evade the police by going to the city zoo. A public announcement to vacate the zoo is made. The search extends until nightfall. Filmed like a safari hunt with tightly held guns ready for instant action, the police meticulously search the zoo. She is found in a vacant animal cell, covered in blood as her child is born.

The persistence of the private defense lawyer proves to be successful when she is reunited with her child after an earlier attempt by the authorities to separate them. More importantly, she is found innocent of the crime. Similar to the staging of the final scene in *Adultery: Aida Macaraeg*, blissful closure is consummated in a park where she is walking with her child amid the crowd of park strollers. What the film does is to create trauma of jail experience as an imperative for justice to prevail. For the heroine, the weight of her subjection inside the jail makes a claim for innocence. For the audience, however, the possibility of this imaginary subjection acts as a preventive screen. The cinematic elaboration of the jail system's infrastructures—as a habitus of hell on earth—becomes the screen to filter the possibility of wrong-doing. After all, moviegoing in the Philippines has become a middle-class activity. The audience's acculturation to the prison underworld via film provides a mortified experience of the possible imaginary of abjection. Thus, the double abjection is metastasized—via abjection of the filmic imaginary, and abjection of poverty that underlies the filmic imaginary. The composition of disempowered female inmates, for example, mainly belongs to the low end of society. What the film unwittingly does is to reinforce the psychical drive of the middle class in its anti-poverty, even anti-poor, stance to life in general. Through the experience of film, the audience is placed as subjects of their class origin, reinforcing the basis for maintaining the abjected subexperience of crime and prison. The viewing of excessive lack reinforces the middle-class excess in Philippine society.

Another film that highlights the prison experience is *Deathrow* (Joel Lamangan, 2000). Sonny Corpuz is a sixteen-year-old boy from the slums who gets entangled in an *akyat-bahay* (home invasion) with his friends. They hogtie the house owner. During a chaotic huddle, a friend shoots the owner. The police arrive and catch the surprised Sonny. He is convicted of homicide with robbery, and is sentenced

Fig. 5: Profiling of a minor, *Deathrow*

to death. The first jail scene, like in *Bulaklak ng City Jail*, shows the procession of Sonny to his cell barracks inside the death row at the national penitentiary. Through his seeing the jail's interiors, the audience is also simultaneously drawn in and out of the experience of incarceration—into the seduction of an abject space and experience, and out into the comforts of their own class origin and middle-class movie watching experience. He is introduced to the mayor, Donald, and the bastonero, Biyo. Like Angela, he is given the first-day, first-time initiation and beatings.

The court scene is typically represented—stark interiors of cold-hearted lawyers and a judge in a huddle about the boy's real age. He had lost his birth certificate in a fire that hit the squatters' community. The only document attesting to his adult age is a forged voter's ID, used to secure a paid vote for a local politician. After formalizing the declaration of his guilt—heralded by the pounding of the gavel—he has an emotional breakdown, pleading his innocence. The gavel interpellates him as a convicted criminal, as much as the court room space and his location in it already foreshadows his status as such. This criminalized body is extended into the space of the prison system. He is assigned menial work, as part of the group being ordered to polish floors and clean toilets. He is as powerless in jail as he was outside. A convicted municipal mayor maintains his status inside jail. His assistant deodorizes the toilet before he uses it; he oversees the drug subeconomy in the prison, even maintaining a guard to work in the drug network.

The patronage of higher male figures safeguards Sonny in jail. He acts as a drug courier for a gang leader, and has impressed him by not squealing when caught by the guards. Through small generous favors by another gang leader, he is given preferential treatment in jail. When this gang leader attempts to extract his payment by sodomizing Sonny, the boy is protected by the most revered older member of a death row section. This last patriarchal figure, Lolo Sinag (Grandpa Sinag), allows Sonny to develop a male bonding relationship. They escape, get caught together, and are beaten by the gang leaders as punishment for their failed escape attempt. Sonny is sodomized again by the gang leader. In his attempt to fight off the assault, Sonny kills the leader. Lolo Sinag takes the blame and fast-tracks his death sentence.

Sonny witnesses Lolo Sinag's procession to the gas chamber. The details of the carrying out of the death sentence are meticulously treated in the film, which shot the scene in the actual chamber in the national penitentiary. The female alcoholic lawyer who fought for Lolo Sinag's appeal case is requested by him to save the boy from death row. The lawyer succeeds, and Sonny is freed. The friend who had shot the homeowner is captured and sentenced to jail. Filmed from an awkward helicopter camera, Sonny enjoys his walk outside the open green space, to chronicle his final journey amid the flurry of grass leaves. He is freed from the rumble and gang wars, sexual and physical violations, demeaning menial work and existence of the jail system.

These films successfully reproduce the prison and crime threat and paranoia as the materialization of the concrete criminal subjects. These films succeed in schematizing the hierarchy and play of power figures and activity inside the prison system. Even in their bed bunks, cells, or sections, their bodies are cast and substantiated as animalized and criminalized subjects. Simultaneously, what is also heralded as middle-class free subjects are the movie audience themselves, concretized through the materiality of their film-going experience. The imaginary of paranoia—represented in film in scenes of brutality and violence in the claustrophobic space of the prison—is anathema to the way the audience views the film text. Seated in a comfortable yet dark constricted space, with the image projected from behind onto a giant screen in front, the audience already has a feel of the imaginary of paranoia. This paranoia, after all, is posed in the very

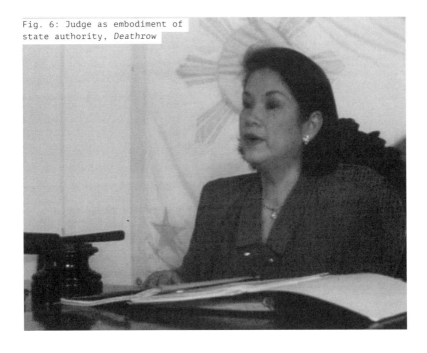

Fig. 6: Judge as embodiment of state authority, *Deathrow*

Fig. 7: Oscillating spaces of court and jail, *Deathrow*

nature of film viewing—experience of that which is there but not fully there, absent but not completely, and present, but not fully.

The nature is also a disciplining mechanism to the very experience of the film machinery—a gentrified activity of imaginary work and labor. The films about the prison system acknowledge the space's disciplining nature. This is because of the police's present absence and absent presence to provide law and order in the incarcerated space. What transpires in film is the police-sanctioned lawlessness that is able to inflict discipline to the historically disenfranchised. Acting out roles of power and powerlessness, the inmates perform the pedagogical construction of the criminalized body by the prison system under police control. What gets instilled is discipline through violence, the ultimate of which is the carrying out of the death sentence. This new law is what Walter Benjamin correctly describes, "For the exercise of violence over life and death, more than in any other legal act, the law reaffirms itself."[30] The corrupt legal system and the more corrupt prison system are legitimized in every police-sanctioned practice of violence.

The government's Commission on Human Rights described the Philippine National Police as "the worst abuser of human rights."[31] The context of poverty is, again, the primordial lack—capped with the maintenance of a pampered military—that is exacerbated by the unabated and excessive abuse of human rights. Because of the continuing global economic crisis, poverty worsened in 2002, reaching 40 percent—54 percent in the rural and 24 percent in the urban population.[32] In order to maintain its hegemony, the state sustains an abusive military. A report in 2002 formalizes the common knowledge that "Some elements of the security services were responsible for arbitrary and unlawful and in some cases extra-judicial killings, disappearances, torture, and arbitrary arrest and detention."[33] More so, "Other physical abuse of suspects and detainees as well as police, prosecutorial, and judicial corruption remained [as] problems."[34] There have been no convictions, for example, for the killings of thirty-eight journalists in the country since 1986.[35]

What aggravates the situation is the slow dispensation of court decisions: "According to the Constitution, cases are to be resolved within set time limits once submitted for decision: 24 months for the Supreme Court; 12 months for the Court of Appeals; and 3 months for the lower courts. There are no time limits for trials."[36] One reason for this delay is the lack of qualified judges. A 2002 report states that "Of the more than 2,100 trial court judgeships nationwide, 32 percent remained vacant at year's end due to lack of qualified applicants. Vacancies in Mindanao and other poorer provinces were particularly unattractive to many jurists, and 38 percent of these judgeships were vacant."[37]

Such condensation of material lack is experienced in films on prison life. The practices of delayed dispensation of justice and excessive abuse of military and state power become the grid to materialize the experience of films on prison—creating the middle-class subject viewing the experience of criminals' subjection. They view the exercise with what Benjamin alludes to as the paradox in the labyrinth of the judicial system, "[The] legal system tries to erect, in all areas where individual ends could be usefully pursued by violence, legal ends that can be realized only by legal power."[38] The prison system—in filmic and material representations—even in its replete performance of police-sanctioned violence, becomes a habitus of legal power: a space that performs the lack and neglect of justice.

Happiness and Redemption

Benjamin also writes as an explanation to one of his theses of history, "Our image of happiness is indissolubly bound up with the image of redemption."[39] Thus, the gritty delivery and non-delivery of justice in legal scenes and prison films suggest—in a perverted instance—an idea of happiness and redemption. These parallel ideas, however, come into greater play when compared with Hollywood, the dominant producer of films, as the apparatus of American cultural global domination. This is especially interesting to the Philippines, given historical colonial and neocolonial relations with the U.S. Contrary to Philippine cinematic and real experience with the legal system, American popular films, from *Philadelphia* (1993) to *Erin Brokovich* (2000) and *Legally Blonde* (2001), attest to the ego-ideal success of the U.S. justice system. Even superhero films—*Batman*, *X-Men*, *Spider-Man*, and *Hulk*—epitomize the efficacy of the institutionalized corporeal justice under siege from legal and illegal attacks. The films highlight the ability of the judicial and prison systems, in the end, to extraordinarily dispense with the process to contain the foreign threat.

This ideal becomes especially interesting as one of the imagined bases for transnational migration to the U.S. by Filipinos. These films reinforce the American ideology on justice against something of a primordial lack in the Philippines. This perpetuates the colonial mentality, of dreaming of moving to the U.S., as some one-and-a-half million Filipinos have already done, or as a constant fantasy of the possible. "Filipino-Americans rank fourth in per capita income ($13,616 or 9 percent lower than white per capita income) among ten Asian groups. They have the second highest median family income at $46,698 in the United States (the median family income for the U.S. is only $35,225). Filipinos have the highest labor participation, at 75.4 percent, among all Asian groups. As a result, the poverty level of Filipinos is the lowest in the nation at only 6.4 percent."[40] In the U.S., Philippine poverty is experienced nominally. As a result, forty thousand new immigrants arrive each year in the U.S., as Filipino-Americans were already expected to hit the two million mark in 2000, and would be doubled to four million by 2030. "Filipino-American's aggregate purchasing power has been estimated at $13 billion a year, and remittances from the U.S. account for 70 percent of remittances to the Philippines."[41]

The gentrification of a small economically powerful sector of Filipinos overseas—in the belly of its colonial and neocolonial master—provides a displacement and projection of the dream of social justice and social mobility. From the homeland, this projection—like film itself—is that which is out there but not fully, absent but not completely. What I hope to achieve in this essay is a postcolonial critique of the Philippine judicial system in film that materializes the continuing U.S. tutelage of politics and economics. Such patronage is drawn both from the primordial national lack in poverty and the excessive abuse of police and state power. The essay draws on a transnational link, beginning with a discussion of film representation of the judicial system, followed by an analysis of judicial lack and excess in contemporary Philippine films, and the further interpellation of the subject as moviegoer and criminal. I imply a further connection of this lack in the excess of justice in American popular films and other media display and representation of Filipinos in the U.S., especially as experienced in the Philippines. This transnational connection of excess and lack results from the same libidinal drive of poverty and power in the nation-space. In viewing Hollywood films that successfully dispense justice, in hearing stories of successful Filipino personalities, of more familial and familiar triumphs, an intimacy of mobile desire is constituted, at once heralding the lack and excess of the national body and the national condition, and the possibility of realizing the lack and excess elsewhere, in the intimate space of Hollywood films and Filipino American success. This relocation of happiness and redemption becomes the simultaneous site for reworking of the play of lack and excess.

1   TxtMANIA, "Understanding Poverty," 2013, http://www.txtmania.com/articles/poverty.php, accessed 4 Dec 2014.

2   Lino Brocka, *Adultery: Aida Macaraeg*, 1984.

3   Lupita Aquino-Kashiwahara, *Once There Was a Moth*, 1976.

4   Augusto Buenaventura, *In the Eagle's Claws*, 1988.

5   John Pike, "Philippine – Government," GlobalSecurity.org, http://www.globalsecurity.org/military/world/philippines/government.htm., accessed 4 Dec 2014,

6   For film notes, see Mao Tumbocon, "Minsa'y Isang Gamu-gamo," *CCP Encyclopedia of Philippine Art: Volume 8 Philippine Film* (Manila: CCP, 1994), 175–76.

7   Ibid.

8   Maritess Sison, "Exodus of Nurses Grows, Health System Feels Effect," May 2002, http://www.cyberdyaryo.com/features/f2002_0508_04.htm (site discontinued). In her report, she mentions that nursing schools produce some nine thousand students per year, of which, only five thousand to seven thousand will become licensed nurses.

9   "A Unique Recruiting Arrangement," *Military.com Unit Pages,* 27 Oct 2000, http://www.military.com/HomePage/UnitPageHistory/1,12506,705117|703463,00.html (site discontinued).

10   "When the U.S. Navy Came Calling . . . ," http://philusnavy.tripod.com/when1.htm, accessed 4 Dec 2014.

11   Ibid.

12   Yna Soriano, "Slavery on the High Seas," http://www.marinongpinoy.com/article7.html (site discontinued). She reports that "Of some 40,000 maritime students who graduate yearly, only 4,000 get employed."

13   E. San Juan, Jr., "Filipino Bodies: From the Philippines to the United States and Around the World," http://www.boondocksnet.com/centennial/sctexts/esj_97a.html (site discontinued).

14   See "U.S. Bases in the Philippines: A Position Paper by the Friends of the Filipino People," http://www.boondocksnet.com/centennial/sctexts/ffp_bases7802.html (site discontinued).

15   Jim Zwick, "Militarization in the Philippines: From Consolidation to Crisis," http://www.boondocksnet.com/centennial/sctexts/zwick85a_b.html (site discontinued).

16   Ibid. The essay also provides the increase in military expenditures, from USD 327 million in 1972 to USD 972 million in 1982.

17   For the arguments against the VFA, see Roland G. Simbulan, "Why the Senate Should Reject the VFA," http://www.boondocksnet.com/centennial/sctexts/simbulan99a.html (site discontinued); and Daniel B. Schirmer, "VFA:

The Shape of Things to Come?" http://www.boondocksnet.com/centennial/sctexts/schirmer99b.html (site discontinued).

18 Citing Sol F. Juvida, quoted in CATW (Coalition Against Trafficking of Women) Factbook, "Philippines," http://www.globalmarch.org/worstforms-reports/world/philippines.html (site discontinued).

19 CATW Factbook, "Philippines," http://www.globalmarch.org/worstforms-reports/world/philippines.html (site discontinued). Three hundred thousand people is the estimate of CATW Fact Book, citing from Gabriela, "The Philippines," http://www.uri.edu/artsci/wms/hughes/philippi.htm (site discontinued). Four hundred thousand to five hundred thousand people is the estimate of the International Labor Organization.

20 Rene Ofreneo, quoted in "The Philippines," http://www.uri.edu/artsci/wms/hughes/philippi.htm (site discontinued).

21 CATW-AP (Coalition Against Trafficking of Women-Asia Pacific), *The Philippine Journal*, quoted in ibid.

22 CATW-AP, quoted in "Philippines."

23 Quoted in "The Philippines."

24 For an argument on the toxic damage and clean-up of the bases' environment, see Admiral Eugene Carroll (ret.), "U.S. Military Bases and the Environment: A Time for Responsibility," http://www.boondocksnet.com/centennial/sctexts/carroll971123.html (site discontinued).

25 Ibid.

26 Jon Mills, "Lacan on Paranoiac Knowledge," accessed 4 Dec 2014, http://www.processpsychology.com/new-articles/Lacan-PP-revised.htm.

27 Louis Althusser, "Ideology and the Ideological State Apparatuses (Notes towards an Investigation)," *Mapping Ideology* (London: Verso, 1994), 100–140.

28 Ibid, 114.

29 Ibid, 123.

30 Walter Benjamin, "Critique of Violence," *Selected Writings: Volume 1: 1913–1926* (Cambridge: Belknap Press, 1996), 242.

31 "Philippines: Country Reports on Human Rights Practices, 2002," *U.S. Department of State,* 31 Mar 2003, http://www.state.gov/g/drl/rls/hrrpt/2002/18261.htm, accessed 4 Dec 2014.

32 Ibid.

33 Ibid.

34 Ibid.

35 Ibid.

36 Ibid.

37 Ibid.

38 Benjamin, "Critique of Violence," 238.

39 Walter Benjamin, "Theses on the Philosophy of History," *Illuminations* (New York: Schocken Books, 1968), 254.

40 Mona Lisa Yuchengco and Rene P. Ciria-Cruz, "The Filipino American Community: New Roles and Challenges," http://www.asiasociety.org/publications/philippines/filipino.html (site discontinued).

41 Ibid.

KEYWORDS

Piracy

Regulation and the Filipino's Historical Response to Globalization

P iracy is popularly defined as "any illegal acts of violence or detention, or any act of depredation, committed for private ends by the crew or the passengers of a private ship or a private aircraft, and directed on the high seas, against another ship or aircraft, or against persons or property on board such ship or aircraft (or) against a ship, aircraft, persons or property in a place outside the jurisdiction of any state."[1] Pirate attacks have tripled between 1993 and 2003, with half the incidents happening in Indonesian waters in 2004, the majority of which were in the Strait of Malacca.[2] There is much to be feared in sea piracy, as some fifty thousand commercial ships ply the routes between the Pacific and Indian Oceans, off the Somali coast, and in the Strait of Malacca and Singapore.[3] These cargo ships, which hold tons of steel containers, are, after all, the backbone of capitalist trade, allowing the transfer of bulk materials, produce, and waste. Media piracy, therefore, would fall into a related definition. This is because it is an act of omission committed against a sovereign body, usually a business corporation holding the intellectual property right to the contested object, and thus protected by the corporation's nation-state. However, media piracy does not only happen through sea lines,[4] it also gets literally and figuratively reproduced technologically. In the Philippines, however, media piracy occurs through sea lines. A duplicating machine can reproduce twenty thousand copies of music, film, games, and software per day. So invested are business corporations and their nation-states that there is almost a paranoia in protecting their objects of profit from any further loss—in seaborne piracy, estimated losses are USD 12 billion per year;[5] in media piracy, U.S. companies lose as much as USD 250 billion per year, although another estimate places it at USD 60 billion.[6]

The person who actively "commits piracy by engaging in robbery, pillaging or plundering at sea is known as a pirate."[7] Who has not been a pirate? Who has not bought pirated music or DVD film from friendly neighborhood Muslim vendors? Who has not downloaded films, television shows, and music from internet sites, has not played pirated computer games, has not used pirated computer software, and has not listened to pirated music played in bars, karaoke, and restaurants, among others? So many people could get arrested for doing what they do with these media texts, but they won't be, at least at this time. This is not because we have formed an alliance similar to the call of The Smiths' song title about shoplifters, "Pirates of the world unite!" but because it has become second-nature in contemporary Philippine society among the middle class. Wanting to become middle class comes with all the fineries of middle-class life (alternative music, art films, cult movies, documentaries, classical films, games), yet by categorization of being middle class in the country, these people cannot afford these markers if it were not for pirated media. The reality of being middle class in this country means that we have to simulate the real with the imaginary, with piracy falling more along the lines of the imaginary than the real, which also means that the imaginary is as real as the real itself for many would be middle-class citizens. Wanting in material economic standards, being middle class means making do with even unacceptable middle-class experiences.

The Philippines' entry to globalization has always historically prefigured the pirates and its activity—piracy as inimical to legitimate claims of participation in world capitalism. This essay traces Filipinos'—specifically, Muslim Filipinos'—historical response to piracy. By being designated as pirates, Moros were emplaced in an orientalist racial profiling of the "bad" colonial subject. The state's creation of the image of the Moro-as-pirate remains integral in the

marginalization of this religious ethnic group, or the exacerbation of
the "Moro/Mindanao" problem as integral to official nation-building.[8] Even in daily life, the consignment of the Moro pirates emplaces
the middle-class-ness of modern Philippine life, i.e., providing the
geopolitical bodies that make illicit yet integral the middle-class
experienciation of national life—becoming middle class with the
middle-class guilt—and legitimation projected unto these racialized
bodies of otherness.[9]

In more recent times, by pioneering media piracy in key cities in
the country, Filipino Muslims also excel in their stereotypical role as
media pirates, which is their niche participation in Philippine capitalism. By being conduits to this pedestrian layer of local capitalism—the site of sale itself undertaken on busy sidewalks and streets—
Filipino Muslims are allowing the national desire of becoming middle
class, illicitly possible for most Filipinos. Businesses also engage the
massive pedestrian layer through the *tingi* (small portion) system,
where everything can be sold and purchased in small quantities
in order to fit the budget. This is also known as "sachet marketing
strategy," or the ability to penetrate even the most disenfranchised
of market profile, with goods and services available for lower price
ranges.[10] In officially recognized businesses, the penetration translates to an experience of conspicuous consumption even for the
underclass. For example, this has allowed, in cell phone industries,
market saturation from 25 percent (what was deemed the regular
market) to 45 percent (to include the majority of daily wage earners)
through micro top-up or sachet solutions, that enabled people, who
were earning on a daily basis, to afford text and airtime services
within their income range.[11] The attempt to regulate piracy, therefore,
is also the nation-state's attempt to regulate Moro identity and to
expound on Filipino Muslim marginal citizenship. My contention is
that media piracy is Filipino Muslims' creative and critical response
that allows them to maneuver into the homogenizing cultural politics
of the Philippine nation-state and neoliberal globalization.

In this essay, I will first map out the historical emplacement of
Moro pirates in early capitalism, including their racialization into the
trade, and then discuss the state's reverse piracy that renders itself
as a disenfranchising unit of the Moro and Chinese participation in
the more recent media trade. My paper focuses on the Moro participation, since the historicizing of the Chinese participation entails a
separate discussion. Lastly, I then turn to the key role of the informal
sector—one where media piracy is an active participant—in the sustenance of the national economy. Through a class analysis that links the

Moro participation in media piracy, one finds an affinity of this act with the other classes involved in the informal sector.

Moro Profiling and Racialization

There have been three trends that historicize the Sulu Sultanate's maritime history: first, the "decay theory," or the theme of the "advent of piracy in the Malay world in the eighteenth and nineteenth centuries and the decline of indigenous maritime power" that concentrated more on the suppression of piracy than the local initiatives; second, the "rivalry theory," or the earlier competition "between the Catholic Spaniards and the Muslim population of the Sultanate" that underestimated local economic activities, like raiding, and enslavement as prime objects of wealth; and third, the "pattern theory," or the mapping out of a local typology of economic, political, and cultural activities as central to state formation.[12] What these studies privilege is not so much the local initiatives as a kind of sustained profiling of the Moro as integral yet marginal to state formation. The term "Moro," after all, refers to "the piratical ethnic groups" designated by the Spaniards, whose social category was not based on religion as certain ethnic groups were not Muslims, and that the "Moro Wars" were not only wars of religion but were "forays for economic purpose."[13]

The Sulu area was a vibrant trading power in the eighteenth century, a major port of entry for Chinese from Mainland China, and of Buginese trade, centered on Southeast Asia. The trade was conceived in a hierarchy of ethnic and economic relations, with the Sultanate of Sulu overseeing the trade. For historian James Warren, trading was as crucial as Moro pirates' raiding and slavery activities. Iranus belonged to the Maranao group, and lived in Mindanao's coastal areas. Their integration provided more supplementary skills to the Sulu Sultanate. Samals collected marine products for the Jolo market, and were under the Tausug datus, who had the authority to give permission for piratical raids. Tiruns conducted raids on their own, even though they were also under the supervision of Tausug datus, who in 1757 allied themselves with the Spaniards to retaliate against the Tiruns for the raid expeditions in other Philippine areas.

Through a system of tributaries and raiding, Sulu's sultan and cohorts were sustained. Local subsistence agriculture was not developed until rice production became necessary to maintain the sultanate's needs, particularly when the Spaniards successfully controlled pirate activities. The main economic activity was raiding, with figures suggesting a sizeable population size and boat fleets: "Ten communities have been located representing a male population of over 4,000 and a fleet of 30 boats for each community, a total of a hundred per boat."[14] Raiding primarily involved enslaving the local population, who were used to serve within households, or were traded as much sought-after commodities for the developing plantation economy within, and for the growing trade of Southeast Asia. A report in 1728 cited that "25 boats attacked various places in the Visayas. They carried 500 Moros plus 800 slaves as oarsmen. They enslaved 450 persons, including three priests, one of whom was sold for 2,500 pesos."[15] The entire coastal area of the Philippines was a raid route, with the Sulu sultanate sanctioning and benefiting from the slave and produce booty. So massive was raiding that "at the end of the eighteenth century, some 500 persons a year would have been captured and enslaved."[16] Politically, "it is more than probable that some skilled pirates did become chiefs and achieved power which was later only justified by blood-ties."[17]

Unable to contain piracy, "Spanish sources stigmatized the pirates as cruel because of the harsh treatment meted out to their captives, and treacherous because often they took Western ships by surprise or by the use of ploys." Spanish colonial rule was not able to protect the Catholic-converted natives. Many natives sought refuge in the hinterlands instead of going back to towns prone to pirate raids. Historian Ghislaine Loyre makes this sweeping claim:

> When the Spaniards arrived in the Philippines, there were no sultanates; instead petty chiefs engaged in piracy with their followers. The influence of Islam, the presence of an enemy, and increasing facilities for piracy enabled the inhabitants to prosper and to organize themselves into sultanates based on piracy. Missionaries gathered people into villages, not allowing them defense for fear they might rebel. Thus targets were 'offered' more easily to the pirates. Spanish sources of this period constantly complained about the raids which destroyed, sometimes more than once, almost all the villages of the central islands of the Philippines and the northern coast of Mindanao. The Spaniards had to exempt the inhabitants from paying taxes because so many people were taken away and some areas were totally devastated.[18]

James Warren writes of the aftermath of raids by pirates:

Some of the old towns were rebuilt on the original site, or on a new one nearby, but Iranun raids put a decisive end to many villages. The search for security and the fear of starvation and disease drove Filipinos [*sic*] to abandon villages that had existed for generations, after they experienced the forced harvesting and burning of their fields, and the slaughter of their plough animals. The dilemma facing stricken villages in the aftermath of a large scale raid was how to resume their original way of life without risking enslavement in the future. Some went to live in larger villages; some looked for new village sites, often on elevated ground; others abandoned the coast altogether for an equally harsh life in the mountain fastness of the interior where sometimes many were reduced to eating grass in order to survive. The Spanish labeled the fugitives *cimarrones* and *remontados*. On islands like Marinduque, Polillo, and Catanduanes, villagers could not readily flee to another area, and were forced to stand and fight. The raids knitted the inhabitants of the coastal towns of smaller islands like these together closely for mutual defense.[19]

The advent of piracy in the area came at the height of Spanish colonial rule, although Loyre mentions that "piracy in the Philippines was not a response to colonialism for it had existed before the arrival in the area of Western empires. However, colonialism altered the rules of political and economic life in several ways."[20] Piracy became the local initiative to hook up with early global capitalism that was then under the shadow of colonialism. It provided natives the opportunity and resources to trade and maintain local political and economic control, despite the Spanish colonial claims on the islands. Until its decline, piracy symbolized the shame of Spanish colonizers' failure to dominate, and its continuance, especially in the enslavement of captives, became the embarrassment to liberal values espoused during the subsequent American colonial period.

Warren states that "the Spanish were, in fact, too weak to prevent the inland seas of the central Philippines from becoming a 'Muslim lake.'"[21] Furthermore, raiding took its toll on colonial and Christian planning in other areas. Warren also cites that "the Bishop of Cebu stated that slave raids were the basic reason for declining parish enrolments and the continued poverty of the churches in Caraga, Iligan, and Panay."[22] The Spanish friars, after all, were instrumental in establishing over a thousand towns and cities in the Philippine lowlands by 1898: "Majority of these communities had less than

2,000 inhabitants; 200 had a population of over 2,000; thirty over 5,000; nine over 10,000."[23] The civilized native would be an appropriate object for exhibition, as the U.S. did with the Moros in the 1904 St. Louis World's Fair. America's "Moroland" was the sore thumb sticking out of its liberal pie. Historian Michael Salman states, "The sultan's 'notoriously deficient' income opened the possibility of forging a relationship through a monetary subsidy. In return, like Spain before it, the United States demanded a cessation of 'piracy,' meaning slave raiding as well as the general plundering of seaborne traffic."[24] Colonial policy shifted from indirect to direct rule, and the Bates Agreement signed in 1899, where the U.S. promised "not to interfere with the religion, law, and commerce (and to pay the sultan and his datus monthly stipends) in exchange for the sultan's acknowledgement of United States sovereignty" was unilaterally abrogated by the U.S. in 1905.[25] Datus were pitted against each other, and new ones were reared through colonial education, while some even became *pensionados* (Filipino scholars in the U.S.).

Postcolonial profiling would be aggravated by the institutionalized practice of distributing lands to new settlers from Luzon and the Visayas, mostly comprised of Christians. Agricultural corporations were also allowed to redevelop Mindanao's rich arable lands into plantation economy geared for export. On the one hand, national policies were also "designed to 'integrate'" Muslims into "national life" by providing an elite few access to postsecondary education.[26] On the other hand, Marcos would intensify the Moro/Muslim/ Mindanao conflict by resorting to militarizing the island. This began with the "Jabidah Massacre," where some 14–28 of the 180 Muslim trainees recruited in 1967 were executed without investigation. The conflation of these two historical junctures provided for the rise of Moro nationalism, the effect of which still continues to shape Mindanao and national politics.

The disjuncture in the signifying practices of colonial rule, as brought about by the experience of piracy, can be used to illuminate contemporary issues where the Moro media pirates continue to undermine the nation-state's practices. Postcolonial national politics would further propel an internal orientalization of the Moro figure—unintegratable in their propensity then to become ethnically at par with national citizenship or to become autonomous subjects in their struggle for self-determination now. Even in this rhetoric of the nation-state, the Moro pirates become the fluid subjects, able to weave through national politicking, the Moro struggle for sovereignty, and global neoliberalism. It is within the shadows of global neoliberalism, that hinges on protecting the innovator-entrepreneur's intellectual property rights—a similar reworking of the laissez-faire philosophy of early capitalism—that the pirates are able to intrude and insert themselves, at least, in Philippine modernism, as the filter to imagine the nation-state and its citizens as having achieved the simulacrum of being middle class.

Philippine State Formation and the "Middle-Class" Affect

"Dividi," pronounced in a low, almost sinister-like whisper, becomes the popular way both to reify and parody the Moro vendors of the pirated media trade. Dividi becomes the translator of the acronym, which, for its seeming technological entwinement, does not have currency in popular culture. Dividi is played on a pirated DVD player—the seller will ask the buyer what brand name should be glued onto the generic player. This player is oftentimes more powerful than regular players, as it can play all regional formats. Dividi—the pirated version—is technologically and commercially supported by other modes of piracy, including the VCD format preferred by most underclass users. An IIPA report states, "Unlike in some other Southeast Asian countries, the VCD format has not yet supplanted VHS videocassettes; but VCD piracy is extending the life of the pirate market in the older format."[27] In fact, dividi, though encompassing of all media forms, is more basically attuned to music CDs and movie VCDs, which are both cheaper than DVD. Dividi, therefore, translates the present technological innovations for the underclass prior to technological developments (VCD) and middle class.

Dividi, said in a whisper, foregrounds what is unsaid, or could not be said, in the discourse of the nation-state: pirated media as basis for non-inclusion or partial exclusion in global neoliberalism. Hovering in the sidelights, the seller—the pirate body no less, selling pirated goods—seduces buyers with the latest markers of middle-class media. It tempts buyers into their own unsaid desire for middle-class mobility—to become participants in piracy, and therefore, to have illicit markers of being middle-class, yet deemed unacceptable in present global capitalism. For the would-be middle class, these products signify both the parallel direction and the disjuncture into actual middle-class-ness. Middle-class contestation on this quasi-middle-class act is rationalized by limited access to genuine goods (where else to buy classics of world cinema?), principled partici-

KEYWORDS

pation (would buy only foreign and not local pirated films), or a
"genuine" manifestation of consumerism, and not by acceptance of
the act as part of "genuine" example of piracy. Positivized, the
middle-class angst for piracy is negated.

In most places, dividi has been publicly displayed in stalls for
prospective buyers. These stalls are within and on the fringes of legitimate local capitalism—Greenhills, Divisoria Mall, Philcoa, Makati
Cinema Square, Metro Walk, and the various sidewalks in Baguio,
Laoag, Davao, and other major Philippine cities. Within the belly of
the Moro enclave in Quiapo, old buildings were refurbished to cater
to new stalls for the aggressive dividi trade. The dividi stalls compete
with jeepneys for constrictive access along Quiapo's thoroughfares.
Not only were infrastructures reconceptualized for the trade, but so,
too, were behaviors and decorum of the trade. During the introduction of many classic films and operas, devoted clients would wait
early in the morning when new titles were released. For pornographic films, a range of new practices surfaced: sellers of pornographic
films whispered to people walking down the street, prospective
clients being brought into more illicit spaces, not opening the package
bought in the site, and, of course, being duped into buying something
other than the pornographic films ordered. Sellers would coalesce
on a minimum price per dividi, and would impose a tough attitude
to those not acceding to the price; even as elsewhere, in Quiapo's
various enclaves, prices varied depending on the stall's location. The
more commercialized the space—if a stall was brand new, with air-
conditioning, and had a television to test the dividi with—the more
expensive the minimum price set.

It is not so much that Moro identity dictates the newer capitalist experience in dividi production and sales. It is the historical
construction of the sinister figure of the Moro pirate that somehow
foregrounds any actual contact and exchange with Moro ethnicity.
Christian and state chauvinism have minoritized the position of Moro
ethnicity, creating it as the other of the national self, an othering
based on ethnicity and religion rather than on class, as compared, for
example, with the assertion by the New People's Army of working
class issues and differences. In asserting the three million Muslims
in the country, or just some 5 percent of the population of predominantly Christian Filipinos,[28] national politics emplaces the Muslim
conflict as something induced by the Muslims themselves, for not
wanting to integrate into the body of national politics that purports
cultural and religious tolerance. In obfuscating class from Moro
ethnicity, Christian and state chauvinism have washed off their own

crucial role in minoritizing the Moro. Difference is posed in terms of religion and ethnicity, all redeemable within the nation-state's developmental objectives.

This chauvinism furthers the middle-class affect or the gentrified feeling of belongingness, and in Filipino colloquial use, "feeling" means to be in the privileged yet inappropriate place of the other—*pa-feeling, feelingera, feeling rich, feeling pretty*. So we add the new feeling: *feeling middle class*, a class affinity that contradicts actual class affiliation—aspiring to become part of this socially mobile group, even with dismal historical class positionings. Middle-class affect becomes the simulacrum to actualized forms of actual social mobility, with dividi forming an integral part of the affect's substantiation. The contradiction of middle-class affect and actual historical class position becomes the tension in the everyday interrogation of national politics and global neoliberalism.

Dividi becomes the marker of the contradiction, poised in the racialization and class depoliticization of the Moro figure that illegally reproduces and sells it as a modality of class subjectivity within the gentrified codification of global neoliberalism. Within national politics, the most infamous case that comes to mind is former President Joseph Estrada's celebration, in a devastated mosque, of his victorious reclaim of an MILF (Moro Islamic Liberation Front) camp: "Erap waged total war against the Abu Sayyaf and the MILF in Mindanao, celebrating his troops' victory by giving away jeeploads of lechon and beer, in a deliberate affront to Muslim sensibilities (about pork and alchohol)."[29] The pirate's turf, Mindanao, is posited as either land of (Christian) opportunity, war-ravaged, or newer site of terrorism, the latter as a result of the larger minoritization of Moros in the global war on terror. Former U.S. chargé d'affaires in Cambodia Joseph Mussomeli has warned that Mindanao "could become the next Afghanistan," and that "Metro Manila could become the next Baghdad."[30] The Autonomous Region of Muslim Mindanao (ARMM) tops the list of provinces with the highest poverty incidence in the country.[31] Also included in the top ten are the Muslim provinces of Tawi-tawi, Maguindanao, and Sultan Kudarat.[32]

Moro involvement in the dividi trade revolved around the ghettoization of the ethnic groups in national identity formation and national development. What Moros undertook, in their infrastructuring of the nation for the dividi trade, was a reproduction of their headquarters ghetto of sorts—their redevelopment of Quiapo's Muslim side as the antithesis to Manila Mayor Lito Atienza's own urban renewal of historical and touristic sites in the capitol—in other

K
E
Y
W
O
R
D
S

sidewalk ghettos in key cities. In the first place, Moro enclaves in the official city have been designated in Maharlika Village, Taguig and Culiat, Tandang Sora areas, prone to periodic raids and "sona" (forced submission of suspects for inspection) by the police. Other informal sites include Baclaran, the island that was part of the reclamation project in Manila Bay, and crosswalks where Badjaos and other ethnic groups brought from Mindanao are made to beg by syndicates or of their own will. The state's own Clark Special Economic Zone was used as a factory site to produce pirated media until it was raided in 2000.[33]

The attempt of the nation-state to weaken Moro ethnicities exhibits the state's own propensity for corruption and its upholding of larger interests. It underwrites, if not supervises, the economic flow of goods and trade by Moros on the one hand, and the social engineering, or the minoritization of the Moros, on the other hand. The Philippine state also functions to discipline and punish the Moros through continuous surveillance and self-vigilance. An uncanny example of the state's policing activities, specifically directed at Moros, are its media piracy raids. In a reversal of roles, the state, through its police apparatus, now undertakes the raiding of pirated media, a piratical act against pirated goods, and pirates themselves. The state's performance of a double-take on piracy, even in its coercive nature, is legitimate. This coercive nature of state function becomes the corrupting impetus for the use of Moros and their trade then and now to signify the state's acquiescence to both the normality of its racializing operation—in the name of protecting the more legitimate individual and corporate claims—and its own corruptible enterprise via individualized or hierarchical interests through pay-offs, cuts, percentages, and illegal claims in exchange for protection. In a report on raids, the racialization of piracy is once again pronounced:

> [US Assistant Secretary of State William] Lash said the Philippines has yet to convict a single person for piracy, even though 280 arrests were made [in 2002]. Almost at the same time as Lash's visit, VRB [Video Regulatory Board] operatives confiscated five truckloads of pirated audio and video tapes and arrested eight people, including a ranking police official from Mindanao, during a raid in Maharlika Village in Taguig. Senior Supt. Laud Sari, Lanao del Sur provincial director, was arrested in one of the houses where the illegal piracy activity was being done. He was immediately relieved by Philippine National

Police Director General Hermogenes Ebdane Jr. for ignorance of the law.

Combined teams from VRB, PNP [Philippine National Police], Presidential Security Group, Special Weapons and Tactics of the Southern Police Disctrict, Philippine Air Force and film stuntmen, joined in the anti-piracy operation on Mindanao Avenue, Maharlika Village. Lawyer Carlo Uminga, VRB chief for legal affairs, said the raid on nine Muslim houses along Mindanao Avenue also yielded 150 units of CD burners, desk computers and master copies of audio and video CDs.

Uminga describe the raid as the biggest "in terms of the number of CD burners and the volume of fake CD and VCD materials." "This is unique in the sense that Maharlika is the biggest supplier of pirated materials to barter centers in Quiapo," he said. Officials said the illegal piracy activity in Maharlika, dubbed Quiapo Dos, has become a cottage industry in the area, serving as main sources of livelihood for jobless residents as well as their relatives in Quiapo.[34]

K
E
Y
W
O
R
D
S

Unlike in usual reportage of crimes, the religious and ethnic backgrounds of the perpetrators are clearly mentioned in the report, and tied to the crime of piracy. Uminga draws the link of Quiapo and Maharlika Village, as well as livelihood for those in the area and their relatives in Quiapo, homogenizing the notion that all Muslims are the same, or at least, in support of their kind. The report spectacularizes the raid, involving even movie personnel as providing the authentic dissent to the crime committed against their industry. A vendor of pirated CDs succinctly puts the reversal at play, again poised in racialized terms, "But they have no right to confiscate what we are selling . . . the police are just like the Abu Sayyaf (a kidnap terrorist group in Southern Philippines), they come and confiscate everything we sell . . . while some of them choose the (pornographic) films and some of the good music CDs and just take (those) away!"[35]

The ebb and flow of raids and raid patterns become normalized, too, with the traders' forewarned knowledge of what to do, why, and how. Raids are staged performances, after all, of the state's display of efficiency to deliver trading practices at par with neoliberal standards. The Chair of the Optical Regulatory Board (ORB) will always be present in these raids denoting the "quite safe" conduct of these police activities. Shops would just pull down their shutters, and street vendors would run with their goods. Actor Ramon Revilla Jr., a Chair of the VRB, would find national political acclaim in these raids, allowing him to run and win a Senate seat. Pirated goods are then seized, and another spectacle will ensue, the bulldozing of the illegal goods. Quantities of the goods destroyed are stated but can never be verified. Viewers are made to assume the enormity of the quantity, and therefore, the moral ground to destroy these. This becomes the moral locus, however, for individual holders of pirated media to justify their collection—the amount they have can never equal the amount produced by pirates that is seized and destroyed by the state. The middle-class reaction mimics the state's own self-preservation agendum—to ensure some compliance to dictates of global capitalism on the one hand, and to ensure that it reaps its share in the illegal trade on the other hand.

Neoliberalism, Informal Sector, and Its World of Piracy

Quiapo derives its name from *kiyapo* or *pistia stratiotes* (scientific name), a floating water plant, "whose leaves are densely clothed on both surfaces with short depressed hairs, (such that) any water falling on the inclined leaf is speedily repelled and the epidermis never wetted. The air layer effectively prevents the plant (from) becoming submerged."[36] The plant has evolved to survive in the area's murky and muddy waters. Its qualities parallel Quiapo's own evolution as a cultural center of modern and postmodern national life.[37] Its first underpass was built by Mayor Arsenio Lacson in the 1950s. In the 1970s, Quiapo was the shopping and leisure district in the pre-mall era. Quiapo was also the site where Marcos built the golden mosque in a gestural attempt to display Muslim recognition. Quiapo also became the site of the first 24/7 Mercury Drug Store branch, the site first redeveloped into Atienza's grand city in the 2000s, and remains the major hub of the present dividi trade. Quiapo's survival rests on its symbolic premodern value to the country's religious and cultural life. It is Quiapo's present enclave of piracy that is most illuminating of the plant's similar characteristic, as a "direct mechanical hindrance to navigation, entangling boat propellers; also leads to loss of crops, flooding."[38] In other words, Quiapo always foregrounds the continuance of piracy, or a double-act, simultaneously showcasing national modernity and its undercurrent: the informal economy that sustains this modernity.

Such informal economy is crucial, as it allows for the cultural maneuvering that postures modernity, and its version of Third World cosmopolitanism, which sustains modernity. Quiapo's habitat is unique yet reproducible in the age of neoliberalism: from the annual procession of the Black Nazarene, Atienza's grand renovation of the Plaza Miranda, to the eclecticism of the space of folk medicine, religiosity, and consumerism; from the old houses in San Miguel, or decaying art nouveau buildings in España, to the in-mixing of Christian and Muslim domains. Neoliberalism seeks to allow the free flow and penetration of global capital, goods, and people through a system where government creates the business and political conditions to ensure this free flow. This is done through laws that support privatization, commercialization, and liberalization of goods and services. Primary to neoliberalism's reproduction of capital via finance markets is its perpetuation of physical and service infrastructures to guarantee capital's smooth flow. Services are franchised to tailor-fit the newer mode of capitalism, and Quiapo retrofits newer modes with an almost premodern variety of services. These services were first negotiated and standardized in Quiapo and other related sites prior to the circulation of these as usual norms of middle-class national experience.

The informal sector that brings about the culture of modern-premodern artifice sustains the national economy. It is by locating the Moro pirate figure within class, and even underclass politics, that another visibilizing trope of identity formation is rendered possible. Indeed, Quiapo's informal sector, in general and media piracy in particular, accounts for a juncture of the economic backdoor's flow, as well as the illegal bringing in, or marketing of, goods and produce. The informal sector projects a double-piracy: the selling of goods brought in illegally, and the selling of illegal goods. Thus, the bringing in and selling of the goods represent the illegal operation in this informal sector. The local movie industry is quick to react to media piracy, given its prominent stature in the culture industry, as some PhP 30 million of its total sales succumb to piracy or 30–35 percent of its entire sales monthly.[39]

The Philippine population profile, a sizeable portion of which is made up of very young people (45.53 percent from ages eighteen and below, or a total of 38.8 million, with zero to four years old being the age group with the largest population), is served by the informal sector, particularly media piracy.[40] The informal sectors in Quiapo and elsewhere eat up the USD 23 billion Hollywood profits, USD 33.6 billion U.S. recording industry, and the USD 189 billion worldwide software industry.[41] Quiapo and the likes were able to bite off USD 116 million worth of sales from U.S. companies in 2002.[42] In

2004, U.S. companies' lost an estimated USD 160 million.[43] Even as early as 1997, USD 177.7 million was already lost in the Philippines due to piracy, USD 107.7 million of which was from media piracy.[44] Specific to software, the piracy rate was a high 71 percent in 2005, with industry losses amounting to USD 76 million.[45] The influence of this sector is so massive that the Philippine government has failed to get the country out of the U.S.'s priority watch list for five years. "Special 301 is the part of the U.S. trade law that requires U.S. Trade Representative to identify countries that deny adequate and effective protection for IPR or that deny fair and equitable market access for U.S. persons who rely on IPR. Once "identified," the country could face bilateral U.S. trade sanctions if changes are not made to address U.S. concerns."[46] It was in February 2006 that the Philippines was "upgraded" to the "Watch List" after having been on the "Priority Watch List" for five consecutive years, but nonetheless, the country remains under close watch by the U.S.[47] The country's inclusion in the Priority Watch List represents the premodern stigma of non-inclusion in the newer global trade, a kind of underclass in the more recent big-league capitalist game. According to Emma Francisco, IPO director general, *Pangit ang* implication *no'n* (the implications are bad), because there is a tendency for people to stay away."[48] The U.S. bluntly declared: "The Philippines has been relatively ineffective in protecting intellectual property rights."[49] Media piracy becomes the pronounced sore in the national leper geobody politics.

By 2001, it was clear that Quiapo was becoming part of the global media piracy network. "The Philippines ranked number three in Asia in manufacturing and selling pirated media materials"[50]; and the "seventh worst Intellectual Property Rights violator," according to Dumlao.[51] No longer simply a distributor, the Philippines was also becoming a supplier of media piracy. However, the ownership of the means of piracy was ethnicized through the "Chinese" (Singapore, Macau, Hong Kong, Taiwan and China) and "Muslim" (Malaysia) connections. This means that the informal sector of media piracy in the country still owed much to illegal foreign capital for funding, signifying that even in the illegal trade, the Philippines was poised low globally. Nonetheless, the country remains crucial—"taking advantage of the country's porous borders, the CD pirates relocated in the Philippines where IPR enforcement is worn to escape tighter enforcement in their own countries. The pirated optical media are sold to Southeast Asian and other global markets, including Latin America."[52]

Fig. 1: Pirated DVDs
(photo by Karl Castro)

Fig. 2: Third-run movie theater in Manila (photo by Karl Castro)

The porousness is experienced twice—in the archipelagic geography that posits the national experience as already open to global ideas and products on the one hand, and in the quasi-effectiveness of governance in law enforcement and in the nature of the informal sector with its very anachronistic use of technology, on the other hand. These include hand-delivering the master dividi copy, folded paper ledgers for *jueteng kubradors* (gambling agents), or marked stones to hide sachets of *shabu* (crystal meth), making the culpability of the illegal perpetrator limited. Yet the porousness is socially allowed, too, because of the informal sector's sizeable contribution, supplying 40–70 percent to the official gross domestic product.[53] The informal sector also constitutes 63 percent of the total labor force, or some fifteen to nineteen million workers.[54] The informal sector does not only supplement the government and private sector's initiatives on employment and individual income, but also provides for the majority of these components.

The history of the informal sector is generated by three major episodes in the national development drive.[55] Even prior to these national drives, the Philippines "is among the most enthusiastic of global players, lowering its tariffs faster than its neighbors and opening its entire economy, including land ownership and retail trade without caution—as if the lesion from 'parity rights' and 'free trade' during the American colonial rule have not been learned."[56] In the postwar period, import substitution restricted imported consumer goods, allowing for monopolies in the manufacture of various basic food and agricultural products. The introduction of machines displaced manual labor, and urban migration intensified. The Marcos period stressed export-oriented economy, with the labor force supplying the needs of multinational corporations in manufacturing and agriculture in the homeland, and the export of Filipino contractual labor in foreign lands. The 1980s up to the present emphasized economic liberalization with government assets and services being privatized (electricity, water, and corporations, among others) leading to mass layoffs, greater contractualization, and reskilling of workers.

Media piracy comes in the aftermath of national development, marking both its failure to fully progress as a nation and its illicit translation of global standards of leisure. Textbook piracy was justified by the tenets of import substitution, and the availability of various media products—including pirated versions—in the 1990s was spurred by economic liberalization and the official drive for global competitiveness. In 1976, the International Labor Organization

(ILO) gave criteria for defining the informal sector, which still applies today, particularly to media piracy:

> 1) family workers in a business (usually paid); 2) less than 10 people are employed in a business; 3) there are no legal regulations or existing regulations are not observed; 4) there are no regular working times; 5) the work is seasonal; and 6) there is no dependency on regular loans.[57]

In 1998, ILO defined the informal sector as "small-scale self-employed activities (with or without hired workers) distributing goods and services at a low level of organization, skills, and technology, with the primary objectives of generating employment and incomes. The activities are usually conducted without proper recognition from authorities, and escape the attention of the administrative machinery responsible for enforcing laws and regulations."[58] What the ILO does is to legitimize the informal sector's contribution, especially in the developing economies, as a struggle for livelihood and the standards of living.

What it also does is highlight a form of primitive accumulation of capital in the intensification of neoliberalism—capital has so penetrated the lives of individuals that even the disenfranchised are made subservient to higher positions of legal and illegal authority to generate vestiges of capital. In *Kubrador* (Jeffrey Jeturian, 2006), there is a scene where coins placed as gambling bets are shoveled into containers. Even the most marginalized sectors are further disenfranchised in finding individual immediate relief from abject reality and access to social mobility. For example, even as *jueteng* (the numbers game) gives a one-in-four-hundred chance of winning, so enticing is the appeal that annual revenues from this small-town lottery amounts to PhP 30 billion annually.[59] According to Isagani Yuzon, the informal sector is "the first casualty of globalization" for the following reasons:

> First, informal sector products have no way of competing in the global market, due to their low-input, low-technology, low capital content . . . [s]econdly, the informal sector bears the brunt of the harsh structural adjustment programs, such as the liberalization of banks and the gobbling up by unibanks and multinational corporations (MNCs) of small banks and rural banks . . . [t]hirdly, the informal sector carries a substantial burden of the country's regressive taxation system . . . [f]ourthly,

the informal sector suffers from the absence of social protection being outside the regulatory coverage of the government. . . .[60]

While the informal sector may not be able to compete head-on with legitimate business entities, it is able to form alternative engagement practices in the service of the consuming public, fulfilling a function both in aid and in contention with government interests. Yuzon writes of the ability of the informal sector to sustain the national economy amidst globalization:

> [T]he informal sector absorbs all the victims of globalization—displaced workers, forced retirees, educated, unemployed, etc. . . .
> [T]he informal sector cushions the impact of globalization on the surviving formal sector . . .
> [T]he informal sector expands the domestic market, spreads the purchasing power among the poor, and brings the products of the formal sector into the poorest segments of society, thus contributing to the health of the formal sector . . .
> [T]he informal sector covers up what government has failed to provide in terms of basic services. . . .[61]

K
E
Y
W
O
R
D
S

What the informal sector does is make employment available, even as some 25 percent of the country's youth are unemployed, and as the youth labor force is expected to expand by 17 percent from 2005 to 2015.[62] It gives alternatives or sustaining options even when the nation-state disenfranchises this massive sector.

On the one hand, the state enforces global IPR dictates of developed nations, showcasing the spectacle of law and order in raiding piracy lairs. On the other hand, the state condones biopiracy, especially those coming from developed nations' corporations. Together with Brazil, the Philippines ranks fifth among the world's biological "hotspots," with an estimated nine thousand species of flora, a third of which is considered endemic.[63] "At least one tree [Philippine yew] with cancer-curing potential, four native vegetables [*ampalaya, talong*], one snail [Conus Magnus] which produces the most effective painkiller, an antibiotic soil fungus, one tree and several rice varieties, have been stolen, and are now owned by foreign pharmaceutical firms."[64] Biopiracy is not said to be new in the country. As early as 1949, Dr. Abelardo Aguilar, who worked for the pharmaceutical firm, Eli Lilly Co., sent samples of an antibiotic isolated from soil in Iloilo. "Ilosone," named after the place where the sample was found, was the "first successful macrolide antibiotic introduced in the U.S. in 1952," allowing an alternative to patients with allergic reactions to penicillin.[65] The drug has earned billions for Eli Lilly, but Aguilar did not receive any royalties. Another celebrated piracy case is Roberto del Rosario's invention of the sing-along system, the precursor of the karaoke, for which he also has not received any royalties.

The issue of piracy renders the state and the higher interests of developed nations and their multinational corporations as officiating gatekeepers that legitimize corporate claims and disenfranchise perpetrators of illegal reproduction. The state straddles the legitimation of the antithetical contest of authentic and illegally reproduceable claims, even as the state seeks to legitimate its own status as an efficient machine that implements global stakes as well as effective local governance. It is not so much a weak state, but a state designed to be weak in order to remain porous in "swinging it both ways," so to speak, to legitimate its own machinery of corruption and politicking. This allows the informal sector to bridge the gap of public service and, therefore, periodic breaths of tolerance in between raids and pillage of pirated goods, and allows capitalist interests to be protected and be expanded nationally.

While the middle-class affect emplaces the national citizen in some nexus of gentrified social being, the informal sector could very well challenge the order of civil society. On the one hand, in the drive against piracy, the government seeks to protect legitimate business and take up the cause of artists in their struggle for economic artistic rights. In this case, the government disenfranchises counterclaims to citizenship, especially the case of media pirates. On the other hand, in the continuance of media piracy, the informal sector asserts its own claims to citizenship, reminding the government and the businesses that it protects of the uneven distribution of wealth and the experience of national life. Poised in issues of social legitimacy and massive poverty, the informal sector, especially the figure of the Moro pirate, trespasses the lines of hegemonic consignment and relegation. Coerced into being minoritized, the informal sector strives to assert its survival on a daily basis. The arrogance of power is to create pejoratives of underclass practices to soothe middle-class identity formation. Middle-class arrogance, for example, will not choose charity, thinking beggars will just gamble their money, or buy drugs, and that the underclass itself should just choose to buy rice and other basic commodities rather than buy pirated DVDs. The underclass is discursively denied access to middle-class lifestyle, yet the intermittent position of the middle class is allowed access to approximate the middle-class experience. There is tolerance for the middle class in downloading media from the internet, as some four hundred thousand to six hundred thousand films were illegally downloaded daily in 2003, even as the box-office and home video sales soared in 2004.[66] However, the homogenizing effect of global popular culture and neoliberalism has allowed the gentrified social imaginaries to be out here and there, even to the underclass that have also begun to dream of "feeling rich." Pirated media become the trace that simulates not the real but the imaginary of the real, "feeling rich" because that is all that it could get at this time.

ENDNOTES:

I am grateful to Professor Tilman Baumgartel for inviting me to share my ideas on media piracy in the Philippines. I am also thankful to Merce Planta for helping me locate sources on sea piracy in the Philippines.

1   Lloyd Duhaime, "Piracy (Maritime Law) Legal Definition," duhaime.org, http://www.duhaime.or/LegalDictionary/P/Piracy Maritime Law.aspx, accessed 28 Oct 2014.

2   Ibid.

3   Ibid.

4   See Tilman Baumgartel, "The Culture of Piracy in the Philippines" (manuscript, 2006). The essay has a primary source discussing the "Muslim connection," including the use of the sea lanes that bring pirated movie sources from Kota Kinabalu, Borneo to Manila. Upon reaching Mindanao territory, the "RoRo" scheme (Roll on, roll off) is used, "where long-distance busses leave Mindanao via ferries, that take them to other islands, in this case the main island of Luzon, where the capital Manila is located."

5   Nishtha Chugh, "Global Piracy: Just a Seaborne Scourge or a Bigger Malady," *Fair Observer,* 7 Apr 2013, http://www.fairobserver.com/region/north_america/global-piracy-just-seaborne-scourge-or-bigger-malady/, accessed 4 Dec 2014,

6   Richard Menta, "Movie and Record Industry Piracy Figures Incendiary, But Not Fact," 15 June 2006, *MP3newswire.net,* http://www.mp3newswire.net/stories/6002/250billion.html, accessed 6 Nov 2006. The USD 60 billion figure is cited in Julie Javellana-Santos, "Optical Media Act Penalizes Film Piracy," *Philippine News,* 18 Feb 2004, http://www.philippinenews.com/, accessed 6 Nov 2014,

7   Wikipedia, "Piracy" Change to Duhaime, ibid.

8   In elite culture, Mindanao is transposed from its ravaged history to a location replete with natural beauty and wonder. See, for example, the coffee-table book *Mindanao: A Portrait* (Manila: Bookmark, Inc, n.d.) that renders an almost invisible history of war and piracy in the island grouping.

9   The characteristic and quality of reproducibility of media in piracy is dis-
     cussed in Scott R. Garceau, "Truth in Advertising," *Philippine Star,* 30 Aug
     2006,   http://www.philstar.com/philstar/LIFESTYLE200505093706.htm,
     accessed 21 Sept 2006 (site discontinued). This was emailed in plaridel_pa-
     pers@yahoogroups.com; Conrado de Quiros, "Out of the Box," *Inquirer,*
     30 Aug 2006, http://opinion.inq7.net/inquireropinion/columns.view_ar-
     ticle.php?article_id=17953, accessed 21 Sept 2006 (site discontinued); and
     "Fighting Pirates," 26 Dec 2003, http://www.asianjournal.com/cgi-bin/
     view_info.cgi?code=00002599, accessed 21 Sept 2006 (site discontinued).

10   Leo Magno, "RP Mobile Phone Penetration Growth Can be Replicated—
     Smart," *Inquirer,* 17 Oct 2006, http://technology.inq7.net/infotech./infotech/
     view_article.php?article_id-27221, accessed 18 Oct 2006 (site discontinued).

11   Ibid.

12   The decay and rivalry theories are drawn from James Francis Warren, *The
     Sulu Zone 1768–1898* (Singapore: Singapore University Press, 1981), xiv–xv.
     To my mind, what Warren undertakes in his study marks off a third theo-
     ry of historiography of Sulu and piracy, "revolving around the interrelated
     themes of external trade, slave raiding, and state formation as the key to
     the general history of the zone" (xv). Subsequent studies include Ghislaine
     Loyre, "Living and Working Conditions in Philippine Pirate Communities,
     1750–1850," *Pirates and Privateers: New Perspectives on the War on Trade in
     the Eighteenth and Nineteenth Centuries* (Devon: University of Exeter Press,
     1997), 69–86, and Thomas M. McKenna, *Muslim Rulers and Rebels: Everyday
     Politics and Armed Separatism in the Southern Philippines* (Berkeley:
     University of California Press, 1998). Also see Warren, *The Sulu Zone: The
     World Capitalist Economy and the Historical Imagination* (Amsterdam: VU
     University Press, 1998), and Peter G. Gowing and Robert D. McAmis, eds.,
     The Muslim Filipinos (Manila: Solidaridad Publishing House, 1974). Local
     historiography of the Moro can also be seen in Samuel K. Tan, *The Filipino
     Muslim Armed Struggle, 1900–1972* (Philippines: Filipinas Foundation, Inc.,
     1977), and Kenneth E. Bauzon, *Liberalism and the Quest for Islamic Identity
     in the Philippines* (Quezon City: Ateneo de Manila University Press, 1991).

13   Loyre, "Living and Working Conditions in Philippine Pirate Communities,
     1750–1850," 72.

14   J. Hunt, "Some Particulars Relating to Sulu in the Archipelago of Felicia,"
     Notices of the Indian Archipelago and Adjacent Countries, ed. J. H. Moor
     (London: Cass, 1967), cited in Loyre, 77.

15   Loyre, "Living and Working Conditions in Philippine Pirate Communities,
     1750–1850," 80.

16   Montero y Vidal, cited in Loyre, 83.

17   Loyre, "Living and Working Conditions in Philippine Pirate Communities,
     1750–1850," 76.

18   Ibid., 81.

19   James Francis Warren, *The Sulu Zone: The World Capitalist Economy and the
     Historical Imagination* (Amsterdam: VU University Press, 1998), 169.

20 Loyre, "Living and Working Conditions in Philippine Pirate Communities, 1750–1850," 81.

21 Warren, *The Sulu Zone*, 170.

22 Parish documents (1779), cited in Warren, *The Sulu Zone*, 171.

23 Robert Reed, cited in Warren, *The Sulu Zone*, 177.

24 Michael Salman, *The Embarrassment of Slavery: Controversies over Bondage and Nationalism in the American Colonial Philippines* (Berkeley: University of California Press, 2001), 68.

25 McKeena, 90.

26 Ibid., 140.

27 International Intellectual Property Alliance, "2001 Special 301 Report Philippines," accessed 6 Nov 2006, http://www.iipa.com/rbc/2001/2001SPEC301PHILIPPINES.pdf, 177.

28 Ibid., 2.

29 Antonio Abaya, "The US Loves Erap?" *Manila Standard Today*, 27 Mar 2005, http://www.manilastandardtoday.com, accessed 27 Sept 2005 (site discontinued).

30 Joseph Mussomeli, cited in Abaya, ibid.

31 This information is from the National Statistics Coordination Board (NSCB), from research conducted in 2006, as cited in Jema M. Pamintuan, "Pagmamapa ng Pagbabagong Heograpikal, Historikal at Kultural ng Quiapo" (manuscript, 2005), 9.

32 Ibid., 16.

33 International Intellectual Property Alliance, "2001 Special 301 Report Philippines," 178.

34 "Piracy Watchdog Backs Bill Regulating Optical Media," *Poblaw Newsletter* 3, no. 24 (April 2003), http://www.poblaw.com/April2003.html, accessed 8 Nov 2006 (site discontinued). U.S. support versus U.S. sanction renders the piracy issue as economically and politically contestable. Even in sea piracy, in the Associated Press, "US Lauds S-E Asia's Anti-Piracy Measures," *The Strait Times,* 4 Nov 2006, 30, U.S. approval premeditates national course of actions among various Southeast Asian nations.

35 Jonas Baes, "Towards a Political Economy of the 'Real': Music Piracy and the Philippine Cultural Imaginary" (manuscript, 2002), 4. For another account of media piracy raid in Baguio City, see Harley Palangchao, "Raid of Pirated CDs, VCDs Nearly Ends in Violence," *Sun Star Baguio,* 5 May 2003, http://www.sunstar.com.ph, accessed 8 Nov 2006.

36 C. P. Sculthorpe, The Biology of Aquatic Vascular Plants (London: E. A. Publishers Ltd., 1967), quoted in Jema M. Pamintuan, "Pagmamapa ng Pagbabagong Heograpikal, Historikal at Kultural ng Quiapo," *Plaridel Journal* 3, no. 1 (Feb 2006): 24.

KEYWORDS

37 For a discussion of the spatialization of Quiapo and media piracy in it, see Pamintuan's essay, "Pagmamapa ng Pagbabagong Heograpikal, Historikal at Kultural ng Quiapo," which astutely examines the site in terms of elixir, capital obsolescence, rise of the informal sector, backdoor policy, and territorialization.

38 Sculthorpe, *Biology of Aquatic Vascular Plants*, quoted in Pamintuan, "Pagmamapa ng Pagbabagong Heograpikal, Historikal at Kultural ng Quiapo."

39 Florence F. Hibionada and Maricar M. Calubiran, "Pirates Go Slow on Movies, 'Get Even' on Music," *News Today,* 23 Dec 2005, http://www.the-newstoday.info/20051223/pirates.go.slow.on.movies.get.even.on.music.html, accessed 8 Nov 2006 (site discontinued).

40 "Figure It Out," *Inquirer,* 5 Nov 2006, http://showbizandstyle.inq7.net/sim/sim/view_article.php?article_id=30587, accessed 5 Nov 2006 (site discontinued).

41 Menta, "Movie and Record Industry Piracy Figures."

42 "Piracy Watchdog Backs Bill Regulating Optical Media."

43 Bureau of Public Affairs, "Philippines," U.S. Department of State, http://www.state.gov/e/eb/ifd/2005/42102.htm, accessed 6 Nov 2006 (site discontinued).

44 International Intellectual Property Association (1997), cited in Baes, "Towards a Political Economy of the 'Real,'" 3.

45 "Software Piracy Rate in the Philippines Remains at 71%," *BSA: The Software Alliance,* http://www.bsa.org/, accessed 6 Nov 2006 (site discontinued).

46 Delia S. Tantuico and Errol Wilfred Zshornack, "Intellectual Property Rights: Talking Points for RP-US FTA Negotiations," *Philippine Institute of Development Studies* (Feb 2006), 16.

47 "Philippines," *Office of the United States Trade Representative,* http://www.ustr.gov/assets/Document_Library/Reports_Publications/2006/2006_NTE_Report/asset_upload_file.223_9202.pdf, accessed 6 Nov 2006.

48 Iris Cecilia C. Gonzales, "RP Still in Priority List of IPR Violators," *Business World,* 15 May 2003.

49 Bureau of Public Affairs, "Philippines."

50 Rep. Imee Marcos, cited in Gonzalez, "RP Still in Priority List."

51 Baes, "Towards a Political Economy of the 'Real,'" 3.

52 "Foreign Pirates Find RP a Lucrative Haven," cited in Baes, "Towards a Political Economy of the 'Real.'"

53 Ma. Rosario K. Garcia, "Hidden No Longer: Beyond Property Rights, The Philippine Informal Sector from a Rights-Based Perspective" (manuscript, 2005), 4; Estellita V. Domingo, "Measuring the Non-Observed Economy (NOE): The Philippine Experience" (manuscript, 2004) estimates the informal sector as 44 percent of GDP.

54 Cited from a study done by the Bureau of Labor and Employment Services of the National Statistics Office, cited in Domingo, "Measuring the Non-Observed Economy."

55 This history of the economic development drives is based in Domingo, "Measuring the Non-Observed Economy."

56 Isagani F. Yuzon, "The Human Resource Development of the Philippine Informal Labor Sector Amidst Globalization and Its Applicability to Developing Economies" (UMP-Asia Occasional Paper, March 2004), 1. His estimate of the informal sector is between 45–55 percent of the labor force.

57 ILO, cited in Garcia, "Hidden No Longer."

58 Ibid.

59 Emil Jurado, "Destroying People's Reputations," *Manila Standard Today*, 1 Jun 2005, http://www.manilastandardtoday.com/?page=emilJurado_june01_200, accessed 22 Nov 2006 (site discontinued).

60 Ibid., 2–3.

61 Ibid., 2.

62 ILO cited in Alastair McIndoe, "Asia Faces Tough Job Finding Work for Its Young," *The Strait Times*, 7 Nov 2006, 2.

63 Norman Myers, et al. "Biodiversity Hotspots for Conservation Priorities," *Nature*, 24 Feb 2000, http://www.equalisambiental.com.br/wp-content/uploads/2013/02/My042.pdf., accessed 4 Dec 2014.

64 Antonio Cerilles, quoted in Myers, "Biodiversity Hotspots."

65 See Myers, "Biodiversity Hotspots," for Dr. Abelardo Aguilar's disenfranchisement in biopiracy.

66 Jie Zhou, "The Economics of Movie Downloads," *Yale Economic Review*, http://www.yaleeconomicreview.com/issues/fall2005/downloads, accessed 6 Nov 2006 (site discontinued).

Vagination

Cinema and Globalization in the Post-Marcos Post-Brocka Era

Based on the range of scholarship undertaken, there seem to be three areas of concern in independent filmmaking—first, digital films as the newer direction for a democratized filmmaking; second, in terms of funding source, independent films or works done by non-mainstream producers; and third, in terms of form and content, alternative films, such as documentaries, experimental, and short animation films. What is common among all three is the notion of empowering marginal voices or the ability to foreground oppressed identities and their condition of oppression.

What I am proposing is a fourth area that remains constant and sustainable in Philippine cinema, especially in times of crisis. Sex-oriented films have remained a standard feature of contemporary Philippine cinema since their inception in the late 1960s. I refer to their continual production amid conditions of economic and political turmoil which, in retrospect, actually signifies the Philippines' national character. The sex-oriented film genre becomes the semi-autonomous sphere that sustains Philippine national cinema. The term "sex films," however, is a misnomer. Mainstream cinema, in particular, may only contain tame sex scenes, including the display of semi-naked and semi-nude bodies or, in recent trends, split-second frontal nudity.

There were only fifty-three Filipino movies shown commercially in 2004. This is low compared to the past when Philippine cinema had an annual output of some two hundred films per year. The once-robust national cinema is truly experiencing a decline. Though its demise has been predicted on and off in the past, the recent steadier slide may just mark the real "death of Philippine cinema." The cause of the decline is economically-rooted. The Philippines has yet to fully recover from the global economic crisis that afflicted most especially the Southeast Asian region in 1997. Although other nations in the region have witnessed the growth of their national economies, the Philippine economy has only grown from 3.5 to 5 percent per annum in the post-crisis era. What sustains its economy is an open secret—the massive deployment of overseas contract work (OCW). With seven million Filipino contract workers abroad, official annual remittance has already hit USD 8 billion, about half of the national budget.[1]

K
E
Y
W
O
R
D
S

This essay discusses the cultural discourse of the libidinal drive of Philippine national development in the film industry. My hypothesis is that the sexualization of its national development produces, among other things, the overt sexualization of Filipino films. Since their appearance and domination of the film industry in the Marcos dictatorship's pre-martial law period (pre-21 September 1972), *bomba* (soft-porn) films have permutated to various subcategories attuned to a range of historical sub-developments of the period. Ferdinand Marcos used such films as basis to declare martial rule, equating sex-oriented films—including the growing communist movement—to the moral decay of the times and thus the need for a clean administrative slate. Immediately after declaring martial law, Marcos banned these films, only for them to reappear in various strains in dialog with the allotted parameters of the period. To this day, sex-oriented films are still plagued by debates on morality, and are often banned. My contention is that the continuing prevalence of sex-oriented films is attuned to the intensifying feminization of Philippine labor, one that has been instrumentalized to characterize the Philippine state as powered by the vaginal economy.

Vaginal economy refers to the intensifying feminized sexualization of Philippine labor that is mobilized in the national development program. This involves the dual transnationalization of Philippine labor—in the homeland, to service the labor needs of multinational capital, whether as factory, service sector, or sex workers; and outside the homeland, with the continued reliance on OCW, especially in times of crisis. In this essay, I will posit a dialog on how the vaginal economy produces a Philippine cinema attuned to the national libidinal drive, and the politics involved in the production of images. If sexualized Philippine labor resuscitates the endless crisis of the national economy, then sex-oriented cinema saves the day for the Philippine movie industry, forestalling its periodically announced death.

I will first map out the Marcos and Brocka debates on the imaging of the nation. I will then examine the intensification of the vaginal economy—how the discourse is carried over in the post-investigation era. Lastly, I will examine sex-oriented films that represent the turn and greater reliance on the vaginal economy, especially noticeable at a time where the economy and its cinema are experiencing their worst lull in the post-war era. This cinema and its cultural discourse represent the newer direction in the post-Marcos and post-Brocka era to dialog and contest the imageries of nation.

Contestation of the Image of the Nation in Marcos and Brocka

After the declaration of martial rule in 1972, then President Ferdinand Marcos established a novel republic called *Bagong Lipunan* (New Society), imagined as the wellspring of the modern Philippine nation. Together with his wife, Imelda, President Marcos designed a fascist rule and utilized edifice showcases like film to beautify the nation's representation despite the mounting international criticism of his rule. Moreover, he institutionalized the circuiting of national laboring bodies to be in the service of international capital. Prior to the declaration of martial rule but during Marcos's second presidential term,[2] Filipino professionals were migrating to the United States under liberalized working and immigration rules. This 1960s diaspora signaled the brain drain phenomenon or the outflux of professionals such as doctors, nurses, accountants, engineers, among others that serviced the needs of already developed nations; and thus, forfeiting the needs of their own nation. What Marcos also institutionalized after the declaration of martial rule was overseas contract work (OCW), initially involving male laborers in Middle Eastern nations' oil-boom economies. It later involved both men and women in more prosperous global sites. The remittance of OCWs' foreign currency earnings was required to prop up his administration, already saddled with corruption and overspending. Historically, OCWs sustained the nation, especially in times of economic and political crises. Multinational investments easily closed shop in the nation-space during economic downturns. This leaves the OCWs to prop up the national economy by deploying their massive accumulated earnings.

The tragedy of the Marcos dictatorship was that it only propelled the megalomania of the already prominent presidential bodies and their cronies, leaving the nation in massive poverty. Added to this, the nation's militarization furthered the disenfranchisement of national bodies, subjugated to serve the dictatorship and its foreign interest. Most of the legacies of the Marcos period—the liberalization of the economy, factionalism of an already small ruling comprador class, pampering of the military, and swelling of poverty—remains in place even to this day. Semi-colonial and semi-feudal infrastructures that negate any turn for genuine social transformation also remain.

Lino Brocka was considered the period's foremost political filmmaker. His films provided the counter-imagery to the Marcosian megalomania of nation-building. While Imelda Marcos in particular focused on an aesthetics of the "true, good, and beautiful" as practiced in state pageantries and edifices, Brocka proliferated images of poverty in film. In *Tinimbang Ka Ngunit Kulang* (Weighed But Found Wanting, 1974), he juxtaposed the desire of a leper and the town's fool for a better, albeit isolated, life amid the Catholic hypocrisy of the small town's elite. In *Macho Dancer* (1989), he told the story of a young man caught in the underground of the sex industry. In *Bayan Ko: Kapit sa Patalim* (My Country: Clutching the Knife's Edge, 1984), he allegorized the travails of a working-class couple caught in a factory strike as well as the kidnapping of the owners. He would be recognized both nationally and internationally for the humanization of subaltern people's experiences against the backdrop of state-sanctioned poverty and human rights abuses.

Brocka and Marcos would eventually usher in the Second Golden Age in Philippine cinema, a sustained production output of both aesthetically and politically attuned films. His films, *Maynila sa Kuko ng Liwanag* (Manila in the Claws of Neon, 1975) and *Orapronobis* (Fight for Us, 1989) would become bookends of the period. He openly protested against the Marcos policies, heading cultural organizations such as PETA (Philippine Educational and Theater Arts) and the Concerned Artists of the Philippines (CAP). Marcos's oppressive regime provided both the impetus to develop quality films as part of the dictatorship's showcase and to regiment the production of imageries of nation with strict censorship rules. The Marcoses revived the Metro Manila Film Festival (MMFF) which reserved entire moviehouses solely to exhibit Filipino films during the peak Christmas holidays, funded quality film initiatives via the Experimental Cinema of the Philippines, and launched the International Manila Film Festival at the height of their political crisis. They also built the infamous Manila Film Center, the floors of which collapsed and killed dozens of workers in the mad dash to finish construction in time for the international film festival's opening. What became of the second golden age was the production of quality films characterized by both artistic and political merit, the latter discussing the dehumanization of individuals, mostly subaltern figures, amid the intensifying crises surrounding them.

Sex-oriented movies, like their predecessors in the pre-martial law era, would not only sustain the film industry but would also be canonized as part of the second renaissance. Films like *Virgin Forest* (1981), *Scorpio Nights* (1985), *Isla* (Isle, 1983), *Ang Pinakamagandang Hayop sa Balat ng Lupa* (The Most Beautiful Animal on the Face of the Earth, 1975), *Burlesk Queen* (1977) and even Lino Brocka's *White Slavery* (1984) combined covert political commentary on the period with numerous sex scenes. In the first two years of martial law, the bomba genre disappeared, with horror films dominating the box-office instead. Gradually, the bomba made a comeback in movie houses, permutating in various forms provided for by the political temper of the Marcos dictatorship. For example, the bold wet look, known for covertly displaying the female body using a wet *kamison*,[3] emerged during 1974–1976. It is considered bold because of the daring display amid stringent censorship regulations. Audiences only witness the spectacle of the heroine's private parts through her drenched *kamison* as she takes a bath or is raped along the river. The first generation of bold actresses were stars who typified the local notions of beauty (brown-skinned, dusky, slim), such as Gloria Diaz, Elizabeth Oropesa, and Daria Ramirez, former beauty pageant winners, and attuned to Marcos's return to the heritage past in Bagong Lipunan. This is in stark contrast to the mestiza bomba actresses of the pre-martial law period, where whiteness was the privileged norm for display.

The second generation of actresses, however, was younger and thus, deemed bold for the period (1976–1983). Chanda Romero and Alma Moreno were the most famous *probinsyana*[4] stars of this gener-ation; they shifted the standard from racial colors to youth. Marcos's emphasis on youth involved forming a youth brigade (Kabataang

Barangay) headed by his eldest daughter, Imee, and lowering the voting age for plebiscites to fourteen years. The empowering of youth was tied to the utilization of able bodies for a transnational national development. The third permutations of the bomba genre was known as the FF (fighting fish) film and the more raucous *penekula*.[5] The launching of the Manila International Film Festival (MIFF) brought a brief censorship-free period. Art films from abroad, which depicted sex in overt ways, were shown in theaters. At other times of the year, local sex films or FF films were shown at the Film Palace, which was exempt from censorship rules. The *penekula*, however, referred to those sex films shown in third-run movie houses that inserted hard-core scenes to soft-porn movies. These inclusions were either taken from foreign porn movies or were actually shot in local films but deleted in its regular run in first-class theaters and reinserted in its third-run theaters. The actresses from this generation of stars were younger, some of them Amerasians[6] using branded product names. A generation of them were known, for example, as soft drink beauties—Coca Nicolas, Sarsi Emmanuel, and Pepsi Paloma.[7]

Like pre-martial rule, bomba films of this period (late 1960s to 1972) proliferated and were met with the censorship agency's blind eye to hide the heightened political unrest. With the assassination of returning political opponent Benigno Aquino in 1983, massive protests that drew hundreds of thousands catalyzed on the streets. After deposing the Marcoses in 1986, Aquino's wife, Corazon, took the helm of power. A devout Catholic and pacifist, Corazon Aquino promised to be the total moral opposite of Marcos. However, this did not spell the end of sex films. Instead, sex films survived by being transformed into the ST (sex-trip) films. ST films involved young actresses from well-to-do-families performing sex on film in what majority of society perceives as the proper place, time, reason, and sexuality—namely, in the bedroom to show love, preferably by a married heterosexual couple. Included in the line-up of actresses were Rita Avila and Gretchen Barreto, both *kolehiyalas*.[8]

The bomba film's last permutation began in 1992, known as the TT (titillating film). Slowly, through the years, the overt display of the female (and sometimes that of the male) body may lead to a split-second frontal nudity shot. Actresses from middle class families like Alma Concepcion, and Filipino-American Amanda Page, were later followed by another expatriate, Joyce Jimenez, and the very loud Rosanna Roces who worked as a "guest relations officer" in a nightclub.[9] These women had not only socially acceptable body types, but also articulate voices that enunciated women's issues and liberal opinions on sex.

While the rest of Southeast Asia enjoyed massive economic booms from the 1980s to the mid-1990s, the Philippines would remain isolated from such robust regional developments. The nation was in several political and economic crises from 1983 to 1992, leading to the sustained systematic export of Philippine labor as geopolitical sites of familial and national relief. The economic take-off in 1994 would be dragged down by the 1997 global crisis that affected the Southeast Asian region in particular. The economic crisis would also take another political toll in 2002 with the deposing of President Joseph Estrada, a former action star, via EDSA 2 (also known as People Power 2), People Power 3, where Estrada's supporters (mostly from the lower economic class) rampaged near the presidential palace. Brocka's death would clearly mark the end of the second golden age. His construction of the imagery of a nation—marked by excessive abuse of power, and suffering in poverty—provided the vital aura to comprehend the times. However, his death brought attention to his films' emphasis on the political, unwittingly cautioned the international film festival audience against understanding any other imagery of the Philippines. Thus, sex-oriented films became more prominent as a form of aesthetic and political articulation of the intensifying Philippine labor export or the of female labor's diasporization. The proliferation of overseas contract workers would financially sustain families and the national economy, providing enough money for non-necessities, such as entertainment.

Overseas contract work has sustained the nation in its crisis and brief take-off. However, the state does not look kindly on OCWs, even when its bureaucracy has institutionalized tags such as *Bagong Bayani* (New Hero) into official state discourse. With domestic worker Flor Contemplacion's execution in Singapore during the year 1995, the plight of OCWs under the nation-state's apathy was politically forefronted as massive protests took place in the streets. This national event led to three biographical films about Contemplacion, the one titled directly after her becoming the year's undisputed box-office earner. It also opened the way for the influx of OCW films, until the novelty ended. Certain sex-oriented films returned to represent the more recent times. In general, the OCW geobody in film is not represented in OCW character-driven films. Instead, the Filipina laboring body is displaced onto sex films.

Vaginal Economy of Women's Migrant Work

The economics of overseas contract work need to be examined in order to generate the material reality of the nation's growing vaginal economic dependence. Overseas contract work represents the politics of hope and its lingering effect in both the family and nation. This resounds with the ethos of bomba films, women becoming eroticized sacrificial lambs in order to redeem the family. Multinational work has brought women into the work area; they are generally underpaid and prone to sexual exploitation. Like the bomba queen, their bodies become magnets for modes of capital accumulation. The nation-state relies on OCWs' remittances to sustain itself. In 2004, the national budget was PhP 864 billion.[10] However, the estimated total annual remittances (bank, non-bank, and non-cash) of all Filipino OCWs is USD 20 billion.[11] OCWs subsidize the cost of running the government. While PhP 875 million was contributed by OCWs to the Overseas Filipino Workers Administration in 2001, only PhP 91 million was allocated by OWWA for OCW benefits in the same year.[12] The Philippines is not only transnationalized from without the nation-space, but also transnationalized from within. On the one hand, multinational work provided by national bodies, especially in the service sector inside the nation-space, has contributed 45 percent of the gross domestic product.[13] In 1999, another estimate pegged the share at 52.9 percent. Multinational work in the nation-space is sexualized work because the criteria of nimble fingers, perfect eyesight, tedious menial work, and healthy bodies—a category related to female domestic work—is engendered for factory work in the garment and electronic industries. Tourism, fastfood, retail, and entertainment industries rework the national body and personality to fit with globally competitive standards, albeit remaining lowly in the global and sexual division of labor. The national body is further engendered in subcontractual/flexible labor practices, reemphasizing overseas labor's exploitative contractualization. Most blatant of the sexualized trade is sex work, which involves some one hundred thousand children and six hundred thousand adults, mostly women.[14]

On the other hand, women have eclipsed men in transnational overseas contract work. "By 1994, almost 60 percent of the 258,984 OCWs who left the country were female. In the first quarter of 1995 alone, there were more women among the 114,566 newly hired OCWs. Of that total, 69,435 or 60 percent were female while only 45,131 were male."[15] In order for men to compete in the OCW trade, they take on feminized work. Demand for menial manual labor has

K
E
Y
W
O
R
D
S

declined worldwide, especially with the lingering effects of the most recent global crisis. OCW work is sexualized work, as women take on home-related work abroad, such as care-giving, nursing, domestic work, hotel bedroom service, entertainment work, and sex work. Some three hundred thousand Filipina nurses practice their profession abroad.[16] Ninety percent of medical school graduates work or reside abroad.[17] In Japan, the estimated number of Filipinas in entertainment work is 150,000.[18] Some 2,670 Filipinos and Filipinas are leaving the nation every day to do overseas contract work.[19] Men have also adapted to the global demand for feminized labor by reskilling themselves along these fields, including the service sector.

A columnist describes the vaginal economy as "how the otherwise legitimate deployment of Filipino women as entertainers has deteriorated into their massive trafficking into sex work."[20] In this economy, laboring women and men are thought of as vaginal commodities.[21] Thus, the columnist calls for the various sectors involved in the massive deployment of overseas contract work "to take [...] performing artists seriously and work determinedly against any further growth of the 'vaginal economy.'"[22] On the one hand, the columnist recognizes the organizing signifier of the recent national development drive—the feminization of Filipino and Filipina labor, either in transnational contract work overseas or multinational work, in various special economic zones inside the nation-space. The Philippines is the third largest exporter of overseas contract work. The female and the feminine become the nexus of national development drives. Women have overtaken men in overseas contract work, and men have opted to do traditionally feminine work for the promise of social mobility.

On the other hand, the columnist makes a belated call for this economy's cessation of imperative—the trafficking of women for sex work. This, of course, is the logical recourse to protect the contract worker abroad. Ethically, however, the recourse becomes entrenched in the bourgeoisie civil society that seeks out the various sectors to protect the unknowing body of the overseas contract worker. Yet the phenomenon of overseas contract work has been heightened, especially in times of both national and global crises. National development has sustained the deployment of women and men in overseas contract work. Filipinas and Filipinos have become sexualized objects in mostly First World sites that negate access to their own national citizenship. What remains of their citizenship claim is transformed to performing citizens in their homeland. Even in multinational work in the homeland, laboring bodies perform sexualized

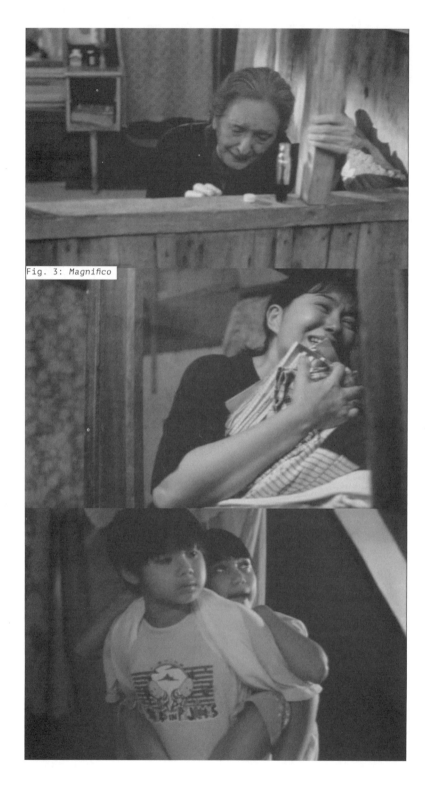

Fig. 3: Magnifico

and gendered feminine work to become abled economic and political citizens. The vaginal economy heralds female and feminine work in diaspora, a process of becoming, or coming to being.

The vaginal economy produces a cultural dialogue that becomes symptomatic of, and receptacle to, the transnationalized national development drive. The vaginal economy provides the drive for women's labor and bodies to proliferate in sites of multinational work and in bomba films. It also implies, especially in recent times, the feminization of Philippine cinema, its decline of what used to be a vibrant national film industry, as Hollywood's share of the market continues to increase. Together with India and the Chinese-speaking nations, the Philippines has sustained its own film industry despite the increasing pressures from the globalized American film industry. Yet, in recent years, the pressures have taken their toll on the national film industry; its output, pegged at 220 films in 1999, dropped to 97 in 2002, making the Philippines the ninth largest producer in 2002, when it used to be fourth from 1997 to 1999.[23] With declining local film production and decreasing costs of foreign film distribution, the national film industry is struggling to survive. Though critics and friends of the national film industry have on-and-off announced the death of Philippine cinema in the past, it is now apparent that the prediction can become a foreseeable reality.

Discourse of Sex in Films and the Recent Nation

Sex has become a byword in recent definitions and operations of the nation. It remains a constant issue in popular discourse, especially as circumscribed by the massive apparatus of the Philippine Catholic Church. Sexual issues have to rely more on popular modes of proliferation, as controlled by the vested interest of the church, state, and businesses. To another extent, hegemonic management of sexual moral panic becomes the mode of creating national safety. What becomes of the Philippines is a sexual nation in popular cultural imagination. This can be gleaned from both work and cultural representations, exuding excess sex. Such excess sex is derived from the material phenomenon—national poverty, wealth abroad—that drives the transnationalized national development. In mainstream cinema, it has become one of two streams of independent filmmaking[24]—one, overt sex-oriented films with artsy style (using modernist artistic styles), a recollection of the Marcos and Brocka aesthetic and commercial production; and two, the artsy attempt to produce not overtly political films but a humanized politics. This is reflected in films such as *Magnifico* (2003), a reworking of the Marcos and Brocka paradigm that shifts the terrain from social to identity politics. Both streams attempt to bring films into national and international prominence in the festival markets. *Magnifico* narrates the story of an innocent optimistic boy persevering to salvage the remnants of his family and his small town, even if it means sacrificing his own life. It is a humanistic telling of optimism even in poverty and death, of innocence even in chaos and disintegration. No major action films have been produced due to high production costs, vested mainly in special effects and action stars' expensive talent fees. Other than the presence of the ever-reliable sex melodrama films, Philippine cinema is dominated by films about teenagers and juvenile adventures.

However, even before and during the martial law era, sex-oriented films provided a democratized access to filmmaking. Done at large by fly-by-night productions, sex-oriented films were the modality in which independent producers participated in commercial filmmaking. It may be possible to read sex films as a realm of another independent public sphere, where contentious issues are brought to the fore and experienced in popular modes. I will briefly examine three sex films, two produced by Regal Films, a mainstream studio, and one produced independently. What I think would be productive in this endeavor is to decipher the substantial development in the more recent independent film to the sex genre, now evolving into the metafilmic genre or self-reflexive film about filmmaking.

Metafilmic Sex-Oriented Films

Live Show (2001) caused a furor when it was commercially exhibited. It was caught in transition between the change of presidential appointees to the censorship board. This film defined Gloria Macapagal Arroyo's relationship with the entertainment industry which she tried to woo against another presidential hopeful, action star Fernando Poe Jr. The film renarrativizes the tale of sex show performers, using the male lead character as a talking head. *Private Show* (1986), an earlier film on the subject, gives the point of view, Fellini style, of a woman performer seeking her humanity in the corrupt trade. *Live Show* does the same but without the connection to reality—by then, the sex show trade had already ceased in the ways imagined in the film. The use of talking heads, however, attempts to

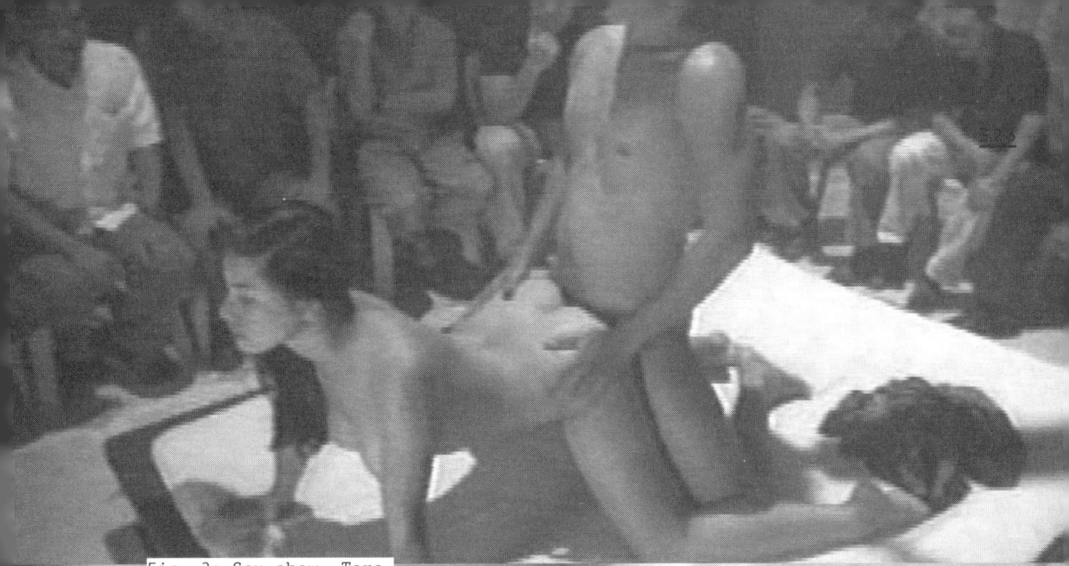

Fig. 2: Sex show, *Toro*

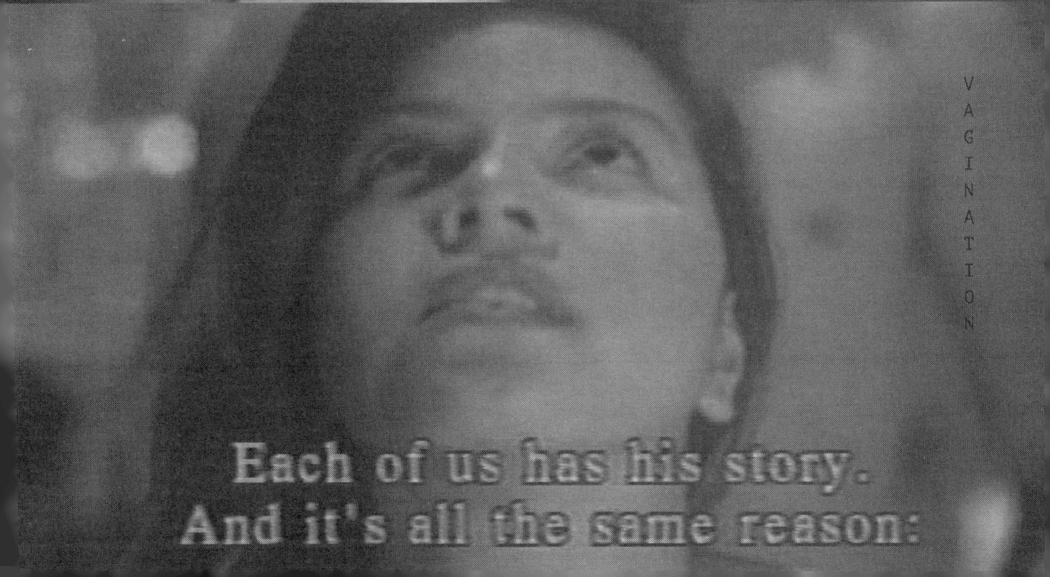

VAGINATION

Each of us has his story.
And it's all the same reason:

324

K
E
Y
W
O
R
D
S

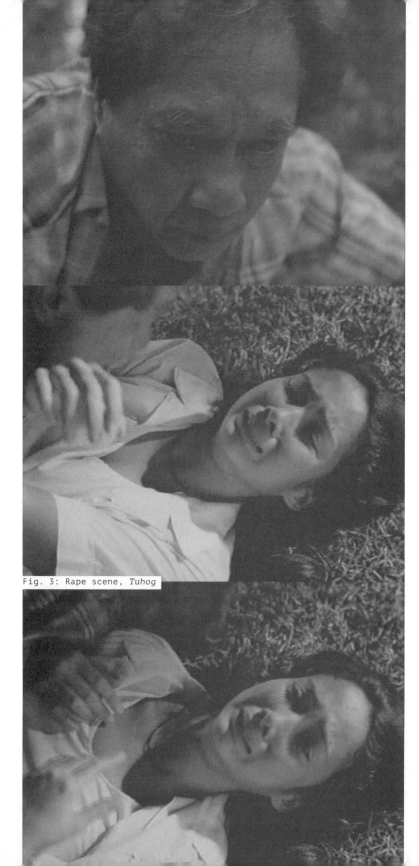

Fig. 3: Rape scene, *Tuhog*

undo its own fictionality—metafilmically trying to implicate the audience in the production and hypocrisy of the sex performer characters' misery. Watching the film, we become the sex show's audience.
For the lead male character, life goes on after the interview. This un-
dermines the cause of implicating the audience, who will simply retain their pre-screening position.

Tuhog (Skewered, 2001) also strives to metafilmically implicate
the audience. The film narrates the story of a young woman who
was raped by her father. The film also tackles the film biography's
production, as well as the woman and her family's reception of the
film. Rape is a common heinous crime in the Philippines, comprising
the majority of death penalty sentences. The film also uses the talking
head style to embellish the metafilmic documentary quality. The final
scene is especially interesting to draw attention to life going on but
on a different level. It shows the family in the van, fresh from viewing
the biography film, disenchanted at how their lives were portrayed
differently. The passenger van maneuvers through a congested street,
and a huge billboard of the biography film becomes the backdrop
of their own congestion and struggle. The film improves on *Live
Show*'s aesthetics—if *Live Show* relinquishes the questions it tries to
raise, *Tuhog* throws the questions back to the audience. If what the
audience sees is the making and reception of an experience within
the real, which is meant to be examined, then the congestion against
the backdrop of the film billboard resurfaces the engagement with
the real—the fictionality of the filmic reality. On the one hand, the
film questions the romance with filmic reality based on a nostalgia
for the real, and how the real becomes the disorganizing presence
in film. On the other hand, the film validates such romantic experience yet leaves the audience feeling queasy just as the characters
are shown leaving the movie house. The psychosomatic romance
becomes indicative of both the possibility and limits of engagement
in film. When the lights are switched off inside the movie theater, the
movie begins and audiences begin to soak in the narrative. Audiences
get a reprieve from themselves, and mis/identify with the characters and narrative of the film. The film becomes both the dream and
dreaming machine of the audience.

In *Babae sa Breakwater* (Woman in the Breakwater, 2003), the
life and love saga of a subaltern couple is told against the backdrop
of Manila's murky bay. It is about a young man's struggle to earn
for his family as he pursues a relationship with a young female sex
worker. Produced independently, the film used unknown actors and
familiar folk music, staged against the unattractiveness of Manila

Bay's polluted waters. The film takes risks by presenting an unattractive theme in an unattractive background that psychosomatically
disturbs the middle-class audience. How could one possibly live,
eat, swim, and die in Manila Bay, which has become the metropolis'
sewer? The connection with the real represents such disturbance. In
the closing credits, footage of both actors—both dead and alive in the
film—vanishes from screen. It calls attention to the inevitability of
the film's conclusion and the realities presented, to linger even after
its own closure. Then, the film presents a choreographed dance scene
of two representational communities—first, a ballroom dance in a
wedding reception at the newly revitalized and gentrified Baywalk,
which used to be portions of the boulevard's breakwater; second,
a mimicry of the subaltern community's own brand of dancing. A
carnivalesque moment ensues, in which subaltern figures figuratively
triumph over the powerful.

Babae sa Breakwater innovates on the sex genre's metafilmic
quality, downplaying sex scenes by its bound failure in presenting sex
as carnivalesque. This is demonstrated by a specific sex scene which
takes place in a pedicab's claustrophobic interiors (a small passenger
cart pulled by a bicycle). Many subaltern figures watch the sex act
from outside, until the cart loses its brakes and slides to the main
street where it is hit by a moving vehicle. This is a film that mimics
the madness of subalternity, a conscious design to link middle-class
angst, sentimentality, and romance with the subalternity. *Live Show*
is a middle-class appropriation of a sex worker's subaltern consciousness, whereas *Tuhog* self-consciously looks at its own attempt to deal
with middle-class subalternized figures. What then transpires is a
pacifist stand on the self-referentiality of film. Primarily because it
is an independent film, *Babae sa Breakwater* navigates the sex genre
with the desire to tell a subaltern story, using a subaltern trope,
thereby producing a quizzical film about the discomfort of the filmic
text and the comfort of watching movies.

These films resonate with the intensified sexuality of the times.
With dwindling film production, however, the heavy weight of sexualized development is metastasized to more accessible media. The
discourse of feminized labor has carried over into other more popular
cultural forms. A recent phenomenon is the domination of novelty
songs with sexual double meanings in tri-media (television, music,
and radio). The SexBomb dancers, stage dancers of the noontime
game show *Eat Bulaga* (the show's name being a play on eating and
surprise), were catapulted to their fifteen minutes of fame via the
song and dance routine "Ispageti" (Spaghetti), now a quadruple

platinum album. Similarly, comedian Bayani Agbayani, of the rival noontime television show, *Magandang Tanghali Bayan* (Good Afternoon, Nation!) became an instant singing sensation with "Otso-Otso" (Eightfold). The songs contained sexual innuendoes, matched with sexualized dance steps. "Ispageti" used the up-and-down sex thrust, represented with gyrating beer house dancing. "Otso-Otso" used the regularized sex act, represented by the butt thrust.

What is especially interesting is how the singers are emplaced in the "sex in the afternoon" trade. The highlight of both noontime shows is the million-peso game segment, choosing guaranteed increasing amounts of money or the greater risk of losing it all for the uncertain jackpot. The emotionally charged segment is triggered by the sub-story of the contestants' poverty. The backdrop for these segments is a cast of some fifteen similar-looking young women in skimpy attire, gyrating to chants and beats. Poverty, hope, and sex are intertwined in the noontime shows daily. The popularity of these shows, and the configuration of a more wholesome variation of sex display on television, further erodes the exclusivity of sex films, rated mostly for adults.

Both adapted from children's rhymes and movements, the songs were reworked by Lito Camo, the new minstrel of the masses.[25] He has also adapted children's nursery rhymes like "Bulaklak" (Flower), "Bakit Papa?" (Why, Love?), and "Pamela," adding sexual innuendoes to innocent tunes. Thus, sex cuts not only through media divides but also through generational divides. With increasing accessibility to genuine and pirated DVDs and VCDs, mainstream production company Viva Films developed the *Viva Hot Babes* (2003) and *Viva Hot Men* (2004) series, both a collection of steamy scenes played by sexy, muscular actors and hopefuls. These titles have sold so well that more are being planned. Within just two days of its debut, *Viva Hot Men* sold some five thousand copies, a box-office success by Philippine standards. Shortly after, it sold around fifteen thousand copies, outselling its female counterpart.[26] The growing interest in model and body searches has showcased feminized male and female bodies on display, including those willing to be displayed, in the pageantries of the sexual nation.

President Gloria Macapagal Arroyo even eyed "Otso-Otso" to be her presidential campaign's official jingle.[27] Her rising ratings in the pre-election surveys sustained an admirable following, providing a mired hope of winning the election just as her strongest contender, Fernando Poe Jr., an iconic action movie star, seemed to have reached the plateau from the initial euphoria. Unlike Poe, his friend and co-actor, action king Joseph Estrada, was a sure-fire win in the election early on because of his strong film and political backgrounds. Despite this, Estrada lacked political experience and was unable to debate with the president, nor control his temper in the campaign routes. Poe became the feminized body as Arroyo sustained her aggressive finance-driven presidential bid.

In October 2003, a film columnist wrote that only eighty films were expected to be produced for that particular year. He further wrote, "The bad news is that something like 50 of those movies are sex flicks. The reason, of course, is that they're cheaper, quicker and easier to make. That does make sense, but it casts a dark, fetid pall over the Filipino movie industry."[28] The pejorative outlook on sex films remains, even as this genre has generally sustained the industry, prolonging its last gasp of breath. It is with this dominant outlook that the need to revaluate sex films along its literal and figurative independent direction—albeit linked with socio-political and economic experiences—becomes necessary. Why, in the first place, are these films produced? How do audiences determine which sex films they will patronize? How do they see their own sexualized lives and the sexual nation represented in these films?

KEYWORDS

ENDNOTES:

I am thankful to Dr. Khoo Gaik Cheng and Professor Joel David for sharing the thoughts on the essay subject, especially on the prevalence of the sex discourse in other media texts.

1   See Roy Mijares, "Philippine Resiliency in the Asian Financial Crises," http://www.jri.co.jp/english/periodical/rim/1999/RIMe199902philippines/, accessed 30 Mar 2015.

2   Marcos's first presidential term was from 1965 to 1969. Before his second term ended, Marcos declared martial law on 21 September 1972 and established himself as virtual dictator via a new constitution in 1973.

3   White camisole, a conservative undergarment for women.

4   Provincial or from the province.

5   Derived from the combination of two words—the word for penetration or sexual contact, and the local word for film, *pelikula*.

6   Mixed-race youth born and raised in U.S. military bases in the Philippines.

7   Names were derivative of leading multinational cola/carbonated drinks such as Coke and Pepsi, and the local Sarsi.

8   Girls who come from convent schools.

9 A female entertainer or an entertainer of male guests.

10 Sol Jose Vanzi, "House Oks P864-B 2004 National Budget," *Philippine Headline News Online*, 19 Dec 2003, http://www.newsflash.org/2003/05/hl/hl019483.htm, accessed 25 Nov 2004.

11 "Startling Statistics," http://www.acountryofourown.com/StartlingStatistics.html, last accessed 25 Nov 2014.

12 Ibid.

13 U.S. State Department, "Philippines: Country Reports on Human Rights Practices, 2002," *U.S. Department of State*, http://www.state.gov/j/drl/rls/hrrpt/2002/18261.htm, accessed 25 Nov 2014.

14 United Nations estimate, quoted in "Startling Statistics."

15 Luz Rimban, "Filipina Diaspora," *Her Stories: Investigative Reports on Filipino Women in the 1990s*, ed. Cecile C. A. Balgos (Quezon City: PCIJ, 1999), 128.

16 Jocelyn Santos, "DoH Also Exports Filipino Nurses Abroad," *Bulatlat*, http://www.bulatlat.com/news/2-38/2-38-nurses.html, last accessed 25 Nov 2004. Other data on overseas contract work were also derived from this article.

17 Grace Chang, "Importing Nurses: A Money-Making Venture," http://www.cpa.org.au/garchves3/1026nse.html, accessed 3 Nov 2004.

18 "Startling Statistics," http://www.acountryofourown.com/StartlingStatistics.html.

19 Ibid.

20 Rina Jimenez-David, "From 'Vaginal' to 'Phenomenal,'" *Philippine Daily Inquirer*, 5 May 2002, A9.

21 Willie Espiritu, quoted in Jimenez-David, "From 'Vaginal' to 'Phenomenal.'"

22 Ibid.

23 Screen Digest, quoted in "Number of Feature Films Produced in Australia and Other Countries, 1997–2002," http://afc.gov.au/, last accessed 3 Nov 2004.

24 Independent filmmaking in the Philippines does not necessarily connote the Western notion of films shot with an artistically independent spirit. The practice could refer to "fly by night" productions done outside of the major studios but with the same intent to generate profit. It could mean film trends outside both Hollywood and mainstream setting, and films that prioritize the moral integrity of the filmmaker and their craft. The negotiation of Philippine independent films becomes a transnational issue in two ways— one, the ethos is derived primarily from feminized OCW phenomenon, and two, filmmakers have to contend with both mainstream Hollywood and art markets. Very little occurs along the lines of foreign funding of local films.

25 Alya B. Honasan, "Minstrel of the Masses," http://www.inq7.net/mag/2004/jan/18/text/mag_2-1-p.htm, last accessed 3 Nov 2004 (site discontinued).

26   Mario E. Bautista, "Hot Men Outsell Hot Babes," *Malaya*, 28 Jul 2004 http://www.malaya.com.ph/jul28/ente_2.htm, accessed 25 Nov 2004 (site discontinued).

27   "Gloria Eyes 'Otso-Otso;' Mar Bags 'Mr. Suave,'" *Malaya*, 18 Dec 2004, http://www.malaya.com.ph.dec18/news5.htm, accessed 25 Nov 2004 (site discontinued).

28   Nestor Torre, "Good News, Bad News," *Inq7.net*, 18 Oct 2003, http://www.inq7.net/ent/2003/oct/18/text/ent_20-1-p.htm (site discontinued).

K
E
Y
W
O
R
D
S

Domesticity

Female Work and
Representation
in Contemporary
Women's Films

The impetus for Philippine national development rests on the export of its laborers. This continually increasing massive export sustains Philippine development through the years. As cultural artifacts of nationhood, films provide a dialog to, and critique of, the economic and political impetus of national development. In this essay, I first map out the context of labor export in the Philippines, then proceed to analyze, in particular, globalized domestic work that emplaces the overseas Filipina domestic worker as a central figure in national development. I then turn to the film subgenre on the overseas contract worker, and locate its development within female and feminist filmmaking in the Philippines. Lastly, I discuss female representation in the films of three younger-generation women directors in the Philippines—Rory Quintos, Olivia Lamasan, and Joyce Bernal—and how their films provide the cultural imaginary that mediates the national development project for film audiences and citizens. What I intend to foreground in the centrality of the overseas Filipina domestic worker is her cultural politics, which renders her as a partial citizen in the homeland and an absent one in the host land. These cultural politics inform the film audience of either their own present predicament or future possibility as both dispossessed transnational professionals and partial citizens, and of the impossibility of hope amid its intimate rendition in filmic melodrama.

Philippine Labor Export

The Philippines is the third largest exporter of labor in the world. In some estimates, the Philippines is a bigger labor-exporting nation than India, considered the second largest exporter globally.[1] In 1998, some 755,000 Filipinos worked overseas, joining the already seven million workers abroad, and helped remit some USD 7.5 billion.[2] Remittance estimate for 2005 is a record-breaking USD 9 billion.[3] As E. San Juan contends, "Since the seventies, Filipino bodies have been the No. 1 Filipino export, and their corpses (about five or six return in coffins daily) are becoming a serious item in the import ledger."[4] Every hour, some one hundred migrant workers leave the country.[5] In 1999, half of overseas Filipino migrant workers were in the Middle East (26.5 percent) and Asia (23.5 percent), 42 percent in North America, and 8 percent in Europe.[6] Since the early 1990s, women comprised 55 percent of overseas contract workers (OCW).[7] By 1994, some 60 percent of Philippine overseas contract workers were women.[8] It is estimated that two-thirds of OCWs are involved in domestic work.

This female domestic work represents the Philippines' niche in the global economy. In 1994, some 120 million people legally and illegally migrated from one country to another, representing 2 percent of the world's population that became geographically mobile and culturally diasporic.[9] In some estimates, it is as high as one in six people; one billion people are migrant workers, with thirteen million coming from Asia, 72 percent of whom are women.[10] A more recent estimate shows that some eight hundred thousand women workers migrate each year, and the figure is gradually rising.[11] Next to foreign direct investments, earnings from migrants working in developing countries amounted to USD 7.2 billion in 2001, representing the second largest source of external revenue.[12] A *Migration News* report provides a more staggering estimate of total world remittances (the sum of workers' remittances, compensation of employees, and migrants' transfers)—at USD

70 billion in 1995 from USD 2 billion in 1970.[13] The United Nations estimates the figure at USD 80 billion in 2002, already exceeding the total for foreign direct investments.[14]

The national link of Philippine female work to the global and sexual division of labor is exemplary of developing nations' link to global capitalism. Up to 70 percent of workers in export-processing zones performing work in the electronics and garments industries— similarly emplaced in the rudiments of paid domestic work—are women; domestic worker contracts represent as high as 70 percent of contracts in the international labor market; and some twenty million people—25 percent of them minors, 90 percent women, and 90 percent women from the Third World—are involved in the global sex industry, another sphere of paid domestic work.[15] It is estimated that some two hundred thousand Filipinas are drawn into the global sex trade as another five hundred thousand perform sex work within the nation-space, with nearly 100 percent coming from the underclass.[16] This figure represents a significant contribution to the estimated USD 7 to 12 billion annual revenues from the global sex industry.[17] Furthermore, in Belgium, one of every twenty Filipinas is a trafficked woman; and in South Korea, Filipinas are increasingly becoming the overwhelming national geobody in the domestic sex trade.[18] Filipina bodies dominated the mail-order bride trade in the 1980s.

Women from various developing nations would outnumber men in overseas 3D (dangerous, dirty, demeaning) jobs. Women from Sri Lanka comprised 84 percent of OCWs; from Indonesia, 70 percent.[19] As men and women in the global cities of postindustrial nations become better educated, earn higher wages, and are freed from mundane domestic work, Saskia Sassen stressed that "globalization's high-end jobs breed low-paying jobs,"[20] with some 30 to 40 percent of new jobs considered low-wage.[21] Compared to Filipino migrants, 77.8 percent of Filipina migrants are in more vulnerable service occupations, such as domestic and entertainment work.[22] With shifts in global economic conditions, creating more demand for flexible (non-unionized, downsized, outsourced, contractual, home-work) labor, women's labor is preferred as periodic employment in works deemed traditionally feminine—like domestic labor, nursing, sex work, and factory work in garments and electronics, among others—to allow them time (albeit limited) to care for their families.[23]

The term "Filipina" has become identical with the geoeconomic and geopolitical figure of the domestic worker in various host countries. It has become synonymous with maid and performer of domestic work in affluent and nouveau rich families in the global economy. Filipina denotes "maid" in Hong Kong and "nanny" in Canada, Taiwan, and Italy.[24] In Greece, a new entry in a local dictionary defines "Filipineza (Filipina) as a 'domestic servant; someone who performs nonessential auxiliary tasks.'"[25] Filipina doll sets, complete with a miniature Philippine passport and work contract, were sold in Hong Kong until public outcry stopped their distribution.[26] As Filomeno Aguilar states, "'Filipina' and 'domestic work' have become reducible and interchangeable."[27]

The configuration is emplaced in global geoeconomics and geopolitics, as global capitalism intensified and became the world dominant in the economic mode of production. This resulted in the Keynesian shift (government as invisible hand) in economic postwar restructuring to Thatcherism and Reaganomics beginning in the 1970s, and the confidence-building of neoliberalism in the post-1997 global crisis management. The last fifty years represent a massive increase in women involved in paid domestic work, from 14 percent of mothers (with children aged six years old and below) in 1950 to today's 65 percent.[28] This represents Filipinas, and other Third World women in domestic work, as major conduits in what is termed the global care chain or the "series of personal links between people across the globe based on the paid or unpaid work of caring."[29]

The beginning of the twentieth century saw the decline in income disparities in Western Europe. Paid domestic work was dwindling with the wide entry of women in the formal labor force and with the technological innovations being massively introduced during the period, such as "the reinvention of the kitchen, the rise of home technologies, the emergence of 'eating out,' and other household labor-saving strategies."[30] It was only in the colonies that "aristocratic pretensions," including the hiring of male and female domestic workers, was being maintained "as hiring in Europe itself was on a decline."[31] Paid domestic work proliferated in mid-1980s post-industrial societies as menial jobs in the service industries, domestic services, and residual industrial activities were delegated to migrant workers. The post-industrialization of Europe, for example, created labor demands to further sustain the integration of its own female work force, which, in turn, created the demand for Third World women to fill the void in domestic work. In the United Kingdom alone, the amount paid to domestic workers quadrupled from £ 1.1 billion in 1987 to £ 4.3 billion in 1996.[32] In the U.S., the postwar upward trend—even when this was halted by a series of events in the 1970s (de-industrialization, oil crisis, national inflation, the end of the Vietnam War, and shifts in global trade)—restructured the national economy, created gaps that both diminished the number of the rising middle class and produced an occupational structure that allowed for migrant workers to come in.[33] By the 1980s and 1990s, the polarization of income in the U.S. further intensified, "setting the stage for further expansion of paid domestic work."[34] In the U.S., there were 540,000 domestic workers in 1998, up by 9 percent from 1996.[35] Domestic workers rode the wave of a new global capitalist dictum of outsourcing, "where labor is cheapest at the expense of the local workers."[36]

There are some 153,000 Filipina *amahs* (doing both nanny and domestic functions) in Hong Kong.[37] Of the 1995 estimated 150,000 domestic workers in Hong Kong, 130,000 of these were Filipinas.[38] Filipinas comprise the largest group of entrants under Canada's Caregiver Programme: 61 percent in 1992, 75 percent in 1995. More Filipinos work illegally in major Canadian cities: up to thirty thousand or 70 percent of nannies work in rich neighborhoods.[39] Of the eight thousand domestic workers in B.C., Canada, 93 percent are Filipinas. Of the eighty thousand registered migrant domestic workers in Taiwan, over half are from the Philippines.[40] In 1996, a survey found that women comprised 83.3 percent of OCWs in Hong Kong, 77.1 percent in Singapore and 78.3 percent in Italy.[41] English fluency and a college degree equip the Filipina with both linguistic and cultural advantage to compete in the global economy. This is due to English becoming a major language of global capital. This is also due to college degrees becoming a differentiating capital that privileges a Filipina from her Third World counterparts. In one study, a scholar found that 80 percent of the Filipina domestic workers interviewed in Italy had a bachelor's degree, and had worked earlier in the homeland as teachers and nurses.[42] Aguilar writes that, in Singapore, Filipina domestic workers are ranked at the top, while Sri Lankans are ranked at the bottom.[43] In Malaysia, a Filipina earns a monthly salary of RM 500, while an Indonesian can be hired to service a household for RM 300-330.[44] The Filipina's competitiveness, itself based on colonial legacies and contemporary cultural history, becomes the benchmark in the social stratification of inequity among Third World women.

However, various businesses, the host state, and the host household or enterprise where the case applies always interpolates the competitiveness of the Filipina domestic worker. Various businesses prey on the Filipina domestic worker and her meager wage. With some 2,500 Filipinos leaving the country daily to work abroad, travel agencies, airlines, caregiving enterprises, land developers, and the telecommunications industry target the wage of the migrant workers even before they leave. These industries even target workers during and after their contractual work abroad.[45] Recruiters, for example, charge placement fees between USD 1,200 to USD 1,500 for migrant workers to get a job in Hong Kong. If applicants cannot raise the amount, they are forced to sign a loan agreement which deducts the charge from their monthly wages, including interests.[46] Singapore's model that provided for a monthly levy for its seventy thousand domestic workers raking in SGD 298.8 million in 1999. Amid the economic crisis, Hong Kong hoped to generate, from its 240,000 foreign domestic workers, an annual revenue of HKD 1.152 billion from a program that started in October 2003.[47] While nation-states can protect themselves from economic crisis, foreign domestic workers remain vulnerable to it. During the height of the post-1997 economic crisis, Hong Kong employers pushed for a 5 percent wage cut in the salary of domestic workers; in South Korea, 10,800 to 18,000 foreign workers were told to leave the country.[48] At the beck-and-call of household owners, the Filipina and her work are highly regimented, in most cases detailed to what she can and cannot do, and in terms of a monitored work and sleeping schedule: "According to the Asian Migrant Centre study, more than 75% of all domestic workers surveyed worked more than 14 hours a day; only about 3% of Filipinas worked fewer than 11 hours a day. Almost a third worked 16 to 17 hours a day, with 4% slaving for more than 18 hours a day."[49] The Filipina domestic worker, like other migrant workers, have yet to be protected by the UN Convention on the Protection of the Rights of All Migrant Workers and Members of Their Families, as only twelve countries (mostly those exporting labor) have ratified the convention, mostly those countries exporting labor.

OCW Film and Women Directors

In the last ten years, Philippine cinema has been substantiated by the experience of globalized domestic work. *The Flor Contemplacion Story* (Joel Lamangan, director, 1995), a film dramatization of the named Filipina domestic worker, who was tried and executed in Singapore. The film became the most commercially and critically acclaimed film of the period, reaching PhP 100 million at the box-office mark, which was a feat unheard of at the time. Flor Contemplacion's case was so politically contested that there were four film versions revolving around her execution. Another film, *Sarah Balabagan Story* (1997), dealt with the murder trial of an underage Filipina domestic worker in the Middle East. Balabagan's employer attempted to rape her. In self-defense, she ended up stabbing said employer. These films would become part of a Philippine melodrama subgenre that deals with the social anxiety of the female overseas contract worker (OCW). The OCW film was the female response to biographical movies typified by male heroism in a form that either represents the moral origin of politicians used as part of the political campaigns for elections, or dramatizes the rise and fall of Robin Hood-type criminals. More recent OCW films turned toward fictional story and characters. The filmic shift was engineered by three contemporary female directors of the newest breed in Philippine cinema.

Joyce Bernal, Rory Quintos, and Olivia Lamasan are three of thirteen female directors in the entire history of Philippine cinema. A characteristic shared by two of the directors is their prior experience as film artisans—Bernal as an editor and actress, Lamasan as a scriptwriter. All three directors specialize in female characters as central in various forms of melodrama. In Bernal's case, she specialized in the romantic melodrama and the female camp comedy. All three have accepted exclusive contracts with ABS-CBN, the largest entertainment media corporation in the Philippines. They all work in both film and television, specializing in the latter's daily melodrama series and *telefantaserye* (fantasy serials). They have also become gatekeepers of film production and television programming, having substantial input in the company's program-shaping and film output.

The three women directors represent the post-second golden age generation. The so-called second golden age of Philippine cinema from the mid-1970s to mid-1980s included directors such as Lino Brocka and Ishmael Bernal, as well as female directors Laurice Guillen and Marilou Diaz-Abaya. This second golden age yielded a body of films that showed aesthetic excellence despite limited budgets as well as engaged in a dialog with the oppressive Marcos dictatorship. Free from the gritty realist politics of the second golden age, a newer generation of directors grappled with other ways of substantiating the national experience in the post-Marcos, post-Brocka era. Director Lino Brocka became the primary aesthetics engineer of the second golden age, with his film *Maynila sa Kuko ng Liwanag* (Manila in the Claws of Neon, 1975) considered the opening film of the generation.

The three female directors veered away from the overtly feminist agenda that helped define the second golden age—whether through films directed by women, such as *Moral* (Marilou Diaz Abaya, 1982) and *Salome* (Laurice Guillen, 1981), or through the sensitive portrayals of men and women in films by critically acclaimed male directors, primarily by Bernal in films like *Himala* (Miracle, 1981), *Relasyon* (Relations, 1982), *Broken Marriage* (1983), *Working Girls* (Bernal, 1984), and *Hinugot sa Langit* (Wrenched from Heaven, 1985). Bernal's legacy on female representation would be taken over by a new generation of directors, the most prominent of whom is Chito Roño with films such as *Private Show* (1986), *Bata, Bata, Pa'no Ka Ginawa?* (Child, Child, How Were You Made, 1998) and *Dekada '70* (70s Decade, 2002).

The later generation of female directors opted to help define newer notions of women's films that focused not so much on works tackling overt social agenda but on the female individual's internalization of the social. Their notion of the individual's social refers to either the tangential (in most romantic melodrama and camp films) or the more overt rendition of the individual's social experience as in Quintos's *Anak* (Child, 2000) and Lamasan's *Milan* (2004).

Globalized Domestic Work and Filmic Female Representation

In women's films, one substantiation of the national experience by the three women directors is the melodramatic mode that harps on youthful heterosexual romance and motherhood. For this essay, what are more instructional are the films that represent mothering and domestic work as newer instances of representing the OCW mode within the national experience. What this section intends to analyze is the pre-empted demise of feminist films and the leap toward an already postfeminist agenda in women's films. This is a kind of nostalgia for genres identifiable with women, in an age where labor is being feminized further to supply global demand.

Quintos's *Anak* centers on the return of a Filipino mother named Josie from contractual domestic work in Hong Kong. The happy return to the homeland in the opening chaotic airport scene provides an analog to the national condition, especially as this familiar familial

Fig. 1: Final scene, actress in company of actual domestic workers, *Anak*

scene is replicated in the entire periphery of the international airport. Airport regulation in Manila somehow preempted the present-day antiterrorism drive in U.S. airports, as families and friends of departing passengers are not allowed to enter the airport's interiors to either send off or pick up their loved ones. Josie is greeted by her children with different reactions: The eldest child, Carla, a troubled teenager, is coldest to her; her son, Michael, is unusually quiet; and her youngest daughter, Daday, treats her as a stranger. Tensions further unfold in the household as Josie discovers that her eldest child is taking drugs, engaging in casual sex, and is skipping school. The son becomes more elusive to her. The two children harbor resentment arising from their mother failing to come home for their father's funeral, due to not being allowed to break her contract in Hong Kong. In a climactic scene, the eldest daughter retorts, *"Bakit ka pa kasi umuwi?"* (Why did you even bother coming home?).

Josie's periodic returns are prompted by her series of failures in the nation. Josie attempts to put up a business, but fails, draining her savings in the process. She is devastated, tries to patch up what she can of the family, and decides to leave for another round of overseas work. In the film's final scene, Josie, in a close-up shot, smiles as she walks past Hong Kong Central, the business district, on a Sunday. The camera tilts up showing Josie among other Filipina domestic workers in their usual Sunday takeover of the Central, engaging in both informal economic activities and camaraderie.

In selecting one of the country's show business superstars to play the role of the migrant domestic worker, the film was naturalizing the experience of the Filipina's globalized domestic work as source of both present-day pleasure and pain, and, therefore, also a source of possibility of a futuristic hope. Like the spectacle of the domestic worker's body that attracts both higher wage and social disdain for domestic chores, Vilma Santos's spectacularized body in its filmic portrayal normalizes the experience of overseas domestic work, making it integral in the discussion of everyday national life. In more recent times, Santos's own spectacular body has crossed over to the political, where she has enjoyed popular support for the mayoralty of the industrial Lipa City in Batangas, south of Manila. In fact, she was already Lipa City mayor when she participated in the film. What then transpired from her engagement in representing the domestic worker was the naturalization of the politics that transposed lesser known women's bodies in overseas work. She simultaneously legitimized the demeaning work, even the contribution of domestic workers abroad, at the same time as she naturalized the politics inherent in the work—

the substantial role of the Philippine nation-state in proliferating access to international domestic work and national female bodies.

After all, the Philippines benefits from all the hardships of OCWs. The steady increase of dollar remittance is a reliable source of income, especially as the national economy is suffering from its worst fiscal crisis. With little resources to finance government spending, President Gloria Macapagal-Arroyo has cultivated the OCW phenomenon like her predecessors have in the past. The USD 8 billion annual remittance is about 45 percent of the 2005 national budget of PhP 957.56 billion or 41 percent of the national deficit of USD 3.2 billion for the same year. While other exports like electronics and garments are also dollar earners, OCW or labor export is more reliable than the undependable demand for traditional exports. Demand for electronics and garments, after all, can easily be eroded by the competitive advantage of Philippine laborers doing 3D work or the lack of research in and upgrade of these commodities. OCWs also sustain the government's questionable activities, as some 30 percent of government budget is lost due to rampant graft and corruption.[50] Furthermore, OCW earnings support the government's debt servicing, as around 30 percent of said earnings are drained from the national budget to support payment of debt interest.

Thus, the film's ending scene exalts the OCW as both resplendent and abject individual and collective entities. The nation's expenses are shouldered by the individuals who are made to personalize the social baggage. In some sense, Quintos's film is a heroic rendering not only of the domestic worker but also of the ethos of personalization and internalization of the social baggage. Made to bear the weight of the national development experience, the OCW figure is milked for all its potential to take on the nation's obligations and excesses, including foreign borrowings, pork barrels, and corruption. It is a patriotic film, geared toward servicing the national development project.

The film focuses on the implications of the Filipino domestic worker's absentee mothering. This, in turn, is legitimized in the process of naturalizing the normativity of the absence of state preventive intervention. Despite all the troubles in the transnationalized home with the transborder mother/domestic worker absenting herself from physically realizing her feminine role, she has no recourse—given the continued bankruptcy of the nation-state—but to persevere and repeat the cycle of her overseas work. Thus, the domestic worker is a partial citizen in her homeland and is an absent citizen doing domestic work in the hostland. The hierarchy in women's reproductive work, which has been termed as the international division of reproductive labor that allows for a three-tier transfer of reproductive labor[51] remains ungrounded in the film even as such layers of transnational mothering become inimical to overseas domestic work.[52] The tensions are poised—the daughter questioning her mother's return and absence, Josie questioning the injustice of being able to care for her foreign employer's children and not her own—yet goes unquestioned in the film. Such tensions are real as various studies on overseas domestic workers' absentee mothering would indicate. Yet the film is silent on both the maternalism of the employer which, as Pierrette Hondagneu-Sotelo argues, "is an important mechanism of employer power" and the "social reproduction and new regimes of inequality" brought about by "transnational motherhood."[53] Just as the nation-state is unquestioned in the film, so, too, does the dimension of transnational politics, that transposes local domestic workers and mothers overseas, remain uninterrogated. As such, when the nation-state heralds OCWs as *bagong bayani* (new heroes), it does so without any reference to historical and contemporary cultural politics that foreground placelessness—why they are there instead of here—yet does not interrogate such movement.

What films undertake through the use of the visual culture's rudiments is an intimate relationship between characters and audience. Such intimacy furthers the already ongoing internationalization of intimacy in overseas domestic work.[54] This includes child care and the false kinship between employer and domestic worker, as demonstrated by the practice of gifting (the passing of second-hand clothes and items to the worker by the employer). However, through the star system that purports to represent the ordinary drama of the new cultural figure in the national experience—the overseas domestic worker—the intimacy is doubly constructed as artifice. In Lamasan's *Milan*, the domestic worker is portrayed by Claudine Barretto, the most bankable young female star of ABS-CBN. She is paired with Piolo Pascual, the most commercially successful young male star of the same company, portraying the illegal worker in Italy.

Milan dramatizes the melodramatic romance of an odd young couple. Barretto's fashionably dressed character, Jenny, is that of a loud-mouthed, street-smart, and fluent Italian-speaking domestic worker in Milan. Pascual's character, Lino, is that of an unsuccessful Filipino engineer who tries his luck working overseas, crossing the Swiss Alps to illegally enter Italy. The two meet, and the relationship becomes initially romantic. Unfortunately, the relationship succumbs

Fig. 2: Transnational spaces of residence and work, *Milan*

to tensions of the male character's inadequacy to deal with his limitations, and the female character's inability to fully comprehend the tensions. In the end, the two characters overcome all odds and decide to remain in Milan.

What becomes of this intimate portrait of romantic love is emplaced in the very notion of domesticity. Domestic work, which provides possibilities and limits to the couple's love, is resolved through a romantic closure of domestic union. Even with a social disdain for domestic work, the audience is pedagogically trained to accept such work as integral in the fashioning of conflict, development, and resolution. Domestic work, after all, remains the work of the maid (*alila, utusan, atsay, katulong, katiwala*) within the nation-space, done mostly by lower-class under-educated youth from the provinces. Yet in film, there is no pejorative connotation in domestic work. What is being transposed in the filmic narrative, combined with a tourist mode and feel for an unknown land like Milan, is a mystification of domestic work as something adverse but not unnatural in the order of transnational experience.

KEYWORDS

What the film creates as absent are the intertwining cultural identities that simultaneously define and negate the Filipina overseas domestic worker: Third World Filipina, migrant, contractual, domestic worker. As Filipina and Third World, she carries with her the historical force of both colonial and neocolonial experiences; as migrant, her status as outsider inside the belly of a former colonizing power becomes prominent; as contractual, her reproduction of the nostalgia for the homeland via periodic returns and departures is the psychical drive; and as domestic worker, her menial and often-times invisible tasks in the 3D service industries in First World sites construct her identity in the postindustrial society. All four identities earmark for the Filipina her emplacement and attempt to locate herself—including her family—in the circuits of the global and sexual division of labor, the gaps created by intensified global capitalist development especially in the First World, and the similar intensified underdevelopment of her homeland. These categories define her cultural politics as a woman.

Instead, what has also been engineered for women's films, especially by Joyce Bernal, is the female camp comedy, with the heroine struggling in similar exacerbated conditions of the homeland. What Bernal undertakes is the comedic turn using the same wellspring of melodrama, and the construction of the figure of ultrasexy yet ultradim-witted female character as heroine. This figure is portrayed by actress Rufa Mae Quinto, who is known for her sexiness and her

Fig. 3: Rufa Mae Quinto, *Masikip sa Dibdib*

broken English. She stars in films such as *Masikip sa Dibdib* (Tight in the Chest, a reference to Quinto's large breasts, 2004), *Super B* (the name of a superheroine, 2002), and *Booba* (a play on "*bobo*" or dumb, 2001). The heroine's narrative punch line in all these films is derived by playing on her innocence and ignorance with the overtly sexual scenes she entangles herself in. She becomes the trespassing subject in sex-oriented films, allowing for her to move through the same space of sexuality through comedy, not through overt sex scenes. However, the similar signification of women's bodies spectacularized in sex films is what makes Quinto equally as objectified as the women in sex-oriented films.

A columnist writes that the difference between more senior female director Diaz-Abaya and the latter generation of female directors (for instance, Bernal and Lamasan) is that Diaz-Abaya started "as an espouser of feminist stances regarding men's brutish treatment of women and the joys of female bonding," then moved on to become "more universal in her interests . . . and also less main-stream and more subjectively venturesome in her choice of subject matter for her movies."[55] Lamasan is "where Diaz-Abaya was a decade ago, working on important themes rather than on spontaneous and relatively unstructured human experience," and Bernal, being "the new kid in town," is "becoming known for her brisk, visual, mod way of telling a film story."[56] While the columnist gives a sweeping overview that privileges the free-flowing realities of less politically themed films, he elides the question of politics that intervenes in the placement of female filmmakers and their female representations. Like scholars of local film studies, even popular film criticism fails to articulate both a political and a feminist agenda in filmmaking.

What becomes of the Filipina's globalized domestic work is a transnational departure for the hostland and the remittance of her hard-earned wage to the homeland. As Barber stated, "Philippine gendered labor migration and its diaspora have become the primary means for servicing Philippine indebtedness; they have also created new conditions and spaces for the reworking of Philippine class, gender, and cultural identities."[57] What then occurs is the return of her capital via the nation's debt repayment to the host land, and the depositing of her earnings through token infrastructuring of the homeland, that which is not drained by graft and corruption. As the host and home nation-states restrict the Filipina domestic worker's access to political citizenship, the Filipina OCW attempts to circumvent the matrix of power—chain immigration not through recruitment agencies but through pre-arranged employment in Italy of Filipina family members in the Philippines,[58] or linguistic supremacy in English of domestic workers over their Taiwanese employers, or reterritorialization of Hong Kong space by Filipina domestics during their days off. However, such subversive acts need to be contextualized in a social politics that is interrogative of everyday and historical engagements with the transnationalized national experience of development.

It may be concluded that the Philippines' biggest export is female labor. This is intimately rendered in film as a natural occurrence in the transnational experience of contemporary nationhood, as part of the global chain of care, and the realization of the Philippine niche in the global economy. Filmic representations of women are in dialogues attuned to the official experience of the nation-state, echoing and humanizing its rhetoric for the contemporary audience—the prospective OCWs among them—and already constraining their access to citizenship.

KEYWORDS

1   Pei-Chia Lan, "Remapping Identities Across Borders and at Home: Filipina Migrant Domestic Workers and Taiwanese Employers," presented at the Fifth Annual Conference on the History and Culture of Taiwan, UCLA (manuscript, Oct 2000), 2.

2   E. San Juan Jr., "Trajectories of the Filipino Diaspora," *Planet Philippines,* http://www.planetphilippines.com/current/features_current/feature8.html, accessed 24 Mar 2005 (site discontinued).

3   National Alliance of Philippine Women in Canada/SIKLAB (Overseas Filipino Workers Group), "Philippine Government Pushing to Get US$9 Billion in Remittances from Overseas Workers" (media statement, 24 Mar 2005). For a discussion of Canada's caregiver program, see "Trafficking in Women in Canada: A Critical Analysis of the Legal Framework Governing Immigrant Live-in Caregivers and Mail-Order Brides," http://www.swc-cfc. gc.ca/pubs/066231252X/200010_066231252x_11_3.html, accessed Mar 2003 (site discontinued).

4   San Juan, "Trajectories of the Filipino Diaspora."

5   National Alliance of Philippine Women in Canada, "Philippine Government Pushing to Get US$9 Billion in Remittances from Overseas Workers."

6   From POEA, in Pei-Chia Lan, "Remapping Identities across Borders and at Home," 3

7   Arlie Hochschild, "The Nanny Chain," http://www.prospect.org/print-friendly/print/V11/4/hochschild-a.html, accessed 24 Mar 2005 (site discontinued).

8   "Labor Exporters Plan for Emigration," *Migration News* 2, no. 12 (December 1995), http://migration.ucdavis.edu/mn/more.php?id=827_0_3_0, last accessed 24 Nov 2005; Stella Go, "The Changing International Migration Landscape: A View from the Philippines," in Pauline Gardiner Barber, "Agency in Philippine Women's Labour Migration and Provisional Diaspora," *Women's Studies International Forum* 23, no. 4 (2000): 400.

9   International Organization for Migration, quoted in Hochschild, "Nanny Chain."

10 "Globalization and Migration" *Women & the Economy,* http://unpac.ca/economy/index2.html, accessed 24 Mar 2005.

11 "Help Wanted: Abuses Against Female Migrant Domestic Workers in Indonesia and Malaysia," *Human Rights Watch* 16, no. 9 (July 2004), http://www.hrw.org/reports/2004/indonesia0704/4.htm, accessed 24 Mar 2005.

12 Ibid.

13 Filomeno V. Aguilar, Jr., "Global Migrations, Old Forms of Labor, and New Transborder Class Relations," *Southeast Asian Studies* 41, no. 2 (Sept 2003): 152.

14 "Faces of Globalization: Home Away from Home," *Global Envision,* 8 Jun 2004, http://www.globalenvision.org/library/8/614, accessed 24 Mar 2005.

15 Ninotchka Rosca, "Globalization's Assault on the Rights of Women," *International League of People's Struggle,* 27 May 2001, http://ilps.info/index.

DOMESTICITY

php/en/contributions-a-speeches/88-globalizations-assault-on-the-rights-of-women, accessed 25 Nov 2014.

16   Ibid.

17   Ibid.

18   Ibid.

19   International Labor Organization, quoted in Migrant Forum in Asia, "Asian Women and Labor Migration: The Beijing plus 5 Review," http://www.aworc.org/bpfa/pub/sec_f/eco0003.html, accessed 24 Mar 2005 (site discontinued).

20   Pierrette Hondagneu-Sotelo, "Domestica," http://www.ucpress.edu/books/pages/9180.9180.ch01.html, accessed 24 Mar 2005   (site discontinued).

21   Melissa Benn, "Review of Global Woman," 2 Aug 2003, *The Independent*, http://www.arlindo-correia.com/global_woman.html,   accessed   24   Mar 2005.

22   Republic of the Philippines, in Rhacel Salazar Parrenas, "Transgressing the Nation-State: The Partial Citizenship and 'Imagined (Global) Community' of Migrant Filipina Domestic Workers," *Signs: Journal of Women in Culture and Society* 26, no. 4 (Summer 2001), http://www.iupui.edu/anthkb/a104/philip-pines/migrationfilipinas.htm, accessed 24 Mar 2005 (site discontinued).

23   For a discussion of issues involving contemporary women's work, see Rosalinda Pineda Ofreneo, "Women in Asia and the Pacific: A   Trade   Union   Perspective,"   https://www.ids.ac.uk/files/dmfile/Ofreneo2011RightsbasedsocialprotectioninPhilippinesCSPconferencedraft.pdf, accessed 25 Nov 2014.

24   Pauline Gardiner Barber, "Agency in Philippine Women's Labour Migration and Provisional Diaspora," *Women's Studies International Forum* 23, no. 4 (Jul-Aug 2000): 400, http://www.sciencedirect.com/science/article/pii/S0277539500001047#, accessed 30 Mar 2015.

25   George Babinotis, *The Dictionary of the Modern Greek Language,* quoted in Ebron, "Not Just the Maid."

26   Ebron, "Not Just the Maid."

27   Aguilar, "Global Migrations," 140.

28   Hochschild, "Nanny Chain."

29   Ibid.

30   Aguilar, "Global Migrations," 145.

31   Quoted in Aguilar, "Global Migrations," 145.

32   From Bridget Anderson, quoted in Aguilar, "Global Migrations" 146.

33   Hondagneu-Sotelo, "Domestica."

34   Ibid.

35 Barbara Ehrenreich, "A Grubby Business," *The Guardian*, 12 Jul 2003, http://www.arlindo-correia.com/global_woman.html, accessed 24 Mar 2005.

36 Ehrenreich, "Grubby Business."

37 Gemma Tulud Cruz, "No Strangers in this Church," *National Catholic Reporter* 1, no. 35, 3 Dec 2003, http://www.nationalcatholicreporter.org/globalpers/gp120303.htm, accessed 24 Mar 2005.

38 Hondagneu-Sotelo, "Domestica."

39 Abigail Bakan and Davia Stasiulis, "Not One of the Family: Foreign Domestic Workers in Canada," in Barber, "Agency in Philippine Women's Labour Migration and Provisional Diaspora."

40 Lan, "Remapping Identities," 1.

41 Republic of the Philippines, in Parrenas, "Transgressing the Nation-State."

42 Ebron, "Not Just the Maid."

43 Aguilar, "Global Migrations," 149.

44 Ibid.

45 In http://www.geocities.com/asti05/Articles.txt, viewed 31 Mar 2005 (site discontinued).

46 "Faces of Globalization"

47 Aguilar, "Global Migrations," 156.

48 Ehrenreich, "Grubby Business."

49 Nicole Constable, "Wash When I Tell You and Don't Talk to Your Friends," *The Guardian*, 14 Jul 2003, http://www.arlindo-correia.com/global_woman.html, accessed 24 Mar 2005. She also cites from the "Maid's Rulebook" the restrictions on the domestic worker's life. For the condition of Filipina nannies in Canada, see "Advocates Call for Changes to Ottawa's 'Nanny' Program," 25 Mar 2005, http://www.cbc.ca/news/canada/advocates-call-for-changes-to-ottawa-s-nanny-program-1.527167, accessed 31 Mar 2005.

50 "PCTC Paper on Graft and Corruption," accessed 25 Nov 2014, http://www.pctc.gov.ph/papers/graft.htm.

51 "First, among middle- and upper-class women in receiving countries; second, migrant Filipina domestic workers; and third, Filipina domestic workers in the Philippines who are too poor to migrate."

52 Rhacel Salazar Parrenas, *Servants of Globalization: Women, Migration and Domestic Work* (Quezon City: Ateneo de Manila University Press, 2003), 72.

53 Hondagneu-Sotelo, "Domestica."

54 Anna Rotkirch, "The Internationalisation of Intimacy: A Study of the Chains of Care," accessed 24 Mar 2005, http://www.valt.helsinki.fi/staff/rotkirch/ESA%20paper.htm (site discontinued).

55 Nestor U. Torre, "Female directors' Films Compared," *Philippine Daily Inquirer*, 27 May 2000, accessed 24 Mar 2005, http://www.inq7.net/saturday/may2000wk4/spc_6.htm (site discontinued).

56   Ibid.

57   Barber, "Agency in Philippine Women's Labour Migration," 399.

58   For subversion of the official chain migration, see Anny Misa Hefti, "Globalization and Migration," accessed 25 Nov 2014, http://unpan1. un.org/intradoc/groups/public/documents/APCITY/UNPAN006918. pdf; for linguistic capital, see Lan, "Remapping Identities"; for Hong Kong Central reterritorialization, see Renato Redentor Constantino, "Winter in Hong Kong," http://www.zmag.org/content/print_article. cfm?itemID=4896&sectionID=13, accessed 24 Mar 2005.

K
E
Y
W
O
R
D
S

BIBLIOGRAPHY

"A Unique Recruiting Arrangement." *Military.com Unit Pages,* 27 Oct 2000. http://www.military.com/HomePage/UnitPageHistory/1,12506, 705117|703463,00.html (site discontinued).

Abaya, Antonio. "The US Loves Erap?" *Manila Standard Today,* 27 Mar 2005. http://www.manilastandardtoday.com (accessed 27 Sep 2005).

"Advocacy Activities on the Filipino 'Comfort Women.'" *War Crimes on Asian Women: Military Sexual Slavery by Japan during World War II: The Case of the Filipino Comfort Women Part II.* Quezon City: Task Force on Filipino Comfort Women-Asian Women Human Rights Council, 1998.

"Advocates Call for Changes to Ottawa's 'Nanny' Program.'" 25 Mar 2005. http://www.cbc.ca/news/canada/advocates-call-for-changes-to-ottawa-s-nanny-program-1.527167 (accessed 31 Mar 2005).

Agoncillo, Teodoro. *The Revolt of the Masses: The Story of Bonifacio and the Katipunan.* Quezon City: University of the Philippines Press, 1996.

Agoncillo, Teodoro, and Milagros Guerrero. *History of the Filipino People.* Quezon City: Malaya Books, 1970.

Aguila, Kap Maceda. "Written and Drawn in Stone." *The Philippine Star,* Sep 1998.

Aguilar, Filomeno V. Jr. "Global Migrations, Old Forms of Labor, and New Transborder Class Relations." *Southeast Asian Studies* 41, no. 2 (Sep 2003): 137–61.

Agulto, Manuel. "UP: Student's Death an 'Isolated Unfortunate' Case." *Sun Star,* 18 Mar 2013. http://www.sunstar.com.ph/breaking-news/2013/03/18/students-death-isolated-unfortunate-case-273547(accessed 12 May 2013).

Alegre, Edilberto N. *Inumang Pinoy.* Metro Manila: Anvil Publishing, 1992.

Althusser, Louis. "Ideology and the Ideological State Apparatuses (Notes towards an Investigation)." In *Mapping Ideology,* edited by Slavoj Zizek, 100–140. London: Verso, 1994.

Amojelar, Darwin G. "Lots of Jobs for College Students but Do They Want the Work?" *InterAksyon,* 14 Jan 2013. http://www.interaksyon.com/business/52619/lots-of-jobs-for-college-grads-but-do-they-want-the-work (accessed 12 May 2013).

Anderson, Benedict. *Imagined Communities.* London: Verso, 1983.

Anderson, Warwick. "'Where Every Prospect Pleases and Only Man is Vile: Laboratory Medicine as Colonial Discourse." In *Discrepant Histories: Translocal Essays on Filipino Cultures,* edited by Vicente Rafael. Philadelphia: Temple University Press, 1995.

"Articulations of the Nation-Space: Cinema, Cultural Politics and Transnationalism in the Philippines." Dissertation, University of Southern California, 1996.

Associated Press. "Kobe Nightmare: Letter-Writer Lays Claim to Beheading." *Philippine Daily Inquirer.* 7 Jun 1997.

———. "US Lauds S-E Asia's Anti-Piracy Measures." *The Strait Times,* 4 Nov 2006.

———. "America Names Its Top Copyright Offenders." *The Independent,* 1 May 2009. http:www.independent.co.uk/life-style/gadgets-and-tech/news/America-names-its-top-copyright-offenders-1677253.html (accessed 29 Jul 2009).

Baes, Jonas. "Towards a Political Economy of the 'Real': Music Piracy and the Philippine Cultural Imaginary." Manuscript. 2002.

Bakhtin, M. M. *The Dialogic Imagination.* Austin: University of Texas Press, 1981.

Balibar, Etienne. "From Class Struggle to Classless Struggle?" *Race, Nation, Class: Ambiguous Identities with Immanuel Wallerstein.* London: Verso, 1991.

———. "Subjection and Subjectivation." *Supposing the Subject,* edited by Joan Copjec. London: Verso, 1994.

Barber, Pauline Gardiner. "Agency in Philippine Women's Labour Migration and Provisional Diaspora." *Women's Studies International Forum* 23, no. 4. (Jul-Aug 2000): 400. http://www.sciencedirect.com/science/article/pii/S0277539500001047# (accessed 30 Mar 2015).

Barker, Chris. *Cultural Studies: Theory and Practice.* 2nd ed. London Sage Publication, 2003.

Barnaouw, Erick. *Documentary: A History of the Non-Fiction Film.* Oxford: Oxford University Press, 1983.

Barrows, David P. "What May Be Expected from Philippine Education?" *The Journal of Race Development* 1, no. 2 (Oct 1910): 159–62.

Bartholet, Jeffrey. "Innocence for Sale." *Newsweek,* 23 Dec 1996.

Baumgartel, Tilman. "The Culture of Piracy in the Philippines." Manuscript. 2006.

Bautista, Mario E. "Hot Men Outsell Hot Babes." *Malaya,* 28 Jul 2004. http://www.malaya.com.ph/jul28/ente_2.htm (accessed 25 Nov 2004, site discontinued).

———. "Gloria Eyes 'Otso-Otso'; Mar Bags 'Mr. Suave.'" *Malaya,* 18 Dec 2004 http://www.malaya.com.ph.dec18/news5.htm (accessed 25 Nov 2004, site discontinued).

Bauzon, Kenneth E. *Liberalism and the Quest for Islamic Identity in the Philippines.* Quezon City: Ateneo de Manila University Press, 1991.

Beller, Jonathan. "Third Cinema in a Global Frame: *Curacha,* Yahoo! and *Manila by Night.*" *Acquiring Eyes: Philippine Visuality, Nationalist Struggle, and the World-Media System.* Quezon City: Ateneo de Manila University Press, 2006.

Benjamin, Walter. "Theses on the Philosophy of History." *Illuminations.* New York: Schocken Books, 1968.

———. "Critique of Violence." *Selected Writings: Volume 1: 1913-1926.* Cambridge: Belknap Press, 1996.

Benn, Melissa. "Review of Global Woman." *The Independent*, 2 Aug 2003. http://www.arlindocorreia.com/global_woman.html (accessed 24 Mar 2005).

Bennett, Tony. "The Exhibitionary Complex." *Culture/Power/History: A Reader in Contemporary Social Theory*. Princeton: New Jersey, 1994.

Beveridge, Alfred J. "Our Philippine Policy." In *The Philippines Reader: A History of Colonialism, Neocolonialism, Dictatorship, and Resistance*, edited by Daniel B. Schirmer and Stephen Rosskamm Shalom. Quezon City: Ken, 1987.

Bhabha, Homi. "Articulating the Archaic: Notes on Colonial Nonsense." *Literary Theory—Today*, edited by Peter Collier and Helga Geyer-Ryan. Ithaca: Cornell University Press, 1990.

———. "Anxious Nations, Nervous States." *Supposing the Subject*, edited by Joan Copjec. London: Verso, 1994.

———. *The Location of Culture*. London: Routledge, 1994.

Biersteker, Thomas, and Cynthia Weber, eds. *State Sovereignty as a Social Construct*. Cambridge: Cambridge University Press, 1996.

"Bodies, Letters, Catalogs: Filipinas in Transnational Space." *Diliman Review* 45, no. 1 (1997).

Bogardus, Emory S. "Anti-Filipino Race Riots." In *The Philippines Reader*, edited by Schirmer and Shalom. Quezon City: Ken, 1987.

Bommes, Michael, and Patrick Wright. "Charm of Residence: The Public and the Past." *Making Histories: Studies in History-Writing and Politics*. London: Hutchinson, 1982.

Borja, Howie. "Chatting with the Chito Chat Guys." *Philippine Daily Inquirer*, 13 Dec 1997.

Broeske, Pat. H. "After Seeing 'Platoon,' Fonda Wept." *Los Angeles Times*, 25 Jan 1987. http://articles.latimes.com/1987-01-25/entertainment/ca-5554_1_jane-fonda (accessed 13 Nov 2014).

Bureau of Public Affairs. "Philippines." *U.S. Department of State*. http://www.state.gov/e/eb/ifd/2005/42102.htm (accessed 6 Nov 2006, site discontinued).

Business Processing Association of the Philippines. "Demand for BPO Work Remains High in 2013." http://www.likejobs.com/articles/demand-for-bpo-employees-remains-high-for-2013 (accessed 12 May 2013).

Businesss Software Alliance. "Software Piracy Rate in the Philippines Remains at 71%." 23 May 2005. http:www.bsa.org (accessed 6 Nov 2006).

Cabacungan, Gil C., and Elena R. Torijos. "Pol Shows More Execs Unhappy Over Economy." *Philippine Daily Inquirer*, 1 Jul 1999.

Caballos, Poch, and Vichael Angelo Roaring. "Comic Quests: Unraveling the Secrets of Fil Cartoons and Alamat." *Philippine Collegian* 176 no. 8 (1998).

Caballos, Poch, and Allan Hernandez. "Romancing the Stone." *Manila Times*, 22 Sep 1998.

Cabanillas, Francisco. "Victor Hernandez Cruz: From Marginality to Twilight." Unpublished. 1993.

Cagahastian, Diego C. "Film Animators Locate in Clark." *Bulletin Today*, Jun 1998.

CATW (Coalition Against Trafficking of Women) Factbook. "Philippines." http://www.globalmarch.org/worstformsreports/world/philippines.html (site discontinued).

Carroll (ret.), Admiral Eugene. "U.S. Military Bases and the Environment: A Time for Responsibility." http://www.boondocksnet.com/centennial/sc-texts/carroll971123.html (site discontinued).

Chang, Grace. "Importing Nurses: A Money-Making Venture." http://www.cpa.org/au/garchves3/1026nse.html (accessed 3 Nov 2004).

Chatterjee, Partha. "The Nation and Its Women." *The Nation and Its Fragments: Colonial and Postcolonial Histories.* Princeton: Princeton University Press, 1993.

CHED. "Roadmap for Public Higher Education Reform." 2011.

Choi, Chungmoo. "The Discourse of Decolonization and Popular Theory: South Korea." *Positions* 1, no. 1 (1993).

Chugh, Nishtha. "Global Piracy: Just a Seaborne Scourge or a Bigger Malady." *Fair Observer,* 7 Apr 1013. http://www.fairobserver.com/region/north_america/global-piracy-just-seaborne-scourge-or-bigger-malady/ (accessed 4 Dec 2014).

———. "The Culture of Piracy in the Philippines." Manuscript. 2006.

Constable, Nicole. "Wash When I Tell You and Don't Talk to Your Friends." *The Guardian.* 14 Jul 2003. http://www.arlindo-correia.com/global_woman.html (accessed 24 Mar 2005).

Constantino, Renato. *Synthetic Culture and Development.* Quezon City: Foundation for Nationalist Studies, 1985.

Constantino, Renato, and Letizia R. Constantino. *The Philippines: A Past Revisited.* Quezon City: Renato Constantino, 1975.

———. *The Philippines: The Continuing Past.* Quezon City: Foundation for Nationalist Studies, 1978.

Constantino, Renato Redentor. "Winter in Hongkong." 2004. http://www.zmag.org/content/print_article.cfm?itemID=4896&sectionID=13 (accessed 24 Mar 2005).

Cooney, Robert P. "Education in the Philippines Part II." *World Education Services.* http://www.wes.org/ewenr/wenarchive/RP_EdInThePhillipPart2Spr89.pdf (accessed 12 May 2013).

Coppola, Eleanor. *Notes on the Making of Apocalypse Now.* New York: Limelight Editions, 1991.

Cordova, Fred. *Filipinos: Forgotten Asian Americans. A Pictorial Essay/1763-Circa-1963.* USA: Demonstration Project for Asian Americans, 1983.

Covar, Prospero R. "Paniniwala, Pananampalataya, at Paninidigan sa Pelikulang Bakbakan." *Unang Pagtingin sa Pelikulang Bakbakan.* Manila: Anvil Publishing, 1992.

Crisostomo, Isabelo T. *President Joseph Ejercito Estrada: From Stardom to History.* Quezon City: J. Kriz Publishing, 1999.

Crowell, Todd, and Antonio Lopez. "Better than Expected." *Asiaweek* 25, no. 26. 1999.

Cruz, Gemma Tulud. "No Strangers in this Church." *National Catholic Reporter* 1, no. 35, 3 Dec 2003. http://www.nationalcatholicreporter.org/globalpers/gp120303.htm (accessed 24 Mar 2005).

Cruz, Isagani. "Si Lam-ang, si Fernando Poe Jr., at si Aquino: Ilang Kurokuro Tungkol sa Epikong Pilipino." *Krisostomo: Mga Teorya at Antolohiya para sa Epektibong Pagtuturong Panitikan.* Metro Manila: Anvil Publishing, 1992.

d'Alpuget, Blanche. "Philippine Dream Feast." *New York Times Book Review.* 25 Mar 1990.

Daroy, Petronilo Bn. "Social Significance and the Filipino Film." In *Readings in Philippine Cinema,* edited by Rafael Ma. Guerrero. Ann Arbor: University of Michigan Press, 2008.

David, Joel. "Men and Myths." *Fields of Vision: Critical Applications in Recent Philippine Cinema.* Quezon City: Ateneo de Manila University Press, 1995.

———. "Ma(so?)chismo." *Fields of Vision: Critical Applications in Recent Philippine Cinema.* Quezon City: Ateneo de Manila University Press, 1995.

———. "Aksyon." *CCP Encyclopedia of Philippine Art: Volume VIII Philippine Film.* Manila: Cultural Center of the Philippines, 1994.

David, Joel, and Lena Pareja. "Animation." *CCP Encyclopedia of Philippine Art, Volume VIII-Philippine Film.* Manila: Cultural Center of the Philippines, 1994.

David-Menard, Monique. *Hysteria from Freud to Lacan.* Ithaca: Cornell University Press, 1989.

"Dawn of Freedom Notes." *Imperial Japan at the Movies.* Yamagata: Yamagata International Documentary Film Festival, 1997.

de Certeau, Michel. *The Practice of Everyday Life.* Translated by Stevan Rendali. Berkeley: University of California Press, 1984.

———. "Walking the City." *The Practice of Everyday Life.* Translated by Stevan Rendali. Berkeley: University of California Press, 1984.

de Manila, Quijano. "Erap in a New Role." *Joseph Estrada and Other Sketches.* Manila: National Bookstore, 1977.

de Quiros, Conrado. "Out of the Box." *Philippine Daily Inquirer,* 30 Aug 2006. http://opinion.inq7.net/inquireropinion/columns.view_article.php?article_id=17953 (accessed 21 Sep 2006, site discontinued).

———. "Fighting Pirates." *Asian Journal,* 26 Dec 2006. http://www.asian-journal.com/cgi-bin/view_info.cgi?code=00002599 (accessed 21 Sept 2006, site discontinued).

Deleuze, Gilles, and Feliz Guattari. *A Thousand Plateaus: Capitalism and Schizophrenia.* Minneapolis: University of Minnesota Press, 1987.

Deocampo, Nick. "From Revolution to Revolution: The Documentary Movement in the Philippines. *Documentary Box #5,* 1994.

Dirlik, Arif, ed. *What is in a Rim? Critical Perspectives on the Pacific Region Idea.* Boulder: West View Press, 1993.

Doeppers, Daniel F. *Manila 1900–1941: Social Change in a Late Colonial Metropolis.* Quezon City: Ateneo de Manila University Press, 1984.

Domingo, Estellita V. "Measuring the Non-Observed Economy (NOE): The Philippine Experience." Manuscript. 2004.

Doty, Roxanne Lynn. "Sovereignty and the Nation: Constructing the Boundaries of National Identity." In *State Sovereignty as Social Construct,* edited by Thomas Bierstecker and Cynthia Weber. New York: Cambridge University Press, 1996.

Duhaime, Lloyd. "Piracy (Maritime Law) Legal Definition." http://www.duhaime.org/LegalDictionary/P/PiracyMaritimeLaw.aspx (accessed 28 Oct 2014).

Dumlao, Doris. "$8B in OFW money seen to prop up RP economy." *Philippine Daily Inquirer,* 1 Oct 1999.

Dumont, Jean-Paul. "Ideas on Philippine Violence: Assertions, Negations, and Narrations." In *Discrepant Histories: Translocal Essays on Filipino Cultures,* edited by Vicente Rafael. Philadelphia: Temple University Press, 1995.

Eagleton, Terry. *Ideology: An Introduction.* London: Verso, 1991.

Ebron, Grace. "Not Just the Maid: Negotiating Filipina Identity in Italy." 2002. http://intersections.anu.edu.au/issue8/ebron.html (accessed 24 Mar 2005).

Ehrenreich, Barbara. "A Grubby Business." *The Guardian,* 12 Jul 2003. http://www.arlindo-correia.com/global_woman.html (accessed 24 Mar 2005).

Eklof, Stefan. *Pirates in Paradise: Modern History of Southeast Asia's Maritime Marauders.* Nordic Institute of Asian Studies, 2006.

Escobar, Arturo. *Encountering Development: The Making and Unmaking of the Third World.* Princeton: Princeton University Press, 1995.

Estopace, Benito. "BPO Workers Opt For Jobs Overseas." *Business Mirror,* 3 Apr 2013. http://www.abs-cbnnews.com/business/04/02/12/bpo-workers -opt-jobs-overseas (accessed 12 May 2013).

Estrada, Joseph. "Speech during the Birthday Celebration of Bro. Mike Velarde." 20 Aug 1999.

"Faces of Globalization: Home Away from Home." *Global Envision.* 8 Jun 2004. http://www.globalenvision.org/library/8/614 (accessed 24 Mar 2005).

Field, Norma. "The Child as Laborer and Consumer: The Disappearance of Childhood in Contemporary Japan." *Children and the Politics of Culture.* Princeton: Princeton University Press, 1995.

"Fighting Pirates." 26 Dec 2003. http://www.asianjournal.com/cgi-bin/view_ info.egi?code=00002599 (accessed 21 Sept 2006).

"Figure It Out." *Philippine Daily Inquirer.* http://showbizandstyle.inq7.net/ sim/sim/view_article.php?article_id=30587 (accessed 5 Nov 2006).

Flores, Patrick. "Plotting the People Out." *Pelikula* 1, no. 1 (1999): 10–13.

Foucault, Michel. *Discipline and Punish.* Translated by Alan Sheridan. New York: Vintage Books, 1979.

———. *The History of Sexuality,* translated by Robert Hurley. New York: Vintage, 1990.

Francisco, Luzviminda. "The Philippine-American War." *The Philippines Reader.* Quezon City: Ken, 1987.

Freud, Sigmund. *Psychopathology of Everyday Life.* New York: Mentor Books, 1964.

Frisch, Michael. "The Memory of History." *A Shared Authority: Essays on the Craft and Meaning of Oral and Public History.* Albany: State University of New York Press, 1990.

Garceau, Scott R. "Truth in Advertising." *Philippine Star,* 30 Aug 2006. http://www.philstar.com/sunday-life/276762/truth-advertising (accessed 21 Sep 2006).

Garcia, Ma. Rosario K. "Hidden No Longer: Beyond Property Rights, The Philippine Informal Sector from a Rights-Based Perspective." Manuscript, 2005.

Garnham, Nicholas. "The Mass Media, Cultural Identity, and the Public Sphere in the Modern World." *Public Culture* 5 (1993): 251–65.

George, Susan. *How the Other Half Dies: The Real Reasons for World Hunger.* New Jersey: Allanheld, Osmun, 1977.

Genrozala, Geraldine G. *"Dawn of Freedom:* Transnasyonalismo sa Pelikulang Propaganda." Unpublished. N.d.

Ginzburg, Carlo. *The Cheese and the Worms: The Cosmos of a 16th Century Miller,* translated by John and Anne Tedeschi. New York: Penguin Books, 1982.

"Global/Local Nation and Hysteria: Japanese Children's Television in the Philippines." In *Image and Reality: Philippine-Japan Relations Towards the 21st Century,* edited by Rolando S. Dela Cruz. Quezon City: Institute of International Legal Studies, U.P., 1997.

"Globalization and Migration." *Women and the Economy.* http://unpac.ca/economoy/index2.html (accessed 24 Mar 2005).

Gonzales, Iris Cecila C. "RP Still in Priority List of IPR Violators." *Business World,* 15 May 2003.

"Gov't Moves to Have RP Delisted as IPR Violator." http://www.poblaw.com/April2003.html (accessed 6 Nov 2006).

Gowing, Peter G., and Robert D. McAmis, eds. *The Muslim Filipinos.* Manila: Solidaridad Publishing House, 1974.

Gramsci, Antonio. *Selections from the Prison Notebooks.* New York: International Publishers, 1971.

Grimes, W. C. "Organization and Administration of Education in the Philippine Islands." *The Phi Delta Kappan* 10, no. 6 (April 1928).

Guillermo, Ramon. "Rationalizing Failures: The Philippine Government in the Education Sector." *Courage Online from Education for Development Magazine, Ibon Databank,* Dec 1997. http://www.skyinet.net/~courage/position/act-edanalysis.htm (accessed 12 May 2013).

Hagedorn, Jessica. *Dogeaters.* New York: Penguin Books, 1990.

Hau, Caroline. "Literature, Nationalism, and the Problem of Consciousness." *Diliman Review* 46 nos. 3–4 (1998): 3–24.

———. *On the Subject of the Nation: Filipino Writings from the Margins 1981–2004.* Quezon City: Ateneo de Manila University Press, 2004.

"Heart of Darkness." Project Gutenberg Ebook. http://www.gutenberg.org/files/219/219-h/219-h.htm (accessed 27 Jan 2015).

Hefti, Anny Misa. "Globalization and Migration." http://unpan1.un.org/intradoc/groups/public/documents/APCITY/UNPAN006918.pdf (accessed 25 Nov 2014).

"Help Wanted: Abused Against Female Migrant Domestic Workers in Indonesia and Malaysia." *Human Rights Watch* 16, no. 9 (Jul 2004) http://www.hrw.org/reports/2004/indonesia0704/4.htm (accessed 24 Mar 2005).

Henson, Maria Rosa. *Comfort Woman: Slave of Destiny.* Pasig: Philippine Center for Investigative Journalism, 1996.

Heston, Charlton. "I'm Ashamed of My Union, Actor's Equity." *Los Angeles Times,* 13 Aug 1990, F4.

Hibionada, Florence F., and Marciar M. Calubiran. "Pirates Go Slow on Movies, 'Get Even' on Music." *News Today,* 23 Dec 2005. http://www.thenewstoday.info/20051223/pirates.go.slow.on.movies.get.even.on.music.html (accessed 8 Nov 2005, site discontinued).

Hochschild, Arlie. "The Nanny Chain." http://www.prospect.org/print-friendly/print/V1/4/hochschild-a.html (accessed 24 Mar 2005, site discontinued).

Honasan, Alya B. "Minstrel of the Masses." http://www.inq7.net/mag/2004/jan/18/text/mag_2-1-p.htm (accessed 3 Nov 2004, site discontinued).

Hondagneu-Sotelo, Pierrette. "Domestica." http://www.ucpress.edu/books/pages/9180.9180.ch01.html (accessed 24 Mar 2005, site discontinued).

Hughes, Katheryn. "Sweet and Sour." *New Statesmen and Society,* 12 Jul 1991.

Hunt, Chester L., and Thomas R. McHale. "Education and Philippine Economic Development." *Comparative Education Review* 9, no. 1 (Feb 1965): 69–70.

Hunt, Michael. *Ideology and U.S. Foreign Policy*. New Haven: Yale University Press, 1987.

Ileto, Reynaldo C. "Cholera and the Origins of the American Sanitary Order in the Philippines." In *Discrepant Histories: Translocal Essays on Filipino Cultures,* edited by Vicente Rafael. Philadelphia: Temple University Press, 1995.

International Intellectual Property Alliance. "2001 Special 201 Report Philippines." http://www.iipa.com/rbc/2001/2001SPEC301PHILIPPINES.pdf (accessed 6 Nov 2006).

Ira, Luning Bonifacio, and Isagani R. Medina. "What Will They Think of Next?" *Turn of the Century*. Quezon City: GCF Books, 1990.

Itoi, Kay. "The Game of Horror." *Newsweek,* 9 Jun 1977.

Ivy, Marilyn. "Formations of Mass Culture." *Postwar Japan as History*. Berkeley: University of California Press, 1993.

Iwabuchi, Koichi. "Complicit Exoticism: Japan and its Other." *Continuum* 8, no. 2. (1994): 49–82.

———. "Genius for 'Glocalisation' or the Sweet Scent of Asian Modernity: Japanese Cultural Export to Asia." Manuscript. 1997.

———. "Return to Asia? Japan in the Global Audiovisual Market." *Media International Australia* 77 (1995): 94–106.

James, Estelle. "Private Higher Education: The Philippines as Prototype." *Higher Education* 21, no. 1 (Mar 1991).

Jameson, Fredric. "The Cultural Logic of Late Capitalism." *Postmodernism or the Cultural Logic of Late Capitalism*. Durham: Duke University Press, 1991.

JanMohamed, Abdul. "The Economy of Manichean Allegory: The Function of Racial Difference in Colonialist Literature." *Critical Inquiry* 12, no. 1 (1985).

"Japanese Legal Culture, Animation Studies, Security and Sovereignty." Manuscript. 1999.

Javellana-Santos, Julie. "Optical Media Act Penalizes Film Piracy." *Philippines News,* 18 Feb 2004. http://www.philippinenews.com (accessed 6 Nov 2014).

Jimenez-David, Rina. "From 'Vaginal' to 'Phenomenal.'" *Philippine Daily Inquirer,* 5 May 2002.

Jurado, Emil. "Destroying People's Reputations." *Manila Standard Today,* 1 Jun 2005. http://www.manilastandardtoday.com/?page=emilJurado_june01_200 (accessed 22 Nov 2006, site discontinued).

Kellman, John. *American Myth and the Legacy of Vietnam*. New York: Columbia University Press, 1986.

Kelly, William W. "Finding a Place in Metropolitan Japan: Ideologies, Institutions, and Everyday Life." *Postwar Japan as History*. Berkeley: University of California Press, 1993.

Kim, Kyung Hung. "Notes on *A Single Spark*." *Post-Colonial Classics of Korean Cinema 1948–1998 Souvenir Program*. 1998.

Kinder, Marsha. "The Power of Adaptation in 'Apocalypse Now.'" *Film Quarterly* 33, no. 2 (Winter 1979–1980): 12–20.

Kristeva, Julia. *Powers of Horror: An Essay on Abjection*. New York: Columbia University Press, 1982.

"Labor Exporters Plan for Emigration." *Migration News* 2, no. 12 (Dec 1995). http://migration.ucdavis.edu/mn/more.php?id=827_0_3_0 (accessed 24 Nov 2005).

Lacaba, Jose F. "Movies, Critics, and the Bakya Crowd." *Readings in Philippine Cinema*. Manila: Experimental Cinema of the Philippines, 1983.

Lacan, Jacques. *Ecrits: A Selection*. New York: W.W. Norton & Company, 1977.

LaCapra, Dominick. *History and Criticism*. Ithaca: Cornell University Press, 1985.

Lan, Pei-Chia. "Remapping Identities across Borders and at Home: Filipina Migrant Domestic Workers and Taiwanese Employers." Presentation at the Fifth Annual Conference on the History and Culture of Taiwan, UCLA, October 2000.

Le Doeuff, Michele. *Hipparchia's Choice: An Essay Concerning Women, Philosophy, Etc.* Cambridge: Blackwell, 1991.

Lefort, Claude. "Outline of the Genesis of Ideology in Modern Society." *The Political Forms of Modern Society: Bureaucracy, Democracy, Totalitarianism*. Cambridge: MIT Press, 1986.

LeRoy, James A. "'Laissez-Faire' in the Philippine Islands." *Journal of Political Economy* 12, no. 2 (Mar 1904): 191–207.

Liao, Ping-hui. "Rewriting Taiwanese National History: The February 28 Incident as Spectacle." *Public Culture* 5, no. 2 (January 1993): 281–96.

Llorito, Dave L. "Loose Rules Make CD Pirates Feel at Home." *The Manila Times*, 2 Jan 2003. http://www.manilatimes.net/others/special/2003/jan/02/20030102spe1.html (accessed 30 Jul 2009).

Lo, Ricky. "Joseph Estrada, Era ni Erap." *Star-Studded*. Makati: Virtusio Books, Inc., 1995.

"Local/Global Hysteria: Japanese Children's Television in the Philippines." *Image and Reality: Philippine-Japan Relations Towards the 21st Century*. Quezon City: Institute of International Legal Relations, University of the Philippines-Diliman, 1997.

Loyre, Ghislaine. "Living and Working Conditions in Philippine Pirate Communities, 1750–1850." *Pirate and Privateers: New Perspectives on the War on Trade in the Eighteenth and Nineteenth Centuries*. Devon: University of Exeter Press, 1997.

Lukacher, Ned. "The Epistemology of Disgust." In *Hysteria from Freud to Lacan: Body and Language in Psychoanalysis,* edited by David Menard. Ithaca: Cornell University Press, 1989.

Lumbera, Bienvenido, and Cynthia Nograles Lumbera, eds. *Philippine Literature: A History and Anthology*. Pasig City: Anvil Publishing, 2005.

Luz, Juan Miguel, and Teodoro Y. Montelibano. *Corporations and Communities in a Developing Country, Case Studies: Philippines*. Manila: Philippine Business for Social Progress and Center for Corporate Citizenship, 1993.

Magno, Leo. "RP Mobile Phone Penetration Growth Can be Replicated—Smart." *Philippine Daily Inquirer,* 17 October 2006. http://technology.inq7.net/infotech./infotech/view_article.php?article_id-27221 (accessed 18 Oct 2006, site discontinued).

Malate, Renato F. "Corporatization of State Universities and Colleges: Impact on Higher Education." *The Threshold* 4 (2009).

Marcuse, Herbert. "Some Social Implications of Modern Technology." *The Essential Frankfurt School Reader.* New York: Continuum, 1993.

Marfil, Martin P. "Estrada Vows to Liberate Poor." *Philippine Daily Inquirer,* 8 July 1999.

Marx, Karl. "Capital, Volume One." *The Marx-Engles Reader.* New York: W. W. Norton & Company, 1978.

———. "Alienation and Social Classes." *The Marx-Engles Reader.* New York: W. W. Norton & Company, 1978.

———. "The Limits of the Working Day." *Capital* 1. http://www.marxists.org./archive/marx/works/1867-c1/ch10.htm (accessed 12 May 2013).

———. "The Modern Theory of Colonization." *Capital* 1. http://www.marxists.org/archive/marx/works/1867-c1/ch33.htm (accessed 12 May 2013).

McClintock, Anne. "The Angel of Progress: Pitfalls of the Term 'Post Colonialism.'" *Social Text* 10, nos. 2 & 3 (1992).

McCoy, Alfred W. "1900–1941: Images of a Changing Nation." *Philippine Cartoons: Political Caricature of the American Era 1900–1941.* Quezon City: Vera-Reyes, Inc., 1985.

McIndoe, Alastair. "Asia Faces Tough Job Finding Work for Its Young." *The Strait Times,* 7 Nov 2006.

McKenna, Thomas M. *Muslim Rulers and Rebels: Everyday Politics and Armed Separatism in the Southern Philippines.* Berkeley: University of California Press, 1998.

McKinley, William. "Remarks to the Methodist Delegation." In *The Philippines Reader,* edited by Daniel B. Schirmer and Stephen Rosskamm Shalom. Quezon City: Ken, 1987.

McLellan, David. "Gramsci." *Marxism After Marx.* Boston: Houghton Mifflin, 1979.

Melencio, Gloria Esguerra. "Almost 3,000 Filipinos Leave for Work Abroad Daily Despite Low Exchange Rate." *Arab News,* 11 Jan 2008.

Menta, Richard. "Movie and Record Industry Piracy Figures Incendiary, But Not Fact." *MP3newswire.net.* 15 Jun 2006. http://www.mp3newswire.net/stories/6002/250billion.html (accessed 6 Nov 2006).

Michio, Arita, and Yamaoka Shunsuke. "The 'Over-Worthy Child' Syndrome." *Asahi Journal* (1992): 11–16.

Migrant Forum in Asia. "Asian Women and Labor Migration: The Beijing plus 5 Review." http://www.aworc.org/bpfa/pub/sec_f/eco0003.html (accessed 24 Mar 2005, site discontinued).

Mills, Jon. "Lacan on Paranoiac Knowledge." http://www.processpsychology.com/new-articles/Lacan-PP-revised.htm (accessed 4 Dec 2014).

Mijares, Roy. "Philippine Resiliency in the Asian Financial Crises." http://www.jri.co.jp/english/periodical/rim/1999/RIMe199902philippines/ (accessed 30 Mar 2015).

Mindanao: A Portrait. Manila: Bookmark, Inc., 1999.

Musser, Charles, and Carol Nelson. *High-Class Moving Pictures: Lyman H. Howe and the Forgotten Era of Traveling Exhibition*, 1880–1920. Princeton: Princeton University Press, 1991.

Myers, Normal, et al. "Biodiversity Hotspots for Conservation Priorities." *Nature*. http://www.nature.com/nature/journal/v403/n6772/full/403853a0.html.

National Alliance of Philippine Women in Canada/SIKLAB (Overseas Filipino Workers Group). "Philippine Government Pushing to Get US$9 Billion in Remittances from Overseas Workers." Media statement. March 2005.

"Number of Feature Films Produced in Australia and Other Countries, 1997–2002." http://afc.gov.au/ (accessed 3 Nov 2004).

Ofreneo, Rene E. "Philippines." *The Handbook of Human Resource Management Policies and Practices in Asia-Pacific Economies*, 390–444. UK: Edward Elgar Publishing, Inc., 2002.

Ofreneo, Rosalinda Pineda. "Women in Asia and the Pacific: A Trade Union Perspective." https://www.ids.ac.uk/files/dmfile/Ofreneo2011Rightsbased socialprotectioninPhilippinesCSPconferencedraft.pdf (accessed 25 Nov 2014).

Niver, Kemp R. *Early Motion Pictures: The Paper Print Collection in the Library of Congress*. Washington: Library of Congress, 1985.

Padua, Reiner, and Evelyn Macairan. "Enrolment Ruling: If Only Kristel had Known." *Philippine Star*, 17 Mar 2013. http://www.philstar.com/headlines/2013/03/17/17/920669/new-enrolment-ruling-if-only-kristel-had-known (accessed 12 May 2013).

Palangchao, Harley. "Raid of Pirated CDs, VCDs Nearly Ends in Violence." *Sun Star Baguio*, 5 May 2003. http://www.sunstar.com.ph (accessed 8 Nov 2006).

Pamintuan, Jema M. "Pagmamapa ng Pagbabagong Heograpikal, Historikal at Kultural ng Quiapo." Manuscript. 2005.

Parrenas, Rhacel Salazar. *Servants of Globalization: Women, Migration and Domestic Work*. Quezon City: Ateneo de Manila University Press, 2003.

———. "Transgressing the Nation-State: The Partial Citizenship and 'Imagined (Global) Community' of Migrant Filipina Domestic Workers." *Signs: Journal of Women in Culture and Society* 26, no. 4 (Summer 2001). http://www.iupui.edu/anthkb/a104/philippines/migrationfilipinas.htm (accessed 24 Mar 2005, site discontinued).

Pazzibugan, Dona Z. "Teachers May Receive P5K to P35K in Bonuses." *Philippine Daily Inquirer*, 5 Mar 2013. http://newsinfo.inquirer.net/368597/teachers-may-receive-p5k-top35k-in-bonuses (accessed 12 May 2013).

PCTP. "PCTC Paper on Graft and Corruption." http://www.pctc.gov.ph/papers/graft.htm (accessed 25 Nov 2014).

Pertierra, Raul. "The Mythology and Politics of Philippine Education." *Kasarinlan: Philippine Journal of Third World Studies* 10, no. 3 (1995). http://journals.upd.edu.ph/index.php/kasarinlan/article/viewArticle/1686 (accessed 12 May 2013).

———. "Political Consciousness Versus Cultural Identity." *Philippine Localities and Global Perspectives*. Quezon City: Ateneo de Manila University Press, 1995.

"Philippines." http://www.ustr.gov/assets/Document_Library/Reports_ Publications/2006/2006_NTE_Report/asset_upload_file.223_9202.pdf (accessed 6 Nov 2006).

"Philippines: Country Reports on Human Rights Practices, 2002." *U.S. Department of State,* 31 Mar 2003. http://www.state.gov/g/drl/rls/ hrrpt/2002/18261.htm (accessed 4 Dec 2014).

Pido, Antonio J. A. *The Pilipinos in America: Macro/Micro Dimensions of Immigration and Integration.* New York: Center for Migration Studies, 1986.

Pike, John. "Philippine–Government." GlobalSecurity.org. http://www.global security.org/military/world/philippines/government.htm (accessed 4 Dec 2014).

"Piracy Watchdog Backs Bills Regulating Optical Media." *Poblaw Newsletter* 3, no. 24 (2003). http://www.poblaw.com/April2003.html (accessed 8 Nov 2006, site discontinued).

"Platoon Troubles S. F. Vets." *The Hollywood Reporter,* 1987.

"Poverty in the Philippines." http://www.txtmania.com/articles/poverty.php.

Rafael, Vicente. *Contracting Colonialism: Translation and Christian Conversion in Tagalog Society Under Early Spanish Rule.* Quezon City: Ateneo de Manila University Press, 1988.

Raman, B. "Taming Terror on the High Seas." *Asia Times Online,* 9 June 2005. http:www.atimes.com/atimes/Southeast_Asia/GF09Ae05.html (accessed 29 Jul 2009).

Reyes, Soledad. "Bagong Historisismo/Pag-aaral na Kultural." *Kritisismo: Mga Teorya at Antolohiya Para Sa Epektibong Pagtuturo ng Panitikan.* Pasig City: Anvil Publishing, 1992.

Rimban, Luz. "Filipina Diaspora." In *Her Stories: Investigative Reports on Filipino Women in the 1990s,* edited by Cecile C. A. Balgos. Quezon City: PCIJ, 1999.

Roces, Alfredo. "Mang Juan and Uncle Sam: The Filipino Caricaturist as Historian." *Philippine Cartoons: Political Caricature of the American Era 1900–1941.* Quezon City: Vera-Reyes, Inc., 1985.

Romero, Paolo. "Angara: Quality Education for All." *Philippine Star,* 30 Apr 2013. http://www.philstar.com/headlines/2013/04/30/936537/angara-quality-education-all (accessed 12 May 2013).

Rosaldo, Renato. *Culture and Truth: The Remaking of Social Analysis.* Boston: Beacon Press, 1989.

Rosca, Ninotchka. "Globalization's Assault on the Rights of Women." *International League of People's Struggle.* 27 May 2001. http://ilps.info/index.php/en/contributions-a-speeches-88-globalizations-assualt-on-the-rights-of-women (accessed 25 Nov 2014).

Rotkirch, Anna. "The Internationalisation of Intimacy: A Study of the Chains of Care." http://www.valt.helsinki.fi/staff/rotkirch/ESA%20paper.htm (accessed 24 Mar 2005, site discontinued).

Roxas, Cynthia, and Joaquin Arevalo Jr. "The Birth of the Komiks." *A History of Komiks of the Philippines and Other Countries.* Quezon City: Islas Filipinas Publishing Co., Inc., 1984.

Rubin, Martin. "The Crowd, the Collective, and the Chorus: Busby Berkeley and the New Deal." *Movies and Mass Culture.* London: Athlone, 1996.

Rubio, Jenalyn. "Philippines Piracy Rate Stays Steady." *Infoworld Applications,*

20 May 2009. http://www.infoworld.com/t/applications/philippines-software-piracy-rate-stays-steady-215 (accessed 30 Jul 2009).

Rydell, Robert W. *All The World's a Fair*. Chicago: University of Chicago Press, 1985.

Sabdesi.net. "On-Set Stitches: 15 Films that Almost Killed Their Stars." http://sabdesi.net/2013/09/on-set-stitches-15-movies-that-almost-killed-their-stars/ (accessed 14 Nov 2014).

Said, Edward. "An Ideology of Difference." *Critical Inquiry* 12, no. 1 (1985).

———. "Representing the Colonized: Anthropology's Interlocutors." *Critical Inquiry* 15, no. 2 (1989).

Salazar, Zeus A. "Ang Kulturang Pilipino sa Harap ng mga Institusyong Panlipunan sa Pelikulang Bakbakan." *Unang Pagtingin sa Pelikulang Bakbakan*. Manila: Anvil Publishing, 1992.

Salman, Michael. *The Embarrassment of Slavery: Controversies over Bondage and Nationalism in American Colonial Philippines*. Berkeley: University of California Press, 2001.

———. "'Nothing Without Labor': Penology, Discipline and Independence in the Philippines under United States Rule." In *Discrepant Histories: Translocal Essays on Filipino Cultures*, edited by Vicente Rafael. Philadelphia: Temple University Press, 1995.

Salterio-Gatdula, Leah. "Look What's Invading the Small Screen." *Philippine Daily Inquirer,* November 1998.

Samonte, Elena L. "Japanese Nationality Law and Japanese-Filipino Children." Manuscript. 1998.

San Juan Jr., Epifanio. "For a Critique of Contemporary Imperial Discourse." *Reading the East/Writing the West*. New York: Peter Lang, 1992.

———. "Filipino Bodies: From the Philippines to the United States and Around the World." http://www.boondocksnet.com/centennial/sctexts/esj_97a.html (site discontinued).

———. "Trajectories of the Filipino Diaspora." *Planet Philippines*. 2000http://www.planetphilippines.com/current/features_current/feature8.html, (accessed 24 Mar 2005, site discontinued).

Santos, Corazon L. "Ang Politisasyon ng Masa at ang Nobelang *Sa mga Kuko ng Liwanag ni* Edgardo M. Reyes." Manuscript. 1999.

Santos, Jocelyn. "DoH Also Exports Filipino Nurses Abroad." *Bulatlat.* http://www.bulatlat.com/news/2-38/2-38-nurses.html (accessed 25 Nov 2004).

Sassen, Saskia. "Whose City Is It? Globalization and the Formation of New Claims." *Public Culture* 8 (1996).

Saud, Lawrence H. *Guts and Glory: The Making of the American Military Image in Film*. Lexington: University of Kentucky Press, 2002.

Schirmer, Daniel B. "VFA: The Shape of Things to Come?" http://www.boondocksnet.com/centennial/sctexts/schirmer99b.html (site discontinued).

Schirmer, Daniel B., and Stephen Rosskamm Shalom, eds. *The Philippines Reader*: A *History of Colonialism, Neocolonialism, Dictatorship, and Resistance*. Quezon City: Ken, 1987.

Sculthorpe, C. P. *The Biology of Aquatic Vascular Plants*. New York: St. Martin's Press, 1967.

Shohat, Ella. "Gender and Culture of Empire: Toward a Feminist Historiography of the Cinema." *Quarterly Review of Film and Video* 13, nos. 1–3 (1991).

Shohat, Ella, and Robert Stam. *Unthinking Eurocentrism: Multiculturalism and the Media*. London, Routledge: 1994.

Shoseki, Nippon. "Descriptions about 'The Forced Comfort Women' in All the Seven Junior High School Textbooks in Japan." *War Crimes on Asian Women*.

Silverman, Kaja. "Masochism and Male Subjectivity." *Male Trouble*. Minneapolis: University of Minnesota Press, 1993.

Simbulan, Roland G. "Why the Senate Should Reject the VFA." http://www.boondocksnet.com/centennial/sctexts/simbulan99a.html (site discontinued).

Sison, Maritess. "Exodus of Nurses Grows, Health System Feels Effect." May 2002. http://www.cyberdyaryo.com/features/f2002_0508_04.htm (site discontinued).

Smith, Pauline Crumb. "A Basic Problem in Philippine Education." *The Far Eastern Quarterly* 4, no. 2 (Feb 1946).

"Software Piracy Rate in the Philippines Remains at 71%." *BSA: The Software Alliance*. http://www.bsa.org/ (accessed 6 Nov 2006).

Soriano, Yna. "Slavery on the High Seas." http://www.marinongpinoy.com/article7.html (site discontinued).

Sotto, Agustin. "Christ Figures in Troubled Land." *Unang Pagtingin sa Pelikulang Bakbakan*. Monograph. Manila: Cultural Center of the Philippines, 1989.

———. "War and the Aftermath in Philippine Cinema." In *Panahon ng Hapon: Sining sa Digmaan, Digmaan sa Sining*, edited by Gina Barte. Manila: Cultural Center of the Philippines, 1992.

Spivak, Gayatri. "The Rani of Sirmur." In Vol. 1 of *Europe and Its Other*, edited by Francis Barker et al. Cholchester: University of Essex Press, 1985.

———. "Can the Subaltern Speak?" In *Marxism and the Interpretation of Culture*, edited by Cary Nelson and Larry Grossberg, 271–313. Chicago: University of Illinois Press, 1988.

Spurr, David. *The Rhetoric of Empire: Colonial Discourse in Journalism, Travel Writing, and Imperial Administration*. Durham: Duke University Press, 1993.

"Startling Statistics." http://www.acountryofourown.com/StartlingStatistics.html (accessed 25 Nov 2014).

Stephanson, Andrew. "Regarding Postmodernism—A Conversation with Fredric Jameson." In *Universal Abandon*, edited by Andrew Ross. Minneapolis: University of Minneosta Press, 1988.

"Stock Estimates on Overseas Filipinos." http://www.poea.gov.ph/Stats/st_stock2000.html.

Subido, Tarrosa. *The Feminist Movement in the Philippines 1905–1955: A Golden Book*. National Federation of Women's Clubs, 1955.

Sulat, Bert B., Jr. "Whilce Myth." *Today's Weekender*, Sep 1998.

Sullivan, Rodney J. *Exemplar of Americanism: The Philippine Career of Dean C. Worcester*. Quezon City: New Day, 1992.

Sussman, Gerald. "Bulls in the (Indo) China Shop." *Journal of Popular Film and Television* 20, no. 1 (1992).

Tadiar, Neferti. *Fantasy-Production: Social Economics and Other Philippine Consequences for the New World Order*. Quezon City: Ateneo de Manila University Press, 2004.

KEYWORDS

———. "*Himala*, 'Miracle': The Heretical Potential of Nora Aunors's Star Power." *Fantasy-Production: Social Economics and Other Philippine Consequences for the New World Order.* Quezon City: Ateneo de Manila University Press, 2004.

Tan, Samuel K. *The Filipino Muslim Armed Struggle, 1900–1972.* Manila: Filipinas Foundation, Inc., 1977.

Tantuico, Delia S., and Errol Wifred Zshornack. "Intellectual Property Rights: Talking Points for RP-US FTA Negotiations." *Philippine Institute of Development Studies*, 2006.

Taussig, Michael. *Mimesis and Alterity: A Particular History of the Sense.* New York: Routledge, 1993.

———. "The Magic of the State." *Public Culture* 5, no. 1 (1992).

Teeuw, A. 1994. *Kamus Indonesia-Belanda* [Indonesian-Dutch Dictionary]. Jakarta: Gramedia.

Tejada, Blesilda. "For Kristel Tejada, Studying Was a Coping Mechanism." *Philippine Daily Inquirer*, 18 Mar 2013. http://newsinfo.inquirer.net/375303/for-kristel-tejada-studying-was-a-coping-mechanism (accessed 12 May 2013).

Terami-Wada, Motoe. "The Cultural Front in the Philippines, 1942–1945: Japanese Propaganda and Filipino Resistance in Mass Media." Ph.D., University of the Philippines, 1984.

———. "Strategy in Culture: Cultural Policy and Propaganda in the Philippines, 1942–1945." In *Panahon ng Hapon: Sining sa Digmaan, Digmaan sa Sining*, edited by Gina Barte. Manila: Cultural Center of the Philippines, 1992.

Tesoro, Jose Manuel. "Asia Says Japan is Top of the Pops." *Asiaweek*, 5 Jan 1996.

"The K to 12 Basic Education Program." *Official Gazette.* http://www.gov.ph/k-12/#Implementation (accessed 12 May 2013).

"The Philippines." http://www.uri.edu/artsci/wms/hughes/philippi.htm (site discontinued).

Tolentino, Rolando. "Articulations of the Nation-Space: Cinema, Cultural Politics and Transnationalism in the Philippines." Dissertation, University of Southern California, 1996.

———. "Mattering National Bodies and Sexualities." PhD diss., University of Southern California, 1996.

———. "Bodies, Letters, Catalogs: Filipinas in Transnational Space." *Diliman Review* 45, no. 1 (1997): 51–67.

———. "Global/Local Nation and Hysteria: Japanese Children's Television in the Philippines." In *Image and Reality: Philippine-Japan Relations Towards the 21st Century,* edited by Rolando S. Dela Cruz. Quezon City: Institute of International Legal Relations, U.P., 1997.

———. "Pagbagsak ng Flight 387 at Edad Ozone: Mga Sangandaang Isyu ng Kulturang Popular, Syensyang Panlipunan at Pangkulturang Pag-aaral." Manuscript. Philippine Social Science Center, 1998.

———. "Japanese Legal Culture, Animation Studies, Security and Sovereignty." Manuscript. 1999.

———. "Film in the Age of Empire: Cinema, Gender and Sexuality in the U.S. Colonization of the Philippines." *Bulawan: Journal of Philippine Arts and Culture.* Manila: National Commission of Culture and the Arts, 2001.

———. "'Inangbayan' in Lino Brocka's *Bayon Ko: Kapit sa Patalim* (1985) and

Oraponobis (1989)." *National/Transnational: Subject Formation and Media in and on the Philippines.* Quezon City: Ateneo de Manila University Press, 2001.

———."Subcontracting Imagination and Imageries of Bodies and Nations: The Philippines in Contemporary Transnational Asia Pacific Cinemas." In *Sites/Sights of Contestation: Localism, Globalism, and Cultural Production,* edited by Kwok-kan Tam. Hong Kong: Chinese University Press, 2002.

Tordesillas, Ellen, and Greg Hutchinson. *Hot Money, Warm Bodies: The Downfall of President Joseph Estrada.* Pasig City: Anvil Publishing, 2011.

Torre, Nestor U. "Filipino Animation Artist at DreamWorks." *Philippine Daily Inquirer,* 24 October 1998, C7 and 31 October 1998, B8.

———. "Female directors' Films Compared." *Philippine Daily Inquirer,* 27 May 2000. http://www.inq7.net/saturday/may 2000wk4/spc_6.htm (accessed 24 Mar 2005, site discontinued).

———. "Good News, Bad News." *Inq7.net.* 18 Oct 2003. http://www.inq7.net/ent/2003/oct/18/text/ent_20-1-p.htm (site discontinued).

Tsuda, Mamoru. *Filipino Diaspora in Asia: Social and Personal Networks, Organizing, Empowerment, Ethnicity, and Culture.* Osaka: Japan Academy for the Promotion of Sciences, 2002.

Tujan, Antonio Jr. "Sizing Up Erap." *Perspectives* 1, no. 13 (1999).

Tumbocon, Mao. "Minsa'y Isang Gamu-gamo." *CCP Encyclopedia of Philippine Art: Volume 8 Philippine Film.* Manila: CCP, 1994.

TxtMANIA. "Understanding Poverty." 2013. http://www.txtmania.com/articles/poverty.php (accessed 4 Dec 2014).

"U.S. Bases in the Philippines: A Position Paper by the Friends of the Filipino People." http://www.boondocksnet.com/centennial/sctexts/ffp_bases7802.html (site discontinued).

"US Lauds S-E Asia's Anti-piracy Measures." *The Strait Times,* 4 Nov 2006.

U.S. State Department. "Philippines: Country Reports on Human Rights Practices, 2002." http://www.state.gov/j/drl/rls/hrrpt/2002/18261.htm (accessed 25 Nov 2015).

Vanzi, Sol Jose. "House Oks P864-B 2004 National Budget." *Philippine Headline News Online.* 19 Dec 2003. http://www.newsflash.org/2003/05/hl/hl019483.htm (accessed 25 Nov 2004).

Velarde, Emmie. "Joseph Estrada." *All Star Cast.* Manila: Cine Gang Publications, 1981.

Vostral, Sharra L. "Imperialism on Display: The Philippine Exhibition at the 1904 World's Fair." *Gateway Heritage* 13, no. 4 (Spring 1993).

Warren, James Francis. *The Sulu Zone 1768–1898.* Singapore: Singapore University Press, 1981.

———. *The Sulu Zone: The World Capitalist Economy and the Historical Imagination.* Amsterdam: VU University Press, 1998.

"When the U.S. Navy Came Calling . . ." http://philusnavy.tripod.com/when1.htm (accessed 4 Dec 2014).

Williams, Raymond. "Masses." *Keywords: A Vocabulary of Culture and Society.* Croom Helm, 1976.

Wilson, Karl. "School Drop-Out Rates Highlight Lost Decade in Philippine Education." *The National,* 28 Jun 2010. http://www.thenational.ae/

news/world/asia-pacific/school-drop-out-rates-highlight-lost-decade-of-education-in-philippines#full (accessed 12 May 2013).

Yoshikawa, Yoko. "The Heat is On, Miss Saigon Coalition." *The State of Asian America: Activism and Resistance in the 1990s*, edited by Karin Aguilar-San Juan. Boston: Southend Press, 1994.

Yu-Jose, Lydia N. *Japan Views the Philippines 1900–1944*. Quezon City: Ateneo de Manila University Press, 1992.

Yuchengco, Mona Lisa, and Rene P. Ciria-Cruz. "The Filipino American Community: New Roles and Challenges." http://www.asiasociety.org/publications/philippines/filipino.html (site discontinued).

Yudice, George. "We Are Not the World" *Social Text* 31/32, 10, nos. 2 & 3 (1992).

Yuzon, Isagani F. "The Human Resource Development of the Philippine Informal Labor Sector Amidst Globalization and its Applicability to Developing Economies." UMP-Asia Occasional Paper. Mar 2004.

Zhou, Jie. "The Economics of Movie Downloads." *Yale Economic Review*. http://www.yaleeconomicreview.com/issues/fall2005/downloads (accessed 6 Nov 2006, site discontinued).

Zizek, Slavoj. "'I or He or It (the Thing) Which Thinks.'" *Tarrying With the Negative*. Durham: Duke University Press, 1993.

———. *Looking Awry: An Introduction to Jacques Lacan through Popular Culture*. London: MIT Press, 1993.

———. "Appendix Taking Sides: A Self-Interview." *The Metastases of Enjoyment*. London: Verso, 1994.

Zwick, Jim. "Militarization in the Philippines: From Consolidation to Crisis." http://www.boondocksnet.com/centennial/sctexts/zwick85a_b.html (site discontinued).

INDEX